Operant Conditioning in the Classroom
INTRODUCTORY READINGS IN EDUCATIONAL PSYCHOLOGY

Operant Conditioning
in the Classroom

edited by CARL E. PITTS

Thomas Y. Crowell Company

INTRODUCTORY READINGS IN
EDUCATIONAL PSYCHOLOGY

United States International University
CALIFORNIA WESTERN CAMPUS

NEW YORK   Established 1834

Preface

In the textbook *Introduction to Educational Psychology: An Operant Conditioning Approach,* for which this reader is an accompaniment, I have tried to make a case for a new approach to the teaching of educational psychology. Starting with the premise that too little is known about human behavior to provide the kind of specific information needed by the teacher in the classroom, I provided instead the "tools" of behavioral description and modification. The position taken was that the science of human behavior can be more profitably used as a *method* for investigating and solving problems than as a fact-filled answer book for the specific kinds of individual and group problems facing teachers daily.

This book of readings is an extension of the text and is a compilation of statements and action research dealing with behavioral description and modification. Here, as in the textbook, the underlying assumption is that the teacher's task is to discover ways of creating the optimal environment for achieving predetermined goals—helping young people become adept at solving problems, thinking logically, critically, analytically, and creatively. The central question to which this reader addresses itself is: *What are the conditions under which teacher-student goals can be achieved?*

Selections have been chosen that support and exemplify the approach to teaching and learning taken in the text, namely that of operant conditioning as developed by B. F. Skinner. Consequently, many of the classical articles usually included in educational psychology readers will not be found here, as it is felt they do not give the teacher guidance in developing a strategy of teaching.

The essays in Part I explore the theoretical aspects of behavior modification. Parts II and III address themselves to the problem of translating this theoretical knowledge into operant conditioning techniques that can be used in the classroom. The articles in Part II discuss techniques for changing behavior in non-school environments; psychotic-neurotic behavior, retarded behavior, stuttering, and delinquency are among those dealt with. The selections in Part III are reports on research carried on in schools, with examples drawn from preschool to university populations. Also included is a section on the use of technical devices and pro-grammed materials in measuring, recording, and describing behavior.

C.E.P.

Contents

I / The Conceptual Tools   1

1 / Innate Intelligence: An Insidious Myth?   3
WILLIAM H. BOYER AND PAUL A. WALSH
2 / The Method   13
ARTHUR W. STAATS AND CAROLYN K. STAATS
3 / The Technology of Teaching   34
B. F. SKINNER
4 / Theoretical Basis for Behavior Modification   54
OGDEN R. LINDSLEY
5 / Analysis of a Teaching Problem in an Educational Perspective   61
FINLEY CARPENTER AND EUGENE HADDEN

II / Using The Conceptual Tools: Out-of-School Settings   75

6 / Operant Group Psychotherapy   77
WILLARD A. MAINORD
7 / The Nightmare of Life with Billy   86
DON MOSER
8 / Screams, Slaps, and Love   91
9 / Behavioural Engineering   94
T. AYLLON AND HEIDI B. HUGHES
10 / Orientation Talk to Relatives of Residents   105
J. MONTGOMERY AND R. McBURNEY
11 / How To Teach Your Pet   113
HELEN KAY

12 / Achievement Place: Token Reinforcement Procedures in a Home-Style Rehabilitation Setting for "Pre-Delinquent" Boys   120
ELERY L. PHILLIPS

III / Using the Conceptual Tools: In-School Settings   137

13 / A Study of Undergraduate Performance in an Incentive Course in Educational Psychology   139
CARL E. PITTS AND MARY ANN POWERS
14 / Establishing Use of Descriptive Adjectives in the Spontaneous Speech of Disadvantaged Preschool Children   147
BETTY M. HART AND TODD R. RISLEY
15 / Production and Elimination of Disruptive Classroom Behavior by Systematically Varying Teacher's Behavior   166
DON R. THOMAS, WESLEY C. BECKER, AND MARIANNE ARMSTRONG
16 / Acceleration of Academic Progress Through the Manipulation of Peer Influence   184
GARY W. EVANS AND GAYLON L. OSWALT
17 / Rules, Praise, and Ignoring: Elements of Elementary Classroom Control   194
CHARLES H. MADSEN, JR., WESLEY C. BECKER, AND DON R. THOMAS
18 / Daily Arithmetic Performance Compared with Teacher Ratings, I.Q., and Achievement Tests   213
NANCY J. ANN JOHNSON
19 / Good-Bye, Teacher . . .   222
FRED S. KELLER
20 / Administration and Precision Teaching   239
ERIC HAUGHTON
21 / Effects of Group Contingent Events upon Classroom Noise   252
GILBERT W. SCHMIDT AND ROGER E. ULRICH
22 / Self-Application of Behavior Modification Techniques by Teenagers   267
ANN DELL DUNCAN
23 / The Role of Social and Material Reinforcers in Increasing Talking of a Disadvantaged Preschool Child   279
NANCY J. REYNOLDS AND TODD R. RISLEY
24 / Effect of Contingent and Non-Contingent Social Reinforcement on the Cooperative Play of a Preschool Chid   294
BETTY M. HART, NANCY J. REYNOLDS, DONALD M. BAER, ELEANOR R. BRAWLEY, AND FLORENCE R. HARRIS
25 / Token Reinforcement Systems in Regular Public School Classrooms   301
R. J. KARRAKER

IV / Hardware and Software   315

26 / Programmed Instruction: An Introduction   317
   EDWARD B. FRY
27 / Using Operant Techniques to Teach Handwriting   329
   TRUDY VILLARS
28 / Autotelic Responsive Environments and Exceptional Children   337
   OMAR KHAYYAM MOORE
29 / Technical Note: A Reliable Wrist Counter for Recording Behavior
   Rates   384
   OGDEN R. LINDSLEY
30 / Technical Note: A Manual Counter for Recording Multiple
   Behavior   386
   ROBERT L. MATTOS

1 / THE CONCEPTUAL TOOLS

This book deals with behavior modification. It rests its case upon the proposal that today more than ever before there is an available social technology ready to be applied by those whom society has set apart to change behavior. Some of these anointed are the clergy, teachers, therapists, personnel directors, managers, and guidance counselors. Their ranks are legion. Just as a carpenter has his tools to facilitate the construction of a building, so must the social technologist have a set of tools—perhaps more abstract but nonetheless important—to achieve with efficiency the goals set for him by his role.

The purpose of this first section, on the conceptual tools, is twofold: to provide a set of behavioral modification concepts and to introduce the reader to the conviction of each writer that predictable change can occur when the concepts are put to use. In short, the theme to be developed here is that the teacher can become a better teacher, the therapist a better therapist, and the guidance expert a better counselor if they begin to see behavior as orderly and malleable rather than random and intractable. Historically, behavioral modification has been more or less by happenstance, and the methods have been the result of natural selection rather than of planned strategy. But current thinking based upon the methods of science has provided an increasing body of evidence that change need not be left to chance.

1 / Innate Intelligence: An Insidious Myth?

WILLIAM H. BOYER AND PAUL A. WALSH

In this article, William Boyer and Paul Walsh launch a powerful attack upon the widely held assumption that people are genetically unequal and that each person has a "top" to his abilities. Educational practice, they state, grows out of the belief that students are innately different and "therefore unequal in capacity to learn." This belief becomes manifest in the schools' practice of ability groupings, track systems, and heavy reliance on tests designed to distinguish ability levels.

But, the authors counter, what if that assumption is incorrect? What if people have inherently equal capacities (barring physiological damage) and they only appear to be unequal because educators have enforced inequality? What if schools were to devote their energies to creating rather than defining abilities, to changing intelligence rather than adjusting curriculum to meet a test score?

If an article is to be measured by the fundamental quality of the questions it raises, this is an important article.

In societies where power and privilege are not equally distributed, it has always been consoling to those with favored positions to assume

Source: William H. Boyer and Paul A. Walsh, published under the title "Are Children Born Unequal?" *Saturday Review,* October 19, 1968, pp. 61-63, 77-79. Copyright © 1968 Saturday Review, Inc. Reprinted by permission of the authors and *Saturday Review.*

3

that nature has caused the disparity. When man himself creates unequal opportunity, he can be obliged or even forced to change his social system. But if nature creates inequality, man need only bow to supreme forces beyond his control, and the less fortunate must resign themselves to their inevitable disadvantage.

The metaphysics of natural inequality has served aristocracies well. The Greeks had wealth and leisure as a result of the labor of slaves. Plato expressed the wisdom of the established order with the claim that nature produces a hierarchy of superiority in which philosophers, such as himself, emerge at the top. Aristotle's belief that all men possess a rational faculty had more heretical potential, but it was not difficult to believe that some men are more rational than others.

In later periods, nations that possessed economic superiority explained their advantages on the basis of innate superiority. Sir Francis Galton was convinced that the English were superior and that the propertied classes were even more superior than the general population. They were the repository of what was the most biologically precious in mankind.

The democracies of the new world shattered many elements of the old order and brought a new, radical, equalitarian outlook. In principle, if not always in practice, man became equal before the law, and the idea of "the worth of the individual" established a principle of moral equality. Yet legal and moral equalitarianism did not necessarily mean that men were intellectually equal. So the assumption upon which American schools and the American market place developed was that democracy should mean *equal opportunity for competition among people who are genetically unequal.* This creed has satisfied the requirements of modern wisdom even for the more liberal founding fathers such as Thomas Jefferson, and it equally fit into the social Darwinism of an emerging industrial society.

In contemporary American education, many of these assumptions remain. People are usually assumed to be not only different in appearance, but also innately unequal in intellectual capacity and therefore unequal in capacity to learn. The contemporary creed urges that schools do all they can to develop *individual* capacities, but it is usually assumed that such capacities vary among individuals. Ability grouping is standard practice and begins in the earliest grades. Intelligence tests and the burgeoning armory of psychometric techniques increasingly facilitate ability tracking, and therefore the potentially prosperous American can usually be identified at an early age. If it is true that people have inherently unequal capacities to learn, the American educational system is built on theoretical bedrock, and it helps construct a social order based on natural superiority. But if people actually have inherently equal capacities, the system is grounded in quicksand and reinforces a system of arbitrary privilege.

Four types of evidence are typically offered to prove that people are innately different in their capacity to learn. The first is self-evidential, the second is observational, the third is logical-theoretical, and the fourth is statistical.

The self-evidential position is based on high levels of certainty which include a strong belief in the obviousness of a conclusion. Many people are very certain that there is an innate difference between people in intellectual capacity. However, such tenacity of feeling is not itself a sufficient basis for evidence, for it offers no method of cross-verification. The mere certainty of a point of view regarding the nature of intelligence must be discounted as an adequate basis for verification.

The observation of individual differences in learning capacity cannot be dismissed as a basis for evidence; useful information for hypothesis requiring further verification can be obtained in this way. For instance, parents may notice different rates of learning among their children. People from different social classes learn and perform at different levels. The city child may learn particular skills more rapidly than the rural child. Observations require some care if they are to produce reliable evidence, but it is possible to observe carefully, and such observation can be cross-verified by other careful observers.

But if people learn particular tasks at different rates, does it follow that people must therefore be *innately* different in their learning capacity? It does *not* necessarily follow. Increasingly, as we know more about the role of environment, we see that there are not only differences between cultures, but also differences within cultures. Even within families, no child has the same environment as the others. Being born first, for instance, makes that child different; he is always the oldest sibling. A whole host of variables operates so that the environment as perceived by an individual child has elements of uniqueness (and similarity) with other children raised in proximity.

Observational evidence can be a useful part of the process of understanding when it raises questions that can be subjected to more conclusive evidence, but it is often used as a way of selectively verifying preconceived notions which are endemic in the culture. Western culture is strongly rooted in the belief in a natural intellectual hierarchy. Few observers have been taught to make observations based on assumptions of natural intellectual equality. Observational evidence must be carefully questioned, for it is often based on a metaphysic of differential capacity which encourages selective perception and a priori categories of explanation. Yet these preconceptions are rarely admitted as an interpretive bias of the observer.

Theories based on carefully obtained data provide a more adequate basis for reaching a defensible position on the nature-nurture controversy than either of the previous procedures. A general theory in the field of genetics or psychology which fits available information would be a relevant instrument for making a deduction about the nature of intelligence. If a logical deduction could be made from a more general theory about heredity and environment to the more specific question of innate intellectual capacity, the conclusion would be as strong as the theory. Such deduction is a commonly used procedure.

Both genetic and psychological theories have often been used to support the belief in inherited intelligence. Genetic connections between physical characteristics such as eye color, hair color, and bodily stature are now clearly established. Certain disease propensity has a genetic basis, yet the best established research is now between single genes and specific physical traits. It is commonplace to assume that if a hereditary basis for differential physical traits has been established, there is a similar connection between genes and intelligence. The conclusion, however, does *not* necessarily follow. Intelligence defined as the capacity to profit by experience or as the ability to solve problems is not a function of a single gene. Whatever, the particular polygenetic basis for learning, it does not follow that intellectual capacity is variable because physical traits are variable. Current genetic theory does not provide an adequate basis for deducing a theory of abilities.

Similarly, the Darwinian theory of natural selection is often used to ascribe superiority to those in the upper strata of a hierarchical society. Yet a system of individual economic competition for survival is actually a very recent phenomenon in human history, characteristic of only a few societies, primarily in the eighteenth, nineteenth, and early twentieth centuries. It is very likely that it is irrelevant to genetic natural selection because of its recent origin. American immigration came largely from the lower classes, a fact which could condemn America to national inferiority if the Darwinian theory were used. In the long span of human history, most societies have relied mainly on cooperative systems or autocratic systems for their survival, and individual competition is an untypical example drawn largely from the unique conditions of Western, particularly American, experience.

Psychological theories which emphasize individual difference have often assumed that the descriptive differences in physical characteristics, personality, and demonstrated ability are all due largely to heredity. Psychology has had strong historical roots in physiology, but as social psychologists and students of culture have provided new understanding of the role of experience, hereditarian explanation has shifted toward environmentalism. Even the chemical and anatomical characteristics of the brain are now known to be modifiable by experience.

Psychologists such as Ann Anastasi point out that, "In view of available genetic knowledge, it appears improbable that social differentiation in physical traits was accompanied by differentiation with regard to genes affecting intellectual or personality development."

Anthropologists, with their awareness of the effects of culture, are the least likely to place credence in the genetic hypothesis. Claude Levi-Strauss, a social anthropologist, claims that all men have equal intellectual potentiality, and have been equal for about a million years. Whether or not this is true, it is clear that the best-supported general genetic or psychological theory does not validate the conclusion that individual intellectual capacity is innately unequal.

Statistical studies under controlled conditions, on the other hand, can provide some of the most reliable information. For instance, when animals are genetically the same, there is the possibility of inferring genetic characteristics through experimental studies. Identical twins develop from the separation of a single egg and have identical genetic inheritance. If human twins could be raised under controlled experimental conditions, much could be learned about the respective role of heredity and environment. Many studies have been made of twins, but none under sufficiently controlled experimental conditions. The results, therefore, permit only speculative conclusions. Most twins are so similar that unless they are separated they are likely to be treated alike. When they are separated, in most cases, one twin is moved to a family of the same social class as the other twin. And people of similar appearance tend to be treated similarly—a large, handsome child is not usually treated the same as a short, unattractive child. The resultant similarity of IQ scores of separate twins has not been surprising.

Even if particular identical twins were to show marked differences in ability when they live in substantially different environments, as they occasionally do, the evidence does not prove the *environmentalist* thesis unless a significantly large number of random cases is compared with a similarly random selection of non-identical twins. In a small sample, difference could be due to the experience deprivation of one twin. It is possible to stultify any type of development, and so the variation between identical twins, identified in some studies up to forty points, by no means disproves the hereditarian position. Consequently, current studies do not provide conclusive statistical evidence to support either position over the other.

The second most commonly used statistical evidence to show the hereditary basis of intelligence is the constancy of IQ scores at different age periods. Usually, IQ scores do not change appreciably, but occasionally the changes are dramatic. It is now understood that a standard IQ test is culturally loaded toward middle-class values, and so the general constancy of most IQ scores can be explained as the expected result of limited mobility between social class and the resultant constancy of sub-cultural experiences. So even the statistical "evidence," so often used to support a belief in innate intelligence, is really not conclusive.

Studies of innate intelligence, then, have not produced conclusive evidence to justify the claim for an innate difference in individual intellectual capacity. Equally, there has not been conclusive evidence that the innate potential between people is equal. The research is heavily marked by the self-serving beliefs of the researchers. Psychologists have usually created "intelligence" tests which reflect their own values, pre-determining that their own scores will be high. When they have discovered they are high, they have often proclaimed such tests to be indicators of innate superiority.

Many studies are built on simple-minded assumptions about the nature of environment. Psychological environment is related to the subject. A researcher who says that two children live in the "same" environment is quite wrong, for the environment that each child perceives may be quite different from that perceived by the researcher.

Also, it is often assumed that environment is only postnatal, but evidence is now available on the role of prenatal environment, both psychologically and nutritionally. Malnutrition of a pregnant mother can, and often does, have permanent debilitating psychological and physiological effects on her child. Certain diseases contracted by the mother (measles, for example) and certain drugs (thalidomide, for instance) can produce destructive "environmental" effects which limit intellectual capacities. Clearly, people do demonstrate varying capacities to learn, but they have had varying prenatal and postnatal opportunities. If they are female, they are generally treated different than if they are male. Negroes are treated different from whites—one social class is treated different from another. The *kind* of employment people engage in has a profound effect on what they become. They probably become different through different treatment and different experience, yet our institutions, reflecting our culture, usually operate on the assumption that such differences in ability are innate.

There are at least three ability models which can be supported by current evidence. [See figure 1.] Each is based on different assumptions about human nature and therefore provides a basis for different social philosophies and different conceptions of government and education.

The first model assumes a great variety of innate ability and a high level of intellectual demand on the average person. In this model, there are hereditary geniuses and idiots, while most people have an intellectual capacity about equal to the demands of their society.

The second model assumes that the innate ability potential of everyone (who has not been injured pre- or postnatally) is equal and far exceeds the normal demand level. (The actual opportunities a person has may produce differential *performance* similar to model No. 1.)

The third model assumes the possibility of some variation, but since all of the ability potential is well beyond the normal demand level, the variation makes virtually no operational difference.

In an economic or educational system, model No. 1 would justify the usual culling, sorting, and excluding through screening devices to create a "natural" hierarchy of ability. It would also justify the common belief in "equal opportunity for competition between unequals," where sorting is achieved through competition.

Both models two and three would justify maximum social effort to develop the abilities of all people, and the failure to achieve high levels of ability in all people would constitute social failure rather than individual failure. American society, with its considerable disparity of wealth and power, is largely a success based on the inequality assumed in the first of the three models. It is largely a failure based on the equality assumed in the second and third models.

Schools make little effort to develop the kind of equal ability

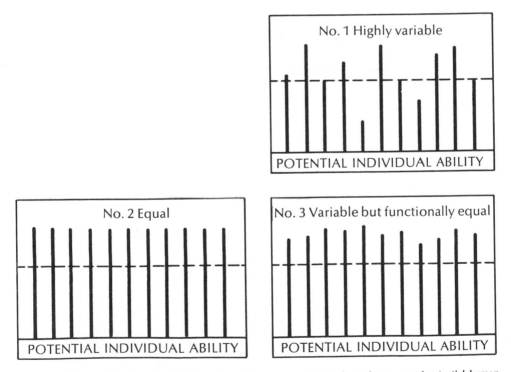

Figure 1. Ability models. Each model is based on different assumptions about the nature of potential human ability. The dotted line indicates the intellectual level at which individuals must function to meet the requirements of society.

assumed in models two and three. IQ tests are widely used to identify presumed differences in innate ability so that culling and grouping can make the management of the school easier and more efficient. The disastrous effects of the schools on lower-class children are now finally becoming known. The "compensatory" concept has gained some headway, but most educators are so overloaded with work and so traditional in outlook that the schools have become partners with the economic system in reinforcing a system of privilege that usually panders to the children of those in power and finds metaphysical excuses to make only minor gestures toward the less fortunate. The "special programs for the gifted" would be more accurately labeled "special programs for the privileged," for the gifted are primarily the children from socio-economic classes which provide the most opportunities. The less fortunate (usually lower-class children) are ordinarily neglected or convinced that they are innately inferior. Once they become convinced, the prophecy is soon realized.

Part of the problem is the way "intelligence" is defined. It can be defined in many different ways, each leading to a somewhat different educational direction. We can view it as environmental adaptation, as ability to solve problems, as ability to use logical convergent thinking, or it can emphasize divergent thinking and the creation of ideas and problems. When intelligence is defined as abstract verbal-conceptual ability drawing on the modal experiences of middle-class environment, as it is in most IQ tests, a selection has been made which excludes many other plausible and often more useful definitions.

The capacity to become intelligent does, of course, have a genetic basis. A cat is not capable of becoming a psychologist. But this does not mean that demonstrated differences in intelligence among psychologists are innate. What is particularly important is whether intelligence is defined primarily as the input or the output. The input is not subject to control, but the output depends on experience; so it is intelligence as output that should be the central concern of the educator.

Until the particular beliefs, which are endemic in many cultures, including American culture, are seen to be part of the heritage of an ancient, anachronistic, elitist tradition, there is little likelihood that the official liberal and equalitarian goals of many modern nations are likely to be realized, even though the wealth of modern technology gives every promise that they are capable of being achieved. Government, industry, education, and virtually all other institutions are now part of the problem, hobbled by a metaphysics of innate inequality. Elitist assumptions about the meaning of ability permeate all fields of education. When teachers of music, mathematics, art, or physical education find that a student doesn't demonstrate the requisite ability, they often reject him (low grades can be a form of rejection). Then counselors shuttle the student to courses where he shows "ability." All this assumes that the school should not develop abilities, but only grant them opportunity to be expressed. The Rousseauian belief in the pre-existing self is widespread.

The environmental hypothesis may be wrong, but if it is, it should be shown to be wrong only after a society has done everything possible to develop the abilities of people. We should begin with prenatal care, and should eliminate the experience of economic deprivation, ghettoized living, and elitist schools and businesses. *Lacking definite scientific evidence about human potentialities, social policy should be based on moral considerations.* We should base our policy on the most generous and promising assumptions about human nature rather than the most niggardly and pessimistic. Men will do their best only when they assume they are capable. Liberal assumptions and conservative assumptions about human nature create their own self-fulfilling prophecies. We now create millions of people who think of themselves as failures—as social rejects. Their sense of frustration and despair is a travesty on the potentialities of an affluent nation.

Poor teaching is protected in the American educational system through the assumption that the child doesn't have the ability. An American environmentalist commitment (toward liberal rather than totalitarian goals) would aim at *creating* ability, at *increasing* intelligence, at *developing* interests. The meaning of "education" would need to be broader than merely institutional schooling. It should also include community responsibility, especially for business and the mass media, which must supplement the work of the school if Americans are to receive more equal educational opportunity. This requires more social planning and more public responsibility than Americans have previously been willing to undertake.

Most American institutions, including the schools, still base their policy largely on the old conservative ideology. This outlook resists change and condemns many to inferiority. Ideological rigidity is not exclusive to the United States; in fact, many other nations are even more rigid. Yet the expanding wealth produced by modern technology is beginning to encourage the have-nots within the United States and throughout the world to demand their share by force and violence if necessary. Violence is likely to be an increasingly common road to social change unless a new public morality based on new assumptions about human potentiality is translated into both foreign and domestic policy. It is not merely racism which bogs down American progress, but also the more pervasive belief in intellectual inequality. The failure to develop the abilities of people was useful to the early American aristocracy and to the power elite of an industrial-scarcity economy. But modern economies of abundance flourish through the maximum development of the abilities of people. There is potentially plenty for all. More widespread development of the capabilities of people would not only add greatly to the wealth of nations, but it can also permit people to participate in a social and cultural renaissance.

Aside from the compelling moral obligation to create equal opportunities within nations and even between nations, the excluded millions in the world are starting to force the changes which should have occurred long ago. Some of them don't believe they are inferior, and they are understandably impatient about changing the old processes of exclusion. All institutions, including the schools, will either need to re-examine their self-consoling elitist beliefs and create real and equal opportunity, or else risk that violence and revolution will increasingly become the dominant instruments of social change.

2 / The Method

ARTHUR W. STAATS AND CAROLYN K. STAATS

This article is an excerpt from Arthur and Carolyn Staats's COMPLEX HUMAN BEHAVIOR. As the title implies, the book deals with the methodological question: "How does one go about the scientific study of another's behavior?" That question necessitates a description of scientific methodology, and distinctions are drawn between science and "common-sense" ways of viewing man's behavior.

It is a demanding article for the neophyte in science because it points out that much of the terminology used to explain man's behavior does not meet the criteria of science. Furthermore, it illustrates how many of our so-called explanations are the result of a tendency to attribute causes to descriptions, to commit the "naming is explaining" fallacy.

It is an article that bears very careful reading because its point of view is central to the following studies and papers.

Man has been seeking explanations of the world about him, including the behavior of other men, for a very long time. The superiority of scientific explanations of nature to prescientific approaches is well documented in all areas of modern life. Our present task is to examine some of the distinctive methods generally used by science to achieve

Source: Arthur W. Staats and Carolyn K. Staats, *Complex Human Behavior* (New York: Holt, Rinehart and Winston, Inc., 1963), pp. 8-26, 32-34. Reprinted by permission of the publisher.

its enormous predictive power so that we may determine what aspects of the method are significant for understanding human behavior. How does one go about establishing a science of human behavior? How do scientific accounts of human behavior differ from nonscientific accounts? The present chapter seeks to discuss in summary fashion some of the questions involved. The discussions are fundamental to those in later chapters of the book.

Observation, Description, Classification

The enormous power over the events of nature that scientific study has provided springs in large part from empirical observations. Because the products of a science—the ability to predict and control—heavily involve observation, the state of development of the observations in a field helps determine the quality and quantity of these products. "[W]e find in the end that discrimination, or differential response, is the fundamental operation [in science]. . . . [T]wo people . . . find that unless they can each discriminate the same simple objects or read the same scales they still will not agree" (Stevens, 1939, p. 228). To appreciate this fully, we now need to examine in greater detail the function of observation in science.

A public record of a simple observation of an event could be said to constitute the first stage in the development of knowledge about the event. When the record of observation is made by using verbal symbols we have a description. Observation and description are thus closely related; description provides a convenient means of permanently recording and publicly communicating our observations. When observation is detailed and systematic, it is possible to prepare detailed and systematic description. Detailed description, in turn, can be very useful, both in its own right and as a step toward the classification of events. In discussing the importance of classification in science, Stevens (1939) points out again that classification depends upon the fundamental operation of discrimination. "If we can discriminate crucial differences between Dobbin and other animals we have named horses, we reject Dobbin as something not horse. In other words, we 'correlate' our discriminations— those made on Dobbin with those made on other objects—and the 'goodness' of the correlation determines where we shall classify the beast" (p. 233).

Let us look at some examples of how this has worked out in practice. Botany is a science in which observation, description, and classification have played an important role. In botany the events of interest are plant life. Important knowledge is derived by accurately observing and describing the characteristics of different plants. The gross events that were of original interest can be seen to consist of finer parts. Detailed descriptions based upon such observation may be organized so that fine similarities and differences (discriminations) are noted and a "class" of plants identified. In this way we now talk about "Eucalyptus, Ash, and Elm" rather than merely about "trees." Thus, detailed observation and description enable us to make comparative examination of the fine parts of which the whole events are constructed, and systematic classification of those parts.

The mere systematic recording and classification of observations is an improvement on nonscientific interest, since it enables observers to notice relationships that would never be apparent on the basis of casual observation. For example, although the conception of the evolution of living organisms had been suggested by Greek philosophers (Reichenbach, 1951, pp. 196–197), it was only after Darwin and others had systematically described many plants and animals and noted their similarities and differences that the concept of the progression which takes place in the evolution of living matter was given a solid foundation. Thus, observation and description may serve an important function by opening the door for a step toward further knowledge.

In addition, however, simple observation and description may have another productive result. Returning to botany as the example, we find that the botanist, in constructing a classification system, may take into consideration physical and functional characteristics of plants. Plants are assigned to a family on the basis of such physical aspects as leaf shape, root type, and flower, as well as on such behavioral characteristics as soil requirements, blooming season, pollination method, etc. Now, with such a classification system, suppose a botanist traveling through foreign terrain comes across a new plant he has not seen before. Upon careful observation, he sees that the plant has certain physical characteristics similar to those of a plant family with which he is familiar. Knowing the characteristics of the general class, he may make predictions about the specific case. He may predict that it will pollinate in the same manner, bear flowers in a certain season of the year, and so on.

Thus, such classification systems may have important practical as well as scientific utility. Knowledge of the general class of events defined by similarities and differences in the observed events may allow prediction about the new individual case. The statements involved in this logic may be put into syllogistic form and have been described as rules of class inference (see Reichenbach, 1951, pp. 215–216). For example, the case we have cited could be put in the following form.

> All plants in class x bear flowers in the spring.
> This new plant is a member of class x.
> The new plant will bear flowers in the spring.

Much of our knowledge in other areas has been developed and

is employed in an analogous fashion. Medicine contains many such examples, for medical diagnosis has typically leaned heavily on this methodology. Having himself observed and described a number of cases of a certain constellation of symptoms, or having studied descriptions made by other qualified observers, a physician includes each new patient who demonstrates a similar symptom pattern in the general class. He now expects the same behaviors in the individual patient that he has found in the general class, and he expects treatments that have been successful for the general class to be successful for the individual case.

The same methodology underlies the efforts expended on observation and classification of abnormal human behavior. It was believed that adequate description of the general class of "schizophrenia," for instance, would enable the clinical psychologist to deal successfully with the individual "schizophrenic."

Detailed observation and comparative description can therefore be a source of powerful information for dealing with new events that man may encounter in life. The novice scientist who inherits someone else's classificatory system is much better able to cope with new events than is the layman who does not have this knowledge.

A word should be said about the importance of the public nature of observations. As was mentioned in the first chapter, it has been found that descriptions based upon public and repeatable observations are the ones which produce the productive fruits of a science. In the history of human knowledge about the natural world there have been many statements based upon "observations" that were neither public nor repeatable. Such statements, however, have not yielded the products— such as prediction—that science has to offer.

Since science is based upon observations, it is of the utmost importance that the observations be reliable. Reliable observations are those that can be obtained again under the same conditions. In the development of a science the search for reliability usually leads to a movement from observations of the event in its natural state to observations in very controlled circumstances—in other words, to the experiment. In addition, there is a movement away from the individual scientist as the "observing instrument," with all his frailties as such an instrument, to the use of mechanical and electronic instruments for observing and recording events.

Furthermore, complex logical methods for deciding whether an observation is reliable have been constructed. Thus, statistical analysis of recorded observations can be used to indicate whether under the same circumstances the same observations would be made, or whether the event was actually due to some uncontrolled factors.

These and other developments are all concerned with insuring that reliable observations are made. Statements about natural events cannot ordinarily include less error than the observations upon which they are based.

Operational Definitions

Science is not an individual matter; it is a social endeavor involving many people. "Science, as we find it, is a set of empirical propositions agreed upon by members of a society" (Stevens, 1939, p. 227). What one observes is significant when it is presented to others. This involves words, as the term "description" implies. The observing behavior of the scientist is important when he responds in some verbal form, which can then affect other people. In order for this to occur, however, his verbal behavior must be very precise. He cannot, for example, report things that are not there or have not occurred. He must respond with the same term to only one object or event. If he responds in the same way to two different events, ambiguity exists. These may seem like commonplace injunctions, but the history of science indicates that they are not, as will be seen. The precise use of terms is very important in scientific endeavor.

Real difficulty is encountered when the terminology used in description is so loose and ambiguous that one cannot be sure what was observed. Greater difficulty is involved when terms occur for which there are no physical counterparts, although they purport to refer to physical events. Descriptions which include ambiguous or empty definitions must be revised so that they use only terms which have been adequately defined. To avoid this methodological difficulty scientists have become very particular about the terminology used in describing events and have established definite criteria for the acceptability of a term.

In psychology one is concerned with the problem of terminology at every stage, but particularly when one seems to be getting away from directly observable events. When we talk about behavior we mean that which man does: the walking, talking, swimming; the being anxious or bright or loyal, and so on, that is observed in men and that behavioral scientists are interested in describing and explaining. The terms "anxious," "bright," and "loyal," however, may not appear to refer to observable behavior in the same direct way as do "walking," "talking," and "swimming." Nevertheless, as long as these former terms are thought of as nothing more than "shorthand" labels for classes of behavior—"anxious" behavior, "loyal" behavior, and so on—we are on safe ground. Unfortunately, in everyday thinking, people commonly act as if the "real" thing to study is not the behavior itself, but rather some inner entity, "anxiety" or "loyalty," which accounts for the behavior observed. Many times, however, no such inferred inner entity is adequately specified by observations. Thus, such an approach may violate a basic scientific dictum that the events of interest must be observable by any investigator sufficiently trained to observe them.

Psychologists have found the logic of *operationism* useful in avoiding this kind of confusion in terminology. *Operational definitions* allow scientists to successfully pursue their activity by providing a framework within which the terms they use in communication are explicitly defined by observable events. A term, accordingly, *means* nothing more than the observations to which the term is attached. An operational definition, in its simplest form, specifies the observational operations used to identify phenomena. As long as these observational operations themselves meet the criteria of the scientific approach, the term introduced may enter into further scientific statements. The canon of operational definition of terms prevents us from composing statements which give the impression that something is being said about empirical events when the statement is really empty of such meaning.

As an example, let us look at a concept that is frequently used, the concept of "emotional maturity." Can this term be appropriately used? As long as the term means only certain observations, the answer might be affirmative. It might be said, for instance, that a child is emotionally mature if he studies by himself without being coerced, if he is not overly demanding, if he has good relationships with other children, etc. On the other hand, a child who does not study well by himself, who is disruptive in his demands, who does not get along with other children, who has temper tantrums, and so on, might be termed "emotionally inmature." At this point the term "emotional maturity" is defined in terms of a number of observable responses. The single term "emotional maturity" now stands for all these separate behaviors that seem to occur concomitantly. As such, it is simply a shorthand label for an elaborate set of observations.

When the definition of a concept consists of the observations that are made and labeled by the concept, the concept is said to be operationally defined. It is necessary to remember, however, that an operational definition is, after all, only a definition; it has no more scientific status than the behaviors observed and described. To attach the label "emotional maturity" to a diverse set of responses is useful only as a classificatory device; it merely classifies many different acts into a single category that may be used in communicating with others who follow the same convention. Operational definitions, then, do not explain the phenomena under consideration. The primary importance of an operational definition is to insure that persons interested in a certain set of phenomena are all talking about the same events (see Mandler and Kessen, 1959, for a discussion of the unambiguous use of terms in psychology). In actual practice, the term "emotional maturity," for example, has been used with a variety of meanings and as a consequence has not acquired much scientific utility.

To summarize, since the events in the natural world are so complex, the conceptual (or symbolic or verbal) terms that are used to stand for the observations will also become quite complex. Because of this, a good deal of attention must be paid to the conceptual, or verbal, tools in a science, in other words, to the way a term is to be introduced, its relations to other terms, and so on. The standards of operational definition help in keeping the conceptual tools distinct. The criteria that a concept must meet in order to gain admission to scientific parlance should be clearly understood. It must be defined by observations that are unique to this term and to no other.

Having arrived at satisfactory observations, then, we are ready to search for explanation; in our terms, to relate the phenomena to the variables of which they are a function. An operational definition is a way of evaluating the terms in the system, of eliminating terms which overlap, and of excluding those which are "fictional," that is, have no observational counterparts. We are still forced, however, to look for those prior conditions that determine the behavior defining the term if explanatory statements concerning the behavior are to be established.

Description as Pseudo Explanation

Solely on the basis of observation and operational definition of the terms, the events in which we are interested may not be fully explored. Although the physician may have learned a description of a certain disease and may be able to treat the individual case on this basis, this is not to say that he has made any explanatory statement about the disease. For example, it has been observed that individuals sometimes exhibit a series of symptoms: the first stage being marked by restlessness, apprehension, and obvious ill health; the second by hyperactivity and spasms of the muscles of swallowing and respiration; and the third by a general paralysis ascending the spinal column and final death. This set of observations, let us say, defines the term "rabies." On observing these symptoms in an individual a physician may accurately label the behavior and consequently state that there is nothing that can be done for the victim. He can then predict the victim's eventual demise. With only this knowledge, however, the physician is incorrect if he says that the patient is going to die because he has rabies; with only a classificatory scheme of diseases he has nothing to explain the death. He can legitimately only describe the disease itself rather than speculate about its "causes."

It is easy, however, to fall into the trap of treating a descriptive term as a pseudo cause. In the field of abnormal psychology, investigators have been concerned with classifying and categorizing different classes of deviant behavior. These classification systems have proved useful for reasons already discussed. One such class includes the behaviors of suspiciousness, envy, extreme jealousy, and stubbornness, as well as delusions of persecution and/or grandeur, and so on. These types of behavior seem to appear together in many cases, and a term has been defined by these observations: *paranoia*. On observing this set of behaviors, the psychologist is in a position to state that the individual concerned is "paranoid," or may be labeled "paranoid." The danger enters when either he or his audience thinks that the undesirable behavior has been explained, *when indeed it has only been named.* The explanatory step of specifying why the individual acts as he does has not yet been taken. There is only a single set of facts: the observations of the behavior of the individual.

Perhaps a diagram will illustrate the faulty logic involved in substituting labeling for explaining. It was said that a certain set of behaviors may be named by one term, "paranoia," because they are related:

$$\left.\begin{array}{l} \text{Beh}_1 \text{ (suspiciousness)} \\ \text{Beh}_2 \text{ (envy)} \\ \text{Beh}_3 \text{ (stubbornness)} \\ \text{Beh}_4 \text{ (delusions)} \end{array}\right\} \text{ Paranoia}$$

The incorrect step in thinking occurs when it is stated that the individual behaves in such fashion because he is "paranoid," inferring now some internal entity "paranoia" to *account* for the behavior. In diagrammatic form it can be seen that in this misuse of the term, "paranoia" is inferred to be inside the organism (as indicated by the circle) and comes before—"causes"—the observed behavior:

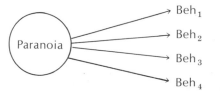

The circularity of this type of thinking is apparent when we ask the investigator, "How do you know that this person is paranoid?" and the answer is, "See how he behaves." The behavior is fallaciously *explained* in terms of the concept, and the concept is verified by the behavior.

Spence (1944) calls such terms "animistic conceptions,"[1] and

---

[1] Terms that are inadequately defined and that suggest unobservable internal processes of a causative nature have been discussed extensively in psychology. See, for example, the discussion of hypothetical constructs by MacCorquodale and Meehl (1948).

Skinner (1953) points to this specious substitution of a definition for a "cause" in his discussion of traits:

> Trait-names usually begin as adjectives—"intelligent," "aggressive," "disorganized," "angry," "introverted," "ravenous," and so on—but the almost inevitable linguistic result is that adjectives give birth to nouns. The things to which these nouns refer are then taken to be the active causes of the aspects. We begin with "intelligent behavior," pass first to "behavior which *shows* intelligence," and then to "behavior which is the *effect* of intelligence." Similarly, we begin by observing a preoccupation with a mirror which recalls the legend of Narcissus; we invent the adjective "narcissistic," and then the noun "narcissism," and finally we assert that the thing presumably referred to by the noun is the cause of the behavior with which we began. But at no point in such a series do we make contact with any event outside the behavior itself which justifies the claim of a causal connection (p. 202).

In our everyday thinking, we can find numerous examples of such faulty explanations. For example, it is observed that people in a situation of danger usually behave in a manner which has the effect of saving their own lives, and this behavior is named "self-preservation." Later, we attempt to explain this behavior with the assertion that all people have an instinct of self-preservation.

In a less dramatic context, the behavior of an individual who spends a large portion of his time practicing the violin may be observed. Consistent, strong, tenacious behavior of this sort has been labeled "interest." A perfect circle in thinking is completed, however, when it is said that the individual plays the violin *because* of his interest.

The teacher who observes eight-year-old Jimmy constantly fighting with other children is concerned with understanding or explaining his behavior in order that she might attempt to change it. For a school psychologist to say that Jimmy is constantly fighting because he is a hostile-aggressive child may sound very impressive, but it really adds no new knowledge, for if we ask how one knows that this is a hostile-aggressive child, the reply is that the child is always fighting. The term "hostile-aggressive," then, is only another name for "one who is always fighting." It does not explain the behavior or indeed add any new information, if the only ways of observing "hostility" are in the behavior itself. In the end, the statement that "Jimmy fights because he is hostile-aggressive" proves to be a tautology: "Jimmy fights because he fights."

Functional Relationships

Now that a type of pseudo explanation has been discussed, we may go on to discuss adequate explanation in psychology that yields the products of scientific laws in general. Explanation in psychology, as in other sciences, is developed upon the basis of systematic observation. That is, when systematic observation of some phenomenon has been made, the second stage in the development of a science may begin: the search for the cause of the phenomenon, or, more accurately, the specification of some independently observed prior event to which it is related.

The stuff out of which the lawful relationships are found are the *observations* of the events in which the scientist is interested and the *independent observations* of the conditions that determine these events. In order to explain an event, then, something more than observing and describing similar events must be done. The *antecedent* conditions under which the event will occur must be known, as well as those conditions under which it will not occur. That is, the relationships between the event of concern and the events determining it must be established.

Let us refer once more to the field of medicine for an example. When it was discovered that infection with a certain virus resulted in the symptoms called rabies, then an explanatory statement of a sort had been made. This is an example of a lawful relationship and may be schematized as follows:

Introduction of virus into body ⟶ Symptoms of rabies

Although this case may seem simple, this is the type of lawful relationship that science seeks to discover. The symptomatic behavior termed "rabies" has been observed to follow upon the independently observed introduction of certain viruses into the body. When it is discovered that the two events are lawfully related, the requirements for a scientific law have been fulfilled.

That this is, in essence, a fundamental task of all science may be shown by examining examples of primitive "laws" from different areas of study. In physics, for example, there was interest in explaining events such as changes in the state of water. It may be observed, on the one hand, that water changes from a liquid to a solid state under certain conditions. It may also be observed, aided by a very simple instrument (a thermometer) that atmospheric temperatures vary. These observations are independent of each other; it is not necessary to see water to know that the temperature has changed, nor is a thermometer necessary in order to observe that water has become solid. However, when it is found that the two events are indeed reliably related, we have the substance of a scientific law. The explanation of the change in state of water is to be found in temperature variations.

Temperature decreases to 32° F. ⟶ Water becomes solid

Turning to biology and the science of genetics, we find the task to be the same: that of finding the relationship between certain events in which one is interested and the events that determine them. Relationships have been found in genetics between certain physical characteristics of the organism and the physical characteristics of its parents. After each phenomenon has been independently observed, the further observation that they are generally related constitutes an empirical law. In genetics one possible lawful relationship might be between certain eye colors of parents and the eye colors of their offspring.

Both parents have blue eyes⸺⟶ Offspring has blue eyes

Having found a lawful relationship between two events, one preceding the other in time—in common-sense terms a "cause"—two powerful products of science may be obtained. First, if the occurrence of event$_1$ is reliably followed by (lawfully related to) event$_2$, knowledge of event$_1$ gives knowledge of what event$_2$ will be. If it can be determined whether or not the particular filterable virus has been introduced into the body of an individual, whether or not the individual will display the symptoms of rabies may be predicted. Thus, when a person is bitten by a dog, the dog is examined to see if it could have transmitted the virus. If the virus has been transmitted, it can be predicted that unless preventive action is taken, rabies symptoms will in due course appear in the person.

In addition to the power of prediction, empirical laws may also yield control. Interest in a particular natural event is often accompanied by an interest in influencing or controlling its occurrence. Now, if there is a lawful relationship between event$_1$ and event$_2$, the second event can be predicted from the first. Moreover, if event$_1$ can be manipulated so that it either does or does not occur, then the control of event$_2$ is achieved. In the above example, if the first event, the introduction of rabies into the body, can be manipulated, then the second event, the occurrence of the disease, can be controlled. (For the sake of simplicity other determining factors have been ignored, such as the treatment that can be inserted between event$_1$ and event$_2$.)

In later discussions event$_1$ will be called the independent variable, or antecedent condition or event. Event$_2$ will be called the consequent condition or event, or the dependent variable.

It should be pointed out that knowledge of empirical laws can take place at different levels, yielding different possibilities for prediction and control. The statement "If a 'mad' dog bites a man, the man will later display the symptoms of rabies" constitutes an important empirical law, yielding the products of prediction and control as discussed. This is a valid and useful empirical law in itself, even though there is no knowledge of the physiological and bacteriological events involved. More detailed observation has, however, indicated that the brain of a "mad" dog contains a certain virus strain which, if injected into the blood of another mammal, results in the occurrence of rabies symptoms in this animal. This constitutes another empirical law, yielding additional products of prediction and control. Applying these empirical laws and others, scientists may develop vaccines for rabies, methods of treatment, and so on. Thus, each empirical law is itself important, but finer and finer detail in the lawful structure should also be sought.

To obtain prediction, one must possess information concerning the *occurrence* of the specific determining event or events, as well as of the lawful relationships involved. If this information is not available prediction is not possible, even though the underlying empirical law is available. For example, the physicist who knows what events determine how a body will fall through space is in a position to predict the course of the fall of a specific body *only* if he is given access to information about the determining events in this case. It is for this reason that the trained physicist may be as helpless in predicting the flight of a stray feather through the air as is the layman. The layman knows neither the determining events nor the laws relating these events to the flight of the feather. The physicist knows the laws relating the events, but without information concerning the occurrence of the actual determining events he is just as powerless as the layman to make predictions.

The psychologist faces the same problem when dealing with the individual case. Although he may be aware of the functional relationships existing between certain behavior and certain environmental conditions, he is powerless to predict the development of the behavior if he is uninformed of these environmental conditions in the life history of a specific individual. It should be emphasized, however, that in many cases the potential for the control of determining events is present but is not utilized because the relationships to the phenomena under consideration have not yet been discovered. Thus, the discovery of empirical laws may have extremely important consequences.

Determinants of Behavior

To explain behavioral phenomena, the task is once more to observe the relationship of the determining events to the behavior of interest. What kinds of events are determinants of behavior? Of course, the first criterion is that the determinants must be independently observable. It is possible, however, to classify the determinants of behavior into two general categories of events acting upon the individual: biological and environmental.

The relationship between behavior and its general determinants can be depicted using a diagram similar to the previous examples. On the one hand there is the biological history of the individual, which may be further subdivided into the individual's membership in a particular species and his personal biological history, such as the genetic endowment determined by his particular parental background. At the same time additional determinants are to be found in the environmental events acting upon, or having acted upon, the individual. The environmental conditions related to behavior start with the prenatal conditions in which the child begins life and continue throughout life. This, of course, includes a great quantity of events that have a determining action upon the behavior of the individual.

1. Heredity ———
                    ——→ Behavior
2. Environment ——

Some disciplines of behavioral science are concerned primarily with heredity and the biological determinants of behavior, while others are interested primarily in environmental determinants. For example, physical anthropologists look for explanations of behavior in the history of the species. Physiological psychologists study behavior as a function of the nervous system, the actions of muscles and glands, and so on. On the other hand, social psychologists, sociologists, and cultural anthropologists are interested in the behavior of man in groups and seek explanations for this behavior in a person's group membership, the institutions that affect him, the "beliefs" and "attitudes" of the culture in which he is raised, and so on.

Psychology is interested in any lawful relationships involving behavior that may be discovered. However, at present, there is relatively little that can be done to manipulate the hereditary or biological events which affect the type of complex behavioral skills we shall be discussing. In attempting to deal with the behavior that is of everyday significance, we are largely restricted to working with environmental variables. For this reason, the present book is concerned with laws involving environmental rather than biological determining events, although it is recognized that the search for lawful relationships between biological events and behavior is very important.

S-R Laws

The independent events we shall be concerned with will be environmental events, to be called stimuli, and behavioral events, to be called responses. As a consequence of this interest in stimulus (S) and response

(R) events, psychology has been concerned with making reliable observations of both. There are therefore operationally defined terms whose referents are observations or measurements of stimulus events, and there are operationally defined terms whose referents are observations of response events.

In addition, there are terms whose operational referents consist of S-R relationships. That is, the term may actually be defined by an S-R law. Such concepts seem even one step further from our original statement that *observability* is the crucial criterion for a term in science. It should be recognized, however, that a term may label a relationship between a set of observable stimulus conditions and a set of observable response conditions. The operational definition of the term in this case is simply the relationship between the two events.

Numerous terms of this sort will be dealt with in this book, but again, we must be sure that they fulfill the essential requirements of scientific methodology before they are accepted. Examples of such terms that are important in psychology are "learning" and "motivation."

Let us examine the concept "learning," for example. In everyday language it is said that a child has "learned" if he is observed to be correctly reciting a poem or if he earns a high mark on an arithmetic test or if he swims with ease and speed. But actually, only a number of different responses have been observed in these cases. Correct use of the term, however, would involve stating the events or conditions that determine these behaviors. For example, if it was pointed out that the child was using a cue card to read the poem or that he copied the answers to the arithmetic problems, one would hardly be satisfied with the statement that he had "learned" the observed adequate responses. In other words, the appropriate behavior by itself is not what is meant by "learning," but rather it is a relationship between a class of antecedent (stimulus) conditions on the one hand and a class of response conditions (behavior) on the other hand that defines the term.

In everyday language, one of the stimulus conditions leading to the "learned" type of behavior described in practice, the repeated presentation of some stimulus material, such as the words in a poem. An oversimplified definition of learning which can be used as an example at this point is that "learning is a relatively permanent change in behavior which occurs as a result of practice." Thus, neither the stimulus conditions alone nor the response conditions alone define the term. Learning is thus defined by *both* a set of stimulus conditions (repeated presentation of stimulus material) and a set of response conditions (the acquired behaviors). This could be called an operational definition of learning.

In the general case, then, concepts are also acceptable in a science when they are defined by an empirical relationship between events—in psychology between stimulus conditions and response conditions. In a diagram form the concept of learning is shown below as such a concept.

Learning

Practice (repeated trials) ⟶ Change in behavior

Of course, the most important aspect of the process for the behavioral scientist is that the relationship between stimulus and response conditions has been observed. Adding the term "learning" has really added nothing of explanatory value. Regardless of the term used, the business of the scientist remains the same—to discover relationships between the events of interest and the events that determine them. The concept is useful, however, as a sort of "shorthand" device. Rather than saying that "the child's behavior has changed as a result of practice," it is simply said that "the child has learned." As a shorthand device, the term allows for the designation of entire sets of stimulus conditions, entire sets of response conditions, and all the relationships between them, with a single term. In the example, all the numerous relationships between the very great number of "practice" situations and the innumerable forms of the consequent permanent changes of behavior have been reduced to a manageable, coherent statement. It must be emphasized, however, that the *only* meaning possessed by the concept as used in this manner is the relationship of the stimulus and response variables.

This type of term, or rather the relationship that defines it, yields the same products as do empirical laws in other sciences. That is, when an S-R law has been found, knowledge of the S conditions will enable the R to be predicted. It may be predicted that if there has been no presentation of the poem stimulus materials, the unprompted recitation behavior will not occur. Or, if the repetitions of the presentation have been few the recitation behavior will be poor, and so on. In addition, the S-R law offers the possibility of the control of behavior. As the presentation of the stimulus material is manipulated, the recitation behavior will vary. The principles to be presented in the next chapter are examples of S-R laws.

R-R Laws

It should be pointed out that there are independently observed events which, although lawfully related, do not provide the possibility of control. Consider, for example, the relationship between teachers' salaries and beer consumption in the United States. As it happens, years in which teachers' salaries are high are also years when beer consumption is high.

Since these two independently observed events are lawfully related, once it is discovered that teachers' salaries are up, it can be predicted that beer consumption will increase. It could be possible that this relationship is a determining one; that teachers are the only ones who drink beer, and as their salaries increase they drink more. If this is the case, control of beer consumption could be obtained through manipulating teachers' salaries.

On the other hand, the relationship may not be a determining one. Economic conditions in the country may be the actual independent variable and both teachers' salaries and beer consumption the dependent variables. Thus, manipulation of economic conditions would result in changes in both teachers' salaries and beer consumption. While these latter two events are, as a consequence, related, they are not in an independent-dependent relationship and are not explanatory in terms of the determining relationships discussed.

There are empirical laws of this sort in psychology also. For example, lawful relationships may exist between two responses of the same person at different times (Spence, 1944). That is, it may be observed that the behavior an individual displays at $time_1$ is related to the behavior he displays later at $time_2$. It might be found, for example, that if an infant displays temper tantrums at $time_1$, the same individual as a school-age child at $time_2$ will periodically explode into "rages."

Sometimes R-R relationships can be found between verbal behavior and subsequent motor behavior, between what a person says at $time_1$ and what he does at $time_2$. Recognizing this relationship, psychologists have attempted to describe verbal behavior precisely, to quantify it, and to relate it to later overt behavior of various kinds. When such a relationship is discovered an observation of behavior at $time_1$ may be used to predict behavior at $time_2$.

Paper and pencil tests may be considered to be measures of verbal behavior that have been found to be related to other behaviors of the individual. For example, obtaining a high score on a test of personality maladjustment (the R_1) might be found, let us say, to be related to other aggressive behaviors (the R_2) (Kimble, 1956).

S-R and R-R Laws Compared

As we have seen, an antecedent event in a functional relationship may be either a stimulus event or a response event. These two types of empirical laws yield different products, however. To illustrate the comparison, the previous example of a boy who fights a great deal in school will be used. Let us assume for a moment that two relationships between fighting behavior and antecedent events had been discovered; one might be a hypothetical S-R relationship. This might consist of the observation that when fighting behavior is rewarded (S) in the home the child will fight (R) in other situations. The R-R relationship might be that a high score on the Rotten Kid Adjustment Test (R_1) is related to frequent fighting behavior (R_2). In either case, the teacher has quite a bit of information. Applying the general S-R law, it is known that if Jimmy comes from a home in which fighting is rewarded he is likely to become engaged in frequent battles. Applying the R-R law yields the same prediction. In other words, having discovered either an S-R or an R-R law one is in a position to predict behavior (Kimble, 1956).

If one is concerned only with predicting behavior, then both types of laws might satisfy the purpose equally well. The criterion for choosing between them would then simply be the amount of error involved in the particular statements, the ease of application of the law, and so on. For example, testing the child might be more practicable than observing home training procedures. In one particular situation it may be the S-R law that is more precise; in another situation it may be the R-R law.

The usefulness of the two types of laws can be further contrasted, however. Is the teacher satisfied simply to predict which child will be aggressive? Probably, it is also important to prevent the undesirable behavior by modifying the conditions that lead to it. With Jimmy, the teacher might, on the basis of the S-R law, have a talk with his parents, explain the situation to them, and suggest other ways of dealing with Jimmy that will have a more desirable effect. If the parents will cooperate, the fighting behavior can be controlled. The R-R law, on the other hand, would be of no help in controlling Jimmy's fighting. Although it may be that when Jimmy makes a certain score on the personality test his behavior is likely to be belligerent, we know too that preventing him from taking the test will hardly prevent the behavior of fighting from occurring. Thus, if we are interested not only in predicting, but also in controlling human behavior, we must search for S-R laws (Kimble, 1956; Spence, 1944).

Unfortunately, the properties of the two kinds of laws are sometimes confused. Although the R-R law is of no value in exercising control of behavior, this is not always clearly understood, and it also may be thought that such a law by itself has this type of explanatory power. Suppose, for example, that an investigator develops a "personality test" which will predict which children are in need of psychological help; he has demonstrated an R-R relationship. At about this point questions of "causation" may arise that are similar to those in our previous discussion of pseudo explanation. It is obvious, of course, that the test behavior (R_1) cannot be regarded as the determinant of R_2, the later maladjustive behavior. Instead of recognizing the limitation of R-R laws and launching a search for S-R relationships, however, there may be in more subtle cases a tendency to infer some causal entity from the test, R_1, which is then thought to *determine* R_2. Following our example, an entity called "weak ego structure" might be inferred from a low score on the personality test, and then the assumption made that a "weak ego" determines the poor behavior in later situations, as in the following diagram. If the term was based solely on the observation of responses, on an R-R relationship itself, a spurious *causative* event would in this way be invented. While this example quite obviously involves improper methods and would be unlikely to actually occur, misuses do occur in real-life cases where the circumstances are more complicated.

R-R laws by themselves simply do not provide information concerning independent variables that offer controlling possibilities. Although it may appear that something has been gained by adding the "weak ego" between R_1 and R_2, no information has actually been gained. The only means of identifying this supposed weak ego is to administer the personality test.

R_1 R_2
Low score on personality test → Weak ego structure → Maladjustive behavior

"Weak ego," then, is nothing more than another name for "low score on personality test." That is, while it is said that the individual has a "weak ego" when he has a low score on the personality test and that the weak ego is the source of his later maladjustive behavior, actually only a single functional relationship has been established, not the two that the previous statement implies.

R-R laws alone always leave unanswered questions concerning the "cause" or "causes" of both R_1 and R_2. In order to answer these questions it is necessary to establish the relationship between antecedent conditions, which are often stimulus events (S), and both R_1 and R_2.

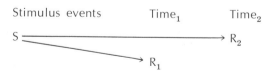

As the diagram indicates, the reason why a lawful relationship exists between R_1 and R_2 may be that they are both determined by the same stimulus conditions. Returning once more to the example of Jimmy's fighting, one of the possible lawful relationships may be diagrammed in the following manner:

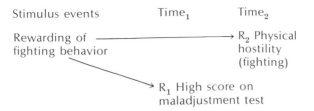

To infer an explanatory concept from R_1 to explain R_2, however, is no improvement over an ad hoc explanation of R_1. It is as circular as the substitution of a label for an explanation, as we showed earlier. Moreover, a disservice is performed when we convince ourselves that we have added anything which will help deal with the behavior, for by convincing ourselves that we have found explanations, we persuade ourselves to discontinue our search for the actual determining events.

This is not to deny the importance of R-R laws in the field of psychology. They are typified in all psychological measurement. It might be pointed out in this context, however, that tests and testing procedures have sometimes fallen into disrepute due to a misunderstanding of the nature of R-R statements. Since tests do not enter into S-R relationships, they cannot be used to manipulate behavior. From R-R laws *alone* no knowledge of how to teach a child arithmetic or how to prevent him from becoming maladjusted in adulthood can be derived. Thus, it is important to use the information yielded by R-R relationships to the full extent possible in prediction, but at the same time their limitations when it comes to explanation (and control) must be recognized and care taken not to infer improperly referenced causal entities.

· · · · ·

The Relationship between Conceptions and Actions

Use of the scientific method has established lawful statements important in everyday life, and the approach and methods seem equally important in understanding actual human behavior. This section will show, in general terms, why a scientific approach to human behavior would be expected to pay practical dividends. Let us consider for a moment how an understanding of the laws underlying phenomena affects the approach to practical problems in other areas of study. Medicine, the applied science built upon the biological sciences of zoology, biochemistry, physiology, botany, and so forth, provides clear illustrations of the relationship between the level of understanding of the laws of the science and the uses to which such understanding can be put. For example, prior to the discovery of the lawful relationship between virus or bacterial infection and the development of certain disease symptoms, there was no understanding of the determinants of disease. Until a patient developed symptoms, therefore, there was no way to predict or control a particular disease. Ignorant of the lawful relationships involved, man had no ability to deal with the events of concern, the occurrence of disease. As is often the case, when people are ignorant of the actual determinants of an event, incorrect conceptions of the determining events arose. These incorrect conceptions then provided a basis for action which, rather than leading to the prediction and control of the events in question, actually compounded the error. Lacking knowledge that explained illness, man attempted to control disease by praying to various gods, by offering sacrifice, by drawing blood from the afflicted, by wearing "protective" garments or jewelry, and so on. For example, the Jivaro Indians of South America are to this day not acquainted with the lawful relationship between antecedent biological events of infection and the resulting illness. They are therefore still unable to deal effectively with disease. To make matters worse, they accept inappropriately defined conceptions which state that illness and death occur because another person directs evil spirits to attack the victim. Because of this conception of death or illness resulting only from evil spirits, when an individual dies or becomes ill the family of the victim attempts to find the responsible evil-doer, and this often results in further occasion for sorrow among the population. The concepts one accepts, good or bad in terms of observational definition, will determine what is done about the event in question.

Let us now turn to human behavior. Here, too, the general system of explanation incorporated into one's thinking helps determine how one deals with practical problems. For example, at one time it was thought that an individual who behaved abnormally was possessed by the devil. This conception led to ways of treating abnormally behaving individuals that are now recognized as inefficient, if not detrimental to advantageous behavior change. At that time, the objective of treatment was to convince the devil that a given body was not a fit place for him to inhabit—that it was too uncomfortable. To prove the point to the devil, "therapy" involved whipping the person, burning him, immersing him in ice water, casting him into a snake-pit, and so on. The treatment was, of course, in line with the prevalent conception of the source of abnormal behavior; it was assumed that the devil would choose to vacate this particular body, and the individual would be "cured."

Today, once again in accord with the prevalent conception of the source of abnormal behavioral phenomena, individuals who behave abnormally are treated as sick people; their behavior is explained in terms of mental illness rather than in terms of possession by the devil. Because of this "illness" concept, mental "hospitals" are provided, drugs that will help an individual regain his "health" are sought, and people are taught to be as kind and thoughtful with the "mentally ill" as with any person suffering from ill health. That this conception may not lead to effective treatment in some cases will be shown in later chapters.

This example illustrates the intimate relationship between the system we use to explain behavior and our reactions to other people. The common-sense conceptions we hold concerning behavior also determine how we respond to others. If our common-sense conceptions correspond to empirical laws concerning behavior, we tend to respond appropriately. If the conceptions are poor, our responses may be inadequate.

The reader should now be able to see the value of establishing empirical laws, whether he be psychologist, parent, teacher, or merely interested in understanding human behavior. Each person's conception of human behavior helps dictate his actions toward others, young and old. For example, a teacher who accepts the premise that the young "mind" must be disciplined like an immature musculature may spend much time drilling on difficult material, regardless of its practicality. On the other hand, a teacher who has been trained in concepts of learning drawn from Gestalt theory will say that drill on individual skills is less important than holistic experiences of a naturalistic sort. In the same way, a parent whose explanatory system involves the terms "personality" and "character" defined as inherited and immutable entities will respond differently to children than will another parent who defines the same terms as a function of the child's past experience and the type of situations with which he is presently confronted. When one's conception of human behavior coincides with the events involved—and, as we have shown, scientific concepts are constructed to do just this— then his actions should in this sense be "good" ones. When the concepts are awry, the actions should be awry.

References

Kimble, G. A. 1956. *Principles of general psychology.* New York: Ronald.
Mandler, E., and Kessen, W. 1959. *The language of psychology.* New York: Wiley.
Reichenbach, H. 1951. *The rise of scientific philosophy.* Berkeley: University of California Press.
Skinner, B. F. 1953. *Science and human behavior.* New York: Macmillan.
Spence, K. W. 1944. The nature of theory construction in contemporary psychology. *Psychology Review* 51: 47–68.
Stevens, S. S. 1939. Psychology and the science of science. *Psychology Bulletin* 36: 221–63.

3 / The Technology of Teaching

B. F. SKINNER

In the first article of this section, "Innate Intelligence: An Insidious Myth?" the environmentalist position was presented. In brief, the thesis is that in terms of today's knowledge behavior modification (learning) is a function of environmental factors more than genetic factors. The person most responsible for extending that thesis is unquestionably B. F. Skinner, the author of this article.

From the experimental laboratory and extensive work with subhuman organisms, Skinner shifted his interest to the problems of human learning. His argument is that by programming reinforcers (scheduling events that increase the probability of the prior behavior) one has the ability to direct behavior toward a predetermined goal.

This article is made up of some vignette examples where the programming of reinforcers has been successful in teaching. It serves as an excellent introduction to the basic terminology and use of operant conditioning techniques.

More than 60 years ago, in his *Talks to teachers on psychology,* William James (1899) said: 'You make a great, a very great mistake, if you think that psychology, being the science of the mind's laws, is something from which you can deduce definite programs and schemes

Source: B. F. Skinner, "The Technology of Teaching," *Proceedings of the Royal Society* (London: The Royal Society, 1965), 162: 427–43. Reprinted by permission of the author and the Royal Society.

and methods of instruction for immediate schoolroom use. Psychology is a science, and teaching is an art; and sciences never generate arts directly out of themselves. An intermediary inventive mind must make the application, by using its originality.' In the years which followed, educational psychology and the experimental psychology of learning did little to prove him wrong. As late as 1962, an American critic, Jacques Barzun (1962), asserted that James's book still contained 'nearly all that anyone need know of educational method'.

Speaking for the psychology of his time James was probably right, but Barzun was clearly wrong. A special branch of psychology, the so-called experimental analysis of behaviour, has produced if not an art at least a technology of teaching from which one can indeed 'deduce programs and schemes and methods of instruction'. The public is aware of this technology through two of its products, teaching machines and programmed instruction. Their rise has been meteoric. Within a single decade hundreds of instructional programmes have been published, many different kinds of teaching machines have been offered for sale, and societies for programmed instruction have been founded in a dozen countries. Unfortunately, much of the technology has lost contact with its basic science.

Teaching machines are widely misunderstood. It is often supposed that they are simply devices which mechanize functions once served by human teachers. Testing is an example. The teacher must discover what the student has learned and can do so with the help of machines; the scoring of multiple-choice tests by machine is now common. Nearly 40 years ago Sidney Pressey (1926) pointed out that a student learned something when told whether his answers are right or wrong and that a *self*-scoring machine could therefore teach. Pressey assumed that the student had studied a subject before coming to the testing machine, but some modern versions also present the material on which the student is to be tested. They thus imitate, and could presumably replace, the teacher. But holding a student responsible for assigned material is not teaching, even though it is a large part of modern school and university practice. It is simply a way of inducing the student to learn without being taught.

Some so-called teaching machines serve another conspicuous function of the teacher: they are designed primarily to attract and hold attention. The television screen is praised for its hypnotic power. A machine has recently been advertised which holds the student's head between earphones and his face a few inches from a brightly lit text. It is intended that he will read a few lines, then listen to his recorded voice as he reads them over again—all in the name of 'concentration.' Machines also have the energy and patience needed for simple exercise or drill. Many language laboratories take the student over the same material again and again, as only a dedicated private tutor could do, on some theory of 'automaticity.'

These are all functions which should never have been served by teachers in the first place, and mechanizing them is small gain.

The programming of instruction has also been widely misunderstood. The first programmes emerging from an experimental analysis of behaviour were copied only in certain superficial aspects. Educational theorists could assimilate the principles they appeared to exemplify to earlier philosophies. Programmed instruction, for example, has been called Socratic. The archetypal pattern is the famous scene in the *Meno* in which Socrates takes the slave boy through Pythagora's theorem on doubling the square. It is one of the great frauds in the history of education. Socrates asks the boy a long series of leading questions and, although the boy makes no response which has not been carefully prepared, insists that he has told him nothing. In any case the boy has learned nothing; he could not have gone through the proof by himself afterwards, and Socrates says as much later in the dialogue. Even if the boy had contributed something to the proof by way of a modest original discovery, it would still be wrong to argue that his behaviour in doing so under Socrates's careful guidance resembled Pythagoras's original unguided achievement.

Other supposed principles of programming have been found in the writings of Comenius in the seventeenth century—for example, that the student should not be asked to take a step he cannot take—and in the work of the American psychologist, E. L. Thorndike, who more than 50 years ago pointed to the value of making sure that the student understood one page of a text before moving on to the next. A good programme does lead the student step by step, each step is within his range, and he usually understands it before moving on; but programming is much more than this. What it is, and how it is related to teaching machines, can be made clear only by returning to the experimental analysis of behaviour which gave rise to the movement.

An important process in human behaviour is attributed, none too accurately, to 'reward and punishment.' Thorndike described it in his Law of Effect. It is now commonly referred to as 'operant conditioning'—not to be confused with the conditioned reflexes of Pavlov. The essentials may be seen in a typical experimental arrangement . . . , a hungry rat in an experimental space which contains a food dispenser. A horizontal bar at the end of a lever projects from one wall. Depression of the lever operates a switch. When the switch is connected with the food dispenser, any behaviour on the part of the rat which depresses the lever is, as we say, 'reinforced with food.' The apparatus simply makes the appearance of food *contingent upon* the occurrence of an arbitrary bit of behaviour. Under such circumstances the probability that a response to the lever will occur again is increased (Skinner 1938).

The basic contingency between an act and its consequences has been studied over a fairly wide range of species. Pigeons have been reinforced for pecking at transilluminated disks, monkeys for operating toggle switches which were first designed for that more advanced primate, man, and so on. Reinforcers which have been studied include water, sexual contact, the opportunity to act aggressively, and—with human subjects—approval of one's fellow men and the universal generalized reinforcer, money.

The relation between a response and its consequences may be simple, and the change in probability of the response is not surprising. It may therefore appear that research of this sort is simply proving the obvious. A critic has recently said that King Solomon must have known all about operant conditioning because he used rewards and punishment. In the same sense his archers must have known all about Hooke's Law because they used bows and arrows. What is technologically useful in operant conditioning is our increasing knowledge of the extraordinarily subtle and complex properties of behaviour which may be traced to subtle and complex features of the contingencies of reinforcement which prevail in the environment.

We may arrange matters, for example, so that the rat will receive food only when it depresses the lever with a given force. Weaker responses then disappear, and exceptionally forceful responses begin to occur and can be selected through further differential reinforcement. Reinforcement may also be made contingent upon the presence of stimuli: depression of the lever operates the food dispenser, for example, only when a tone of a given pitch is sounding. As a result the rat is much more likely to respond when a tone of that pitch is sounding. Response may also be reinforced only intermittently. Some common schedules of reinforcement are the subject of probability theory. Gambling devices often provide for the reinforcement of varying numbers of responses in an unpredictable sequence. Comparable schedules are programmed in the laboratory by interposing counters between the operandum and the reinforcing device. The extensive literature on schedules of reinforcement (see, for example, Ferster & Skinner 1957) also covers intermittent reinforcement arranged by clocks and speedometers.

A more complex experimental space contains two operanda— two levers to be pressed, for example, or two disks to be pecked. Some of the resulting contingencies are the subject of decision-making theory. Responses may also be chained together, so that responding in one way produces the opportunity to respond in another. A still more complex experimental space contains two organisms with their respective operanda and with interlocking schedules of reinforcement. Game theory is concerned with contingencies of this sort. The study of operant behaviour, however, goes beyond an analysis of possible contingencies to the behaviour generated.

The application of operant conditioning to education is simple and direct. Teaching is the arrangement of contingencies of reinforcement under which students learn. They learn without teaching in their natural environments, but teachers arrange special contingencies which expedite learning, hastening the appearance of behaviour which would otherwise be acquired slowly or making sure of the appearance of behaviour which might otherwise never occur.

A teaching machine is simply any device which arranges contingencies of reinforcement. There are as many different kinds of machines as there are different kinds of contingencies. In this sense the apparatuses developed for the experimental analysis of behaviour were the first teaching machines. They remain much more complex and subtle than the devices currently available in education—a state of affairs to be regretted by anyone who is concerned with making education as effective as possible. Both the basic analysis and its technological applications require instrumental aid. Early experimenters manipulated stimuli and reinforcers and recorded responses by hand, but current research without the help of extensive apparatus is unthinkable. The teacher needs similar instrumental support, for it is impossible to arrange many of the contingencies of reinforcement which expedite learning without it. Adequate apparatus has not eliminated the researcher, and teaching machines will not eliminate the teacher. But both teacher and researcher must have such equipment if they are to work effectively.

Programmed instruction also made its first appearance in the laboratory in the form of programmed contingencies of reinforcement. The almost miraculous power to change behaviour which frequently emerges is perhaps the most conspicuous contribution to date of an experimental analysis of behaviour. There are at least four different kinds of programming. One is concerned with generating new and complex patterns or 'topographies' of behaviour. It is in the nature of operant conditioning that a response cannot be reinforced until it has occurred. For experimental purposes a response is chosen which presents no problem (a rat is likely to press a sensitive lever within a short time), but we could easily specify responses which never occur in this way. Can they then never be reinforced?

The programming of a rare topography of response is sometimes demonstrated in the classroom in the following way. A hungry pigeon is placed in an enclosed space where it is visible to the class. A food dispenser can be operated with a handswitch held by the demonstrator. The pigeon has learned to eat from the food dispenser without being disturbed by its operation, but it has not been conditioned in any other way. The class is asked to specify a response which is not part of the current repertoire of the pigeon. Suppose, for example, it is decided that the pigeon is to pace a figure eight. The demonstrator cannot simply wait for this response to occur and then reinforce it. Instead he reinforces any current response which may contribute to the final pattern— possibly simply turning the head or taking a step in, say, a clockwise direction. The reinforced response will quickly be repeated (one can actually see learning take place under these circumstances), and reinforcement is then withheld until a more marked movement in the same direction is made. Eventually only a complete turn is reinforced. Similar responses in a counterclockwise direction are then strengthened, the clockwise movement suffering partial 'extinction.' When a complete counterclockwise movement has thus been 'shaped', the clockwise turn is reinstated, and eventually the pigeon makes both turns in succession and is reinforced. The whole pattern is then quickly repeated. Q.E.D. The process of 'shaping' a response of this complexity should take no more than five or ten minutes. The demonstrator's only contact with the pigeon is by way of the handswitch, which permits him to determine the exact moment of operation of the food dispenser. By selecting responses to be reinforced he improvises a programme of contingencies, at each stage of which a response is reinforced which makes it possible to move on to a more demanding stage. The contingencies gradually approach those which generate the final specified response.

This method of shaping a topography of response has been used by Wolf, Mees & Risley (1964) to solve a difficult behaviour problem. A boy was born blind with cataracts. Before he was of an age at which an operation was feasible, he had begun to display severe temper tantrums, and after the operation he remained unmanageable. It was impossible to get him to wear the glasses without which he would soon become permanently blind. His tantrums included serious self-destructive behaviour, and he was admitted to a hospital with a diagnosis of 'child schizophrenia.' Two principles of operant conditioning were applied. The temper tantrums were extinguished by making sure that they were never followed by reinforcing consequences. A programme of contingencies of reinforcement was then designed to shape the desired behaviour of wearing glasses. It was necessary to allow the child to go hungry so that food could be used as an effective reinforcer. Empty glass frames were placed about the room and any response which made contact with them was reinforced with food. Reinforcement was then made contingent on picking up the frames, carrying them about, and so on, in a programmed sequence. Some difficulty was encountered in shaping the response of putting the frames on the face in the proper position. When this was eventually achieved, the prescription lenses were put in the frames. Wolf et al. publish a cumulative curve (figure 1) showing the number of hours per day the glasses were worn. The final slope represents essentially all the child's waking hours.

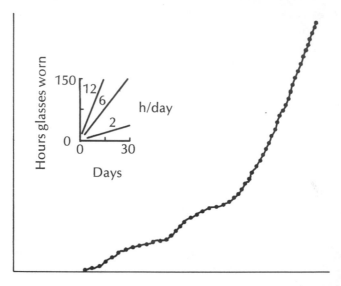

Figure 1. Curve showing the number of hours per day during which glasses were worn, plotted cumulatively. The final slope is about twelve hours per day.

Operant techniques were first applied to psychotic subjects in the pioneering work of Lindsley (1960). Azrin and others have programmed contingencies of reinforcement to solve certain management problems in institutions for the psychotic (Ayllon & Azrin 1965). The techniques are not designed to cure psychoses but to generate trouble-free behaviour. In one experiment a whole ward was placed on an economic basis. Patients were reinforced with tokens when they behaved in ways which made for simpler management, and in turn paid for services received, such as meals or consultations with psychiatrists. Such an economic system, like any economic system in the world at large, represents a special set of terminal contingencies which in neither system guarantee appropriate behaviour. The contingencies must be made effective by appropriate programmes.

A second kind of programming is used to alter temporal or intensive properties of behaviour. By differentially reinforcing only the more vigorous instances in which a pigeon pecks a disk and by advancing the minimum requirement very slowly, a pigeon can be induced to peck so energetically that the base of its beak becomes inflamed. If one were to begin with this terminal contingency, the behaviour would never develop. There is nothing new about the necessary programming. An athletic coach may train a high jumper simply by moving the bar higher by small increments, each setting permitting some successful jumps to occur. But many intensive and temporal contingencies—such as those seen in the arts, crafts, and music—are very subtle and must be carefully analyzed if they are to be properly programmed.

Another kind of programming is concerned with bringing behaviour under the control of stimuli. We could determine a rat's sensitivity to tones of different pitches by reinforcing responses made when one tone is sounding and extinguishing all responses made when other tones are sounding. We may wish to avoid extinction, however; the organism is to acquire the discrimination without making any 'errors.' An effective procedure has been analysed by Terrace (1963). Suppose we are to condition a pigeon to peck a red disk but not a green. If we simply reinforce it for pecking the red disk, it will almost certainly peck the green as well and these 'errors' must be extinguished. Terrace begins with disks which are as different as possible. One is illuminated by a red light, but the other is dark. Although reinforced for pecking the red disk, the pigeon is not likely to peck the dark disk, at least during a period of a few seconds. When the disk again becomes red, a response is immediately made. It is possible to extend the length of time the disk remains dark. Eventually the pigeon pecks the red disk instantly, but does not peck the dark disk no matter how long it remains dark. The important point is that it has never pecked the dark disk at any time.

A faint green light is then added to the dark disk. Over a period of time the green light becomes brighter and eventually is as bright as the red. The pigeon now responds instantly to the red disk but not to the green *and has never responded to the green.*

A second and more difficult discrimination can then be taught without errors by transferring control from the red and green disks. Let us say that the pigeon is to respond to a white vertical bar projected on a black disk but not to a horizontal. These patterns are first superimposed upon red and green backgrounds, and the pigeon is reinforced when it responds to red-vertical but not to green-horizontal. The intensity of the colour is then slowly reduced. Eventually the pigeon responds to the black and white vertical bar, does not respond to the black and white horizontal bar, *and has never done so.* The result could perhaps be achieved more rapidly by permitting errors to occur and extinguishing them, but other issues may need be taken into account. When extinction is used, the pigeon shows powerful emotional responses to the wrong stimulus; when the Terrace technique is used it remains quite indifferent. It is, so to speak, 'not afraid of making a mistake'. The difference is relevant to education, where the anxiety generated by current methods constitutes a serious problem. There are those who would defend a certain amount of anxiety as a good thing, but we may still envy the occasionally happy man who readily responds when the occasion is appropriate but is otherwise both emotionally and intellectually disengaged. The important point is that the terminal contingencies controlling the behaviour of both anxious and nonanxious students are the same; the difference is to be traced to the programme by way of which the terminal behaviour has been reached.

The discriminative capacities of lower organisms have been investigated with methods which require very skillful programming. Blough (1956), for example, has developed a technique in which a pigeon maintains a spot of light at an intensity at which it can just be seen. By using a range of monochromatic lights he has shown that the spectral sensitivity of the pigeon is very close to that of man. Several other techniques are available which make it possible to use lower organisms as sensitive psychophysical observers. They are available, however, only to those who understand the principles of programming.

Some current work by Murray Sidman provides a dramatic example of programming a subtle discrimination in a microcephalic idiot. At the start of the experiment Sidman's subject was 40 years old. He was said to have a mental age of about 18 months. He was partially toilet trained and dressed himself with help. To judge from the brain of his sister, now available for post-mortem study, his brain is probably about one-third the normal size. Sidman investigated his ability to discriminate circular forms projected on translucent vertical panels. Small pieces of chocolate were used as reinforcers. At first any pressure against a single large vertical panel (figure 2A) operated the device which dropped a bit of chocolate into a cup within reach. Though showing relatively poor motor co-ordination, the subject eventually executed the required, rather delicate response. The panel was subdivided into a three by three set of smaller panels (represented schematically in figure 2B), the central panel not being used in what follows. The subject was first reinforced when he pressed any of the eight remaining panels. A single panel was then lit at random, a circle being projected on it (figure 2C). The subject learned to press the lighted panel. Flat ellipses were then projected on the other panels at a low illumination (figure 2D). In subsequent settings the ellipses, now brightly illuminated, progressively approached circles (figure 2E to G). Each stage was maintained until the subject had formed the necessary discrimination, all correct responses being reinforced with chocolate. Eventually the subject could successfully select a circle from an array approximately like that shown in figure 2H. Using similar shaping techniques Sidman and his associates have conditioned the subject to pick up and use a pencil appropriately, tracing letters faintly projected on a sheet of paper.

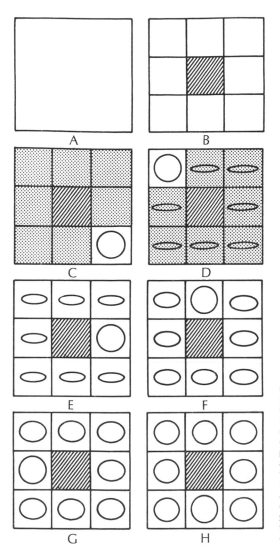

Figure 2. A programme designed to teach subtle form discrimination. Reinforcement was contingent on: (A) a response moving a large panel; (B) a response moving any one of nine smaller panels (with the exception of the centre panel); (C) a response moving only the one panel on which a circle is projected; (D) as before except that flat ellipses appear faintly on the other panels; (E, F, G) a response to the panel bearing a circle, appearing in random position among ellipses the shorter axis of which is progressively lengthening; (H) a response to the panel bearing a circle among ellipses closely approximating circles.

The intellectual accomplishments of this microcephalic idiot in the forty-first year of his life have exceeded all those of his first 40 years. They were possible only because he has lived a few hours of each week of that year in a well-programmed environment. No very bright future beckons (he has already lived longer than most people of his kind), and it is impossible to say what he might have achieved if he had been subjected to a similar programme from birth, but he has contributed to our knowledge by demonstrating the power of a method of instruction which could scarcely be tested on a less promising case. (The bright futures belong to the normal and exceptional children who will be fortunate enough to live in environments which have been designed to maximize *their* development, and of whose potential achievements we have now scarcely any conception.)

A fourth kind of programming has to do with maintaining behaviour under infrequent reinforcement. A pigeon will continue to respond even though only one response in every hundred, say, is reinforced, but it will not do so unless the contingencies have been programmed. A fresh pigeon is no more likely to peck a disk a hundred times than to pace a figure eight. The behaviour is built up by reinforcing every response, then every other response, then every fifth response, and so on, waiting at each stage until the behaviour is reasonably stable. Under careful programming pigeons have continued to respond when only every ten-thousandth response has been reinforced, and this is certainly not the limit. An observer might say that the pigeon is 'greatly interested in his work', 'industrious', 'remarkably tolerant to frustration', 'free from discouragement', 'dedicated to his task', and so on. These expressions are commonly applied to students who have had the benefit of similar programming, accidental or arranged.

The effective scheduling of reinforcement is an important element in educational design. Suppose we wish to teach a student to read 'good books'—books which, almost by definition, do not reinforce the reader sentence by sentence or even paragraph by paragraph but only when possibly hundreds of pages have prepared him for a convincing or moving dénouement. The student must be exposed to a programme of materials which build up a tendency to read in the absence of reinforcement. Such programmes are seldom constructed deliberately and seldom arise by accident, and it is therefore not surprising that few students even in good universities learn to read books of this sort and continue to do so for the rest of their lives. In their pride, schools are likely to arrange just the wrong conditions; they are likely to maintain so-called 'standards' under which books are forced upon students before they have had adequate preparation.

Other objectives in education need similar programming. The dedicated scientist who works for years in spite of repeated failures is often looked upon as a happy accident, but he may well be the product of a happy if accidental history of reinforcement. A programme in which exciting results were first common but became less and less frequent could generate the capacity to continue in the absence of reinforcement for long periods of time. Such programmes should arise naturally as scientists turn to more and more difficult areas. Perhaps not many effective programmes are to be expected for this reason, and they are only rarely designed by teachers of science. This may explain why there are so few dedicated scientists. Maintaining a high level of activity is one of the more important achievements of programming. Repeatedly, in its long history, education has resorted to aversive control to keep its students at work. A proper understanding of the scheduling of reinforcement may lead at long last to a better solution of this problem.

Let us look at these principles of programming at work in one or two traditional educational assignments. Instruction in handwriting will serve as one example. To say that a child is to learn 'how to write' tells us very little. The so-called signs of 'knowing how to write' provide a more useful set of behavioural specifications. The child is to form letters and words which are legible and graceful according to taste. He is to do this first in copying a model, then in writing to dictation (or self-dictation as he spells out words he would otherwise speak), and eventually in writing as a separate nonvocal form of verbal behaviour. A common method is to ask the child to copy letters or words and to approve or otherwise reinforce his approximations to good copy. More and more exact copies are demanded as the hand improves—in a crude sort of programming. The method is ineffective largely because the reinforcements are too long deferred. The parent or teacher comments upon or corrects the child's work long after it has been performed.

A possible solution is to teach the child to discriminate between good and bad form before he starts to write. Acceptable behaviour should then generate immediate, automatic self-reinforcement. This is seldom done. Another possibility is to make reinforcement immediately contingent upon successful responses. One method now being tested is to treat paper chemically so that the pen the child uses writes in dark blue when a response is correct and yellow when it is incorrect. The dark blue line is made automatically reinforcing through generous commendation. Under such contingencies the proper execution of a letter can be programmed; at first the child makes a very small contribution in completing a letter, but through progressive stages he approaches the point at which he composes the letter as a whole, the chemical response of the paper differentially reinforcing good form throughout. The model to be copied is then made progressively less important by separating it in both time and space from the child's work. Eventually words are written to dictation, letter by letter, in spelling dictated words, and in describing pictures. The same kind of differential reinforcement can be used to teach good form, proper spacing, and so on. The child is eventually forming letters skilfully under continuous automatic reinforcement. The method is directed as much toward motivation as toward good form. Even quite young children remain busily at work for long periods of time without coercion or threat, showing few signs of fatigue, nervousness, or other forms of escape.

As a second example we may consider the acquisition of a simple form of verbal behaviour. A behavioural specification is here likely to be especially strongly resisted. It is much more in line with traditional educational policy to say that the student is to 'know facts, understand principles, be able to put ideas into words, express meanings, or communicate information.' In *Verbal behaviour* (Skinner 1957) I tried to show how the behaviour exhibited in such activities could be formulated without reference to ideas, meanings, or information, and many of the principles currently used in programming verbal knowledge have been drawn from that analysis. The field is too large to be adequately covered here, but two examples may suggest the direction of the approach.

What happens when a student memorizes a poem? Let us say that he begins by reading the poem from a text. His behaviour is at that time under the control of the text, and it is to be accounted for by examining the process through which he has learned to read. When he eventually speaks the poem in the absence of a text, the same form of verbal behaviour has come under the control of other stimuli. He may begin to recite when asked to do so—he is then under control of an external verbal stimulus—but, as he continues to recite, his behaviour comes under the control of stimuli he himself is generating (not necessarily in a crude word-by-word chaining of responses). In the process of 'memorizing' the poem, control passes from one kind of stimulus to another.

A classroom demonstration of the transfer of control from text to self-generated stimuli illustrates the process. A short poem is projected on a screen or written on a chalkboard. A few unnecessary letters are omitted. The class read the poem in chorus. A second slide is then projected in which other letters are missing (or letters erased from the chalkboard). The class could not have read the poem correctly if this form had been presented first, but because of its recent history it is able to do so. (Some members undoubtedly receive help from others in the process of choral reading.) In a third setting still other letters are omitted, and after a series of five or six settings the text has completely disappeared. The class is nevertheless able to 'read' the poem. Control has passed mainly to self-generated stimuli.

As another example, consider what a student learns when he consults an illustrated dictionary. After looking at a labelled picture, as in figure 3, we say that he knows something he did not know before. This is another of those vague expressions which have done so much harm to education. The 'signs or symptoms of such knowledge' are of two sorts. Shown the picture in figure 3 without the text the student can say 'caduceus' (we say that he now knows what the object pictured in the figure is called) or, shown the word *caduceus,* he can now describe or reconstruct the picture (we say that he now knows what the word *caduceus* means). But what has actually happened?

The basic process is similar to that of transferring discriminative

Figure 3. Caduceus.

control in the Terrace experiment. To begin with, the student can respond to the picture in various ways: he can describe it without naming it, he can find a similar picture in an array, he can draw a fair copy, and so on. He can also speak the name by reading the printed word. When he first looks at the picture and reads the word, his verbal response is primarily under the control of the text, but it must eventually be controlled by the picture. As in transferring the control exerted by red and green to vertical and horizontal lines, we can change the control efficiently by making the text gradually less important, covering part of it, removing some of the letters, or fogging it with a translucent mask. As the picture acquires control the student can speak the name with less and less help from the text. Eventually, when the picture exerts enough control, he 'knows the name of the pictured object.' The normal student can learn the name of one object so quickly that the 'vanishing' technique may not be needed, but it is a highly effective procedure in learning the names of a large number of objects. The good student learns how to make progressive reductions in the effectiveness of a text by himself: he may glance at the text out of the corner of his eye, uncover it bit by bit, and so on. In this way he improvises his own programme in making the text less and less important as the picture acquires control of the verbal response.

In teaching the student 'the meaning of the word *caduceus*' we could slowly obscure the picture, asking the student to respond to the name by completing a drawing or description or by finding a matching picture in an array. Eventually in answer to the question *What is a caduceus?* he describes the object, makes a crude sketch, or points to the picture of a caduceus. The skilful student uses techniques of this sort in studying unprogrammed material.

'Knowing what a caduceus is' or 'knowing the meaning of the word caduceus' is probably more than responding in these ways to picture or text. In other words, there are other 'signs of knowledge.' That is one reason why the concept of knowledge is so inadequate.

But other relevant behaviour must be taught, if at all, in substantially the same way.

These examples do scant justice to the many hundreds of effective programmes now available or to the techniques which many of them use so effectively, but they must suffice as a basis for discussing a few general issues. An effective technology of teaching, derived not from philosophical principles but from a realistic analysis of human behaviour, has much to contribute, but as its nature has come to be clearly seen, strong opposition has arisen.

A common objection is that most of the early work responsible for the basic formulation of behaviour was done on so-called lower animals. It has been argued that the procedures are therefore appropriate only to animals and that to use them in education is to treat the student like an animal. So far as I know, no one argues that because something is true of a pigeon, it is therefore true of a man. There are enormous differences in the topographies of the behaviours of man and pigeon and in the kinds of environmental events which are relevant to that behaviour—differences which, if anatomy and physiology were adequate to the task, we could probably compare with differences in the mediating substrata—but the basic processes in behaviour, as in neural tissue, show helpful similarities. Relatively simple organisms have many advantages in early stages of research, but they impose no limit on that research. Complex processes are met and dealt with as the analysis proceeds. Experiments on pigeons may not throw much light on the 'nature' of man, but they are extraordinarily helpful in enabling us to analyse man's environment more effectively. What is common to pigeon and man is a world in which certain contingencies of reinforcement prevail. The schedule of reinforcement which makes a pigeon a pathological gambler is to be found at race track and roulette table, where it has a comparable effect.

Another objection is to the use of contrived contingencies of reinforcement. In daily life one does not wear glasses in order to get food or point to circles in order to receive chocolate. Such reinforcers are not naturally contingent on the behaviour and there may seem to be something synthetic, spurious, or even fraudulent about them. The attack on contrived contingencies of reinforcement may be traced to Rousseau and his amazing book, Émile. Rousseau wanted to avoid the punitive systems of his day. Convinced as he was that civilization corrupts, he was also afraid of all social reinforcers. His plan was to make the student dependent upon *things* rather than people. John Dewey restated the principle by emphasizing real life experiences in the schoolroom. In American education it is commonly argued that a child must be taught nothing until he can reap natural benefits from knowing it. He is not to learn to write until he can take satisfaction in writing his name in his books, or notes to his friends. Producing a purple rather than a yellow line is irrelevant to handwriting. Unfortunately, the teacher who confines himself to natural reinforcers is often ineffective, particularly because only certain subjects can be taught through their use, and he eventually falls back upon some form of punishment. But aversive control is the most shameful of irrelevancies: it is only in school that one parses a Latin sentence to avoid the cane.

The objection to contrived reinforcers arises from a misunderstanding of the nature of teaching. The teacher expedites learning by arranging special contingencies of reinforcement, which may not resemble the contingencies under which the behaviour is eventually useful. Parents teach a baby to talk by reinforcing its first efforts with approval and affection, but these are not natural consequences of speech. The baby learns to say *mama, dada, spoon,* or *cup* months before he ever calls to his father or mother or identifies them to a passing stranger or asks for a spoon or cup or reports their presence to someone who cannot see them. The contrived reinforcement shapes the topography of verbal behaviour long before that behaviour can produce its normal consequences in a verbal community. In the same way a child reinforced for the proper formation of letters by a chemical reaction is prepared to write long before the natural consequences of effective writing take over. It was necessary to use a 'spurious' reinforcer to get the boy to wear glasses, but once the behaviour had been shaped and maintained for a period of time, the natural reinforcers which follow from improved vision could take over. The real issue is whether the teacher prepares the student for the natural reinforcers which are to replace the contrived reinforcers used in teaching. The behaviour which is expedited in the teaching process would be useless if it were not to be effective in the world at large in the absence of instructional contingencies.

Another objection to effective programmed instruction is that it does not teach certain important activities. When required to learn unprogrammed material for an impending examination the student learns how to study, how to clear up puzzling matters, how to work under puzzlement, and so on. These may be as important as the subject-matter itself. The same argument could have been raised with respect to a modern experimental analysis of learning when contrasted with early studies of that process. Almost all early investigators of learning constructed what we now call terminal contingencies of reinforcement to which an organism was immediately subjected. Thus, a rat was put into a maze, a cat was put into a puzzle box, and so on. The organism possessed little if any behaviour appropriate to such a 'problem', but some responses were reinforced, and over a period of time an acceptable terminal performance might be reached. The procedure was called 'trial and error.' A programme of contingencies of reinforcement would have brought the organism to the same terminal performance much more rapidly and efficiently and without trial and error, but in doing so it could have been said to deprive the organism of the opportunity to learn how to try, how to explore—indeed, how to solve problems.

The educator who assigns material to be studied for an impending test presents the student with an opportunity to learn to examine the material in a special way which facilitates recall, to work industriously at something which is not currently reinforcing, and so on. It is true that a programme designed simply to impart knowledge of a subject-matter does not do any of this. It does not because it is not designed to do so. Programming undertakes to reach one goal at a time. Efficient ways of studying and thinking are separate goals. A crude parallel is offered by the current argument in favour of the cane or related aversive practices on the ground that they build character; they teach a boy to take punishment and to accept responsibility for his conduct. These are worthwhile goals, but they should not necessarily be taught at the same time as, say, Latin grammar or mathematics. Rousseau suggested a relevant form of programming through which a child could be taught to submit to aversive stimuli without alarm or panic. He pointed out that a baby dropped into a cold bath will probably be frightened and cry, but that if one begins with water at body temperature and cools it one degree per day, the baby will eventually not be disturbed by cold water. The programme must be carefully followed. (In his enthusiasm for the new science, Rousseau exclaimed 'Use a thermometer!') Similar programmes can teach a tolerance for painful stimuli, but caning a boy for idleness, forgetfulness, or bad spelling is an unlikely example. It only occasional builds what the eighteenth century called "bottom', as it only occasionally eliminates idleness, forgetfulness, or bad spelling.

It is important to teach careful observation, exploration, and inquiry, but they are not well taught by submitting a student to material which he must observe and explore effectively or suffer the consequences. Better methods are available. There are two ways to teach a man to look before leaping: he may be severely punished when he leaps without looking or he may be positively reinforced (possibly 'spuriously') for looking before leaping. He may learn to look in both cases, but when simply punished for leaping without looking he must discover for himself the art of careful observation, and he is not likely to profit from the experience of others. When he is reinforced for looking, a suitable programme will transmit earlier discoveries in the art of observation. (Incidentally, the audiovisual devices mentioned earlier which undertake to attract attention do not teach careful observation. On the contrary, they are much more likely to deprive the student of the opportunity to learn such skills than effective programming of subject-matters.)

Learning how to study is another example. When a teacher simply tests students on assigned material, few ever learn to study well, and many never learn at all. One may read for the momentary effect and forget what one has read almost immediately; one obviously reads in a very different way for retention. As we have seen, many of the practices of the good student resemble those of the programmer. The student can in a sense programme material as he goes, rehearsing what he has learned, glancing at a text only as needed, and so on. These practices can be separately programmed as an important part of the student's education and can be much more effectively taught than by punishing the student for reading without remembering.

It would be pleasant to be able to say that punishing the student for not thinking is also not the only way to teach thinking. Some relevant behaviours have been analysed and can therefore be explicitly programmed. Algorithmic methods of problem-solving are examples. Simply leading the student through a solution in the traditional way is one kind of programming. Requiring him to solve a series of problems of graded difficulty is another. More effective programmes can certainly be prepared. Unfortunately, they would only emphasize the rather mechanical nature of alorithmic problem-solving. Real thinking seems to be something else. It is sometimes said to be a matter of 'heuristics.' But relevant practices can be formulated as techniques of solving the problem of solving problems. Once a heuristic device or practice is formulated and programmed, it cannot be distinguished in any important way from algorithmic problem-solving. The will-of-the-wisp of creative thinking still leads us on.

Human behaviour often assumes novel forms, some of which are valuable. The teaching of truly creative behaviour is, nevertheless, a contradiction in terms. Original discovery is seldom if ever guaranteed in the classroom. In Polya's little book, *How to solve it* (Polya 1945), a few boys in a class eventually arrive at the formula for the diagonal of a parallelopiped. It is possible that the teacher did not tell them the formula, but it is unlikely that the course they followed under his guidance resembled that of the original discoverer. Efforts to teach creativity have sacrificed the teaching of subject-matter. The teacher steers a delicate course between two great fears—on the one hand that he may not teach and on the other that he may tell the student something. Until we know more about creative thinking, we may need to confine ourselves to making sure that the student is in full possession of the contributions of earlier thinkers, that he has been abundantly reinforced for careful observation and inquiry, that he has the interest and industry generated by a fortunate history of successes.

It has been said that an education is what survives when a man has forgotten all he has been taught. Certainly few students could pass their final examinations even a year or two after leaving school or the university. What has been learned of permanent value must therefore not be the facts and principles covered by examinations but certain other kinds of behaviour often ascribed to special abilities. Far from neglecting these kinds of behaviour, careful programming reveals the need to teach them as explicit educational objectives. For example, two programmes prepared with the help of the Committee on Programmed Instruction at Harvard—a programme in crystallography constructed by Bruce Chalmers and James G. Holland and a programme in neuroanatomy by Murray and Richard Sidman—both reveal the importance of special skills in three-dimensional thinking. As measured by available tests, these skills vary enormously even among scientists who presumably make special use of them. They can be taught with separate programmes or as part of crystallography or neuroanatomy when specifically recognized as relevant skills. It is possible that education will eventually concentrate on those forms of behaviour which 'survive when all one has learned has been forgotten.'

The argument that effective teaching is inimical to thinking, whether creative or not, raises a final point. We fear effective teaching, as we fear all effective means of changing human behaviour. Power not only corrupts, it frightens; and absolute power frightens absolutely. We take another—and very long—look at educational policy when we conceive of teaching which really works. It has been said that teaching machines and programmed instruction will mean regimentation (it is sometimes added that regimentation is the goal of those who propose such methods), but in principle nothing could be more regimented than education as it now stands. School and state authorities draw up syllabuses specifying what students are to learn year by year. Universities insist upon 'requirements' which are presumably to be met by all students applying for admission. Examinations are 'standard.' Certificates, diplomas, and honours testify to the completion of specified work. We do not worry about all this because we know that students never learn what they are required to learn, but some other safeguard must be found when education is effective.

It could well be that an effective technology of teaching will be unwisely used. It could destroy initiative and creativity, it could make men all alike (and not necessarily in being equally excellent), it could suppress the beneficial effect of accidents upon the development of the individual and upon the evolution of a culture. On the other hand, it could maximize the genetic endowment of each student, it could make him as skilful, competent, and informed as possible, it could build the greatest diversity of interests, it could lead him to make the greatest possible contribution to the survival and development of his culture. Which of these futures lies before us will not be determined by the mere availability of effective instruction. The use to which a technology of teaching is to be put will depend upon other matters. We cannot avoid the decisions which now face us by putting a stop to the scientific study of human behaviour or by refusing to make use of the technology which inevitably flows from such a science.

The experimental analysis of behaviour is a vigorous young science which will inevitably find practical applications. Important extensions have already been made in such fields as psychopharmacology and psychotherapy. Its bearing on economics, government, law, and even religion are beginning to attract attention. It is thus concerned with government in the broadest possible sense. In the government of the future the techniques we associate with education are most likely to prevail. That is why it is so important that this young science has begun by taking its most effective technological step in the development of a technology of teaching.

Preparation of this lecture has been supported by Grant K6-MH-21,775-01 of the National Institute of Mental Health of the U.S. Public Health Service, and by the Human Ecology Fund.

References

Ayllon, T., and Azrin, N. H. 1965. An objective method for the measurement and reinforcement of adaptive behaviour of psychotics. *J. Exp. Anal. Beh.* (In the Press.)

Barzun, J. 1963. Review of J. S. Bruner, *Essays for the left hand, Science* 25:323.

Blough, D. 1956. Dark adaptation in the pigeon. *J. Comp. Physiol. Psychol.* 49:425–30.

Ferster, C. B., and Skinner, B. F. 1957. *Schedules of reinforcement.* New York: Appleton-Century-Crofts.

James, W. 1889. *Talks to teachers on psychology.* New York: Henry Holt.

Lindsley, Ogden R. 1960. Characterization of the behavior of chronic psychotics as revealed by free operant conditioning methods. *Diseases of the Nervous System,* Monograph Supplement 21:66–78.

Polya, G. 1945. *How to solve it.* Princeton, New Jersey: Princeton University Press.

Pressey, S. J. 1926. A simple apparatus which gives tests and scores—and teaches. *Sch. Soc.* 23:373–76.

Rousseau, J. J. 1762. *Émile ou de l'éducation.* Le Haye: Néaulme.

Skinner, B. F. 1938. *The behaviour of organisms.* New York: Appleton-Century-Crofts.

Skinner, B. F. 1957. *Verbal behaviour.* New York: Appleton-Century-Crofts.

Sidman, M. 1964. Personal communication.

Terrace, H. S. 1963. Errorless transfer of a discrimination across two continua. *J. Exp. Anal. Behav.* 6:223–32.

Wolf, M., Mees, H., and Risley, T. 1964. Application of operant conditioning procedures to the behaviour problems in the autistic child. *Behav. Res. Therapy* 1:305–12.

4 / Theoretical Basis for Behavior Modification

OGDEN R. LINDSLEY

Ogden R. Lindsley was a colleague of B. F. Skinner who later coauthored several books with him. Like Skinner, his early work in the laboratory developed into an interest in applied psychology and the uses of operant conditioning techniques.

Here Lindsley takes to task many academic psychologists in his claim that they are often concerned about supporting their theories of behavior rather than about learning from the observation of behavior. In his refreshingly uncomplicated style he calls psychological terminology atrocious and points out that the best way to teach the use of an applied psychology is to use it, a point made in the early pages of this text.

When you think about dying, you want to feel some sort of assurance that what you have done will flourish, that the corn you planted will be harvested. Such has been true of my own professional life. I spent

Source: Ogden R. Lindsley, "Theoretical Basis for Behavior Modification," an address given at the School of Education, University of Oregon, May 1967. This is the first publication. The research was supported by Training Grant NB-05362, National Institute of Neurological Diseases and Blindness, and Research Grant HD-00870, National Institute of Child Health and Human Development from the U. S. Public Health Service, Dept. of Health, Education, and Welfare to the Bureau of Child Research, University of Kansas. The writer is indebted to the graduate students in his education classes and the fathers in his "father's groups" for making it possible to obtain this data.

the first five or six years of it convincing myself that the procedures we were using had great potential for helping man do something about his problems. During the next few years, I found out that there are just too many exciting things to be done for any one man to be able to cope with all of them. After still more years, I found out that there is too much to be done for any one profession to accomplish. This holds true for the application of free-operant techniques and procedures. Thus, I have been spending less time in advancing the subdiscipline in which I personally work in order to train others. I would like to discuss how to teach these people most efficiently and effectively.

One of the difficult problems with which we are faced is that some of the people who shared with me the teachings of B. F. Skinner have become professionalized and are teaching their students to do things in exactly the same way in which they were taught. In other words, many people are spending most of their energy trying to make sure that Osgood's theory of perception does not die in our time, that Skinner's book *The Behavior of Organisms* will live without change, or that our own words of ten years ago will still be held valid. Instructors are actually teaching only the history of operant conditioning. This concerns me greatly. We are an infant with a potential that exceeds my imagination. To cut this up into courses, start testing for it, in other words, to dress it up in academic paraphernalia, is ridiculous!

Associated with a strong academic orientation are other problems with which a professional becomes involved today. I have found that in maintaining my own behavior it is extremely difficult to discover which habits, which behaviors, can be dispensed with and which are absolutely necessary to perform the current tasks that I have assigned myself. Professionalism seems to be one of the major problems facing all the disciplines concerned with behavior today—psychology, education, nursing, psychiatry, and so forth. The argument is not over how we can change the child. Rather it is over who is going to get the major share of a mental retardation center or how is the proposal going to be written up. The discussion is not over how we can *help* the child or *teach* the teacher. The fight seems to be over who is going to have three semester hours for student teaching, what is going to be said, and which textbook is going to be used.

I think, however, education is in a better position in regard to this issue than academic psychology. Education is oriented towards service. Probably this is what keeps people in education from spending over four hours a day in concern with personal power. My own hunch is that if psychology had produced a large group of service personnel in the last two or three decades, it would not be stifled by professionalism. For example, there was a tremendous pressure put on psychology after it "sold" tests to *give* these tests. Some people, who were mostly practitioners, thought it might be feasible to use terminal masters students as testers. However, the academicians won that battle when they demanded that every practitioner be a purple-hooded Ph.D. Because the academicians won, we have a structure in which there are all peers and no troops, all generals and no one to go out to the front-line trenches.

Another problem in psychology and the other disciplines concerned with behavior is commitment. The committed person is the kind of fellow who thinks about his work on Saturday or even early in the morning while he shaves. He has a high rate of performance with respect to his profession. However, there is differential commitment among our professionals. So within these disciplines, for descriptive purposes, I talk about *theoretical commitment, methodological commitment,* or *problem* or *field commitment.*

I think education and psychology are too much theoretically and methodologically committed. If a professional group is primarily theoretically committed, as are the Freudians and the clinical psychologists, their approach cannot long endure. It will not endure when other approaches can be demonstrated to work immediately, efficiently, and more effectively. What we need is to develop an orientation which allows the people who are working with problem children or adults to use any technique, any tools at their disposal, that will enable them to perform most proficiently in a given situation. Such an orientation would be *field commitment.* We have far too few people in this category in our professions.

What I am concerned about and what I want to share with you are some of the ways that you can keep an original element of operant conditioning. Skinner used to say, "The rat knows best; that is why we have him in the experiment. If we knew so much, we could put a mechanical rat in, or make predictions ourselves." Translated to human behavior, what this means is that the child knows best.

This original element of operant conditioning allows us to learn *from* the child, *from* observation of human behavior. For example, if one child shows you that the approval of another child is more powerful than all the M&M's you have ever brought, and you still persist with M&M's or tokens, then you are committed to a method or theory, not to the best way to work with this child! If, on the other hand, you realize *what* is significant to the child, you throw away the M&M's for a better technique. That would be an example of being child-committed and field-oriented.

It has been my experience that there are far too few professionals to work with the behavior problems of our children in the homes and schools today. And I have concluded that if we are going to do anything about behaviorally managing the children of this country, it has got to be done with teachers and parents as agents. They are the ones who work directly with the children.

When I began to teach teachers, one of the first things I found out was that the language we were going to use was atrocious. Not only did it fail to build on the language they had already learned; it actually worked counter to their language. We spoke of stimuli that followed responses. That is a difficult way to talk about behavior. If I tell a teacher, "One thing about behavior is that there is a stimulus, a response, and a stimulus that is a reinforcing stimulus," she looks at me perplexed for a minute before she concludes that she doesn't want to go back to school and buy new textbooks before she can even understand the language. Furthermore, that kind of talk is a bad instructional system—it does not produce the behavior that we want. Once when instructors were trying to teach pilots in the Air Force, they used a system where red meant "right" and green meant "left." This system wasn't functional because pilots knew that the red light was always on the left wing and the green light was on the right wing. They couldn't learn another system that went counter to the "color language" that they had known for years. Similarly, the red and green traffic signals are intregal with our driving behavior, and we couldn't very well change the meaning of these lights.

Therefore we decided not to speak about *stimuli* and *reinforcing stimuli*. We decided that a reinforcing stimulus is the powerful thing which builds behavior. You follow a certain behavior with it to increase the probability of the occurrence of the movement or response on future occasions. In searching for a term that would mean precisely that, we wondered what is wrong with *acceleration*? If you have a reinforcing stimulus, or a consequence, that increases the probability of the occurrence of a behavior on future occasions, you know it. No one asks, "How you can tell if a consequence is accelerating?" Obviously, the consequence is accelerating when the behavior increases on future occasions. Conversely, *deceleration* is the lessening of or decreasing of the probability of a recurrence on future occasions.

The reason *acceleration* and *deceleration* or *accelerating* and *decelerating consequences* are good terms to use with teachers is that they are functional. They mean something from the teacher's point of view, and they mean something from the child's point of view. The teacher and the child are immediately aware of the effect. I find it very easy to teach functional behavior analysis in one hour or two hours to parents and teachers for two reasons: (1) if the teacher or if the child himself chooses a consequence that is meaningful for him, then there is a high probability that it is going to work; and (2) if it doesn't work, then we know something else is happening.

We know, from the child's point of view, if he has the teacher

under his control instead of vice versa. She may be maintaining his talking-out behavior by the very attention she pays to him to get him to
stop it. In order for teachers to understand what may be happening, we
have worked out a few simple functional ways to analyze behavior. You
have to realize that if the child is in a room and now and then a candy
drops and he is not even aware that he is wriggling, you have no behavior control. You should not assert the consequence, but you might
try other movements. We have techniques for response building, consequence building, and stimulus building.

  These terms are about all we talk about because if you stress
talk with your class of teachers, only about thirty percent of them are
going to change the behavior of the children in the classroom as a
result. The reason it is not enough to teach "verbal behavior" is: What
are the consequences for the teacher? Talk only stimulates behavior; it
does not consequate it. Therefore I stopped explaining behavior when
questions were asked. Now the first thing I require is that my students
find a child who has a behavior they wish to accelerate or decelerate.
They cannot come back to class until they have chosen this behavior
as a target for deceleration or acceleration. Also they must have a record
of the frequency of the behavior. How often does it occur? Is it cyclical?
The record or the graph can tell us the answers to these questions
precisely.

  The graduate courses I teach now have two grades that I have
never used before, *I* and *F*. The *I* represents "incomplete modification
of a child's behavior." The *F* is given for "falsified data." By the eighth
meeting of last semester, one hundred percent of the students in one
of my classes had a behavior modification case under surveillance. This
class no longer has lectures. Students bring their graphs in and show
them on a large screen with an opaque projector. They describe where
they are having difficulty or why a particular approach did not work.
Only after the class has exhausted its ability to comment and suggest
will I comment. On the basis of this approach to teaching, I gave a
pen-and-pencil test that I have given before to groups taught by other
procedures. This last class, which had never had formal instruction in
symbolic behavioral analysis, outperformed groups that had. I believe
they did so because they had higher motivation and because natural
consequences were operating. Natural consequences mean that the students were affected by the success of their projects, by the knowledge
that they had modified the behavior of a child, and that they had the
records to prove it. A teacher can take these records to a principal and
say, "This is what was happening with Billy before I tried such and
such for so many days, and this was the result of my modification. Now
Billy is no longer a problem. I have thirty days of post-modification
data to show this." The most important aspect of the natural conse-

quences is that Billy is no longer a problem to the teacher. Now she can work more effectively with the twenty-six other students in her classroom.

Another aspect of natural consequation is allied with an interesting dimension of my current teaching. When I was younger, I was told that the last patient in the world you should work with was your wife or yourself because of your bias. Now, however, we know how to observe and to record behavior with techniques that eliminate this bias. There is an advantage in working with people close to you because you are able to maximize the consequences. When my graduate students come to me and say, "I want to work with my daughter's speech problem or my sister's weight problem or my own smoking," I tell them, "That is fine. Someone near you is the best person you can work with. When you have succeeded in changing that person's behavior, you yourself are consequated. What you have done means something to you." This is another instance of the greater power natural consequences put into our instructional system than synthetic ones ever could.

The class that I referred to was composed of thirty-four graduate students. One hundred percent of them successfully modified children's behavior in a fifteen-week semester course, which met two hours each week. The median number of successful cases when only one was requested was 3.2 per student. I think that next semester I might ask for four cases, two of which are to have acceleration targets, and two deceleration. I used to be happy with a thirty percent modification of a single case. Now I want one hundred percent modification. I really don't know what the upper limit is in the number of behavior problems a single individual can handle in a certain length of time. I do know that I am getting many more successful cases than I would have expected. I handled a father's group in this manner, and again one hundred percent of the fathers succeeded with the deceleration target for the behaviors of their retarded children. I never saw any of these children. I just talked with the fathers. It is these kinds of findings that convince me a lot of time is being wasted teaching the "history" of our science.

From our point of view, the only measure of a good teacher or good methods or good schools is the performance, the *daily* performance of the children. Most teachers will tell you, "We do not have any measure of daily performance. It just would be impossible to measure the behavior of every child every day." Many teachers have been told that the way you measure a child's performance is to give him a test. Tests are not measurements of a child's performance—just samples of it! We have been working on the direct measurement of children's behavior in the classroom. We feel we have had some success.

We have found that there is a lot of recording skill available in the classroom which has never been tapped. If a child can add and subtract and divide and tell time, then he can record his own behavior. He can record the time it takes him to do a certain number of arithmetic problems and divide that into the number of correct problems to get the rate of correct problems per minute. This self-recording of data acts as a big accelerating consequence. We have been able to accelerate performance in children with whom we had originally failed while the teacher was recording the behavior. I wish to stress, however, that recording numbers alone is not a sufficient consequence. By making a graph of his performance, the child can see how much he has improved. It seems to me that we should make graphs instead of tables because graphs change behavior many times when tables do not. We now have fourth- and and fifth-grade children plotting semi-log plots of their own performance.

Summary

I have given examples of what I call field commitment. I believe that academic psychology and education lack this kind of commitment. Until the members of these professions spend more time really watching and recording behavior, more time in the classroom and wherever field commitment may lead them, we will not get many new ideas. Instead, we will have some more big buildings. It is possible to teach effective, functional behavior analysis and management to teachers and parents in ten to twenty hours of instruction; in some cases, in two to four hours. One short-range reason this is possible is by employing a common functional language for analyzing behavior. Another reason, more important perhaps from the long-range viewpoint, is that natural consequences have proven to be extremely effective. Significant findings indicate the accelerating effect of self-graphing. We have had teachers, parents, graduate students, and school psychologists successfully modify behavior. There is a common dictum that the proof is in the pudding. We feel that the proof is in the classroom and in the home.

5 / Analysis of a Teaching Problem in an Educational Perspective

FINLEY CARPENTER AND EUGENE HADDEN

A criticism of educational psychology as it has been presented in the past is that, by and large, it has been made up of vague statements about learning that have minimal applicability. Finley Carpenter and Eugene Hadden share that opinion and in this article address themselves to a strategy whereby psychology can have a direct application to learning.

Beginning with the objective that one of the teacher's functions is to help students acquire subject matter efficiently, the authors tear apart the significant words "acquire," "help," and "efficient" and translate these into concrete signs so that the teacher can know with some assurance when or if the objective has been reached. A careful reading should give you a fairly insightful ability to discriminate between functional and nonfunctional principles of psychology.

The road to making useful operating rules begins with a practical problem. Trying to apply principles of psychology to teaching without first locating a teaching problem is like trying to apply paint to an imaginary

Source: Finley Carpenter and Eugene Hadden, *Systematic Application of Psychology to Education* (New York: The Macmillan Company; 1964), chap. 2. Copyright © 1964 The Macmillan Company. Reprinted by permission of the publisher.

house. The first step, therefore, is to locate a specific question or diffi-culty. One important question in education can be stated as follows: *How can the teacher help students acquire subject matter efficiently?* Not only do teachers accept the question as an important problem, but it is also the basis of much current criticism of education. The charge of a lack of progress in the efficiency of teaching has gained such in-tensity that educators have been forced to recognize the problem with grave concern. Whether or not the charge is valid cannot be deter-mined by verbal rebuttals, but only through exhaustive research efforts.

AN EDUCATIONAL PERSPECTIVE

After a problem has been chosen, the next step is that of providing suffi-cient context for viewing the problem in a meaningful perspective. The context will be only partly developed here because it will be expanded in greater detail in Part II of the book as a prelude for the analyses of teaching practices.

Let us consider the purpose of teaching content as having four phases:

a. *Acquiring information* is that stage in which the learner comes in contact with the new facts, terms, principles, and theories in the subject matter. Unless the pupil succeeds in acquiring the necessary information, he cannot be expected to manipulate it critically and creatively, nor even to use it effectively in practical situations.

b. *Using the information* is the stage of putting the information to work toward solving problems that exist outside the subject matter itself. Most viewpoints on education accept the view that the learning of subject matter should have some value for meeting problems in every-day living. While there are differences of opinions as to the degree to which school learning should meet the standard of practical utility, virtually all thinkers on education agree that information holds a sig-nificance that extends beyond the mere acquiring of it.

c. *Analyzing the content critically* is a valuable phase for deep-ening the learner's understanding. Skill in making searching analyses provides the pupil with a measure of self-confidence because it places him in a more commanding role in relation to the subject matter than does mere acquisition of information. Fruitful analysis requires a skill that seems to bring its own reward by revealing considerations of con-tent that previously were not apparent. Somehow the act of finding imperfections in a topic seems not only to help bolster the learner's self-confidence, but to stimulate attempts to improve that which is being analyzed. Thus, important functions of analysis are clarifying the nature and significance of a subject matter and preparing the way for posing new and searching questions.

d. *Manipulating the content creatively* is a goal phase that has perhaps given the learner his greatest feeling of satisfaction. Our perspective of content learning asserts that movement toward creativity should be stimulated as early as possible so that the learner can experience the most intense reward available in the educative process. Early satisfaction in creativity is believed to be the kind of stimulation that will sustain the growth of learning throughout the productive life of the person. Not all learners produce high-level creations, but it is believed that all learners can develop the kind of behavior that predisposes them to create, with consequent satisfaction and sustained learning effort.

Our perspective indicates that the teacher's problem, *as limited by our definition,* is contained largely in the first phase of learning—acquiring information. The problem occupies only the initial corner of education in subject matter, but it should suffice to help in illustrating an approach to the application of psychology to teaching.

ANALYSIS OF THE TEACHER'S PROBLEM

The purpose of this analysis is to show which kinds of psychological tools would be most promising for use in dealing with the problem. Some tools (concepts) in psychology are more useful than others for attacking the chosen group of teaching difficulties. A careful inspection of the problem should help in selecting the more promising concepts. The point of all this reduces to an axiom which provides an important support for our effort: *The appropriateness of any tool is determined by the needs found in the problem to be solved.* If the problem is to change a tire, then only tools with certain qualities can be used effectively. Analysis of such a problem is quite simple and easy, for the needs are readily discovered. Likewise, analysis of the teaching problem is undertaken in order to determine which needs are to be satisfied.

Of what value is the analysis of the chosen teaching problem? Instead of trying to answer in the abstract, we shall proceed to examine the problem and to identify the kind of decisions that can be facilitated by analysis.

ANALYSIS OF THE PROBLEM

There are three phases involved: defining key terms; identifying the assumptions on which the problem rests; identifying the facts central to the problem. A final task will be to tie the definitions, assumptions, and facts together to describe the kind and form of psychological knowledge which seems to be needed to develop useful operating rules.

Defining the key terms. Let us first repeat the statement of the problem and underline the terms in that statement which seem to warrant special treatment. "How can the teacher *help the pupil acquire subject matter efficiently?*" Special definitions are in order when processes such as analysis, measurement, and evaluation are involved. Let us proceed with the key terms in our problem.

Acquire. The meaning of this term is rooted in both a process and an outcome of education. As a process "acquire" refers to the presentation of course content plus the reactions of the learner leading to a demonstration of proof that learning has occurred. There are two common standards used to measure acquisition. They consist of tests of *recall* and *recognition*. Recall tests require the learner to supply a sample of material to which he has been exposed. A recognition test requires the learner to identify one or more correct answers embedded in a set of answers furnished by the test item. *Correctness* is the degree of correspondence between responses or answers chosen by the learner and those listed in a key as most appropriate.

Efficient. This term is concerned with the teacher's effect on the pupil in the acquisition process. The teacher influences efficiency when the things that he injects into the acquisition process save time and effort for the student in reaching the goals of recognition and recall.

Help. To help a pupil is to stimulate him to behave in a way that represents desirable educational outcomes without negative effects on attitude and motivation.

The terms *pupil* and *teacher* need no special definition in the present analysis.

IMPORTANT ASSUMPTIONS

Every query rests on certain assumptions. If an assumption is false then the intent of the question is not compatible with the facts. Our teaching problem rests on two assumptions:

a. The first assumption is that the teacher can do something to help students acquire subject matter. Such an assumption is important because, for one thing, it is used in hiring teachers. If the assumption is false, then it would be appropriate to redefine the things that teachers are expected to do. One of the most significant tasks facing education today is the clarification of the teacher's role. We shall have some suggestions concerning role clarification in a later chapter.

b. A second assumption, which follows from the first, is that how the teacher behaves makes a difference in the pupil's learning efficiency. If this is true, then some things that the teacher does may lead to positive results, while other forms of action may bring negative or neutral outcomes. "Positive" and "negative" refer to the kinds of changes in behavior actually occurring in the pupil as compared with changes which the teacher has tried to help the pupil establish. A "positive" change is movement toward a goal, while a "negative" changes arises from strengthening of behavior that is incompatible with the educational aim.

c. Facts. A worthwhile analysis of any practical problem must emphasize certain facts. Only from the study of important facts can a clear view of the nature of the problem be seen. The demands of the problem should determine the useful properties of the psychological tools.

The aim of the teacher is to help the pupil change his behavior along certain lines. It is not enough to identify behavioral change as the goal. We must be more specific and locate the kinds of change that teachers try to promote. These changes may be classed as follows:

a. *Helping the pupil acquire new ways of behaving.* Some of the ways used by teachers to bring about new ways of behaving can be identified in everyday language. They explain, demonstrate, provide hints, encourage the pupil to try, verbally approve correct performance, assign homework, and the like. Each of these things is often done in the hope that acquiring new behavior will be facilitated.

b. *Helping the pupil strengthen behavior which he already shows but expresses in a precarious or weak way.* When the teacher helps pupils to build skills in reading, writing, computation, and spelling, he is achieving the present goal. While the teacher explains, demonstrates, encourages, gives hints and in other ways seeks to improve skills as well as to increase acquisition, there is a special class of additional things that teachers do for skill building. They provide conditions for practice and inform the pupil how he can alter specific acts or movements or symbolic responses to increase his skill. Teachers give the learner information that is usually detailed and is often accompanied by suggestions to the pupil as to how he can judge his own performance and alter it accordingly. The aim of skill building is efficient performance.

c. *Helping the learner weaken undesirable behavior.* While this is a part of skill improvement, it deserves special mention because it can be a desirable goal without involving skill. The teacher tries to discourage, for example, immature and inappropriate habits which annoy others and which inhibit efficient learning. Inappropriate techniques, however, are often selected by the teacher. The common practices include mild disapproval, calling attention to the negative side of the habits, shaming, warnings, and reprimands.

d. *Helping the pupil to increase his self-control.* The intent is to help the child act in an approved way without his being directed or commanded. Many teachers do not seem to have special methods to promote this goal other than exhortation, reminders, and warnings. They harbor a vague hope that with the getting of more knowledge and academic skills, the pupil will somehow succeed in acquiring self-control. Often, much of this hope is invested in growth of socialization as a road to self-control.

We have selected the above as aspects of the teacher's intent. Let us now try to draw together the facts under a single concept. We have noted before that the teacher's efforts are indicated by such terms as *explains, demonstrates, describes, requests,* and *suggests*. These actions are attempts to *influence* pupils to change certain behaviors. Since the aim of teaching is to help the pupil through acquisition, strengthening, weakening, and self-control, "teaching influence" has meaning in both intent and outcome.

A formal definition of "teacher's influence" should help us move toward a clearer understanding of its connection with psychological terms. "Teacher's influence" is defined as *a deliberate attempt to manage stimuli so that the learner alters his behavior in some desired way.* It should be clear that the meaning of "teacher's influence" is rooted in the facts of teaching, in the things teachers try to accomplish, and in the ways adopted to realize goals. The following features of useful tools for getting at our problem are worth identifying specifically.

Properties of Teacher's Influence

OBSERVABLE OPERATIONS

The things that teachers do to influence students should be observable. When a stimulus is observable it has an effect on some sense organ such as the eye, ear, nose, and skin. Things that teachers do which influence must have some effect on the senses of the students, else they do not qualify as effective stimuli.

DELIBERATE MANIPULATION

Some actions of the teachers are not under his conscious control. An example of such an action would be a facial tic. We may say that a tic is not something that a teacher *deliberately* uses to influence the student. We rule out unconscious actions on the part of the teacher from the meaning of "teacher's influence" because the main interest here is toward *controlled* application of psychology. Those positive effects of teaching that are beyond the conscious control of the teacher furnish an index of the nonprofessional activity of the teacher. There are those who believe that the teacher's influence is entirely a matter of nondeliberate, unconscious, and uncontrolled behavior by the teacher. Does it follow then that rational, articulate, and controlled attempts to influence pupils are a waste of time? Another claim is that teachers should be selected mostly on the basis of their personality traits. Our claim is that effective teaching is largely a product of deliberate, rational, and systematic decision making.

"Deliberate manipulation" also points up the fact that teachers also consciously control *things* to influence the pupil. For example, a textbook can be manipulated or controlled in a variety of ways by the teacher. He may use it to stimulate careful reading, for critical analysis, and for dealing with practical problems. Or he may be so noncommittal on how to use the book that most pupils fail to read it. *We believe that some influences of the teacher which are presently "unconscious" can come under deliberate control as the means for effective application are identified.* It is conceivable, for example, that new techniques in the management of textbooks—techniques that some teachers may now be using, but with only a dim awareness of important controls involved—may greatly increase their stimulus value for efficient learning.

Teaching functions are embodied in ways of stimulating the learner. We have noted that the stimuli in teaching should be observable and manipulable. It is important to show why the psychological tools must represent observable and manipulable things in the teacher's environment. The next section is intended to make this clear.

WHY SOME PRINCIPLES WORK AND OTHERS DO NOT

When we put psychology to use in teaching, we are dealing with verbal expressions. We have seen earlier that a word cannot be directly applied like a material tool such as a screwdriver, hammer, or saw. A verbal expression however, can stimulate a person to act out something that the words represent or to make some overt reply. It is such a form of application that we are concerned with in building the bridge of application between psychology and education.

A principle is a statement that is supposed to describe a relationship between two or more things that exist in nature. It is supposed to identify some uniformity. Sometimes one or more of the key terms may represent only presumed or hypothetical things, that is, they may not be seen directly, but only inferred. A good example in psychology of something inferred is "motivation." We do not see motivation. We infer it from the way one behaves. It follows that motivation is not *directly* manipulated by the teacher in a fashion similar to the manipulation of chalk, erasers, books, maps, verbal symbols (words), and the like. Motivation is the *result* of influence brought about by manipulation of stimuli rather than by manipulating the motivation itself directly. To apply principles of motivation in teaching means to arrange conditions so that students want to act differently. The practical significance of the problem of motivation lies in *how* the teacher can influence the student so that he behaves in a way that reflects a desire to learn. All "how" problems are resolved by manipulation of things in ways effectively suiting the aim.

Let us examine some typical statements that are sometimes presented as principles in educational psychology.

   a. All learning is motivated.
   b. Purpose serves to unify experiences in learning.
   c. A response becomes progressively less likely to occur as it is repeated
      without reward.

Can we determine why some principles are serviceable in solving problems and other principles fail to be useful? The quest should lead us to
locate properties shared by useful principles (as well as those features
which contribute nothing toward application). Let us again look at the
three principles stated above.

"All learning is motivated." In what way can this statement be
put to work by the teacher? What features does it have that either make
it applicable or prevent it from being useful? The two questions should
be answered in relation to the "teacher's problem" as we have defined
it. We have shown two central features of the problem: observable operations and deliberate manipulation. Now let us identify some specific
rules that can be used to help us decide on the usefulness of the principle which we are examining.

Teacher influence is found in those actions of the teacher that
stimulate the pupil. Our first rule, therefore, can be stated: *The applicable principle should indicate or imply a form of stimulation.* The principle "all learning is motivated" can be interpreted to mean that all
learning is stimulated, making the terms *motivated* and *stimulated* inter-
changeable. An examination of motivation, however, reveals several
different reference points. Some psychologists use "motivation" to refer
to a physiological state such as hunger. Others use a mentalistic reference point, meaning that a motive is some conscious intent. Many
psychologists, however, say that most motives are unconscious and
arise from a psychic energy which causes behavior but which can never
be observed itself. Still other psychologists view motives as referring to
environmental influences and therefore see the management of external
stimuli as ways of motivating.

The fact that the status of "motivation" in psychology lacks
clarity and a standard meaning makes its application in teaching difficult unless it is borrowed from a psychology that restricts the meaning
of the term. A difficulty, however, in the notion that all learning is
motivated is that it is not a principle for action but a kind of definition.
It says that whatever learning may be it cannot exist without being
motivated. The real function of the principle should be to classify events
called "learning" under a class of the "motivated." But since the principle does not do this, does not suggest a particular form of motivation,
then it does not seem relevant to our first rule.

Our second rule is that *the stimulus operations must be observable.* Since there are no stimulus operations that seem to be implied by the principle which we are analyzing, the second rule cannot be satisfied by the principle "all learning is motivated."

THE STIMULUS OPERATIONS SHOULD BE MANIPULABLE

This third rule is not satisfied by the principle we are examining because no stimulus operations can be deduced.

We conclude that the principle "all learning is motivated," taken as an isolated statement, has little application value for the teacher when it comes to dealing with our chosen problem (what the teacher can do to influence behavioral changes in pupils). It does little good to emphasize the principle that all learning is motivated because there is nothing in it that provides a handle and fulcrum for application. The handle which is called for by the selected teacher's problem is something that can be manipulated which can serve to stimulate. The fulcrum is the point or place of stimulus contact. Roughly, our rules of application may be represented by the lever as a simple machine. Figure 1 is a crude model to illustrate the meaning of application of a concept to a problem which requires the manipulation of something in the environment to change the behavior of the student. "All learning is motivated" has no handle or stimulus for the teacher to grasp as a means for inducing a desired change. (Technically speaking, when a principle has no handle that can be controlled it has no manipulable independent variable.)

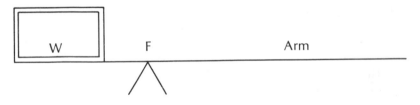

Figure 1. Weight is moved (influenced) by manipulation of arm ("F" is the fulcrum).

Let us inspect briefly the second principle, "purpose serves to unify experiences in the learning situation." Does this have a handle? Yes, the intended handle is indicated by the word "purpose" because it is the thing that is supposed to bring about a change ("the unification of experiences").

Can this handle be manipulated by the teacher? The answer is "no," because there seems to be no direct way of manipulating purpose. Apparently "purpose" in the principle refers to the purpose of the learner. The teacher cannot manipulate purpose as a stimulus object.

He may do things, however, to influence the student's purpose. This principle has little power for the teacher because there happens to be no handle at all, but rather, something that is influenced by other unspecified handles. Principles that use purpose as causes for behavior *seem* to be supplying something useful, but upon close inspection they turn out to be truisms or platitudes, in many cases. Many people probably accept them, but they provide no power for bringing about desired changes.

Now, let us analyze the third principle: "A response becomes progressively less likely to occur as it is repeated without being rewarded." Where is the handle here? We find it by noting which term in the principle refers to the apparent cause of something. We see that the result of the cause is "a response becomes progressively less likely to occur." It is clear that when a response becomes less likely to be made by a given pupil then some change in behavior is indicated. What is supposed to be responsible for the change? We find the handle located in the latter part of the principle (although the causal term may be found in any part). The handle is "without being rewarded," which is presented as the something which brings about decreased chance of the response. Can rewards be manipulated by teachers? Certainly, some kinds of reward can be controlled, such as words of approval, commendation, granting special privileges, and the like. While the stated principle does not specify the reward that is to be controlled, it does indicate the *effect* of withholding reward, that is, a lessening of the chance that the response will occur. The principle, then, seems to have definite power for indicating how the teacher can deal with the problem of weakening undesirable behavior. It is clear that rewards which are controlled by the teacher can be withheld as well as presented.

The Different Kinds of Principles Found in Educational Psychology

Statements presented as principles in educational psychology seem to conform to no single pattern. They can be classified in several ways. We shall sort them according to the ways in which they seem to function. It has not been established that principles *ought* to have all the functions indicated. Let us merely identify the different statements that are currently being treated as principles.

PRINCIPLES THAT FUNCTION AS DEFINITIONS

A definition is a statement that is intended to provide a clear meaning of a word or term. Meanings, however, are determined in an arbitrary fashion and resolve themselves into *decisions* on how a term is to be used. In the sciences and other growing disciplines, it is often necessary to create new terms which have precise definitions. Also, many familiar words are redefined for special purposes; in psychology, for example, many common words are given technical meanings. The following instances of definitions used as principles are found in educational psychology:

> Learning is experiencing and doing.
> Learning is complex and dynamic.

The first statement is a definition that states the components of learning, that is, the components which someone has *decided* should be so regarded. The statement seems to mean that when there is both experiencing and doing there is also learning because experiencing and doing compose or define learning.

The second statement is another kind of definition. It indicates the *qualities* which have been assigned to "learning." The words *complex* and *dynamic* do not equal learning; they are only properties of it. Learning is the process and *complex* and *dynamic* indicate two features of the process. Therefore, the statement is not a complete definition. It does, however, serve to delimit and sharpen the meaning of learning; and so in that sense it functions as a definition despite the fact that it lacks completeness; that is, it fails to furnish words that can be fully substituted for *learning*.

It is the opinion of the authors that definitions should *not* be treated as principles because the term *principle* should be reserved for those statements that can be verified by empirical evidence. A definition is an arbitrary rule concerning how a term is to be used. A principle, on the other hand, often starts as a hypothesis, gains support from observed facts, and thereby is given the status of a "principle." A principle *depends on evidence* to determine its validity. A definition is made by fiat, decree, arbitrary choice. Its survival depends on whether people are willing to accept it and use it according to the original decree. Dictionary definitions amount to meanings that have gained some acceptance without guarantee that future arbitrary decisions will not be made to add new meanings that may supersede the old.

PRINCIPLES THAT FUNCTION AS TRUISMS

A statement that is self-evident is a truism. The function of a truism is not an informative one, but it serves as a memorandum about something that is deemed worth keeping in mind. It can be argued strongly that truisms ought not to be presented as principles, which should at least be informative and capable of being demonstrated. The following are examples of truisms which have been treated as principles:

The goals and methods of teaching should be geared to the developmental level of the learner.

The end products of learning which are accepted by the learner are those which are meaningful to him and which satisfy certain needs.

The learner will stick to a learning task to the extent that he values the goal.

The first one is a truism because not even beginning education students need any supporting evidence in order to accept it. It stimulates unanimous agreement, but it does not have power because it does not suggest *how* the teacher should gear the methods of teaching.

Sometimes a statement is a truism because it is circular. Upon inspection it is seen to be something like the statement "all soldiers are soldiers." The third example above is virtually circular. It states that the learner will keep trying to the extent that he values the goal. But what is the evidence that he values the goal? If we say that the evidence is found in how persistent he is in trying, then we have a truism that is circular because it amounts to this: A learner will keep trying to the extent that he keeps trying. Principles that function as truisms are statements that are self-evident, that is, they are only pseudo principles.

PRINCIPLES THAT FUNCTION AS ARTICLES OF FAITH

The central value of articles of faith in science is that they serve as longitudinal stimuli, that is, they tend to sustain action in a certain direction. Prime examples of articles of faith are found in religions. Faith stimulates perseverance, which can be fruitful when the energy is spent on solving problems that add both knowledge and power to the reservoir of a culture.

Let us examine just one article of faith that could serve to mobilize energy to bring about a revolutionary change in education and modern culture. The article is simply the belief that *the average person has only a small fraction of his learning potential actually developed.* There is no overwhelming evidence for such a belief. However its acceptance by able researchers in education and learning could conceivably lead to discoveries that may eventually verify it. If the point could be reached such that the learning potential of people could be increased ten-, twenty-, or thirtyfold, then the ensuing social revolution would make the current nuclear age seem a rather mild development.

PRINCIPLES THAT FUNCTION AS "STATIC" INFORMATION

Perhaps the majority of statements treated as principles in education's psychology can be classed as "static" information. We mean by "static" information that knowledge which is meaningful to the practitioner but which has no application for him. It can be irrelevant, that is, beside the point, or it can be quite relevant without adding any power in decision making and action toward solving practical problems. Perhaps one reason why some able students in educational psychology express discontent with course content is that they see much "static" information which either cannot be used in teaching or which has not been processed to the point where its use is apparent.

Examples of "static" information principles include the following:

Differences in school achievement among students are related to individual differences in personality traits.

The effect of a teacher on a pupil depends in part on the background of both the teacher and pupil.

The first principle is static to the extent that the teacher is unable to use the information to make any practical decision. The statement is too indefinite to be functional. Secondly, if teachers cannot do much about the personality traits of pupils, then the information emphasizes an area in which the teacher has virtually no power. Although the teacher may derive some rules about how to group pupils from such knowledge, the principle would be more meaningful if it indicated which traits influence school achievement.

Some statements are both informative and instrumental. Others lack one or both of these aspects. If a principle points up a reliable relationship which can be controlled by the teacher to improve or understand some condition then that principle has application value. It is believed that many "static" principles could become functional through a processing that would begin by developing some "how" statements, which would act as hunches or hypotheses and be tested in practical situations. Knowledge that is relevant but nonfunctional in solving problems we call "static" information.

PRINCIPLES THAT FUNCTION AS SOURCES OF POWER

When a statement is informative, instrumental, and pertinent to a family of problems, then it is a potential source of power in dealing with the set of problems. As mentioned before, power principles should deal with a descriptive relation between at least two key terms, which can be used to name things in the practical situation. In addition, the key term which acts as the "cause" of an indicated change should be manipulable or come under the control of the practitioner. A power principle, then, can be processed to function as a useful tool. Since most of this book is given to the processing of power principles into operating rules, no examples will be treated here. Principles that function as sources of power are found in statements which are informative, instrumental, and pertinent to a family of problems.

Summary

In this chapter we have chosen a practical problem of the teacher. The problem was stated in the form of a question, namely: How can the teacher help students acquire subject matter efficiently? A viewpoint of the educational phases in learning subject matter was outlined to provide a perspective for seeing how the chosen problem is related to other aspects of academic learning. An attempt was made to clarify the key terms in the problem and to point up two assumptions basic to the query. The analysis of the problem continued with identification of certain facts that represent the aims of teachers. Those aims were attempts to help the pupil acquire new ways of behaving, to strengthen existing weak responses, to weaken undesirable acts, and to promote self-control. Further analysis revealed that all forms of teacher influence can be reduced to ways of stimulating students. Also, before any given principle can be applied it should contain some indication or suggestion of the kind of things that can be manipulated by the teacher to stimulate the desired behavior. Examination of three principles illustrated the value of rules derived from features called "observable operations" and "deliberate manipulation." A final section identified several kinds of statements which are presented as principles in educational psychology. Reasons were given as to why some of the statements should not be accepted as principles.

References

Anderson, H., ed. 1959. *Creativity and its cultivation.* New York: Harper & Bros.
Barnes, F. P. 1952. Materials of learning—and learning. *Educational Leadership* 9:402–8.
Bruce, R. W. Conditions of transfer of training. *Journal of Experimental Psychology* 16:343–61.
Hayakawa, S. I. 1949. *Language in thought and action.* New York: Harcourt, Brace & Co.
Scott, W., Hill, C. M., and Burns, H. W. 1959. *The great debate.* Englewood Cliffs, N.J.: Prentice-Hall.

II / USING THE CONCEPTUAL TOOLS: OUT-OF-SCHOOL SETTINGS

As important as abstract-conceptual knowledge is, it has little value for the practitioner unless it is translated operationally. Parts II and III are devoted to that translation process; their purpose is to answer the inevitable question: "Yes, but what do I do now? How do I make it work?"

Part II consists of translations for behavior outside the regular school, for example, psychotic-neurotic behavior, retarded behavior, stuttering, delinquency, and nonhuman behavior in "How to Teach Your Pet," the only such article in the book.

Part III contains research carried on in schools. Examples are drawn from preschool to university populations. Each model is exportable to other settings in which you may be interested.

In short, these two parts focus on action, where an investigator has seen a problem, devised a strategy for change based upon learning theory, and has set out to modify the behavior in question.

6 / Operant Group Psychotherapy

WILLARD A. MAINORD

In a very straightforward way, Willard A. Mainord makes the case
for the therapist as teacher rather than as healer. For many, such a
thought is a violation of traditional psychological therapy and an
almost total decimation of Sigmund Freud. So be it, Mainord seems
to say.

The treatment borders on the shocking. The patient is told
that he is in the hospital because of a lack of personal assets and
imperfect behavior, that therapy is designed to remove his defects,
and that his institutionalization should be viewed "in the light of his
own inadequate handling of situations. . . ."

But read on. The technique is a unique and effective use of
behavior modification principles with groups of institutionalized
patients.

Operating as I do on the assumption that maladaptive behavior is
learned in a social context, *elicited* in a social context, and *maintained*
by a social context, it appears altogether logical to me that corrective
learning also will and can most efficiently occur in a social context. And
this—an artificially created specialized society with a set of three fixed

Source: Willard A. Mainord, "Operant Group Therapy in a Total Institution
Setting," *The Discoverer* 5 (March 1968): 1-6. Reprinted by permission of the
author and *The Discoverer.*

social rules—is the basis upon which I build what might be called the *teaching community.*

This teaching community is intended to reflect accurately the larger society in terms of critical interpersonal problems, contingencies created by these problems, and successful solutions. Yet, it differs from the larger, "real" community in two important respects. The first difference: in *this* community the learner is protected against the usual disastrous consequences of observed maladaptive behavior. Second: because of its capacity to respond instantly to new conditions, the teaching community curriculum can be altered to "fit" each patient when and as he exhibits behavior patterns that show up as needing modification.

The program—or curriculum—used in this small teaching community ideally will elicit and actually trigger undesirable behaviors among its "pupils," because there is no other currently feasible method for identifying such behavior than direct observation. Such a group as I am describing here has the potential to apply almost every type of social pressure, while at the same time theoretically providing the most accurate and *functional* diagnosis of social malfunction that can be obtained.

This, by the way, is why it seems inevitable to me that group psychotherapeutic approaches will in times to come be preferred over traditional individual approaches—not as a second-best expedient caused by a shortage of therapists nor as a stopgap measure to meet emergency needs, but as the *strategy of choice.*

The teaching mini-community I postulate here can vary all the way from a total-institutional, 24-hour-a-day setting (such as found in Synanon and Daytop) to a small group meeting together only intermittently. But what must be present is a *reacting social body* that will promptly respond to the patient's behavior with alert and helpful feedback and reinforcements. When functioning optimally this remedial teaching community will insist on adequate performance and productivity from each of its members. At the same time, it will encourage unfolding of the patient's skills through the warm, affectionate, genuinely valuable human relationships that invariably blossom in the group. Our illustrations will be based mainly on the institutional program.

The role of the therapist as I conceive and practice it definitely is not that of a *healer.* To me it is more compatible with the *social learning conceptualization of psychotherapy* to see the therapist as a teacher. In this frame of reference, the therapist's most effective tools quite naturally can be expected to originate in the world of pedagogy. He is a particular kind of teacher, functioning in a social learning situation. One of the imperatives for controlled learning lies in the teacher's ability to manipulate consequences systematically. So must the therapist-teacher necessarily command the choice of determining when, where, and what the pay-off will be for both adaptive or maladaptive behavior.

Unless the consequences of behavior are under the direct or indirect management of the therapist, the patient's day will furnish him with an overload of either irrelevant or contradictory "lessons." Lessons of this sort lead to unnecessary frustrations for patient and therapist alike. Much of the therapist's and group's efforts involve helping the patient extinguish the lessons he learns between group meetings.

This need to counteract unprogrammed learning graphically demonstrates why it is necessary for the therapist's administrative scope to be wide and strong enough to set up and maintain reliable lines of feedback from any person in the patient's environment who can observe his progress—or lack of it.

Luckily, however, the therapist does not need absolute power to enforce total consistency in the patient's environment. I say "luckily" because, in the first place, it is impossible to get such consistency. In the second place, it should be understood that inconsistency is a vital part of the patient's program to learn new and better ways of dealing with the world as he will find it when he leaves the institution. Only through challenge and learning new responses will he be able to change his habitual mismanagement of behavior.

Any skill training program involves some combination of new knowledge and the acquisition of numerous new technical abilities. The therapist will find his task including both of these two pedagogical properties in liberal doses. Most patients are in critical need of new knowledge about what survival in the social world requires and how it operates, of new skills allowing alternate ways of behaving and responding. Patients quickly and naturally come to look upon their therapist-teacher as a prime purveyor of new social knowledge and as a trainer in better social skills than they have had. The therapist needs to be keenly alert to feedback information from the environment in which the patient spends the most hours in his day outside the therapeutic sessions.

After one or two group sessions in which he has the opportunity to observe the patient "in action" the therapist invariably will form certain tentative assessments of the kinds of behavior that have caused the patient the most trouble in his social relationships.

But the therapist must (or should) be prepared to continually modify his tactics in accordance with new information that will flow back to him—both from the patient and from the significant others in his life. I think the role of the therapist is perhaps more clearly defined by the terms of the therapeutic contract.

The following description of the intake interview should help clarify what I consider to be the manner in which the therapist should and can best function as leader of the teaching community group. As mentioned earlier, control of learning is obtained by the therapist being able to manipulate reinforcement in the best ways indicated as determined by his observations of the behavior of the patient. Clearly, a passive, nonresponding patient will prove to be extremely difficult to teach because he resists doing anything that can be reinforced. For rapid behavior changes it is essential to have responsive subjects, whether they be man or beast.

Yet it is not necessary for patient responsiveness to be centered entirely around pleasant stimuli. In the beginning of therapy it is perfectly acceptable if only verbally noxious stimuli are available to induce responsiveness. When the therapist can stimulate the patient to express anger or grief he will find himself with a *behavioral baseline* that will prove sufficiently rich for rapid teaching and learning.

The only personality trait I require from the potential new group member is that he be of near average intelligence or better Since group participation is centered around verbal interchanges, some ability to verbally abstract is decreed.

The institutionalized patient should be reached as soon after admission as possible. It is important to do this because the typical mental hospital is all too diligent at teaching newcomers how to be "good patients." This usually does not promote a good foundation for lively therapy progress. With this in mind, the therapist should arrange for access to all new admissions and should recruit candidates for his program inside of a very few days after their admission. Naturally, the therapist should also be responsive to referrals, diagnostic evaluations, and the like. But if he relies on them exclusively he will pass up many patients who meet the criteria for success in the teaching community.

First Interview Strategy

My interview strategy has become quite routinized so that by now it can usually be completed within half an hour. I break the ice by informing the patient that he is being considered for a special intensive program that is designed to get patients out of the hospital as soon as possible. Then I lay the groundwork for the procedures to come. I casually remark that, whatever it was that got him in trouble, it undoubtedly was not any excess of personal assets or his perfect behavior that landed him in the institution. It is a rare patient indeed who will not agree with this conclusion. And then, without too much resistance he will generally agree with my next point. This point is that the logical focus of therapy should be on removing his defects, helping him reach the point where he will be better able to cope with the outside world.

Following nailing down these two agreements, I ask the patient for his own explanation of what brought him to the hospital.

In spite of his previous admission that he is not in the hospital because of his assets, at this point I expect him to launch into a tirade against the others who misunderstood him and mistreated him, or the hostile social environment that brought about his downfall and final incarceration. He will describe his current situation in *any* terms other than his own inadequacies. At this time I have my first real opportunity to suggest to the patient that his plight might be more usefully examined in the light of his own inadequate handling of the situations leading up to his arrival at the hospital—the possible mistake that *he* made instead of the mistakes the others have made.

The generally effective argument I use here is that neither I nor the patient has the power to change the world to our liking, but we *do* have the power to make some desirable changes in ourselves by learning to behave more effectually and skillfully. When the patient indicates he buys the notion of his own need to change, I mark this point as the beginning of therapy. He has received his *first lesson,* which is simply that hereafter everything he says or does for which he assigns responsibility to someone else will be retranslated to his own accountability.

Just as any pupil will forget some of the information he has acquired, so will the patient suffer mental lapses in which he totally banishes from his memory a position he has only recently accepted as valid. Like a fish on a line, he will twist and turn, seek in innumerable ways to escape having to answer for his actions. Again and again he will reactivate one of his customary modes for disavowing responsibility for his own misjudgments and mistaken behavior. He will plead helplessness because of "sickness." He will whine and complain about the others who let him down, who treated him shabbily—but *less and less will he fall back on such dodges as he receives no reinforcement for his efforts to lay the blame outside of his own skin.* One of the more common excuses the patient will offer is that he is sick. When the rationalization is sickness, I ask the patient to explain what he means—in what *way* is he sick? Predictably, the patient will fumble around a bit and finally lay his claim of sickness on the fact that he *feels* bad—or because he just doesn't know "why" he behaves the way he does—or because he can't seem to control behaviors that are classifiable as symptoms. Following my policy of redefining everything in terms of the patient's responsibility, I am likely to respond by inisisting that one does not have to feel good to behave adequately, that one does not have to know the *whys* of behavior in order to learn how to behave better, and that the word "can't" is a euphemism for "don't" or "won't."

The patient's claim of helplessness, of course, must be treated as an alibi, offered, perhaps, to convince himself and the therapist that he can't control his behavior. But as time goes on he will learn that his behavior clearly is under his control as he learns to maximize his pay-offs.

Obviously, it is impossible to describe every device for avoiding responsibility and every method for countering all of the devices. But I have found that, if the therapist will gird himself *always to insist upon patient responsibility,* it is not difficult to handle any rationalization patients will offer. Furthermore—and this is particularly helpful—the therapist should carefully explain to his patients that he is not an expert in nor competent to deal with any kind of illness. I tell patients, however, that I *am* an expert in helping people with emotional difficulties and behavior problems. What I am stressing here is the vital importance of continually chipping away at the medical model if personal responsibility is to become the dominant theme in the psychotherapeutic relationship.

Nevertheless, many patients are shocked when I deny illness as the cause of their predicament. Often they ask me: "What *am* I if I'm not sick?" After experimenting with a variety of answers, I have more or less settled on this stock reply: "No, you're not sick—you're *crazy.*" This response, as one might imagine, usually has considerable impact. When a patient indignantly takes exception to this label applied to his condition and demands to be excluded from the crazy group, I explain to him that I use the term "crazy" only because he has indulged in foolish behaviors or made foolish decisions—or both. I should mention here that both the Synanon and Daytop programs, dealing with drug addicts, routinely use the word "stupid" to label addicts' behavior, but the term is employed with substantially the same aim and results I seek when I use the word "crazy."

What if the patient insists on evidence that he is crazy? I merely remind him of where he is and the kind of people confined there. Although startled at my blunt and certainly unexpected reference to them and their condition, most patients, after the initial shock wears off, can accept this conceptualization rather quickly and gracefully. Many of them even accept it *with relief,* apparently encouraged by the prospect of being able to discard their socially unacceptable, absurd behavior and becoming able to make better choices of actions—losing their "craziness," in the process.

If the prospective group member has come this far along with me—and this really is all that is necessary—I then proceed to the next part of the recruitment procedure.

The patient is told that the program requires acceptance by all members of three primary rules. And this I stress as a mandatory requirement. Although the patient does not at this time realize it, these three rules are the indispensable instruments that arm the therapist with the power to manipulate reinforcements with the necessary authority to promote change in the patient.

My first requirement—the *first rule—is that the patient must agree* (actually commit himself) *to be completely honest with his group and with each other member in it.*

Later, the patient (often much to his chagrin) will discover that the joker in this agreement is that his *group* includes all of the significant other people in his environment. But the demand that he extends his honesty to this degree is reserved until the patient has experienced the logic and value of the first rule through his participation in the training community.

It is interesting that in this culture of ours, practically everyone will vocally agree that he should be honest. Patients usually will prove no exception on this score. So I immediately follow up by advising the patient that fulfillment of this obligation means that he must surrender his freedom merely to remain silent, or to withhold information that anyone in the group, including myself, might seek from him. His commitment to follow Rule One means that he agrees to make all information about himself and his behavior accurately available to whomever it may be of concern.

Anything of personal concern and importance will be of concern to the group. Probably because of his lack of full understanding of the revolutionary nature of the behavior being required of him, the patient most often will surmount this hurdle with little hesitation. The next requirement also is generally accepted with little to-do and with the same lack of patient understanding of the behavioral modifications entailed in following the rule to its logical conclusion.

The second group rule is that the patient agrees to accept total responsibility for all of his behavior—24 hours a day.

Operationally, responsibility may be defined as behaving in congruence with the patient's own ethical code. Upon his acceptance (if only with tongue in cheek) of Rule Two, another significant therapeutic step has been taken: the patient has unwittingly agreed that he *is* capable of producing behavior that will meet the terms of a social contract. And this is a capability in direct contradiction to the self-concept of helplessness patients normally exhibit initially.

*The third requirement—his agreement to assume responsibility for every other patient in the program—*is often bewildering to the new candidate. I justify this requirement by explaining to the patient that I will consider it my obligation to do whatever I believe to be in the best interest of each patient in the group—whether he likes it or not. In the same manner, I tell him, each patient also is expected to take whatever action he believes to be best for other patients—whether *they* like it or not. Not only does this rule make social responsibility a given in the total program, but it also sets up a system of action, reaction, and feedback that is of supreme importance to the therapist if he is to function with optimum scope, flexibility, and impact.

My final condition for membership in the social training community is that the patient consider it a part of our contract that all decisions will be made by me except for those necessary to maintain physical health. I impress upon him that it will be a violation of extreme seriousness for any patient to try to bypass me for any nonmedical decisions.

By the end of the intake interview, the patient actually has committed himself to the primary essentials of effective social functioning—both in our training community and the real, outside world as well. I contend that it is impossible to hold to the concepts I have here outlined as the core of my therapeutic approach—and not dramatically improve in social activity, problem solving, and in social interdependence. In our training community, the day-to-day mechanics of the program will vary, naturally. But I have found the implementation of these three rules exceedingly useful for every type of patient in every type of program I have been associated with, in or out of an institution.

You have perhaps noticed that I make no promise of confidentiality. When the question of confidentiality arises—usually in a group meeting—I simply state that in fulfilling my obligation of responsibility to the patient I must and will communicate with whomever and about whatever I think will be helpful for him. But I also pledge that I will be neither secretive nor gossipy, that I will always inform the patient about any communications with others that I have had about him.

Whenever possible, I try to carry on conversations about the patient only in his presence. When it isn't possible, but if the communication about the patient is significant, I attempt to set up a face-to-face confrontation when all involved persons can be present.

I should mention, incidentally, that I make every effort to subject members of the patient's family to the same three rules that govern the patient's social behavior. It is my conviction that any information given to the therapist by the family, but which the family declines to allow quoted, is worse than no information at all. Once the therapist agrees to enter into even a petty conspiracy against the patient, the therapist needlessly jeopardizes his own credibility. His honesty thereafter is suspect. When the therapist finds himself involved with a family that demands secrecy, such a demand is clearly revealing of the character of the environment in which the patient lives and must function on release.

Another lesson on patient recruiting procedure I have learned is that a patient who shows initial reluctance to go along with my group membership requisites is much more likely to be moved by challenging, and even sharply judgmental statements, than if I placate him in his unacceptable pattern of behavior. Just to mention one example that supports this thesis: a female patient spitefully decided to join our group after she became furious at the therapist for accusing her of not having enough "guts" to go through with a difficult program, even though she had first claimed she was desperate enough to go through *anything* if it even remotely indicated a possible solution to her hopeless problem. Her determination to prove the therapist wrong in no way seemed to obstruct her ability to benefit from the program. When an initially hostile patient has to be bribed into cooperating by making concessions to his objections, he is thereby taught to expect the program to be modified to meet *his* terms, rather than the therapist's terms. Operating on the principle of propitiation, no psychotherapy can be expected to produce worthwhile results, including those based on extreme permissiveness.

If a psychotherapeutic program is a good one, it will still generate results even if a patient needs some degree of "selling" or even coercion to get him involved. If the program is a poor one, all of the initial enthusiasm in the world will be unhappily wasted when the patient ends up disillusioned, discouraged, and untouched by change.

7 / The Nightmare of Life with Billy

DON MOSER

The article you are about to read is almost unbelievable, for it describes a young child slowly but surely developing into a cunning and diabolical monster. Though unusual, the story is not unfamiliar to child psychiatrists and psychologists. Treatment with such a child has generally been unsuccessful, and, more often than not, parents have been advised to "put him away" in institutional isolation, as were the parents of this child.

"When his father's car pulled out of the driveway, I'd bolt the doors, lock the windows and the nightmare would begin." Thus Billy's mother, Pat, describes a terrifying existence in which she was at the mercy of a small boy so cunning and so violent that he almost propelled her into a nervous breakdown.

Pat's story is significant in two respects. First, it indicates that it is virtually impossible for an intelligent, well-intentioned parent to cope with an autistic youngster. Second, it shows why Pat and her husband, along with the parents of the other children, so eagerly embraced Lovaas' program even though it involved shock and other forms of punishment.

The causes of autism are no clearer with Billy than with the other children. He had suffered a traumatic birth, one that places great strain on the infant. Pat was 17 hours in labor, and when doctors had

Source: Don Moser, "The Nightmare of Life with Billy," *Life*, May 7, 1965, pp. 96–100. Copyright © 1965 Time Inc. Reprinted by permission of *Life*.

finally delivered him by Caesarean section, it was 90 seconds before he breathed, another 90 before he cried. Nor was his early environment always pleasant. His parents' marriage was going through a difficult period. His father, a doctor, was serving his internship; every other night he was at the hospital, and when he came home he had no energy left to do anything but fall into bed. Later, called into the Navy, he was separated from Billy and Pat for long periods.

Whatever the causes—organic, environmental, or both—it was clear by the time Billy was 2 years old that something was very wrong with him. He had not started to speak. He threw uncontrollable tantrums. He never seemed to sleep. Pat and her husband took the child from one psychiatrist or neurologist to another. All gave the same analysis: Billy was retarded.

Before long, however, Pat realized that Billy was diabolically clever and hell-bent on destroying her. Whenever her husband was home, Billy was a model youngster. He knew that his father would punish him quickly and dispassionately for misbehaving. But when his father left the house, Billy would go to the window and watch until the car pulled out. As soon as it did, he was suddenly transformed. "It was like living with the devil," Pat remembers. "He'd go into my closet and tear up my evening dresses and urinate on my clothes. He'd smash furniture and run around biting the walls until the house was destruction from one end to the other. He knew that I liked to dress him in nice clothes, so he used to rip the buttons off his shirts and used to go in his pants." When he got violent Pat punished him. But she got terribly distraught, and for Billy the pleasure of seeing her upset made any punishment worthwhile. Sometimes he attacked her with all the fury in his small body, once going for her throat with his teeth. Anything that wasn't nailed down or locked up—soap powder, breakfast food—he strewed all over the floors. Then, laughing wildly, he dragged Pat to come to see it.

She had to face her problems alone. It was impossible for her to keep any household help. Once Billy tripped a maid at the head of the stairs, then lay on the floor doubled up with laughter as she tumbled down. And Billy was so cunning that his father didn't know what was going on. "Pat would tell me about the things he did while I was away, but I couldn't believe her," he says.

As time went on, even his father realized that they had a monster on their hands. Enrolled at a school for retarded children, Billy threw the whole institution into an uproar. Obsessed with a certain record, he insisted on playing it over and over for hours. He sent the children in his class into fits of screaming misbehavior. "He was just like a stallion in a herd of horses," his mother says. Billy ruled his teacher with his tantrums until, a nervous wreck herself, she could no longer stand to have him in the class. "He became a school dropout at the age of 5," says Pat.

At home things were taking a macabre twist. Billy had a baby brother now, and at any opportunity he tried to stuff the infant into the toy box and shut the lid on him. His parents had bought him a doll which resembled the baby, and which they called by the baby's name, Patrick. Every morning Pat found Patrick doll head down in the toilet bowl. Terrified of what might happen, she never left the two children alone together.

As he grew older Billy's machinations seemed far too clever for a retarded child, and so his parents took him to see another expert. There, given a puzzle to test his intelligence, Billy simply threw the pieces against the wall. The expert delivered the same old verdict: Billy was retarded.

At the retarded children's school, the youngsters occasionally got hamburgers for lunch from a drive-in chain. Inexplicably, Billy became hooked on them—hooked to the point that he would starve himself rather than eat anything else. Within a few weeks Pat and her husband became slaves to Billy's hamburger habit. Every morning and every night Billy's father stood in line at the drive-in and bought cheap hamburgers by the sack. Eventually he became so embarrassed—he is a small, thin man, and the waitresses had begun to look at him curiously—that he cruised the city looking for drive-ins where he wasn't known. Billy ate three cold, greasy hamburgers for breakfast, more for lunch, more for dinner. "He was like Ray Milland in *The Lost Weekend,*" Pat shudders. "To make sure he wouldn't eat them all at once I'd hide them all over the house—in the oven and up on shelves. In the middle of the night he'd be up prowling around, looking for them. A month later I'd find ossified hamburgers in hiding places I'd forgotten."

When they were out driving with Billy, they had to detour around any drive-ins. Billy flew into such a frenzy at the sight of one that he frothed at the mouth and tried to jump out of the moving car.

Pat knew that the boy could not survive on a diet of cheap hamburgers. She took him to places where they served hamburgers of better quality; Billy refused to eat them. Frantic, she contrived an elaborate ruse. Buying relish and buns from the drive-ins, she bought good meat and made the patties herself. She put them into sacks from the drive-in, even inserting the little menu cards that came with the drive-in's orders. When she presented this carefully recreated drive-in hamburger to Billy, he took one sniff and threw it on the floor.

Then there was Billy's Winnie-the-Pooh period. Billy had become obsessed with a particular kind of Teddy bear, marketed under the trade name of Winnie the Pooh. Without it, he'd go berserk. The family was moving about a good deal then, and Pat was terrified that she would have no replacement when Billy lost his bear or tore it up. "Just to make sure I'd never run out, I found where to buy a Winnie wherever we might be going. I knew a place in San Diego and a place in La Jolla and a place in San Francisco. I even knew where to buy a Winnie in Las Vegas. I always kept some in reserve just so we wouldn't run short in a hotel. Our whole life became one long Winnie trip. Once, when we were moving, Winnie got put into the van by mistake, and we had to have the movers take everything out so we could find it. We were afraid to make the trip with Billy without a Winnie bear—we were starting to go nutty ourselves."

Pat became so desperate that when she found something that frightened the boy, she used it as a weapon of self-defense. The one thing that did the trick, appropriately enough, was Alfred Hitchcock. For some reason, when Hitchcock came on television Billy took off like a rocket and hid under the bed. When Pat learned that photographs of Hitchcock had the same effect, she started cutting them out of TV magazines. When Hitchcock appeared on *Life*'s cover, she bought a whole stack of magazines and stuck the covers up all over the house— on the icebox to keep Billy from opening it, on the fireplace to keep him from crawling around in it. When she took a bath she put Hitchcock pictures outside the bathroom door so Billy would leave her in peace.

"It was crazy," Pat remembers. She was at bay in a house with the doors bolted and the windows locked, the baby stuffed in the toy box and the Patrick doll with its head in the toilet, hamburgers hidden on shelves and a closet full of cast-off Pooh bears and the breakfast food strewn all over the floor, and little Billy raging around like an animal, attacking pictures of Alfred Hitchcock with a long stick.

By now Billy was getting so big and strong that Pat could hardly control him physically, and she and her husband were thinking of building a fence around their house to keep him from endangering others. But before doing so, they took him to one more psychiatrist. "You can't build a fence high enough," the psychiatrist said flatly. "He'll be a Frankenstein monster. Put him away."

Miserable though they were, Pat and her husband couldn't stand the thought of abandoning the boy to an institution. "We were supposed to put him away and throw away the home movies and tear up the scrapbook pictures," she said. "We just couldn't do it."

A few weeks later a psychiatrist connected with the retarded children's school told Pat and her husband that Billy might not be retarded but autistic. He suggested they take him to the Neuropsychiatric Institute at UCLA where Dr. Lovaas and his colleague, Dr. James Simmons, a psychiatrist, were choosing autistic children for a new experimental program. Pat and her husband were enthusiastic, even though they knew about the punishment that Billy would be subjected to.

Their fear was that Billy, erratic child that he was, would flunk his audition in front of Lovaas. But they knew that one of the criteria was that the children accepted must like to eat, and must be willing to expend a lot of energy to obtain food. So Pat and her husband talked things over, and they had an idea.

When they took Billy to see Dr. Lovaas, they made a stop on the way at the drive-in. Billy, given the hamburgers during the interview, passed the entrance exam with flying colors.

8 / Screams, Slaps, and Love

An extreme case such as that of "The Nightmare of Life with Billy"
obviously needs extreme therapy. This article describes the work
of Ivar Lovaas, a behavioral psychologist who has been successful
with children like Billy. You may find Lovaas' form of treatment
disturbing, as it often seems on first contact. But more disturbing is
that there are no known alternatives for these children other than
institutional isolation and restraint.

Enraged bellows at the boy, then a sharp slap in the face. This deliberate, calculated harshness is part of an extraordinary new treatment
for mentally crippled children. It is based on the old-fashioned idea that
the way to bring up children is to reward them when they're good,
punish them when they're bad. At the University of California in Los
Angeles, a team of researchers is applying this precept to extreme cases.
They have taken on three boys and a girl with a special form of schizophrenia called autism—utterly withdrawn children whose minds are
sealed against all human contact and whose uncontrolled madness had
turned their homes into hells. And, by alternating methods of shocking
roughness with persistent and loving attention, the researchers have
broken through the first barriers.

At the beginning of the UCLA tests last June [1964] the four
autistic children were assembled in a small room bare of playthings—
such children do not play. Closeted in their private bedlams, they went

Source: "Screams, Slaps, and Love," *Life,* May 7, 1965, pp. 90A–95. Copyright © 1965 Time Inc. Reprinted by permission of *Life.*

through their endless, senseless activities. Pamela, 9, performed her macabre pantomime, and Ricky, 8, loved to flop his arms, waggle his fingers, cover his head with a blanket. Chuck, 7, would alternate his rocking with spells of sucking his thumb and whimpering. Billy, 7, like so many of the thousands of autistic children in the U.S., would go into gigantic tantrums and fits of self-destruction, beating his head black and blue against walls.

Billy and Chuck could not talk at all. Pamela would infuriatingly parrot back everything said to her. Ricky had a photographic memory for jingles and ads which he chanted hour after hour.

The causes of their strange affliction are uncertain. Like most other autistic children, these four are healthy and coordinated, neither brain-damaged or retarded. But the team conducting the experiment at UCLA is not interested in causes. In this, their approach goes against the grain of almost all other modern psychiatric treatment, which tries first to find the child's "core neurosis" and then treats that.

Dr. Ivar Lovaas, the 38-year-old creator of the UCLA project, argues that "you have to put out the fire first before you worry how it started." An assistant professor of psychology at the UCLA Neuropsychiatric Institute, Lovaas believes the whole present concept of "mental illness" is flawed because it relieves the patient of responsibility for his actions. Lovaas is convinced, on the basis of his experience and that of other researchers, that by forcing a change in a child's outward behavior he can effect an inward psychological change. For example, if he could make Pamela go through the motions of paying attention, she would begin eventually to pay genuine attention. Lovaas feels that by (1) holding any mentally crippled child accountable for his behavior and (2) forcing him to act normal, he can push the child toward normality.

The most drastic innovation in Lovaas' technique is punishment—instantly, immutably dished out to break down the habits of madness. His rarely used last resort is the shock room. At one point Pamela had been making progress, learning to read a little, speak a few words sensibly. But then she came to a blank wall, drifting off during lessons into her wild expressions and gesticulations. Scoldings and stern shaking did nothing. Like many autistic children, Pamela simply did not have enough anxiety to be frightened.

To give her something to be anxious about, she was taken to the shock room, where the floor is laced with metallic strips. Two electrodes were put on her bare back, and her shoes removed.

When she resumed her habit of staring at her hand, Lovaas sent a mild jolt of current through the floor into her bare feet. It was harmless but uncomfortable. With instinctive cunning, Pamela sought to mollify Lovaas with hugs. But he insisted she go on with her reading lesson. She read for a while, then lapsed into a screaming fit. Lovaas, yelling

"No!", turned on the current. Pamela jumped—learned a new respect for "No."

Even more than punishment, patience and tenderness are lavished on the children by the staff. Every hour of lesson time has a 10-minute break for affectionate play. The key to the program is a painstaking system of rewarding the children—first with food and later with approval —whenever they do something correctly. These four were picked because they are avid eaters to whom food is very important. In the first months they got no regular meals. Spoonfuls of food were doled out only for right answers.

A case in point was teaching Billy to talk. First he had to learn how to mimic the sounds of speech. He started by learning to blow out a match with a sound like *who*. Every *who* was rewarded with food. Next he was encouraged to babble these sounds aimlessly. From time to time he would accidentally form a word. Each word got its reward. So he would repeat the accident and after weeks had a vocabulary of words like *ball, milk, mama, me*.

Then they tried to teach meaning. When a ball was held up, Billy would just as likely say milk. This went on for five frustrating weeks. In the sixth week the staff realized Billy was smarter than they had thought. When he gave the wrong word, the researcher would prompt him with the right word. When he echoed it, he was fed. Changing the method, the researcher held up a ball. Billy said, "Me," and got nothing. He fidgeted. Desperately he began going through his whole vocabulary. When he hit *ball* he was fed. In an hour Billy had caught on and could find the right word immediately. Today he can ask for any food by name, ask to go out, to go to the bathroom. In short, Billy can talk. All it took was ingenuity—and some 90,000 trials.

Chuck's mother watched her son and her excitement grew. After six weeks, Chuck was beginning to behave like a normal 7-year-old. He had learned to show affection and for the first time talked in simple phrases. The two other boys had also progressed remarkably. Ricky appeared before a UCLA seminar and told them, "I am 4 feet, 3 inches tall. I'm wearing black and white tennis shoes!" Billy may go to a special school next year. Pamela, the oldest, can read now but left alone still reverts to her bizarre autistic ways.

One of the leading authorities on autism has called the UCLA project "a tremendous accomplishment." There are not yet plans for a clinic to offer general treatment, but Lovaas hopes he has found a way to help any child with a broken mind more quickly and simply than with methods now used.

9 / Behavioural Engineering

T. AYLLON AND HEIDI B. HUGHES

The work of Ted Ayllon and his coinvestigators is considered by
many to be on the cutting edge of research in behavioral
modification. His contributions stem mainly from investigations
with psychiatric patients in a hospital ward. The article you are
about to read is an excellent review of operant principles as they
apply to an experimental hospital ward located at Anna State Hospital, Anna, Illinois. The pattern developed there has been widely
copied by other mental institutions.

Again one sees the emphasis on an overarching theoretical
position as that position applies to a specific setting. Ayllon, himself,
makes that point when he states in his last paragraph that the same
principles he uses are provocative for work in education, slum-
clearance, underprivileged areas, and criminology. "These are questions," he says, "we cannot answer by pondering them in our hearts.
They warrant careful empirical study."

Over the past 50 years many scientists have studied the variables
which seem to affect the learning of behaviour. This is no easy task since
behaviour itself ranges from simple involuntary reflexes to complex voluntary motor acts such as walking, eating, talking and manipulation. In

Source: T. Ayllon and Heidi B. Hughes, "Behavioural Engineering," *Science Journal,*
October 1965, pp. 69–73. Reprinted by permission of the authors and *Science
Journal.*

this article we will consider 'voluntary' acts—those which are traditionally regarded as being initiated by the subject itself. Experimental investigations have shown, however, that the acquisition and maintenance of these behaviour patterns is based on processes which obey definable laws. They are also, to a large extent, determined by their consequences.

Work with laboratory animals and humans shows that behaviour can be modified fairly simply once the basic operations are understood. This, of course, has very important implications for the treatment of the mentally ill. Many attempts have to be made to induce a socially desirable response from mental patients. Often, however, it seems that the treatment given only worsens their condition. Humouring a patient, by talking nonsense to a nonsensically talking psychotic, only makes things worse. If the nonsense is ignored, however, and the realistic conversation is emphasized—or reinforced—desirable results can be obtained. It seems to us that the application of such reinforcement systems could find wide applications in the teaching of human behaviour at all levels.

In 1938 B. F. Skinner, now at Harvard University, published "The Behaviour of Organisms" which constitutes an analysis of the variables governing behaviour. He concentrated on a type of learning involving voluntary behaviour and called it 'operant conditioning'—operant because the organism operates on its environment, that is to say, it does something to it which results in specific consequences. These consequences are commonly referred to as reinforcement, and a specific item of behaviour shown by an organism is called a response, whereas the process of response modification or 'teaching' is known as shaping.

In this type of behavioural investigation described by Skinner, an animal (pigeon or rat) which has been deprived of food is placed in a small experimental chamber where it will learn to operate a device in order to receive food. The moment-by-moment behaviour of the animal is recorded automatically by means of electrical impulse counters and relay circuits. The device is constructed in accordance with each organism's 'natural' response tendencies—levers are provided for rats to press, chains for monkeys to pull and plastic disks for birds to peck. The same electronic instrumentation also permits studies of response characteristics such as rate, force and duration (which are units of behavioural measurement); the instantaneous delivery of the reinforcer; and the automatic programming of different reinforcement contingencies.

By examining the records produced one can see that, in the absence of any consequences or reinforcers, behaviour is more or less random. Numerous responses, such as sniffing, pecking, clawing and grooming occur randomly. However, as soon as a reinforcer is made contingent on the display of a specific response the frequency with which that response is displayed is found to change drastically. An effective reinforcer increases the frequency of the response it follows, and the rate of non-reinforced responses decreases progressively until they extinguish. Since the reinforcer has to be effective—and not all consequences are—experimental animals are usually deprived of the substance, such as food or water, the experimenter wishes to use as a reinforcer.

It is theoretically possible for any organism in an experimental enclosure to 'discover' what produces reinforcement and so learn to give the appropriate response in order to obtain reinforcement. But, in practice, the organism might starve to death—or go insane—before accidentally hitting on the correct behaviour. To facilitate the acquisition of a new response the experimenter uses a micro-switch which, when hand pressed, delivers the reinforcement. The 'shaping' procedure consists of reinforcing mere approximations to the desired behaviour.

Take the pigeon as an example. In the experimental chamber it pecks here and there and generally explores the new surroundings. To teach it to peck on a disk, usually located a few inches above the grain dish, any movement in the direction of the disk or the dish is reinforced with a small amount of food which is automatically dropped into the dish. Soon the animal will spend most of its time in the vicinity of the dish looking for food. After this initial step the bird is taught to peck at the disk which closes a micro-switch that will deliver reinforcement automatically. Here again, successive approximations are used. All pecking responses near and gradually only on the disk are followed immediately by reinforcement. All other behaviours, including pecking anywhere except near the disk, are not so reinforced and hence diminish in frequency and extinguish. Thus within a relatively short time, the pigeon will learn to peck vigorously at the disk and abstain from any other behaviour.

This differential reinforcement of the 'correct' or appropriate response—the one that the experimenter desires to shape—along with simultaneous extinction of all other responses through lack of reinforcement, is a vital aspect of the shaping process. Since extinction of inappropriate or irrelevant responses is involved in any shaping procedure it is easy to lose the behaviour altogether and special care must be taken in planning the successive steps in shaping a response. The steps must not be too large and the experimenter must make certain that each approximation to the final response is well established before moving on to the next.

Once a response has been shaped and is firmly established, the requirements for reinforcement can be raised. Indeed, the reinforcement of every single response, vital as it is to the initial shaping procedure, is a rather ineffective and uneconomical way of maintaining behaviour. The maintenance and persistence of behaviour is dependent upon reinforcement which is delivered intermittently rather than for each response. Thus the pigeon may now have to peck the disk several times before producing a reinforcement, or it may have to peck for a specified period of time. Furthermore, special programmes of intermittent reinforcement affect the response rate in very specific ways. Subjects can be shaped to respond at fast or slow rates, steadily or in spurts, or the behaviour can be made to occur only in the presence of specific environmental cues, known as 'discriminative stimuli' because the animal learns to discriminate between cues during which it pays off to respond and others, during which responding is not reinforced.

Animal trainers in the circus utilize some of these techniques either implicitly or explicitly. The elephant who makes a graceful handstand on one foot, balancing his bulk on a small tub, and then takes a bow before the applauding audience is exhibiting a long, complex chain of responses, each link of which has been shaped through successive approximations by making a reinforcer—usually food—contingent on the specific response and, as training progresses, on several responses emitted in proper sequence and in the presence of appropriate discriminative stimuli. Acquisition of a response, then, is not dependent on repetition or simple practice of the response but is a function of the reinforcement contingencies.

But what about humans? O. Lindsley, at the Harvard Medical School, was the first to extend the methodology of operant conditioning to human behaviour. He utilized essentially the same type of automatic instrumentation, with appropriate modifications, and proceeded to collect records of an arbitrary but experimentally useful response such as plunger-pulling in psychotic subjects. When candy or cigarettes were made contingent on the plunger-pulling response, that response could be shaped in the same manner as pecking in birds or leverpressing in rats. The response rate could be manipulated in a reliable and lawful fashion by varying the reinforcement contingencies. Here, then, was the first indication that human behaviour defied neither measurement nor lawfulness.

It was Lindsley's procedure that inspired one of us (Ayllon) to translate the basic principles of operant conditioning into a situation where human behaviour patterns might be studied and shaped, outside the laboratory, in a more or less free field environment. A treatment programme for psychiatric patients in a hospital ward provided the setting.

The implementation of such a programme requires some systematic changes from the techniques of behavioural measurement usually employed in an experimental laboratory. Instead of the automatic counters and electronic timing devices, nurses and attendants have to be trained as 'behavioural engineers' who count responses and deliver reinforcements accurately and with precision. Of course, this

kind of a behavioural study is not, nor ever will be, accurate to a milli-
second or within a fraction of an inch, but this type of accuracy is
hardly necessary when dealing with gross behavioural changes. However, the basic principles of measurement must be retained. There is no
substitute for objective assessments of observable behaviour, whether
these be obtained through electronic recordings or through tally marks
charted by well-trained human observers. This kind of an assessment
and behavioural engineering must meet several requirements of which
the following are examples. There must be specification and unequivocal
definition of an observable behaviour, such as entering the ward dining
room. An objective record must be kept of the frequency with which the
behaviour was exhibited during a given time period, for example, the
patient entered the dining room for 25 out of 42 consecutive meals.
The empirical determination of an effective reinforcer must be made
which will, for example, isolate either social reinforcement or food to
determine whether they control the patients' frequency of entering the
dining room to eat. There must also be a mechanical or human agent
which will deliver the reinforcer as an immediate consequence of the
specified response according to defined schedules.

These prerequisites are not usually available in a mental hospital
where records typically consist of casual recollections made by hospital
staff. Unfortunately such testimonials are not to be trusted as a basis
for reliable information. We have compared the estimates of numerous
employees about the frequency with which certain behaviours occur
among patients with the actual frequencies obtained by scanning the
hospital records. Despite the fact that the employees were well acquainted with their patients, and had worked with them for at least
one year, they tended to show a systematic bias in reporting the average number of incidents over a period of time. The frequency of behavioural types reflecting pathology in the patients—fighting, seizures
and injuries—was over-estimated, and the estimated number of times
the same employees thought they took refuge in the action of extra
sedation fell drastically short of the actual figure. We thought this
was an interesting finding because attendants and nurses are said to
know their patients well and, often enough, clinical judgments are
made on the basis of such testimonial reports which reflect the staff's
training bias—rather than a patient's condition and progress.

Despite the uselessness of such procedures, and the danger of
distorting facts, nurses all over the world are at this very moment being
carefully trained to write delightful short stories. This is particularly
unfortunate because it is no more difficult to train nurses to become
effective behavioural engineers than it is to make dynamic fiction
writers out of them! What we call 'engineering ability' is absolutely

essential for behavioural measurement and modification which plays such an important role in the rehabilitation of patients.

Intuitively attendants realize the differential effects of reward and punishment but, in practice, these reinforcers are meted out in almost random fashion totally independent of the behaviour rather than as an immediate consequence of it. The intermittent smile by a nurse or the extra cup of coffee, cigarette or candy bar handed out in a moment of good humour may reinforce and maintain precisely that behaviour pattern which is keeping the patient hospitalized. We found,

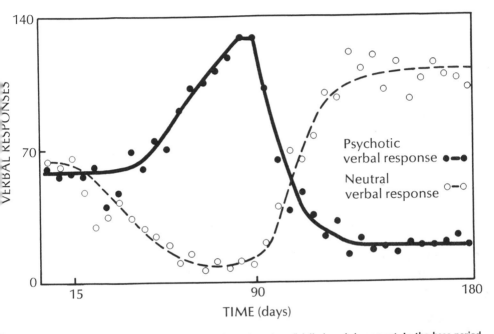

Figure 1. Behaviour of patient can be influenced adversely or beneficially by reinforcement. In the base period up to the 15th day psychotic and neutral verbal behaviour were present in equal strength. During the second period—up to the 90th day—reinforcing the psychotic behaviour by talking nonsense to the patient increased the psychotic verbal behaviour and decreased the neutral one. In the final period—up to the 180th day—this procedure was reversed. The neutral behaviour was then increased and the psychotic behaviour diminished.

for example, that the frequency with which a patient uttered psychotic statements could be increased dramatically simply by listening and giving attention to the patient whenever she talked nonsense. Conversely, the frequency of psychotic statements could be reduced by not listening and by withdrawing attention, while selectively reinforcing conversation which was based on more realistic topics.

In one particular case, a bizarre form of behaviour was shaped to test the effects of an occasional cigarette offered by an attendant 'accidentally' (in our case it was a deliberate accident) at the precise time when the odd behaviour was displayed. As expected, the patient 'learned' to behave in a bizarre manner carrying a broom around in a purposeless fashion wherever she went. The psychiatrist interpreted this behaviour as a symbolic act indicative of the patient's unconscious needs. Symptom and symbol, however, disappeared quite quickly as soon as the reinforcer was withdrawn completely.

One wonders how many so-called 'symbolic acts' in psychiatric patients have anything at all to do with unconscious needs. It seems much more likely that the very environment, which was designed to rehabilitate the patient, maintains such bizarre behaviour through inadvertent reinforcement contingencies. The fact that new and worse 'symptoms' can be shaped within the hospital setting is particularly deplorable. We are convinced that in some cases it is not despite treatment that patients deteriorate over the years, but because of it!

Since bizarre patterns of behaviour are frequently the only indication of psychotic disturbances, it would seem sensible to look for the reinforcers which maintain them and design an environment where contingencies are placed on behaviour patterns which are condoned by society. We have seen that social interaction plays an important role among the environmental contingencies. In fact, the first applications involved the delivery of social reinforcement for specific behaviours. We have found, however, that unless the reinforcer is effective, the behaviour under consideration cannot be dealt with successfully. When we found that a large class of psychotic patients showed little if any change in behaviour through the use of social reinforcers, we started to look for something more effective.

Lindsley circumvented this problem by carefully selecting subjects with a clear and long history of consuming large quantities of cigarettes or candy. But the number of human subjects for whom candy or cigarettes are effective reinforcers is obviously restricted. The relative difficulty in finding effective reinforcers for patients who exhibited an awesome lack of motivation resulted in an adaptation of the original laboratory procedure in which food was used as the reinforcer. Regular meals served in a dining room obviously have more generality as a reinforcer than does candy.

However, some patients even have a long and persistent habit of refusing to eat, and this difficulty also had to be overcome before food could be used as an effective reinforcer for all patients. The typical treatment for patients suffering from chronic anorexia consists of coaxing, spoon or tube feeding or, in extreme cases, providing nourishment intravenously. Fortunately it was found that anorexia could be brought under the control of the environment rather easily. Indeed, the factors that maintain the behaviour are again the powerful reinforcing agents of social attention and nursing care which are inadvertently made contingent on the response of not-eating. When such reinforcement is withdrawn, the response will extinguish—the patients will cease to 'not-eat' and start eating again without assistance from nursing personnel. Once the problem of anorexia was overcome, food or access to the dining room could be used as an effective reinforcer for all patients.

Not only did patients learn to eat on their own without coaxing or coercion, but they also learned to meet a deadline which was progressively shortened from 30 minutes to 5 minutes after the meal call until the dining room doors closed. The patients who served as subjects in these early experiments had been hospitalized for many, many years and were generally considered to be hopeless cases who received only custodial care. Despite the severity of their disturbance and deterioration the patients learned to perform a simple motor response—putting a coin into the slot of a collection can, when food was used as a reinforcer to shape the response. Even social co-operation between two patients could be shaped when access to the meal was made contingent on the response. The co-operation consisted of the two patients pressing a button simultaneously in order to obtain the coin which they could use to gain access to the dining room.

The powerful effects of food as a reinforcer for human subjects was further observed in some individual cases. A patient whom nothing could stop from stealing food off the counter, or from other patients' trays, was placed under close scrutiny. As soon as she was seen to move in the direction of a tray other than her own she was

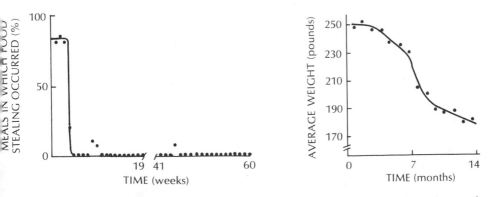

Figure 2. Food stealing by a psychotic patient occurred in about 85 per cent of meals during a three week control period but was eliminated when it resulted in the withdrawal of food reinforcement (left). In only three instances were there occasions during which food stealing occurred. The effective control of food stealing resulted in a reduction of body weight (right).

taken from the dining room and hence missed the remainder of that meal. Within two weeks her food stealing stopped and her diet, which previously had presented quite a problem, was brought under control without further problems of management.

Another individual case involved a patient who wrapped herself in an excessive amount of clothing. This is not an uncommon 'symptom' among patients in psychiatric hospitals. This particular patient, when fully attired, weighed an average of 25 pounds above her normal body weight. When access to the dining room was made contingent on a gradual reduction in weight the patient soon learned to discard her excess clothing. After 14 weeks of shaping she dressed normally and her clothes accounted for only three pounds.

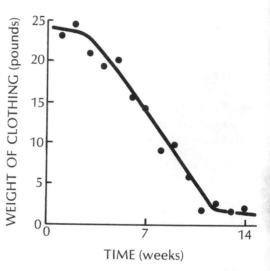

Figure 3. Response of excessive dressing—a not uncommon symptom among patients in psychiatric hospitals—is eliminated when reinforcement in the form of meals is made dependent upon the removal of superfluous clothing.

Studies of this nature illustrate the effectiveness of food as a reinforcer in shaping complex behaviour patterns in humans. But this does not imply that food is the only effective and suitable reinforcer. Most of the behaviour we perform daily is not maintained by food but by a variety of other reinforcers. We may not always be aware of them but this does not mean that they do not exist. For example, we might never think about what maintains such complex human behaviour as playing golf, reading a book or taking a walk. We merely accept the fact that normal human beings seem to do all sorts of things for the sheer pleasure of doing them. This does not mean that doing something for the sake of it means that reinforcement principles are not applicable. Some behaviour can in and of itself be reinforcing, as a look at the animal laboratory will show. Even such animals as rats seem to do things for fun.

D. Premack, at the University of Missouri, discovered that one activity could be utilized as an effective reinforcer for another one. Intuitively, mothers have known this, or they would not have made 'playing outside' contingent on the dishes being washed first. Premack analysed this phenomenon in the laboratory and found that a rat who has free access to food and water will learn to press a lever in order to release the brake of an activity wheel on which it can run to its heart's content. Premack's work demonstrates the fact that the powerful effects of reinforcement contingencies are not restricted to the use of drive-reducing substances like food or water. This has important implications for human learning especially since humans, at least in a reasonably affluent society, are rarely deprived of basic reinforcing stimuli such as food. The scope of operant conditioning techniques applied to humans can be broadened considerably if reinforcement is defined as any kind of pay-off the individual considers to be worthwhile, be it money, consumables, the choice of living quarters or the opportunity to engage in self-chosen behaviour.

Frequency counts obtained from careful and systematic observations of our patients at regular intervals over long periods of time have taught us that they treasure a little corner they can call their own, a cabinet with locks and keys, the choice of bed and dormitory or of roommates and meal-partners. Some patients 'love' to go outside, others prefer to stay in and drink coffee, some enjoy talking to the professional staff and covet social attention and others would just as soon be left alone. All of these phenomena have been used as effective reinforcers to modify behaviour patterns of psychiatric patients. There are, however, some obstacles to be overcome when reinforcement contingencies are to be programmed for an entire hospital ward. For one man's meat may be another man's poison, and it becomes an impossible task for the attendants to sort out the various reinforcers to be utilized in each particular case. The solution to this problem lies in the use of a generalized, conditioned reinforcer.

Any neutral stimulus associated with one that is inherently reinforcing acquires conditioned reinforcing properties of its own. Thus metal tokens, which could be exchanged for things the patients wanted, have been found to be very effective as a reinforcer. Not only can the distribution of these tokens be programmed readily according to well-defined schedules, easy to implement by attendants, but such conditioned reinforcers also eliminate the concern over their effectiveness, since patients can exchange them whenever they so desire and for whatever suits their fancy at any given moment—be this extra food, the choice of a roommate, a talk with a professional person or a walk in the hospital grounds. Patients reinforce themselves, so to speak, and hence there can be no doubt about the value of the reinforcer.

It is wise to remember, however, that the most powerful reinforcers, from food to tokens, are wasted unless they are made contingent on a well-defined and specified response. If the operant conditioner is careless in this regard, he may find that he has shaped all sorts of bizarre and superstitious behaviour patterns rather than the desired response. Such a disillusioned experimenter is quite likely to claim that operant techniques are useless, without ever recognizing that his contingencies were faulty.

Operant conditioning techniques may not be the answer to all the ills of mankind. Indeed, ethologists tell us that some behaviour patterns seem to be innate or imprinted at an early age. Recent work on brain stimulation also suggests that behavioural changes can be brought about without manipulation of environmental consequences. But the great majority of behaviour patterns found in our daily routines are subject to modification through systematic application of reinforcement contingencies.

How much more efficient our educational systems might be if the simple rules that govern learning were applied consistently. Much pain as well as time and effort wasted in tedious practice that leads nowhere could be eliminated. And might not the wearisome procedure of learning to use prosthetic devices be facilitated by proper reinforcement contingencies in the rehabilitation process for the physically disabled? Has anyone ever considered that slum-clearance projects are doomed to fail unless the reinforcement contingencies which maintain 'slumming behaviour' are altered? What principles do societies follow in upgrading the underprivileged? How is the behaviour of criminals shaped and maintained? These are questions we cannot answer by pondering them in our hearts. They warrant careful empirical study. We hope the techniques described in this article may serve as an illustration of how such empirical studies might be conducted.

Further Reading

Ayllon, T., Haughton, E., and Osmond, H. C. 1964. Chronic anorexia: a behaviour problem. *Canadian Psychiatric Association Journal* 9:147–54.
Eysenck, H. J. 1964. *Experiments in behaviour therapy.* Oxford: Pergamon Press.
Ferster, C. B., and Skinner, B. F. 1957. *Schedules of reinforcement.* New York: Appleton-Century-Crofts.
Skinner, B. F. 1938. *The behavior of organisms: an experimental analysis.* New York: Appleton-Century-Crofts.

10 / Orientation Talk to Relatives of Residents

J. MONTGOMERY AND R. McBURNEY

In the preceding article, Ayllon and Hughes discuss the use of an operant-token technique developed for use with psychotic patients. This technique has been widely adopted because of its apparent success. The following article is a slightly abridged form of an address given to parents and relatives of mentally retarded children at Camarillo State Hospital, Camarillo, California, for the purpose of explaining operant conditioning techniques and how they would be used in a new program about to be instituted by the hospital. This presentation was made before the program was begun, to allow parents and relatives to decide whether their children would take part in an experimental ward or remain in the regular program.

The address is noteworthy because of the clarity and simplicity with which it presents a rather sophisticated system.

A program such as we are instituting in the Mental Retardation Division of Camarillo State Hospital requires the understanding of all those concerned. The reason you relatives of the residents on the two units concerned have been asked here today is three-fold. First, we wish to explain our program to you in detail. Second, we wish to enlist your complete and enthusiastic cooperation. Third, we would be remiss in our duties if we failed to take this opportunity of making a little pitch.

Source: J. Montgomery and R. McBurney, "Orientation Talk to Relatives of Residents," an address given at Camarillo State Hospital, Camarillo, California, 1968. This is the first publication.

In our contacts with the relatives of our residents, there are frequently asked questions. Some of these refer to clothes, lockers, the school program, unit programs and therapy, and locked doors. We will most likely answer most of these questions during the course of this discussion, and you will then have the opportunity of asking any other questions you wish.

There are two main philosophies of treatment of the mentally retarded patient. The first is custodial. The patient is fed, clothed, taken care of, and waited on. The second is active treatment. In this philosophy our goal is to aim for the highest potential, to develop the highest skills, and to teach the realities of life.

Our ultimate aim is to prepare the resident for release from the hospital. If this goal is unattainable, the resident will at least have every effort made to help him reach his highest potential. To accomplish this, all modern treatment modalities will be used, and in addition to this we have instituted a well-structured operant-conditioning program.

Some tend to confuse operant conditioning with traditional, or classical conditioning. An example of traditional conditioning is shown by the hungry dog who salivates when confronted with a dish of meat. If a bell is rung each time meat is brought to the hungry dog, eventually the dog will salivate when the bell is rung. The stimulus produces the action.

Operant conditioning differs in that the behavior produces the reinforcement. It also deals with voluntary behavior as opposed to involuntary behavior such as appropriate salivation. Operant conditioning is really a positive behavior-shaping program, in which appropriate behaviors are reinforced, and in our programs the resident may select, by his or her behavior, the type of surroundings preferred.

The advantages of this program are three-fold. The residents profit by increased and specialized attention. The nursing staff, though working harder, is happier, and morale is better. The hospital therefore benefits from both factors.

We must remember also that all the nursing personnel working in this division asked to work here, and unhappy ones have been transferred.

As a therapeutic reinforcement for operant conditioning, we are instituting a token economy. This is a supplemental means of stimulating and reinforcing operant conditioning. It helps the resident approach a more realistic life by working for tokens to pay for everything obtained. By this means the residents set their own standards of living.

The token economy also has a three-fold aim. The first is to establish a higher level of behavior and appearance. Next, to instill progressive improvement aimed at reaching the resident's highest potential in reinforcing and furthering subsidiary programs, which include speech therapy, sensory-motor training—school—and individual behavior-shaping plans.

We realize that not every resident has the potential to absorb the rudiments of the token economy. These residents are not neglected and do not suffer. They are handled as a separate group, and a modified therapeutic approach is used suited to their current level of functioning. They are not deprived of privileges they do not have the capacity to earn.

A therapeutic program such as operant conditioning with the token economy cannot function without the total, complete, and enthusiastic cooperation of all parents. The following reasons will explain this. First, the program is somewhat restrictive. As most of our residents have been used to receiving everything with little required of them, it is somewhat disturbing for them to realize that life is not that way now. Second, privileges must be earned, which is also a departure from the previous mode of living our residents have learned. They say they will tell their fathers or mothers if they are not pleased. It is so comforting to us to have the parents quite aware of our program. As must be obvious, the program cannot function with complaints of irate parents. The program is very strong, and at the same time extremely fragile, as it is so easily sabotaged.

May I ask if there is anyone here who has never missed a meal? [None admitted to this.]

Food is our best reinforcer, and one missed meal is worth a thousand exhortations. A resident who refuses to get up and thereby misses his breakfast will usually never miss another. Refusal to work for a token to pay for a meal is usually not repeated if a meal is missed. We are especially careful to see that all who could be harmed in any way by such a procedure—for example, a resident with diabetes—never miss any meal.

The set-up of operant conditioning is an exacting and closely structured procedure. The most important fundamental is the establishment of nursing groups, each with a nursing leader and alternate. There are corresponding leaders and alternates for these same groups in the afternoon shift. The autonomy of the group leaders is imperative, and the leader is responsible for all activities and medication of the group. The leaders bring problems to the team meetings and no problem of a resident is handled without both day and P.M. leaders present. Each leader is responsible for the group's reinforcements, and no one else is to interfere unless the leader requests it.

Each nursing leader will work with individual behavior-shaping programs directed by the psychologist. Each leader receives instructions from the speech therapist. Each leader works with the rehabilitation therapist in learning the techniques of sensory-motor training.

The set-up for the token economy is also closely structured. The unit is set up in three levels—A, B, and C—the lowest being C. These levels apply to dormitories and dining room. In the C-level dormitory, there are no spreads and the beds are closer together. In B-level, there are spreads, more space between beds, and there are privileges not available for those in C-level. In A-level, there is more room, bedspreads, pictures, and a sitting and reading corner with lamps. Our aim is to make the differences between the levels as noticeable and outstanding as possible within our means. Perhaps you parents might have suggestions for even more distinguished additions to the A-level dormitories. In the dining room, C-level sits closer together, goes through the line and picks up food on compartmented trays. B-level residents have tables for six, more room, and pick up their food on trays with dishes. A-level residents sit at tables for four, are served their food on Corning Ware dishes, and do not have to bus the tables. A-level beds and table service cost more than C-level.

The great problem in our economy is to establish and maintain the value of the token. Residents are reinforced for personal hygiene, personal appearance, general behavior, and general functioning. The residents are reinforced for getting up on time, for bed-making, personal hygiene, including teeth and bathing. Dressing should be complete, with shoes on and tied, belts buckled and buttons buttoned. In the school and on details, residents are given a performance rating and reinforced according to the performance. To stimulate energy and initiative, the residents are charged for meals, privileges, activities, trips, etc. For activities deemed beneficial but in which the residents may show little interest, they are charged more to remain on the unit than they are to participate. Operant conditioning and the token economy are more than programs. They constitute a way of life.

As was mentioned earlier, a most important part of our program is the establishment of the value of the token. A successful means of doing this has been by the use of our unit canteen. Without complete understanding of the purposes of the canteen, it is liable to potential criticism because of what we might facetiously refer to as "double jeopardy." The unit canteen must not be confused with the large hospital canteen. All purchases made by the residents in the hospital canteen must be turned in to their group leaders and the articles are placed in a box belonging to the person who bought them. He must then pay for them with tokens at the regular canteen periods on the unit. Relatives are asked to give any gifts for the residents to the nursing staff in order that they also may be paid for by tokens. Only the resident for whom the gifts are intended is able to procure them. In some ways this may seem unfair, but practically the therapeutic results more than recommend it.

A resident is not permitted to buy from the canteen if he has not obtained sufficient tokens to pay for his next meal.

We have two daily canteen periods on the unit, one in the morning and one in the evening. In our canteen, the residents who receive no money or gifts are enabled to purchase items with tokens earned. The success of the canteen depends on its being well-stocked and therein lies our problem. There are no funds allotted for a purpose such as this. It is only through the generosity of relatives, friends, business houses, *anyone* who may give money or goods for the stocking of the canteen, that the plan can function. Regularly planned monthly contributions to the canteen fund on our token economy units would help us immeasurably. Any gifts of money should be sent to the Unit (your unit) Special Residents' fund, Unit X, Camarillo State Hospital. An ideal situation would be a regular stocking with desirable items for both sexes. Choice items are cookies, candy, gum, Fritos, and any packaged articles of food. For the boys: combs, toothpaste, hair oil, nail-clippers, deodorants—and all items of personal hygiene—transistor batteries, flashlights, billfolds, and numerous miscellaneous items that would interest the males. For the girls: all items of personal hygiene, hair curlers, cosmetics, toothpaste, costume jewelry, purses, etc.

To encourage thrift and to prevent loss and theft of tokens, we have established the First Token Bank of Camarillo State Hospital. We have bank books for each resident, and an account is kept of all deposits and withdrawals. Residents are encouraged to save ahead for visits and various occurrences that cost tokens.

One may say, "It sounds good, but will it work?" There are spot programs throughout the United States in both the divisions of mental illness and mental retardation. It has worked on two units for the mentally ill at Camarillo State Hospital. It is in operation on three mental retardation units, with a fourth due to start soon. One of the most noticeable features of the program is the enthusiasm of those who work with it. The relatives of our residents have been very commendatory in their comments. Progress with this type of resident will, of course, be slow.

Our group-nursing techniques permit a never-ending check of physical problems. Our residents have dental check-ups, and constant attention is paid to feet, hands, and any other ailments which may appear. The whole division has been evaluated by the chief of the Physical Medicine Department and treatment arranged for all those who present treatable conditions.

A survey is in progress throughout the division of speech problems. Our speech therapist is instructing group leaders in the techniques necessary to treat the remedial situations. Two units have been surveyed and others will follow the course of token economy units. A long-range program is being arranged and has and will involve graduate students from surrounding colleges. We also hope to enlist the aid of interested parents and volunteers, who can also be trained.

A program of sensory-motor training is also in operation. Our rehabilitation supervisor and occupational therapist are instructing the nursing leaders in these techniques. This will follow the token economy units but hopefully will outrun them. The nursing leaders, working with a consultant, will carry on this important training. Again, we welcome volunteers who would be willing to undergo a little training and be regular in appearance.

Swimming classes are already in operation.

Our school is functioning. At the present time, we have forty to fifty residents in classes, and on-unit educational programs are to be established, and soon three-fourths of the residents will be involved in educational programs.

Several residents are being transported daily to and from the Sheltered Workshop in Ventura, where a large number of projects are available.

Our own sheltered workshop on the grounds is now in operation and a large number of our residents are being given training there.

There are music-therapy groups on each unit, with group singing and rhythm bands. Twice a week a group goes to the hospital's TV Studio, a closed circuit, and a program is beamed to the hospital, which the residents on the units enjoy thoroughly since they recognize their colleagues.

The entire operant-conditioning program is structured by the division's senior psychologist. This program is constantly being revised and updated to handle changing individual needs in general and in specific behavior-shaping programs.

This program requires the most intense enthusiasm, cooperation, and communication of everyone concerned. It is an extremely strong program, yet a very fragile one, as one person can sabotage it, not necessarily by active obstructionism but by passive footdragging.

May I philosophize a little? As I have mentioned before, this program is unique in that all nursing personnel asked to come to this division and anyone who has become unhappy has been transferred. Our nursing supervisors have been very cooperative in this matter. With this type of care and with the increased individual supervision available with the group-nursing situation, we feel our residents receive a high degree of service. One must remember that these residents are being cared for here because of the impossibility of being in their own homes. Each nurse is rendering total care to several residents. There are all sorts of problems presented from complete inertia to hyperactivity, from complete passiveness to overt combativeness. It is so easy to have a shoe tucked into some obscure corner or to have a sock flushed down a toilet. I think it is somewhat thoughtless under these circumstances for a disturbed parent to take a half-hour or more of a busy nurse's time to complain about a minor detail. Clothes are marked, they are kept in locked lockers, are washed on the unit and despite this care, they disappear. Please, kind parents, we are all human, and it is not only in hospitals that clothes disappear. The nurses render as cooperative attention as possible, and it is hoped that this spirit of cooperation on both parents' and nurses' parts can be encouraged and grow. Understanding, cooperation, and a minimum of criticism will do much to accomplish this. I think we have a tremendous program with endless possibilities, and given just a few months to get rolling we should make you all happy.

Now in regard to the most frequently asked questions. We now have lockers on some of the units, and by the end of the year they should be on all the units. They will be kept locked, with each nurse having a key. On my unit, if a resident is deemed responsible enough to have a key, I think it will be well for us to obtain the parents' permission for him to have it, lest there be subsequent criticism if anything is lost.

Clothes are all marked. Washing is done in the unit washers, but ironing is a problem that we have not as yet solved. It would be well for all relatives purchasing clothes to consider the wash-and-wear type.

We have mentioned the various unit programs. Activities are numerous and include sightseeing, picnics, and fishing trips. There are walks, dances, and movies. Those who earn the privilege and have money make trips to the hospital canteen. Swimming groups and swimming classes are in operation.

As mentioned previously, these privileges are enjoyed if paid for by tokens earned. In the lower, or C, level, those who should be earning their way into a higher level are not permitted some of these privileges. Those activities that are considered to have advisable therapeutic benefit are not on the restricted list. Also, the residents incapable of absorbing the rudiments of our program are not penalized and enjoy all available activities, if they are able.

Our locked doors are at times questioned. Camarillo State Hospital is unique in its open-door policy, but many of our residents have been on security units before coming here, and if doors are left open indiscriminately, the resident is gone and a search must be made. We have one open unit, and others have a partial open-door policy with a monitor to stop those who should not leave. Those who deserve ground privileges have them and are allowed out. Ground privileges on our token economy units must be paid for by earned tokens. The chief complaint about our policy comes from impatient parents who resent the inconvenience of ringing or knocking, but we hope that with this discussion of our program and its goals, and the therapeutic benefits to be derived from it, that there would be a spreading attitude of cooperation.

All medical problems should be discussed with the unit physician. The question regarding unit behavior, socialization, etc., can be quite adequately discussed by the resident's group leader. . . .

Having tried to give you a concise, yet complete résumé of our program, may I once again ask, "Is there anyone here who has any objections to having his or her relative enlisted?" [Not one person objected.]

11 / How to Teach Your Pet

HELEN KAY

You are in for a change of pace with this article. First of all, it is the
only article in the book dealing with subhuman organisms. Second,
it was written for children and first appeared in the delightful book
How Smart Are Animals? by Helen Kay. The book's dedication
indicates its purpose:

> TO THE CHILD
> with the pet of a dog
> cat
> rat
> hamster
> mouse
> rabbit
> duck
> parakeet
> pigeon
> guinea pig
> monkey
> (or what have you?)

WHO IS THE POTENTIAL SCIENTIST OF TOMORROW.

Its appearance here is intended to acquaint you with a
sample of the social-behavioral science books available to elementary
school children that you may want to use someday, and to help
you try out some of the principles discussed.

If you have a teaching machine in your classroom, it is all because some years ago a psychologist put a rat in a box.

How can a rat in a box have anything to do with a teaching machine in a classroom?

The rat was in a special box, called a Skinner Box after the psychologist who made it. His full name is Dr. Burrhus Frederic Skinner, and he is head of the psychology department of Harvard University.

The box was very simple. It had a small bar on which a rat could put its forefeet. If the rat, while running around in the box happened to press the bar, a small bit of food dropped in front of it. Of course, the rat soon caught on and pressed the bar again to get more food. It got only a little bit each time, so it stayed hungry and kept working on the bar. All the while an electrical instrument recorded just how many times the bar was pressed and how much the rat ate.

Something else could be added to the experiment. There was an electric light in the box that could be turned on and off. The experimenter could arrange to give a pellet of food only if the rat pressed the bar while the light was on; if it hit the bar in the dark, it got no reward. The rat then learned to work on the bar only in the light.

Suppose no food came out when the rat pressed the bar, even in the light? The rat would then stop working.

With his useful little box, Dr. Skinner showed that any animal will work for success and will stop doing the things that result in failure. He went beyond Pavlov's experiments in conditioning. He developed a system of conditioned learning which applied not to reflexes, such as a dog's drooling, but the more complicated behavior.

Skinner has been interested in training animals ever since he was a small boy in the Pennsylvania town where he grew up. After he became a psychologist, he developed animal training into a system. He has worked out some brand new methods of training which are more efficient than the old ways. He says that with these methods anyone can quickly train an animal to do all kinds of things.

Do you want to try this system? Would you like to train your pet?

What kind of pet do you have? A dog? A cat? A parakeet? A rat? It doesn't matter. Any animal will do, whether it runs, trots, walks, crawls, or flies. It doesn't even have to be smart. Just choose your animal and decide what you are going to teach it.

Dr. Skinner has worked in the laboratory with all kinds of animals: rats, dogs, cats, monkeys, ducks, pigeons, and what-not. Incidentally, Dr. Skinner, unlike Pavlov, considers dogs the "least reliable" subjects

Source: Helen Kay, *How Smart Are Animals?* (New York: Basic Books, Inc., 1962), pp. 70–80. Copyright © 1962 by Basic Books Publishing Co., Inc., New York. Reprinted by permission of the publisher.

for experiments. Don't let that bother you, if you like dogs. Dr. Skinner won't argue with you. He is really a kindly man and glad to share what he knows. He'll be glad to tell you how to teach a dog.

Dr. Skinner is slight, wiry, and a fast talker. He has a nice sense of humor. "Your first move," he says, "is to choose some available animals as your experimental subject." He adds with a smile:

"Children and other members of your family may also be available, but it is suggested that you save them until you had practice with less valuable material."

What are you choosing?

Your dog?

"Fine," says Dr. Skinner.

What kind is it?

It doesn't matter. It can be chow, collie, terrier, or bulldog; a pedigreed dog or a mixed breed, like Caroline Kennedy's puppy, born of Strelka, the Russian dog that came back from space.

So yours is a mutt, too?

That will do.

Dr. Skinner says that you will have to have several things for the experiment: (1) a quiet place to work, (2) something to reward the dog with for working well, (3) a noise-maker of some kind, and (4) a task to be taught.

You don't need a box for this experiment. Just a quiet room where you and the dog can be alone for five minutes. We'll suppose your dog's name is Bingo.

"The second thing you will need," says Dr. Skinner, "is something your subject wants, say food." This will serve, he explains, as "a reinforcement for desired behavior."

If food is your reward, then the time of day is important. Remember the hungry rat? Remember hungry Viki? Bingo should be hungry, too. Unless the dog is hungry, he will not work. If Bingo is usually fed in the morning, do the experiment early in the morning before he eats. If his feeding time is in the evening, you can give the lesson any time during the day.

For the experiment you'll need about 40 small bits of food, close at hand. Now there is just one more thing—the noise-maker. What shall it be? Well, you may clap your hands, stamp your feet, or use a bell or a buzzer. Dr. Skinner likes a toy cricket, which makes a quick clicking sound.

The noise-maker will be what Dr. Skinner calls a "conditioned reinforcer."

Now you are ready to start. All quiet? No distractions? Pet Bingo. Is he relaxed and happy? Fine.

Begin by tossing Bingo a few bits of food, one at a time. Give him one piece every half-minute. He'll love it, of course, and beg eagerly for the next piece, with his mouth open and drooling.

Now snap the cricket just before you throw the piece of food. Wait half a minute and do it again. Bingo will now come for the food right after he hears the cricket. Don't sound the cricket or give food when the dog is close to you or facing you. You don't want him to jump on you or come up to watch you snap the cricket, because that will spoil the experiment. Wait until Bingo turns away, then sound the cricket and toss the food. Soon, the instant he hears the cricket he will turn toward you and run to the spot where you have been tossing the food. He will do this even if you don't throw him food.

Bingo is now conditioned to the cricket as a reinforcer. You are ready to use it to teach him the behavior you have chosen as a goal. Dr. Skinner suggests that a good goal to start with is getting the dog to lay his nose on some object within his reach, such as the handle of a drawer or cupboard.

Watch Bingo as he moves about the room. Dr. Skinner warns that you must not touch or pet the dog or talk to him. Speak to him only with the cricket and feed him when he comes to you. Whenever he moves toward the cupboard, sound the cricket. In a minute or two Bingo will be standing close to the cupboard.

Now watch for any movement of the dog that brings his nose closer to the cupboard handle. When that happens, snap the cricket quickly and feed him. Timing is very important. The sound must come just as Bingo's nose moves toward the handle.

He will move closer and closer to it. When at last he does rest his nose on the handle, reinforce this at once with the cricket and give a generous food reward. Bingo will soon do it again. He will go and lay his nose on the handle if you continue to sound the cricket as he does, so long as he is hungry enough to want the food.

You should be able to teach this lesson to your dog in only five minutes. With Bingo trained to the cricket as a conditioner, you can go on in other sessions to get him to do many other interesting things.

Dr. Skinner likes to work with pigeons. He finds them more satisfactory than rats—a favorite laboratory animal of psychologists. Pigeons live longer (up to 24 years) and can be used for more kinds of experiments. In Dr. Skinner's laboratory at Harvard, the pigeons outnumber the rats almost six to one. Everything in his lab is covered with white dust, like chalk, from his healthy pigeons.

If you happen to have a pigeon or can catch and tame one, you may want to try some of Dr. Skinner's experiments.

You can make a homemade box for the experiments out of a carton. Use a screen for the roof of the box. Cut some windows in the sides, placing them so that you can watch the bird but it can't see you.

Put a cup inside the box under a hole in the side through which you can drop in food.

The only other things you will need are a handful of grain and a noise-maker. For you are going to teach the pigeon in the same way you taught your dog.

Drop a few grains slowly into the cup just after sounding the cricket. Dò this again and again until the bird learns to eat the food immediately whenever, you snap the cricket.

Now you are ready to begin teaching the pigeon.

Would you like to teach it to play cards with you? This is a favorite experiment of Dr. Skinner.

First you will need to train it to peck at a card. Take any card out of a deck and hang it on a nail in the box where the pigeon can peck it. Then watch the bird; whenever its head approaches the card, sound the cricket and drop some food in the cup. Keep doing this until the pigeon pecks the card.

"After you have trained the bird to peck the card by reinforcing the movements that lead to that end, change the card and again reinforce the peck," Dr. Skinner explains. "If you shuffle the cards and present them at random, the pigeon will learn to peck any card offered."

Now you can go on to teach the bird to choose a particular suit—say hearts. Put a card of the heart suit on the nail. Sound the cricket and feed the bird when it pecks at the card. Replace the heart with a spade card. This time don't give the bird any food if it pecks the card. Continue offering hearts and spades, each time rewarding a peck at a heart but giving no food when it pecks a spade. Gradually the pigeon will refuse to peck spades and will peck only hearts.

The pigeon in your box has shown that, like a rat or a dog, it, too, will work for a reward and will learn what you want it to.

Have you always wanted to be a magician? Magicians pull pigeons out of hats. You can perform a trick for an audience that will be even more startling and amusing than pulling a pigeon out of a hat.

Take two blank cards, and write PECK on one of them and DON'T PECK on the other.

Now, by the same method you used to teach your pigeon to peck at hearts, train it to peck only at the card that says PECK. Sound the cricket and feed the bird when it pecks that card. Don't reward it when it pecks DON'T PECK.

Soon the pigeon will peck only when it sees PECK and will not do so when it sees DON'T PECK.

The people who watch your pigeon's act will marvel at the pigeon that can "read." They will certainly applaud you as a magician.

Dr. Skinner has many more tricks in his bag. This master magician even taught pigeons how to play ping-pong.

Instead of rackets, they use their bills to hit the ball. They play at a pigeon-sized board, knocking the ball back and forth across a small net.

Dr. Skinner started training the pigeons by rewarding them with food every time they hit the ball with their bill. Then he got them to peck the ball back and forth at each other. After that he rewarded a player only when the other bird missed. Both of them learned to play a real game of ball. Pigeons, like anyone else, want to be winners!

Does this sound familiar? Don't you play to win?

Dr. Skinner's method of teaching works with people as well as with animals. Remember, he said you might try this system on children, too.

Some psychologists tried an experiment with nursery-school children between two and five years of age.

They didn't put the children in a box; they put a box in the nursery-school room. It was an experimental box like the one the rat was placed in at the beginning of this chapter.

There was a lever on the box, and when a child found it and accidentally pressed it, a small piece of candy would drop out. Of course, the child then would press it again.

The results were quite the same as with rats.

The child would work faster and faster to get more and more candy. When the candy stopped coming, he would stop working.

So all the subjects responded the same way.

The rat worked to get its crumb of food.

The dog worked to get its tidbit.

The pigeon worked for its grain.

The child worked for his candy.

So it is also with pigs, platypuses, porpoises, porcupines—the whole animal kingdom. All of them learn to repeat behavior that has won them success.

Dr. Skinner thought about this for a long time. How could this law of learning be used as a teaching aid? Finally he invented a way. He adapted his Skinner Box to make a teaching machine.

Perhaps your classroom already has such a machine?

Most of these machines consist of a box with a window through which you can see a question. You write your answer and then turn a shutter to read the correct answer in the machine. If your answer was right, you move on to the next question. You can take as long as you want for each question and do as many as you like.

Boys and girls will work at this machine for various kinds of reward—candy, a pat on the back for the right answer, or just the satisfaction of solving the problems.

All this has come from Dr. Skinner's experiments with a rat in a box. His experiments have shown that a reward helps learning. Every animal, and every child, will work for a reward. Even a pigeon can learn to do complicated things, such as recognizing cards and playing ping-pong. And each pupil learns at his own pace.

12 / Achievement Place: Token Reinforcement Procedures in a Home-Style Rehabilitation Setting for "Pre-Delinquent" Boys

ELERY L. PHILLIPS

While still a graduate student at the University of Kansas, Phillips took on the responsibility of working with a small group of adolescent juvenile delinquents, wards of the court, asking them to live in his home. It soon occurred to him that the rehabilitation program he was to carry out with them was an ideal setting to gather data for his M.A. thesis. The report you are about to read is the product of that endeavor.

This study is particularly interesting because of its dramatic results. The figures demonstrate how his contingencies effectively changed behavior. Also of note is the phasing-out process where he moves from "unnatural" to natural (societal) reinforcers.

Token reinforcement procedures were designed to modify the behavior of "pre-delinquent" boys residing in a community-based, home-style

Source: Elery L. Phillips, "Achievement Place: Token Reinforcement Procedures in a Home-Style Rehabilitation Setting for 'Pre-Delinquent' Boys," *Journal of Applied Behavior Analysis* 1 (Fall 1968): 213–23. Copyright © 1968 by the Society for the Experimental Analysis of Behavior, Inc. Reprinted by permission of the author and the *Journal of Applied Behavior Analysis*.

rehabilitation setting. Points (the tokens) were redeemable for various privileges such as visiting their families, watching TV, and riding bicycles. Points were given by the house-parents contingent upon specified appropriate behavior and taken away for specified inappropriate behavior. The frequency of aggressive statements and poor grammar decreased while tidiness, punctuality, and amount of homework completed increased. It was concluded that a token reinforcement procedure, entirely dependent upon back-up reinforcers naturally available in a home-style treatment setting, could contribute to an effective and economical rehabilitation program for pre-delinquents.[1]

Introduction

Alternatives are being sought to the placement of juvenile delinquents in large state reformatories. While reformatories are steadily increasing their standards they still have had less than adequate records of success (Block and Flynn, 1966; Berelson and Steiner, 1964).

The current trend away from the reformatory can be seen in the establishment of small home-style, residential treatment programs by individual communities. These often involve a pair of house-parents and from three to eight youths. The adjudicated youths live in these homes, attend the local schools, and continue to participate in their communities.

Achievement Place, the program described in this report, is an example of a home-style, community based, treatment facility. The treatment program at Achievement Place employed a "token economy" based on those described by Cohen, Filipczak, and Bis (1965), and Burchard (1967) for institutionalized delinquents; by Ayllon and Azrin (1965) for institutionalized psychotics; and by Wolf, Giles, and Hall (1968), Clark, Lachowicz, and Wolf (1968), and Birnbrauer, Wolf, Kidder, and Tague (1965) for classroom management.

The aim of the present research was to develop and evaluate the effects of a token economy (based on naturally available reinforcers) in a home-style, residential treatment program for "pre-delinquent" boys.

[1] I wish to thank Montrose M. Wolf for his advice and guidance throughout this research. I am also indebted to Elaine Phillips for assistance in conducting the experiments and in preparing this manuscript. This study is based on a thesis submitted to the Department of Human Development in partial fulfillment of the requirements of the Master of Arts degree. The research was partially supported by a grant (HD 03144) from the National Institute of Child Health and Human Development to the Bureau of Child Research and the Department of Human Development, University of Kansas. Reprints may be obtained from the author, 23 East Eleventh St., Lawrence, Kansas 66044.

Program

SUBJECTS

Three boys who had been declared dependent-neglected by the County Court and placed in Achievement Place served as subjects. The boys, all from low-income families, had committed minor offenses ("thefts," "fighting," and "general disruptive behavior") and had histories of "school truancy" and "academic failure."

Jack was 13 years old. His school records reported an I.Q. of 85 and a second-grade reading level. Concern had been noted regarding a "speech problem," "poor grammar," "aggressiveness," "poor motivation," and "a general lack of cleanliness."

Don was 14 years old. School records indicated that academically he was performing two years below his grade placement, but that he had a normal I.Q. rating. Reports from school also described this youth as "possessing an inferior attitude," "rejected" by his classmates, and "aggressive."

Tom, who was 12, was described as having an I.Q. of approximately 120. His disruptive behavior in school had resulted in his being placed in the fifth grade, three years below his level of achievement as indicated by the Iowa Basic Skills Test. School records also noted that he was "dangerous to other children" and "openly hostile toward teachers."

FACILITIES AND DAILY ROUTINE

The purpose of Achievement Place was to provide a home situation in the community for boys who had been termed pre-delinquents by local juvenile authorities (boys who had committed only minor offenses thus far, but whom the Court felt would probably advance to more serious crimes unless steps were taken to modify their behavior). The author and his wife were the house-parents.

The daily routine was similar to that of many families. The boys arose at 7 A.M. They showered, dressed, and cleaned their bedrooms and bathrooms. After breakfast, some of the boys had kitchen clean-up duties before leaving for school. After school the boys returned home and prepared their homework, after which they could watch TV, play games, or engage in other recreational activities if these privileges had been earned via the token economy. Some boys were assigned kitchen clean-up duties after the evening meal. Bedtime was 9:30 P.M. Trips, athletic events, and jobs, both around the home and away from the home, were scheduled for weekends and school holidays.

THE TARGET BEHAVIORS AND THE TOKEN REINFORCEMENT SYSTEM

Target behaviors were selected in social, self-care, and academic areas considered to be important to the youths in their current or future environment. A further requirement was that a target behavior had to be definable in terms of observable events and measurable with a high degree of inter-observer agreement.

Token reinforcers were used which could be easily and rapidly administered and thus could bridge the delay between the target behavior and the remote back-up reinforcing events. The tokens took the form of points. The boys earned points for specified appropriate behavior and lost points for specified inappropriate behavior. Points were tallied on 3-by-5-inch index cards that the boys always carried with them. Thus, the points could be earned or lost immediately and points later redeemed for the back-up reinforcers.

Items and events which were naturally available in the home and which appeared to be important to the boys were the back-up reinforcers. Access to these privileges was obtained on a weekly basis. At the end of each week the boys could trade the points they had earned that week for privileges during the next week. Some of the privileges are described in Table 1.

Table 1   Privileges That Could Be Earned Each Week with Points

Privileges for the Week	Price in Points
Allowance	1000
Bicycle	1000
TV	1000
Games	500
Tools	500
Snacks	1000
Permission to go downtown	1000
Permission to stay up past bedtime	1000
Permission to come home late after school	1000

The prices of the privileges were relatively constant from week to week, although they were occasionally adjusted as their importance appeared to vary. For example, during the winter the price of television was increased.

The economy of the system (the relationship between the total number of points that could be earned and the total cost of all the privileges) was arranged in such a manner that if a youth performed all the tasks expected of him and lost a minimum of points in fines, he could expect to obtain all the privileges without performing any extra tasks.

There was another set of privileges for "one-of-a-kind" opportunities which had no fixed price but which were instead sold to the highest bidder, auction style. One example was the "car privilege" which entitled the purchaser to his choice of seating in the car for the week. Another auctioned privilege was the opportunity for a boy to obtain authority over the other boys in the execution of some household chore. Each week these managerships were auctioned. The purchaser was made responsible for the maintenance of the basement, the yard, or the bathrooms. Each manager had authority to reward or fine the other boys under his direction for their work at the task. The manager, in turn, earned or lost points as a result of the quality of the job done (as judged by the house-parents).

Most of the behaviors which earned or lost points were formalized and explicit to the extent of being advertised on the bulletin board. Rewards and fines ranged from 10 to 10,000 points. Some of the behaviors and approximate points gained are indicated in Table 2.

A few other contingencies were less formalized but still resulted in point consequences. For example, even though there was no formal rule the boys would sometimes earn or lose points as a result of their overall manners while guests were in the home.

Table 2   Behaviors and the Number of Points That They Earned or Lost

Behaviors That Earned Points	Points
1) Watching news on TV or reading the newspaper	300 per day
2) Cleaning and maintaining neatness in one's room	500 per day
3) Keeping one's person neat and clean	500 per day
4) Reading books	5 to 10 per page
5) Aiding house-parents in various household tasks	20 to 1000 per task
6) Doing dishes	500 to 1000 per meal
7) Being well dressed for an evening meal	100 to 500 per meal
8) Performing homework	500 per day
9) Obtaining desirable grades on school report cards	500 to 1000 per grade
10) Turning out lights when not in use	25 per light

Behaviors That Lost Points	Points
1) Failing grades on the report card	500 to 1000 per grade
2) Speaking aggressively	20 to 50 per response
3) Forgetting to wash hands before meals	100 to 300 per meal
4) Arguing	300 per response
5) Disobeying	100 to 1000 per response
6) Being late	10 per minute
7) Displaying poor manners	50 to 100 per response
8) Engaging in poor posture	50 to 100 per response
9) Using poor grammar	20 to 50 per response
10) Stealing, lying, or cheating	10,000 per response

Experiment I: Aggressive Statements

One behavior pattern that had led to the classification of these youths as deviant juveniles had been the "aggressiveness" they exhibited. The terms "aggression" and "aggressiveness" were noted in school records, psychological test reports, Court notes, and in general comments from individuals who were familiar with the youths. Inquiry into the nature of this "aggressiveness" revealed it to be inferred almost completely from comments the boys emitted such as: "I'll smash that car if it gets in my way" or "I'll kill you." The following experiment describes the house-parents' program to measure and to reduce the aggressive verbal behavior.

PROCEDURES AND RESULTS

"Aggressive" phrases were recorded for the three boys simultaneously for 3 hours each day (one session) while the youths were engaged in wood-working activities in the basement workshop.

RESPONSE DEFINITION

Phrases or clauses emitted by the youths were considered to be aggressive statements if they stated or threatened inappropriate destruction or damage to any object, person, or animal. For example, the statement "Be quiet" was not counted as an aggressive response, while "If you don't shut up, I'll kill you" was recorded as an aggressive statement. Over 70% of the aggressive statements were from a list of 19 phrases used repeatedly.

CONDITIONS

Baseline. No contingencies were placed on the youths' responses.

Correction. The boys were told what an aggressive statement was and that such statements were not to be used. A corrective statement by one of the house-parents, such as "That's not the way to talk" or "Stop that kind of talk," was made contingent on the youths' responses. An arbitrary period of approximately 3 to 5 seconds was allowed to elapse after a response (or responses) before the corrective comment was made. This meant that a correction did not follow every aggressive statement; sometimes many responses were emitted before a corrective statement was made. The delay interval was employed in order to increase the chance that the boy would have completed his speech episode before correction was administered by the parent.

Fines. A fine of 20 points was made contingent on each response. The fines, like the corrections of the previous condition, were not delivered until approximately 3 to 5 seconds had passed without a response. No announcement of this condition was made in advance.

No fines. No fines or corrections were levied on responses. This condition was introduced unannounced. There were occasional threats to reinstate the Fines condition if the rate of responding did not decrease. The threats were worded approximately as follows: "If you boys continue to use that aggressive talk, I will have no other choice but to take away points." These threats were not carried out.

Fines. This condition was identical to the first Fines condition except that fines were 50 points instead of 25. The onset of this condition was announced.

In Figure 1 it can be seen, by comparing Correction rate with the

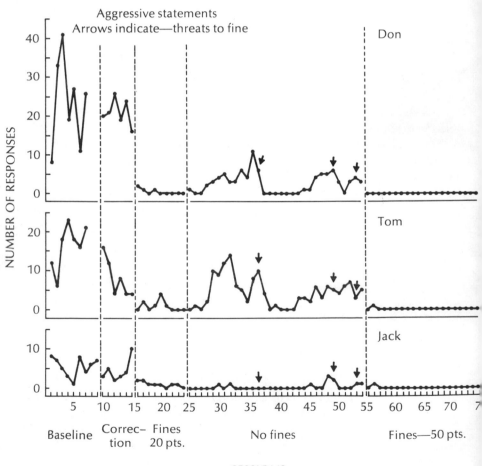

Figure 1. Number of aggressive statements per 3-hr session for each youth under each condition.

Baseline rate, that Correction reduced the responding of only one boy, while Fines (20 points per response) produced an immediate and dramatic decline in each youth's aggressive statements. Responses gradually returned when fines were no longer levied but were eliminated when the Fines condition was reinstated. Although the first threat (indicated by the arrows) in the No Fines condition did appear to have a large suppressive effect on the rate of behavior, the last two threats appeared to have much less, possibly due to the fact that the first threat had not been carried out.

Inter-observer agreement about the occurrence of aggressive statements was measured by the use of a second observer during 14 of the 75 sessions. Agreement averaged 92%.

Experiment II: Bathroom Cleaning

The youths in the home were assigned a number of household chores, such as aiding in the upkeep of the yard and cleaning their rooms and bathrooms. They originally failed to complete these chores in most instances. Programs involving the point system were designed to increase the boys' contribution to the maintenance of these areas. The cleaning of the bathrooms was studied under a number of conditions.

PROCEDURES AND RESULTS

Sixteen cleaning tasks in the bathroom involving the sinks, stools, floors, etc., were scored as accomplished or not accomplished. The bathrooms were scored every day between 12:00 and 12:30 P.M., except in the Baseline condition, where recording was done as soon as the boys reported that the cleaning had been completed (usually before noon). Consequences, if there were any, were levied immediately after inspection.

RESPONSE DEFINITION

As stated above, the bathroom cleaning was divided into 16 tasks. In order to obtain a high degree of inter-observer agreement, each task had a specified set of criteria to be met in order to be considered accomplished. For example, one of the 16 tasks was described in the following manner:

Floor and Rugs—The floor has to be clear of all objects greater than ¼ by ¼ by ¼ inch and clear of all visible water. If rugs were removed for cleaning, they should be replaced and centered under the sink within one foot of the wall.

CONDITIONS

Baseline. The baseline condition consisted of instructing all the boys to clean the bathrooms. No consequences were contingent on their behavior other than the instruction that they clean the bathrooms again, if fewer than four of the tasks had been accomplished.

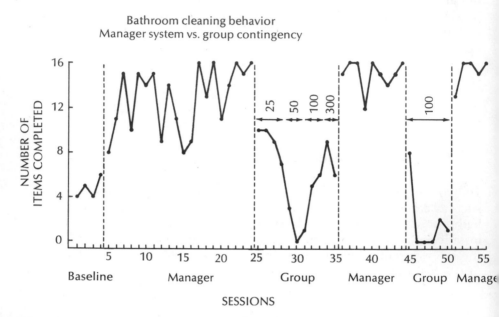

Bathroom cleaning behavior
Manager system vs. group contingency

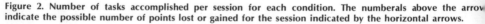

Figure 2. Number of tasks accomplished per session for each condition. The numerals above the arrow indicate the possible number of points lost or gained for the session indicated by the horizontal arrows.

Manager. During the Manager condition one boy was given the responsibility for cleaning the bathrooms daily. He picked the individual, or individuals, to clean the bathrooms each day and then paid or fined the workers (20 points lost or gained per task) according to the quality of their work as judged by him. Later, when the bathrooms were checked by the house-parents, the manager received or lost points (20 points per task). The manager earned points only if 75% or more of the tasks were completed. The privilege of being manager was auctioned each week.

Group. The Group condition consisted of all boys being responsible for cleaning the bathrooms and subject to the same fines. There was no manager. The boys were fined when less than 75% of the 16 tasks were completed. The amount of the fines varied from 25 to 300 points.

Manager. This condition was identical to the first Manager condition.

Group. Identical to the first Group condition except that the fines were 100 points.

Manager. Identical to the first and second Manager conditions.

The point contingencies levied by the manager under the Manager condition were more effective than the fines administered by the house-parents under the Group condition, even when the values of the fines under the Group condition were greater than those administered by the manager. The greater effectiveness of the manager condition may have been the result of the differential contingencies for each boy administered by the manager.

Table 3 shows the average number of points lost per boy each day under each condition. Table 3 shows clearly that the managership was not purchased because it was possible to earn a large number of points as a manager. The manager consistently lost more points than the workers he supervised.

Item by item, inter-observer agreement about the accomplishment of the bathroom cleaning tasks for 20 sessions ranged from 83% to 100% agreement and averaged 97%.

Table 3   Average Number of Points Lost per Session by Workers and Manager under Each Condition

	Baseline	First Manager	First Group	Second Manager	Second Group	Third Manager
Worker	0	18	73	13	100	0
Manager	0	64	—	20	—	16

Experiment III: Punctuality

One of the boys in particular failed to respond to instructions about promptness. This led to an analysis, over a series of behaviors, of the effectiveness of point contingencies on punctuality.

PROCEDURES AND RESULTS

Promptness was recorded for three separate behaviors:

1. Returning home from school.
2. Going to bed.
3. Returning home from errands.

Instructions were posted which stated times to be home from school and to retire to their bedrooms at night. When a boy was sent on an errand the time he was due to return was determined before he departed.

The house-parents recorded the number of minutes late or early up to 30 minutes.

CONDITIONS

Before Fines. If the boy was late from school or an errand, he was reprimanded by one of the house-parents, "Why are you late? You know what time I told you to be here." Tardiness in going to their bedrooms resulted in a reminder every 10 minutes, "Go to bed; it's past your bedtime." No other contingencies were involved.

Fines. The youths were fined 20 points for every minute that they were late. Other than being initially informed of the change in contingencies, they were given no reminders or verbal reprimands. The fines were dispensed when the youths returned home or departed for bed. There were no programmed consequences for being early.

Punctuality for school was dealt with first. The termination of the baseline (Before Fines) involving school marked the beginning of

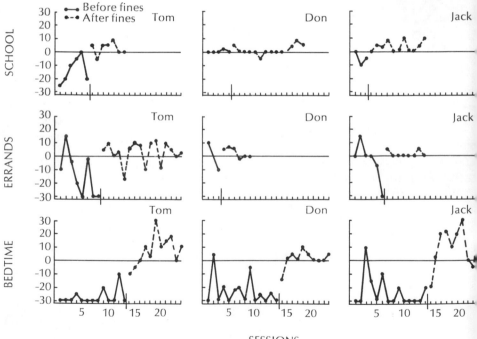

Figure 3. Number of minutes early or late before and after the application of point contingencies. Each youth's punctuality was measured for school, errands, and bedtime.

the baseline of errands. Completion of the baseline for errands corresponded to initiation of the baseline for bedtime behavior.

The development of Tom's punctuality in all three areas can be seen in Figure 3. The other two boys had a consistent punctuality problem only at bedtime, and this disappeared at the onset of the Fines condition. The fines were very specific in their effect on the subjects' behavior. Fining tardiness from school had no apparent effect on promptness in returning from errands, and punishing lateness from errands did not seem to produce punctuality at bedtime. Inter-observer agreement was greater than 95% for the 53 checks which occurred throughout the study.

Experiment IV: Homework

Failure in school is frequently associated with juvenile delinquency. The school records of the boys sent to Achievement Place all contained accounts of truancy and lack of academic success throughout the boys' school years. One apparently severe deficiency in their school repertoires involved their failure to prepare routine classroom assignments and homework. This experiment compared the effect of several contingencies on preparation of homework tasks.

PROCEDURES AND RESULTS

The study was carried out during the summer, when the youths were not in school. Daily assignments were described on 3-by-5-inch index cards which were available after 8:00 A.M. each morning. The work was scored at 5:00 P.M. of the same day. Each boy was instructed that failure to pick up an assignment card during the day would result in a fine equal to the number of points he would have received if he had completed the assignment. None of the youths ever failed to pick up his assignment card. The house-parents were available to aid in the preparation of the assignments during two periods each day, 10:00 to 11:00 A.M. and 2:00 to 3:00 P.M.

RESPONSE DEFINITION

The assignments were pages out of self-teaching workbooks which required approximately 1 hour to complete. The workbooks used were *The Practice Workbook of Arithmetic*, Grade 5 and 6, Treasure Books, Inc., 1107 Broadway, New York, N.Y., and *The Practice Workbook of Reading*, Grades 2 and 3, also by Treasure Books, Inc.

The assignments, usually two or three pages, were divided into five approximately equal parts on the assignment cards. Each part required an accuracy of 75% to be considered complete. The boys received one fifth of the maximum number of points, money, or time obtainable for each assignment completed, as explained below.

CONDITIONS

Money. Under this condition each boy could earn 25 cents for each day's assignment if he had completed the assignment with less than 25% errors. The youths had the choice of receiving the money daily or at the end of the week. All three chose the latter, and the amount of money they earned was accumulated on an index card carried by each boy.

Weekly late-time. The boys had the opportunity to earn up to 1 hour of late-time per assignment. Late-time could be spent on the weekends to stay up beyond the youth's normal bedtime (9:30 P.M.). A maximum of 7 hours could be spent by a boy during a weekend and the boys could share their late-time with each other.

Daily late-time. Throughout this condition the boys could use the late-time the same day earned or save it for the weekend.

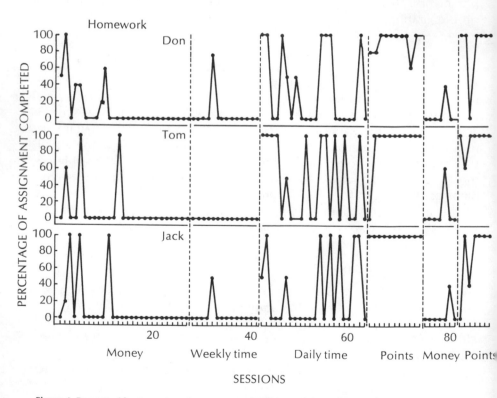

Figure 4. Percent of homework assignment completed by each boy under each of several conditions.

Points. The points phase allowed the youths to earn 500 points per assignment.

Money. This was the same as the first Money condition.

Points. This was the same as the first Points condition.

Figure 4 shows that the Points condition was by far the most effective in producing homework preparation. Daily Late-Time compared favorably to other conditions. Money, at the one value tested, yielded relatively poor results.

It should be noted that no effort was made to equate the points with the money and it seemed quite likely that at some higher value money would have been as effective as points. It was thought that the low rate of behavior in the first Money condition might have been due to the youths' lack of experience in using money. Thus, after the first condition, an allowance of $1.50 was given each week until the second Money condition (a period of seven weeks). During this interim the youths spent their money and appeared to understand what could be obtained with money. However, the reinstatement of the Money condition produced no better performance than the original Money condition.

Observer agreement in scoring the assignments was measured for four separate sessions, one in each of the first four conditions. The agreement on the proportion of the assignment completed was 100%.

Experiment V: "Ain't"

Poor grammar was an obvious problem for one of the boys. The present study describes a program designed to correct a grammatical problem both with and without manipulation of the point system.

PROCEDURES AND RESULTS

The verbal response "ain't" was recorded for one boy for 3 hours (one session) each day. The 3 hours were not consecutive, nor the time of day consistent. Responses were registered on a silent counter which appeared to be unnoticed by the youth.

RESPONSE DEFINITION

It was necessary to differentiate between "ain't" used in normal conversation and the "ain'ts" used in discussions about the incorrect responses. Thus, "ain'ts" used as verbs were considered responses, while "ain'ts" employed as nouns or other parts of speech were not recorded.

CONDITIONS

Baseline. No contingencies were placed on the youth's responses.

Correction. The correction procedure consisted of either house-parent's interrupting the boy's conversation, informing him of his error, suggesting an appropriate alternative, and requiring the youth to repeat the sentence using the correction. The house-parents corrected the mistake in a matter-of-fact manner. The subject's peers were also encouraged to assist in informing the boy of his errors.

Correction and Fines. This condition was identical to the previous phase except that a 20-point fine was levied on each response heard throughout the day. The "ain'ts" from each 3-hour session were recorded as above. Also, the total number of responses fined for the entire day was available by tallying the entries noted on the point card. Again, the other boys were told to inform the house-parents of any responses which occurred when they were not present. These responses were also fined.

Post Check. One month after the final session of the Correction and Fine condition the response was again recorded for five days (3 hours each day).

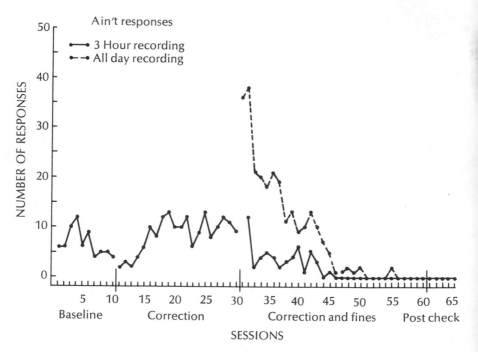

Figure 5. Number of responses per day (3-hr session) for one youth under: (1) no consequences (baseline); (2) correction by the house-parents and other boys; and (3) correction and a 20-point fine for each response. Post checks of the behavior were taken 30 days later. The dashed line indicates the total number of responses for the entire day.

As can be seen in Figure 5, no effect was evident from the Correction condition but when the 20-point fine was made contingent on the youth's behavior, there was an immediate and consistent decline in the frequency of the inappropriate behavior, until, by the end of the second week, the response, "ain't," was eliminated. It was the impression of the house-parents that this effect was not accompanied by any noticeable decline in the youth's overall rate of speech. The dashed line in Figure 5 indicates the course of the decline in "ain'ts" recorded throughout each day during this condition.

The Post Check condition, 30 days after the elimination of "ain'ts," revealed no trace of the response.

Observer reliability was recorded for over one fourth of the sessions. The observer recorded data simultaneously with the primary recorder, but recording was independent. Agreement was never less than 93%, and the overall average was 99%.

Discussion

The token economy (point system), which was designed to deal with a variety of social, self-care, and academic behaviors in the home-style treatment program for pre-delinquent boys, proved to be practicable, economical, and effective. The points seemed almost as convenient to administer as verbal consequences. In the series of experiments presented, the house-parents removed or presented points by requesting the youth's point card and recording the consequence. Subsequent to these studies, the youths themselves have performed the recording tasks equally well. The house-parents have simply instructed the boys to "take off" or "give yourself" points. Cheating has not appeared to be a problem, possibly because of the extremely heavy fine if caught. The privileges for which the points were traded cost nothing, since they were all naturally available in the home as they would be in almost any middle-class home. Since the privileges could be purchased only for a week at a time, they were available over and over again as reinforcers, thus providing an almost unending supply.

The programs involving the point system successfully modified aggressive verbal behavior, bathroom tidiness, punctuality, homework preparation, and poor grammar. The research goals remain of expanding the program to include more boys and more behaviors as well as developing means of transferring the newly established repertories to the natural contingencies of reinforcement. If these goals can be achieved, token reinforcement procedures should become a basic feature of home-style treatment programs for delinquents.

References

Ayllon, T., and Azrin, N. H. 1965. The measurement and reinforcement of behavior of psychotics. *Journal of the Experimental Analysis of Behavior* 2: 357–83.

Berelson, B., and Steiner, G. A. 1964. *Human behavior: an inventory of scientific findings*. New York: Harcourt, Brace & World, Inc.

Birnbrauer, J. S., Wolf, M. M., Kidder, J. D., and Tague, C. E. 1965. Classroom behavior of retarded pupils with token reinforcement. *Journal of Experimental Child Psychology* 2: 219–35.

Bloch, H. A., and Flynn, F. T. 1956. *Delinquency: the juvenile offender in America today*. New York: Random House.

Burchard, J. D. 1967. Systematic socialization: a programmed environment for the habilitation of antisocial retardates. *The Psychological Record* 17: 641–76.

Burchard, J. D., and Tyler, V. O. 1965. The modification of delinquent behavior through operant conditioning. *Behavior Research and Therapy* 2: 245–50.

Clark, M., Lachowicz, J., and Wolf, M. M. 1968. A pilot basic education program for school dropouts incorporating a token reinforcement system. *Behavior Research and Therapy* 6: 183–88.

Cohen, A. K., and Short, J. F. 1961. Juvenile delinquency. In *Contemporay social problems*, R. E. Melton and R. A. Nisbet, eds., pp. 77–126. New York: Harcourt, Brace & World.

Cohen, H. L., Filipczak, J. A., and Bis, J. S. 1965. Case project: contingencies application for special education. Progress Report, U.S. Department of Health, Education, and Welfare.

Glueck, S., and Glueck, E. 1950. *Unraveling juvenile delinquency*. Cambridge, Mass.: Harvard University Press.

McCord, W., McCord, J., and Zola, I. K. 1959. *Origins of crimes: a new evaluation of the Cambridge-Sommerville youth study*. New York: Columbia University Press.

Powers, E., and Witmer, H. 1951. *An experiment in prevention of delinquency: the Cambridge-Sommerville youth study*. New York: Columbia University Press.

Schwitzgebel, R. L. 1964. *Street corner research: an experimental approach to juvenile delinquency*. Cambridge, Mass.: Harvard University Press.

Slack, C. W. 1960. Experimenter-subject psychology: a new method of introducing intensive office treatment for unreachable cases. *Mental Hygiene* 44: 238–56.

Staats, A. W., and Butterfield, W. H. 1965. Treatment of non-reading in a culturally deprived juvenile delinquent: an application of reinforcement principles. *Child Development* 36: 925–42.

Thorne, G. L., Tharp, R. G., and Wetzel, R. J. 1967. Behavior modification techniques: new tools for probation officers. *Federal Probation,* June 1967.

Wetzel, R. 1966. Use of behavioral techniques in a case of compulsive stealing. *Journal of Consulting Psychology* 30: 367–74.

Wolf, M. M., Giles, D. J., and Hall, R. B. 1968. Experiments with token reinforcement in a remedial classroom. *Behavior Research and Therapy* 6: 51–64.

III / USING THE CONCEPTUAL TOOLS: IN-SCHOOL SETTINGS

The next eleven articles are empirical studies conducted in schools. They include examples from preschool to college-university settings. They are not specific how-to procedures ready for duplication in the classroom, but they can serve as models for adaptation with slightly different problems, settings, and contingencies.

Nonetheless, these are examples right out of the classroom. As such, they are close to home and are as amenable to adaptation as any in the literature of educational research.

13 / A Study of Undergraduate Performance in an Incentive Course in Educational Psychology

CARL E. PITTS AND MARY ANN POWERS

The idea for this study began when a graduate psychology student entered the principal author's home, flopped down on the couch, and in response to a How's-it-going question said, "If they're supposed to know so much about human learning, why don't they do something with their graduate classes!" (An expression of appreciation is in order to Miss Pam Tracy for forcing the principal author to reconsider his own classroom practices.)

Introduction

This study was an attempt to introduce more tangible variables into an undergraduate class to increase learning and positive effect for a course by the use of a set of incentives and the reduction of a fear of failure. The purpose was to create a learning environment with some components of the ideal; students learn and they like it. The model is derived from learning theory, particularly Skinnerian operant conditioning, where the major educational emphasis has been upon providing reinforcing consequences for appropriate behavior, neutral consequences for inappropriate behavior.

Source: This is the first publication of "A Study of Undergraduate Performance in an Incentive Course in Educational Psychology," written especially for this volume.

Background

The principal investigator, who has had some disquiet with his prior teaching, used for several semesters a technique to remove some of the aversive qualities of the grading system. Students were informed at the beginning of a semester that the only two grades to be given were an A or a B. For performance below a B on any test, the student would be branched to a remedial program prepared ahead of time and available at the library. The program consisted of a "talk-through" tape made by the instructor in which the test was discussed in detail and guidance was given along with supplementary material for preparing for an alternate test to be taken within the week.

At midsemester another method was introduced because of the apparent success of the after-test tape. This time a discussion tape of about forty-five minutes was made available *before* the test where, using assigned material as the springboard, emphasis was given to those areas considered important by citing names, concepts, major ideas, and so on, along with occasional elaboration of material beyond that provided by the text. Again, for those who did not meet criterion performance on the test (those below B), there was available a taped discussion of the test and an alternate test to be taken within the week.

Although the study was not designed with the care one would normally take in a research study, an informal finding was that the number not meeting criterion performance on each of the three tests dropped steadily. On the first test, 37 of the 55 students failed to make a B (34 correct out of 40 questions); 23 received deferred grades on the second test, and 12 on the last test. By semester's end all students had earned a B grade and there were no incompletes.

Those findings were encouraging, but it was felt that there was more that could be added to the classroom climate to enhance learning. In the classic paradigm for operant conditioning, the subject is usually deprived and the reinforcer is contingent upon desired behavior. But, partly because deprivation can hardly be used when students are paying $150.00 for the three-hour course, it was decided that the environment needed positive rather than negatively reinforcing consequences. In addition, there could be added a set of incentives related to the subject material, which the student could, by choice, work to achieve, contingent upon predetermined criterion performance.

The students for this study came from an educational psychology class. There were 69 students, of which 7 were male, 62 female, ranging from sophomore to senior level. At the first class students were informed of the necessity to reach B-level performance and the procedures by which this would be achieved. The method was as described above; talk-through tapes before each test, remedial tapes, and make-up tests for those not meeting criterion (24 out of 30 correct responses), and everyone was eventually to meet criterion. In addition, the class was told there was to be a set of experimental field extensions to material considered in the classroom. Anyone in the class was eligible to sign up for one, several, all, or none of the incentives. They were informed that signing up or not signing up had nothing to do with the grade. The incentives were for those who wished to go, who demonstrated an average of 27 out of 30 correct responses on tests related to the incentive for which they had signed up, and who could afford the time. Expenses for the incentives such as travel, lodging, meals, and entertainment were to come out of a $500 fund available to the class.

After discussing a variety of incentives, it was mutually decided upon by class and instructor that the incentive would be (a) a conducted tour through the local mental hospital personally directed by a staff psychologist; (b) an afternoon psychodrama experience led by the director of psychodrama from the state hospital; (c) a tour through the research and school section of Central Institute for the Deaf, St. Louis, Missouri; (d) a trip to Anna State Hospital, Anna, Illinois, to see work in behavioral modification with institutionalized mental patients; (e) an overnight trip to Kansas City and the University of Kansas, Lawrence, Kansas, to learn about the use of operant conditioning in a variety of settings sponsored by the University.[1]

The five incentives were spread throughout the 15-week semester, affording several test periods prior to each incentive for the student to "earn" the opportunity to go.

It is clear that the incentives carried more than just an opportunity to go more deeply into an area. Several included travel outside the city, there was an opportunity to get to know one's classmates better, and there was even a cocktail party on one of the incentive trips, arranged by the local staff members. A multidimensional reinforcer was considered important in order to attract a wider variety of students than those who would do well regardless of the incentives described above.

Hypothesis

The hypothesis for this study was that in a regular academic course where there is an incentive system, those who choose to work toward achievement of incentives will do better on tests, will use ancillary aids more frequently, and will rate more highly than those who do not so

[1] The success of this program is due in no small part to the following persons, who were primarily responsible for off-campus arrangements and hospitality: Dr. Marguerite Craft, State Hospital #1; Dr. Lois Elliot, Research Psychologist, CID; Dr. Nate Azrin and Dr. Harry Rubin, Anna State Hospital; Dr. Donald Bushell, Jr., and Miss Joan Jacobson, University of Kansas.

choose. Operationally, the independent variable consisted of the student's choice of whether or not to work for an incentive. The dependent variables were test performance and the use of auxiliary aids designed to ensure as nearly as possible that the student would succeed in meeting criteria.

Design

The experimental period covered one semester consisting of 15 weeks. Since the course was taught once a week in a three-hour block, there were 15 class sessions. Incentives were spaced as shown in Figure 1, usually with two or three weeks between the choice to work for the incentive and the "consummatory response." With the exception of a few class periods, a 30-point objective test was administered each meeting. Tests were graded and returned that same period to provide rapid feedback.

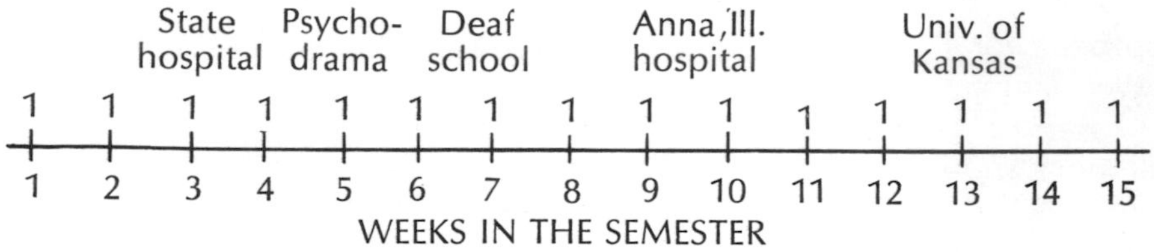

```
        State    Psycho-  Deaf          Anna,'III.         Univ. of
        hospital drama    school        hospital            Kansas

  1   1    1    1    1    1    1    1    1    1    1    1    1    1    1
  +----+----+----+----+----+----+----+----+----+----+----+----+----+----+
  1    2    3    4    5    6    7    8    9   10   11   12   13   14   15
                     WEEKS IN THE SEMESTER
```

Figure 1. The experimental semester by weeks and incentive conditions.

Incentives were scheduled for Friday afternoons except for the Anna, Illinois, trip (early Friday morning to late evening) and the Kansas trip (Friday evening to Saturday evening).

The measures taken were first and primarily test performance, but there were other unobtrusive measures about which the students had no knowledge.

1. Prior to each test a half-hour period was set aside for members of the class to ask questions about the material on which they were to be tested. The class was arranged into three groups before the instructor's entrance; those who signed up for the incentive, those who would like to go on the incentive but who for some reason or another were unable, and those who were not interested. From the back of the classroom an observer gathered data consisting of the number of questions asked by each group. The placement of the groups was unknown to the instructor.

2. A record was kept of the students who made office or coffee shop appointments with the instructor to discuss course material.

3. The library kept a record of all students who used the pre-test talk-through tapes.

Findings

The main hypothesis, the relationships of test performance and choosing or not choosing an incentive, was upheld. That is, there was a statistically significant difference in the expected direction when performance scores under incentive conditions were compared to performance scores under nonincentive conditions ($t = 2.2$ with 97 df yielding a significance level of $<.025$).

This finding could be misleading, however. The "bright" students might have been the ones who signed up for the incentives. To test for this possibility, performance scores of those students who were under two incentive and two nonincentive conditions during the semester were compared (n = 30 out of 69). This allowed each student to serve as his own control. Using the Sandler A (an equivalent but simplified form of the t test for correlated samples) there was found to be a $<.05$ level of significance (A = .305, 29 df). The predicted differences in incentive and nonincentive scores did not seem to be a function of chance.

A further check on the problem of identifying the incentive as the main variable was made by correlating the students' cumulative grade-point averages and the number of incentives for which they signed up (N = 60; there were 9 for whom accurate grade-point averages were not available). A low correlation would further substantiate the fact that it was not just the academically successful who signed up. The correlation coefficient was .113. To reach the .05 level of significance with 60 df, the coefficient should have been .2108.

The incentives had other effects. As the number of incentive periods increased for a student, his score on the final comprehensive test tended to increase ($r = .322$; significant at $<.01$ level). Furthermore, those who signed up for incentives used auxiliary aids more often than those in the nonincentive group even though the aids were equally accessible to both. In comparing the use of talk-through tapes, the difference in use between the two groups was significant using the two variables X^2 test ($X^2 = 6.25$ with 1 df $<.01$ level). See Table 1. Use of these tapes, also, was related to final performance. The correlation between number of times a student used the tape and final test performance was .304 (significant at $<.01$ level).

Table 1   Frequency of Tape Use by Incentive and Nonincentive Conditions

	Used tape	Did not use tape	Row totals
Incentive	132	57	189
Nonincentive	138	99	237
Column totals	270	156	426

When students signed up for an incentive, they made significantly more appointments with the instructor to talk over various aspects of the course (22 versus 6, giving $<.005$ on the X^2 one-variable test). During the half-hour question-answer period prior to each test, those who had signed up for the incentive asked 116 questions; those who were interested in the incentive yet could not go asked 74; and those who were uninterested asked 54. Analysis of these data indicated that the observed distribution does not fit the theoretical distribution. The X^2 one-variable statistic yielded a significance level of $<.0005$ ($X^2 = 24.63$ with 2 df) between the interested and noninterested groups.

A week after the course was completed, students were sent a questionnaire. They were requested not to sign their responses. Among other things, students were asked to evaluate the course on a five-point scale. "How does this course compare to other courses taken in college?" Of the 50 respondents the distribution was a J-shaped curve with preponderant weight on the positive side. See Figure 2.

The questionnaire also asked students to state the number of incentives on which they had gone. The purpose in getting these data was to determine if there was a functional relationship between greater investment in the course, as measured by the number of incentives for which a student signed up, and the student's attitude toward the course, as measured by the scalar evaluation. The correlation between these two variables was .456, significant at $<.005$ level, 47 df.

In sum, it was found that:

1. Choosing an incentive significantly increases test performance.
2. The student's grade-point average was not related to signing up for incentives.
3. Signing up for incentives was significantly and positively related to the final, comprehensive test.
4. Signing up for incentives was significantly and positively related to use of ancillary aids, that is, talk-through tapes and appointments with instructor.
5. Interest in the incentive was significantly and positively related to questions asked in class.
6. The more students took part in incentives, the higher they rated the course in comparison to their other courses.

Discussion

The analysis of the direct and indirect measures taken during the experimental semester tends to support the hypotheses posed at the beginning of the study. Under the conditions described here, incentives appear to be viable tools to increase performance and develop a more positive

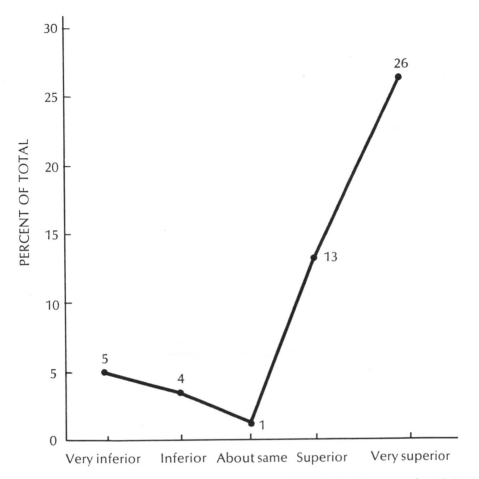

Figure 2. Response to post-course questionnaire (N = 49, 23 of which had not been on an incentive). Students were asked to evaluate the course in terms of their other college courses.

attitude toward required teacher-education courses, which have a long history of inadequacy in most educational programs.

This is not to suggest that The Answer has now been found and is ready to be exported to the world of academia. The human organism is, as any researcher well knows, an infinitely complex being, not about to be understood by a few principles. Nevertheless, the findings here are provocative in several ways. Teaching can be better understood from the point of view of deliberate strategies rather than from that of artistry, and the world of education might profit greatly by turning some of its attention to entrepreneurship, wherein lies virtually untapped a vast knowledge about the use of incentives to stimulate behavior.

Summary

An undergraduate class in educational psychology was used for an investigation to determine how incentives affect performance and attitudes toward a course. Three hypotheses were projected; when students sign up for incentives, they (a) perform better academically, (b) make more use of ancillary aids, and (c) rate the course more highly than those who do not sign up. All three hypotheses were supported at statistically significant levels. The implications of an incentive program for educational settings were considered.

14 / Establishing Use of Descriptive Adjectives in the Spontaneous Speech of Disadvantaged Preschool Children

BETTY M. HART AND TODD R. RISLEY

Poor children characteristically have a paucity of descriptive adjectives in their verbal repertoire. Recognizing this problem and that the usual teaching procedures had little effect, Betty M. Hart and Todd R. Risley set out to increase the use of adjectives by making preschool materials contingent upon the use of adjectives. That is, no longer could a child get a toy by pointing and saying, "Uh"; he was trained to ask for it with descriptive adjectives.

This study demonstrates a standard research paradigm: initial baseline measures, environmental contingencies for some items, no contingencies for others (to determine if the contingencies account for the change), and periodic measurement of change as a function of the manipulated contingencies.

From observer records, a count was made for each child, in a group of disadvantaged children in an experimental preschool, of usage and acquisition of descriptive adjectives, with and without noun referents.

Source: Betty M. Hart and Todd R. Risley, "Establishing Use of Descriptive Adjectives in the Spontaneous Speech of Disadvantaged Preschool Children," *Journal of Applied Behavior Analysis* 1 (Summer 1968): 109–20. Copyright © 1968 by the Society for the Experimental Analysis of Behavior, Inc. Reprinted by permission of the authors and the *Journal of Applied Behavior Analysis*.

Procedures were sought which would effectively modify the low rates of adjective-noun combinations in the everyday language of all the children. Time in school, intermittent teacher praise, and social and intellectual stimulation were not effective in changing the low rates of using adjectives of size and shape. Group teaching effectively increased rates of using color- and number-noun combinations in the group-teaching situation, but was ineffective in changing rates of usage in the children's "spontaneous" vocabularies. By operating directly on the children's language in the free-play situation, making access to preschool materials contingent upon use of a color-noun combination, significant increases in such usage were effected in the spontaneous vocabularies of all the children. Preschool materials apparently functioned as powerful reinforcers. Though traditional teaching procedures were effective in generating adjective-noun combinations in that restricted situation, it was only through application of environmental contingencies that color names as descriptive adjectives were effectively and durably established in all the children's spontaneous vocabularies.[1]

Reflected in the national concern for the scholastic retardation of culturally deprived children is the contemporary conviction that the sources of academic failure are primarily environmental rather than genetic (Bijou, 1963). That the environment of the culturally deprived child can, and should, be changed, is not an issue; rather the questions are ones of defining and producing those environmental changes which will generate academic success. The present consensus is that the behavior most correlated with public school success is verbal behavior, skill in language (Weikart, 1966). As opposed to the linguistically skillful and academically successful middle-class child, the culturally deprived child is characterized as having a language environment which is both "restricted" in terms of range and detail of concept (Hess and Shipman, 1965), and rich in forms of expressive speech which are not used in middle-class-oriented school books and systems (Riessman, 1962). Thus, programs for the development of language skills, the core of all preschool programs for culturally deprived children, seek to give the children educationally appropriate forms of speech, and to enrich their descriptive vocabularies. In such programs the children are directly taught, for instance,

[1] This study is based upon a thesis submitted by the senior author to the Department of Human Development in partial fulfillment of the requirements for the Master of Arts degree. The authors express appreciation to Nancy Reynolds, Dianetta Coates, and Maxine Preuitt for their able assistance in all aspects of the study. This research was supported by Grants (HD 03144) from the National Institute of Child Health and Human Development and (CG-8474) from the office of Economic Opportunity, Headstart Research and Demonstration to the Bureau of Child Research and the Department of Human Development at the University of Kansas. Reprints may be obtained from Todd Risley, Juniper Gardens Children's Project, 2021 North Third St., Kansas City, Kansas 66101.

the appropriate use of adjectives of color, number, size, shape, etc., and the preschool environment is arranged so that they will use them in conversation and narration. That is, "knowing"—the ability to respond correctly when asked—is not considered sufficient; the criterion for "skill" is usage, spontaneous emission as functional language in everyday situations.

There is general agreement concerning what should be taught to culturally deprived children but considerably less agreement about how to teach it most effectively. Many methodologies have been employed, with varying degrees of success (Weikart, 1966). The urgency of the problem, and the need for practical solutions has led, however, for the first time in the long history of preschool education, to empirical evaluation of the effectiveness of traditional teaching procedures. Such evaluation has frequently resulted in pervasive restructuring of the preschool environment in order to achieve the behavioral goals set for the culturally deprived child (Bereiter and Engelmann, 1966). Most important, it has resulted in introducing into the time-honored preschool program those procedures which experimental research has demonstrated to be effective in teaching children.

Research has repeatedly demonstrated that a child's behavior can be modified by its consequences. Such demonstrations have been made in a multiplicity of settings: in the laboratory (Lindsley, 1966), in institutions (Wolf, Risley, and Mees, 1964; Lovaas, Freitag, Kinder, Rubenstein, Schaeffer, and Simmons, 1966), in preschools (Harris, Wolf, and Baer, 1964; Brown and Elliot, 1965), in the classroom (Zimmerman and Zimmerman, 1962), in the clinic (Wahler, Winkel, Peterson, and Morrison, 1965), and in the home (Allen and Harris, 1966). The behaviors so modified have included verbal (Risley and Wolf, 1967), motor (Johnston, Kelley, Harris, and Wolf, 1966), social (Allen, Hart, Buell, Harris, and Wolf, 1964), and academic behaviors (Wolf, Giles, and Hall, 1968; Birnbrauer, Wolf, Kidder, and Tague, 1965). The general principles of reinforcement, which were the basis of all of the above-mentioned studies, were also the basis of the present study. That is, the present investigation involved: defining an observable terminal behavior, the use of descriptive adjectives during free play; devising a method of recording and measuring important categories of spontaneous verbal behavior; and manipulating the consequences of the children's use of language, the presentation of social reinforcement and access to materials contingent on a specified form of verbal behavior. The effectiveness of these procedures is evaluated in terms of the behavioral goals defined, and compared to the effectiveness of traditional preschool procedures in the attainment of these goals. The implications of the study thus relate not only to the problem of cultural deprivation, but to preschool practice in general.

Method

SETTING AND SUBJECTS

The study was conducted at the Turner House preschool of the Juniper Gardens Children's Project in Kansas City, Kansas, and involved 15 children, all Negroes, from a lower-class community, selected from large families with extremely low incomes. There were eight boys and seven girls in the group, all aged from four to five years. The average IQ, as measured by the Peabody Picture Vocabulary Test, was 79.

The preschool sessions were three hours long, from 8:30 to 11:30 A.M., five days per week. The daily program was: breakfast, then free play indoors, then group time, then free play outdoors, followed by story time at the end of the morning. During indoor and outdoor free play the children could interact with materials and with other children in one or more of the unstructured activities normally provided in the preschool program, e.g., blocks, painting, sand play, etc. Most, but not all, materials were available to the children during free play; items such as water and paint were dispensed by teachers.

Breakfast, story time, and group time were teacher-structured situations. At group time, eight or fewer children sat on a rug with a teacher who formally presented stimuli for identification and description. Children were called on individually by the teacher, and were presented with a food snack and teacher praise for correct responses. The classes of responses reinforced at group time were first, identification of pictures and objects, then description of objects in terms of color, and finally description of objects in terms of number. Stimuli for a given class of responses, such as identification, were presented daily at varying levels of difficulty for several months, until all children in the group had attained a certain criterion of response accuracy.

PROCEDURES

Recording. At group time throughout the year an observer recorded on a check sheet whether each response of each child in the group was designated by teacher feedback to the child as "right" or "wrong."

During four periods within the school year, daily samples were taken of children's verbalizations during free play. A sample was recorded by one of four observers, who moved with the child being observed from one activity to another, and for 15 minutes wrote down in longhand "everything" the child said. Two observers recorded throughout the school year; the third was replaced by the fourth observer for two months in mid-year (February and March).

Each child in the group was assigned for observation approximately every other day during the periods of sampling; roughly two observations were made indoors for every one made outdoors because of the sequence of the preschool program. Observation was discontinued whenever free play ended; therefore samples were occasionally of less than 15 minutes when, for example, outdoor play was curtailed by rain, or a child was removed from the group for a test. Usually a given child was assigned for observation to each of the observers in turn. This was done to minimize the development of any observer bias concerning a given child, and to distribute the writing load of high-rate verbalizers versus low-rate.

The sampling periods were:

1. 7 days (August 31–September 9; days 3 through 9 of school).
2. 18 days (October 3–October 26; days 25 through 42 of school).
3. 10 days (December 12–December 23; days 71 through 80 of school).
4. 99 days (January 17–June 9; days 91 through 189 of school).

From the samples were extracted for each child lists of vocabulary entries in the classes of nouns, verbs, and adjectives. Only certain categories of adjectives were counted: size, color, number, and shape, i.e., the descriptive categories usually directly taught in preschool programs. Within each of the categories of descriptive adjectives (color, number, size, and shape) separate counts were made for:

1. All adjectives of that category. Every use of an adjective in each of the four categories was counted regardless of the context in which it appeared, i.e., whether or not it was followed by a noun, or was used with a verb. The categories of descriptive adjectives thus counted were defined as:

All color adjectives: e.g., "red," "red one," "red paint."
All number adjectives: e.g., "one," "two blocks," "three billion" (counted as a single number), "one-two-three" (counted as three numbers).
All size adjectives: e.g., "big," "little one," "He is big," "long time."
All shape adjectives: e.g., "round," "square one," "round circle."

2. All adjective-noun combinations of that category. Every use of an adjective in each of the four categories was counted only if it was followed by a noun. The categories of descriptive adjectives so counted were defined as:

All color-noun combinations, as "red paint."
All number-noun combinations, as "two blocks."
All size-noun combinations, as "long time."
All shape adjectives: e.g., "round," "square one," "round circle."

3. All new adjective-noun combinations of that category. Every use of an adjective in each of the four categories was counted for a given child only if it was followed by a noun and that combination of adjective and noun had never been recorded in any previous sample on that child. The categories of descriptive adjectives so counted were defined as:

New color-noun combinations.
New number-noun combinations.
New size-noun combinations.
New shape-noun combinations.

Thus, for example, if an observer recorded a child's having said, "I want red paint," and the adjective-noun combination *red paint* had never appeared in any prior sample on that child, it would be listed as a new color-noun combination (in addition to being counted as another use in all color adjectives and in all color-noun combinations).

Periodic reliability checks were taken among the three observers (the third and fourth observers were considered, over the year, as a single observer). Periodically, two or more observers were assigned to observe the same child at the same time, each observer recording independently all that child's verbalizations during a given 15-minute period. In addition, a volunteer observer made once-weekly reliability checks, in the same manner, with one or more of the regular observers; this volunteer had almost no contact with either the teachers, the other observers, or any changes in preschool conditions. From the two or more records obtained, all instances of adjective usage in any of the four categories of color, number, size, and shape, were totaled. The record of Observer 1 was always taken as standard, whenever she and any other observer recorded on the same child. When Observers 2 and 3 took reliability checks together the record of that observer who had taken the majority of samples on the given child was taken as standard. Product-moment correlations of the reliability of the total adjective usage over samples was calculated for the regular observers in relation to one another, and for the volunteer observer in relation to the three regular observers.

Baseline. From the beginning of the school year, teachers attended to children when they heard them use descriptive adjectives during free play. The appropriate use of such adjectives was thus followed intermittently by teacher approval, and incorrect use was followed intermittently by teacher correction. If the adjective used was part of a request for a material, the child almost always obtained the object requested; no differential attention was given for use of adjective-noun combinations. The observer samples of the children's verbalizations during free play, however, revealed continuously low rates of use of all descriptive adjectives, whether of color, number, size, or shape. Teachers hypothesized that the limited use of these adjectives might be due to limited repertoires of appropriate labels. Therefore it was decided to systematically teach adjectival labels, starting with colors.

Baseline: color naming at group time. Beginning on day 103 of school, colors were presented every day at group time. The number of colors presented simultaneously was gradually increased from the initial three up to nine, but the manner of presentation remained essentially the same. In presenting each color, the teacher first named each object of that color (i.e., "The car is red"), and placed it with others of the same color. Then she indicated, or had a child indicate, one object in a group and name it and its color (i.e., "The car is red"). Every time a child correctly identified both an object and its color, the teacher praised him and passed him a snack. A complete sentence was always required; if a child named the correct color without naming the object, the teacher praised him and told him he was right, and then asked for the complete sentence before passing him a snack.

Thus, in the group-time situation, teachers prescribed the terminal form of the behavior which they hoped to see in the free-play situation, that is, color-noun combination. Only by requiring that the referent for an adjective be named can a teacher be (fairly) certain that a child has made an appropriate discrimination. Subsequently, a teacher can judge the extent to which a child is forming a concept of a given property (such as "redness") only on the basis of that child's verbal behavior of attributing that property ("red") to a variety of objects ("apple," "car," etc.). When a child merely names the property ("red") or names the property with an indefinite word such as "one" ("the red one"), the teacher must make an assumption concerning the referent, and thus guess both that the child is making a discrimination and that he is forming a concept.

At group time, while presenting colors in the general manner described above, the teacher employed various levels of prompts in order to ensure each child's giving a correct response each time he was called on to name an object and its color. The level of prompt was adjusted to each child's need for such prompts, and every time a new color was introduced, the teacher dropped back, for the whole group, to the more obvious levels of prompts. In the most obvious prompt, the teacher gave the child the correct response immediately before the question, i.e., "The car is red. What color is the car?" In less obvious prompts, the teacher asked a child to name a color and then if he hesitated, mouthed the color word, or gave its initial sound; often, she asked a child to name the color of an object which another child had named correctly immediately before.

Throughout the period of naming colors at group time, any color naming during free play was attended to by teachers, whether the child specified a referent for the color named or not. The teacher praised the child who named a color and told him he was right if this were the case, or corrected him and then praised his repetition of the appropriate color name.

After two months (50 school days) of naming colors daily at group time, seven of the 15 children were reliably naming nine colors in that situation (red, yellow, blue, green, purple, orange, brown, white, and black). The other eight children were being presented only six colors at group time (red, yellow, blue, green, purple, and orange).

During this time, the children's rate of using color adjectives in the free-play situation showed no general change; however, teachers did note on two occasions late in this period sudden and marked increases in color naming by several children in the free-play situation. Both of these occasions involved a teacher dispensing vari-colored pegboard materials to children who, in order to obtain a specific item, had to ask for it by color. This procedure, of a teacher withholding materials until they were requested by a color-noun combination, appeared effective, at least on these occasions, in generating use of such combinations by children in the free situation.

Materials contingent on color naming. It was decided to apply this procedure throughout the preschool situation, and have teachers withhold materials until children asked for them by a color-noun combination. Therefore, beginning on day 153 of school, all of the children in the group could obtain a snack outdoors and certain materials and equipment indoors and out only if they named the desired object and described it by its color. Outdoor items such as trikes, wagons, balls, and shovels were not placed outside the storage shed as usual; rather, a child wanting to use them had to ask a teacher for them and employ an appropriate color-noun combination. A child desiring a snack from the basket held by the teacher had to ask, not for a snack or a cookie, but for a "brown" cookie (if the cookies were of that color), or a "yellow" banana. Indoors, items such as dress-up clothes in the doll house, pegboard materials, parquetry blocks, toy animals, and cars, etc., all had to be named by a color-noun combination before a child was allowed to use them. These materials were not removed from the children's reach; rather, when a child approached one of these materials, a teacher put her hand on the material the child was reaching for. During the first three days of the procedure, the teacher prompted the desired behavior, asking the child, "What do you want?" and then, if the child named the object without naming its color, the teacher asked, "What color of a . . . ?" and supplied the color name if the child either did not respond or responded incorrectly. After the third day teachers no longer prompted; if a child asked for an object without naming its color, or reached for certain objects, the teacher simply put her hand on the object and looked expectantly at the child until he named the object and its color.

Certain materials such as paint and water, which had never been freely available to children, were dispensed only when asked for by color-noun combination, the teacher being "too busy" to attend to requests stated in any other form. The water which children regularly used to "cook" in the doll house was colored with food coloring, so that children had to specify the color or colors of water they wanted to use.

This procedure was continued for 19 days. Throughout, teachers praised every use of color adjectives. Whenever a child asked for a material by naming its color, the teacher verbalized her approval simultaneously with either dispensing the material to him or removing her hand so that he could take the object he had asked for. Spontaneous use of color adjectives on occasions unrelated to the contingency (i.e., occasions other than those when the child "wanted something") were also praised; praise for such usage was given whether or not the child named a noun referent for the color.

Five days after introducing the requirement for naming colors in free play, the naming of colors at group times was discontinued for those seven children reliably discriminating all nine colors, and naming objects by number (counting) was substituted. A second group of eight children continued to have colors presented at group time; children moved from this group into the number-naming group as soon as they had demonstrated mastery of all nine colors. At the end of the school year 10 children were naming objects by number at group time and four children were naming objects by color at group time. One child was sick for the last month of school.

Materials not contingent on color naming. When stable changes were noted in all of the children's spontaneous vocabularies of color adjectives, the contingency of naming colors to obtain materials in the free-play situation was removed. This was done in order to evaluate whether the use of color-noun combinations during free play was maintained solely by the contingencies presented by teachers. Thus, from the 172nd to the 189th and final day of school, all requirements for color naming during free play were discontinued; children were given snacks and materials whenever they asked for them either with a noun alone or with an adjective-noun combination. None of the materials ordinarily made available in the free-play situation were withheld by teachers. The consequences of color naming were essentially those which existed during the first baseline period. That is, correct color naming in the free situation was followed intermittently by teacher approval and usually by obtaining an object (if the color name was part of a request for a material). Incorrect naming of a color was followed intermittently by correction from a teacher, and often by obtaining an object (whatever object the teacher assumed the child to be requesting).

Results

RECORDING

Reliability checks taken periodically over the year by having two observers simultaneously record the behavior of a given child yielded the following product-moment correlation coefficients between observers for the total number of descriptive adjectives of color, number, size, and shape used by all the children in the group:

Observer 1—Observer 2   0.96
Observer 1—Observer 3   0.99
Observer 2—Observer 3   0.86.

The correlation between the volunteer observer and all of the three regular observers was 0.89.

Since most of the children were rotated for observation among the three observers, the correspondence of observations taken by the different observers during each of the four conditions provides another assessment or reliability. Figure 1 (top) shows the correspondence of observations taken by the three observers on all children in the group during each experimental condition. In each of the conditions the total number of color adjectives used per sample hour, and the total number of color-noun combinations used per sample hour for all children, as recorded by each observer, is shown. The bottom of Figure 1 shows the correspondence of observations of a single child taken by the three observers on different days during each experimental condition. This child, whose individual data are plotted in Figure 3, is the median child in the group (number 8 in Table 1) in terms of overall rate of using color adjectives across all conditions; he is representative of the group also in terms of correspondence between observers in each condition.

BASELINE

Figure 2 shows the average rate of use of descriptive adjectives of color, number, and size per sample hour by all the children during each of the four experimental conditions of the study. In each case, the white bar (all adjectives) includes the black bar (adjective-noun combinations). Use of adjectives of shape was not graphed, since the total was only 19 instances over the whole year for the whole group.

During the first baseline (102 school days), the average use of all color adjectives was 0.5 per sample hour, with a range from 0 to 2.3 per sample hour. Table 1 presents the exact rates per sample hour for each child in the group. The average rate of all color-noun combina-

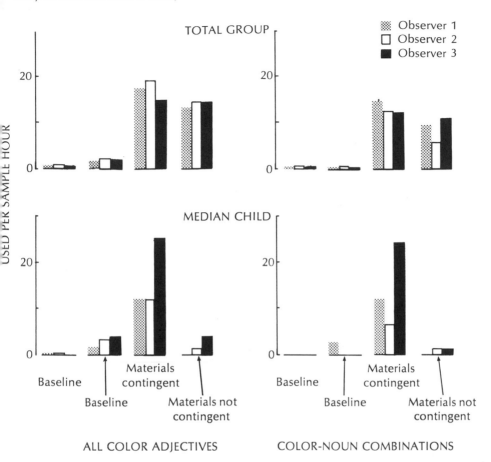

Figure 1. Correspondence of observations by the three observers across conditions for the total group and for the representative median child. Top shows the correspondence of observations taken by each of the three observers on all the children in the group during each experimental condition. Bottom shows the correspondence of observations of a single child taken by the three observers on different days during each experimental condition.

tions was 0.2 per sample hour, the highest rate being one color-noun combination used per sample hour by one child, the lowest rate zero per sample hour by 10 children. The average rate of new color-noun combinations (those not previously recorded for the given child) was 0.1 per sample hour (range 0, to 0.7 per sample hour). Average use of all number adjectives was 3.4 per sample hour (range 0 to 8.8) with average use of all number-noun combinations at 0.5 per sample hour (range 0 to 1.4). All size adjectives were used at an average rate of two per sample hour (range 0.9 to 7.5): all size-noun combinations were used at an average rate of 1.5 per sample hour (range 0 to 7.1). Thus,

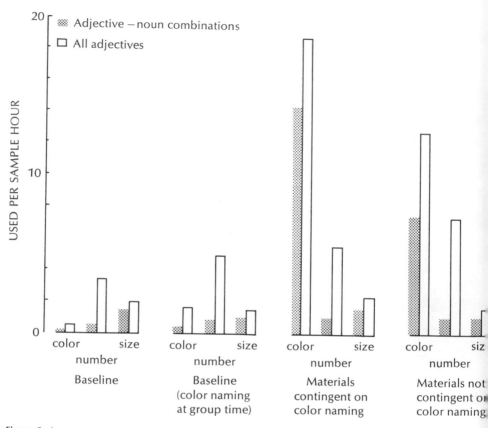

Figure 2. Average use per sample hour of descriptive adjectives of color, number, and size for a group of 1 children. The first baseline was from the first to the 102nd day of school. The second baseline (color namin at group time) was from school days 103 through 152. The condition of access to materials contingent o color-naming was from school days 153 through 171. From school days 172 through 189 materials were n longer contingent on color naming. All samples were of approximately 15 minutes.

the rates of using descriptive adjectives as a class were low, and rates of naming colors were considerably lower than rates of naming number and size attributes. For a third of the children, use of a color adjective had never been recorded during five months of school. No trend toward increased use of descriptive adjectives was observed for any of the children.

Figure 3 shows use of color adjectives by the child (child 8, Table 1) with the median overall rate across all experimental conditions. For this child only two instances of usage of a color adjective had been recorded during the first baseline period, and there were no instances of color adjectives used with a noun.

BASELINE: COLOR NAMING AT GROUP TIME

During the 50-school-day period of naming colors at group time, the group average for use of all color adjectives increased to 1.8 per sample hour. The range was from 0 (for two children) to 4.2 color adjectives used per sample hour. The average rate of using all color-noun combinations rose from 0.2 to 0.4 per sample hour; the range was from a low of zero comparable to the first baseline condition to a high of 1.2 as compared to the high of 1.0 per sample hour during the first baseline condition. New color-noun combinations were used at an average rate of 0.3 per sample hour (range 0 to 0.9). The average rate of using all number adjectives rose from 3.4 to 4.9 per sample hour (range 0.5 to 14.7), and all number-noun combinations were used at an average rate of 0.9 per sample hour (range 0 to 3.2). These average increases in use

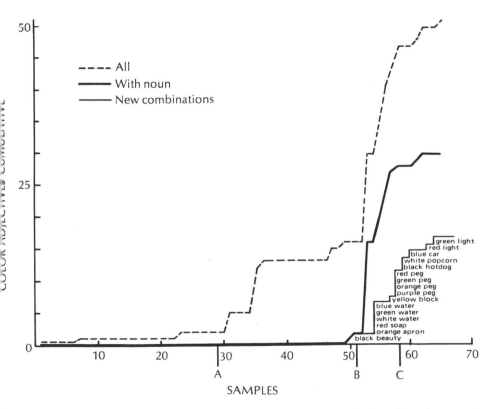

Figure 3. Cumulative use of color adjectives by the child with the median rate. The dotted line shows use of all color adjectives; the solid line shows use of all color-noun combinations. New color-noun combinations are printed in above the samples in which they were first recorded. Samples 1-6 were taken during days 3-9 of school. Samples 7-21 were taken during days 25-42 of school. Samples 22-26 were taken during days 71-80 of school. Samples 27-65 were taken during days 91-189 of school. All samples were of approximately 15 minutes. Baseline is samples 1-29. At A the naming of colors at group time was begun. At B access to materials was contingent on use of color-noun combinations. At C materials were not contingent on color naming.

of number adjectives, in which no training was given, were as great as the increases in use of color adjectives; the rate of using color adjectives during this period was most comparable to the average rate of using size adjectives (1.5 per sample hour, range 0 to 5.6) in which, like number adjectives, no training had been given. Thus, it is not demonstrated that the increased use of color adjectives during this condition was affected by the group time procedures.

Figure 3 shows an increased rate of spontaneous usage of color adjectives in the free-play situation by the child with the median rate. The increase however, was entirely in color adjectives used without a succeeding noun, a form which did not correspond to the behavioral goal (color-noun combinations) set by the teachers. This child was among the seven children who had demonstrated mastery of nine colors by the end of the second baseline condition. Table 1, however, shows that increased color naming was not restricted to those children (marked by asterisks) who had mastered naming all nine colors at group time. It can be seen that the greatest increase in color naming was by a child (7) who was not yet correctly naming nine colors at group time. There seemed to be little continuity between "knowing" colors, as demonstrated at group time, and "using" them in the free situation.

MATERIALS CONTINGENT ON COLOR NAMING

During the 19 days when access to snacks and materials was contingent upon use of a color noun combination, there was a marked increase in such usage. As can be seen in Figure 2, the average use of all color adjectives rose to 18.6 per sample hour (ranging from 2.1 to 56.7). The average rate of using all color-noun combinations was 14.2 per sample hour (range 2.1 to 30.5). In contrast, the use of number and size adjectives during this period showed little change from the preceding periods; average use of number adjectives was 5.5 per sample hour while size adjectives were used on an average of 2.1 per sample hour.

During the second baseline condition, only 22% of color adjectives were followed by noun referents. When obtaining an object required naming the object and its color, 75% of the color adjectives used were followed by a noun. The marked rise in new color-noun combinations (to an average of 5.1 per sample hour) can be seen in Figure 4; more than a third of the objects named by color during the condition of making materials contingent on color-naming constituted new color-noun combinations.

Table 1 shows the changes in rate for individual children during this experimental condition. Though the magnitudes of the increases vary, the increase in use of color adjectives can be seen to be general across the group. The new color-noun combinations, as they appear

Table 1 Use of Color Adjectives per Sample Hour

Child	Baseline All Color	All Color-Noun	New Color-Noun	Baseline (Color Naming at Group Time) All Color	All Color-Noun	New Color-Noun	Materials Contingent on Color Naming All Color	All Color-Noun	New Color-Noun	Materials Not Contingent on Color Naming All Color	All Color-Noun	New Color-Noun
* 1.	1.1	1.0	0.7	2.0	0.0	0.0	46.7	30.0	1.0	5.0	5.0	1.1
* 2.	1.3	0.0	0.0	2.2	0.4	0.4	8.2	5.4	2.9	54.5	33.1	6.8
3.	0.4	0.1	0.1	1.3	0.2	0.2	23.3	17.4	8.9	25.6	7.8	1.1
* 4.	0.0	0.0	0.0	3.0	0.3	0.3	33.5	30.5	13.0	13.0	12.0	1.0
5.	1.3	0.7	0.4	3.1	1.2	0.6	25.7	24.5	1.0	0.7	0.0	0.0
6.	0.2	0.0	0.0	0.8	0.2	0.2	31.2	15.9	7.7	15.0	15.0	4.5
7.	0.5	0.0	0.0	4.2	0.9	0.9	7.5	2.2	2.2	3.1	3.1	2.1
* 8.	0.3	0.0	0.0	3.1	0.4	0.2	18.2	15.3	7.7	2.2	1.1	1.1
* 9.	0.2	0.0	0.0	3.3	0.6	0.6	15.9	13.6	3.6	2.2	1.7	1.7
10.	0.1	0.1	0.1	0.0	0.0	0.0	29.2	25.0	12.3	11.8	3.2	1.4
*11.	0.0	0.0	0.0	0.6	0.0	0.0	8.9	8.4	3.2	21.6	16.3	4.5
*12.	0.0	0.0	0.0	0.5	0.5	0.5	11.1	11.1	4.8	10.8	3.8	2.3
13.	0.0	0.0	0.0	1.3	0.6	0.6	2.1	2.1	2.1	3.8	0.8	0.8
14.	0.0	0.0	0.0	0.0	0.0	0.0	2.5	2.5	2.5	8.7	1.3	0.7
*15.	2.3	0.5	0.4	1.1	0.3	0.3	14.5	9.3	3.1	Not in school		
Average	0.5	0.2	0.1	1.8	0.4	0.3	18.6	14.2	5.1	12.7	7.4	1.9
Range: High	2.3	1.0	0.7	4.2	1.2	0.9	46.7	30.5	13.0	54.5	33.1	6.8
Low	0.0	0.0	0.0	0.0	0.0	0.0	2.1	2.1	1.0	0.7	0.0	0.0

in Figure 3 for the representative median child, indicate usage of a variety of color names, applied to a variety of objects, in most cases appropriately. The onset of this behavior among the children during this experimental condition permitted an empirical assessment of the extent of their knowledge of the different colors.

MATERIALS NOT CONTINGENT ON COLOR NAMING

During the 18 days after the contingencies for color naming were removed, the overall rate of using all color adjectives decreased to an average of 12.7 per sample hour. The rate of using all color-noun combinations decreased to an average of 7.4 per sample hour; that is, 58% of colors named were followed by the name of an object referred to. Though both of these rates show declines from the condition of making materials contingent on color naming, they are well above the rates during either the first or second baseline conditions, indicating that once the behavior was generated in the free-play situation it tended to be maintained, at least in some children. Table 1 shows that there was more inter-subject variation when materials were no longer contingent on color naming, than in any prior condition. The higest rates of color naming, 54.5 per sample hour for all color adjectives used and 33.1 per sample hour for all color-noun combinations used, were higher than during the condition of making materials contingent on color naming; the lowest rate, zero per sample hour for all color-noun combinations, was at the level of the first baseline.

The overall rate of new color-noun combinations was 1.9 per sample hour (see Figure 4), with the highest rate 6.8 per sample hour for one child and the lowest rate zero for one child. That is, even after the contingency was removed, one quarter of all the color-noun combinations employed were new combinations.

Figure 2 shows that even with an overall decrease the rates of using color adjectives were markedly higher than the rates of using adjectives of size and number. Average use of size adjectives continued at approximately the same rate as during the first baseline condition: 1.6 per sample hour. All number adjectives were used at an average rate of 7.3 per sample hour.

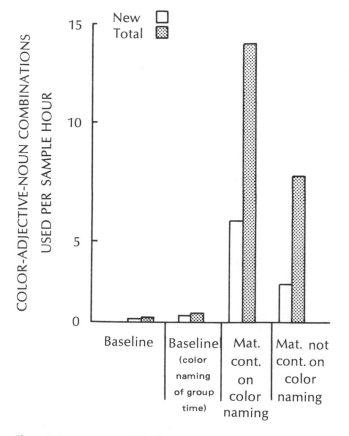

Figure 4. Average new and all color-noun combinations used per sample hour for a group of 15 children. The conditions were: Baseline (color naming at group time), materials contingent on color naming, and materials no longer contingent on color naming.

Discussion

This study demonstrated that traditional preschool methods were ineffective in modifying the children's spontaneous speech. These methods assume, as it was assumed by teachers in this study, that what is "known" will be "used," given the appropriate stimulus conditions. Thus, in the usual preschool during and after teaching a skill in a group situation, teachers arrange stimuli in the free situation—a variety of sizes, colors, and shapes of materials, for instance, and social attention and approval—so as to foster usage in that situation of the skill trained in the group situation. The present study gives evidence that, despite this usual arrangement, such usage in the free situation seldom occurred. An examination of the group and free-play stimulus situations, however, indicates that they may have been so dissimilar as to make transfer between them difficult and hence unlikely.

The verbal behavior reinforced in the group situation was of the form: noun-verb-adjective ("the car is red"). This form, in which the adjective stands alone as predicate adjective rather than as a modifier, is the form called for by the stimulus question, "What color is this (car)?" There is no simple stimulus question in English which necessarily calls for a response form in which an adjective, such as a color name, modifies a noun: the question "What is this?" calls for a noun response ("a car") rather than, necessarily, for a modified noun ("a red car"). In group teaching, prompting the response form of a modified noun concurrently with prompting color responses, while feasible, is rarely done in traditional preschool practice.

For descriptive speech to be "spontaneous," however, the stimulus situation controlling the behavior cannot be a direct question concerning an object. Rather, the stimulus situation must involve an object plus the necessity (not provoked by a question) of singling out that object from one or more other objects. This is the function of descriptive language. Most children come into contact with this function casually, over time, both inside and outside of preschools, and often even before they "know" the precise meaning of the descriptive language used. Since the children in the present study were termed "culturally deprived," an appellation indicating that their environment was in some way deficient in the stimulus conditions conducive to the development and maintenance of complex language skills, it seemed contradictory to teach them a skill such as color naming and then rely on unsystematic environmental events to make that skill functional. Rather, the environment was deliberately structured so that the children would come into contact with the function of descriptive adjectives: the stimulus situation which hopefully would control some rate of the behavior outside of school was created on a massive scale inside of school when access to materials was made contingent on naming them by color.

That the behavior continued in some strength after the contingencies were removed seems to indicate that once color description was generated, there were enough "natural" contingencies in the preschool situation to maintain it. Even after removal of the contingency, children did obtain an object when they asked for it by color; though teachers discriminated the removal of the contingency, not all of the children may have done so. By the end of the contingency period teachers were rarely withholding materials in the obvious manner of the beginning of that period; rather, most of the children were spontaneously naming the color of the object whenever they requested an object from a teacher. This verbal topography was the one most regularly and promptly reinforced. Even after removal of the contingency for color naming this was probably often the case.

There are two implications of this study for preschool practice. The first is that of creating for children a functional environment where the contingencies for pre-academic behavior approximate those applied to such behavior in the "beyond-preschool" environment. The teachers in this study felt, in fact, that the whole process of teaching colors could have been more efficiently and painlessly done by making access to materials contingent on color naming even before the children knew the names of any colors. Prompting and reinforcing in the free situation was little different than that done at group time, except that children did not have to wait for their "turn," and teachers were able to make use of reinforcers such as materials in the free-play situation. The generalization from free-situation naming to test-situation naming seemed more easily made, perhaps because the spontaneous response form is appropriate to both stimulus situations.

The second implication is that preschool materials may function as reinforcers for many children, and for some children may be even more powerful than the social reinforcement and/or food presented in the preschool situation. Some of the children in the present study appeared to teachers to have "really learned" colors only when required to name them in connection with objects they wanted to use; these were the children whose behavior in the group time situation was not well controlled by the praise and food presented there (for neither of which they were deprived, at least in the preschool environment). As reinforcers, materials are not only inherent in the preschool, but are uniquely appropriate to the development of descriptive vocabulary since they are the same class of reinforcers which maintain the behavior in everyday situations.

References

Allen, K. Eileen, and Harris, Florence R. 1966. Elimination of a child's excessive scratching by training the mother in reinforcement procedures. *Behaviour Research and Therapy* 4: 79-84.

Allen, K. Eileen, Hart, Betty M., Buell, Joan S., Harris, Florence R., and Wolf, M. M. 1964. Effects of social reinforcement on isolate behavior of a nursery school child. *Child Development* 35: 511-18.

Bereiter, C., and Engelmann, S. 1966. *Teaching disadvantaged children in the preschool.* Englewood Cliffs, N.J.: Prentice-Hall.

Bijou, S. W. 1963. Theory and research in mental (developmental) retardation. *Psychological Record* 13: 95-110.

Birnbrauer, J. S., Wolf, M. M., Kidder, J. D., and Tague, Cecilia E. 1965. Classroom behavior of retarded pupils with token reinforcement. *Journal of Experimental Child Psychology* 2: 219-35.

Brown, P., and Elliott, R. 1965. Control of aggression in a nursery school class. *Journal of Experimental Child Psychology* 2: 103-07.

Harris, Florence R., Wolf, M. M., and Baer, D. M. 1964. Effects of adult social reinforcement on child behavior. *Young Children* 20: 8-17.

Hess, R. D., and Shipman, Virginia C. 1965. Early experience and the socialization of cognitive modes in children. *Child Development* 36: 869-86.

Johnston, Margaret K., Kelley, C. Susan; Harris, Florence R., and Wolf, M. M. 1966. An application of reinforcement principles to development of motor skills in a young child. *Child Development* 37: 379-87.

Lindsley, O. R. 1966. Experimental analysis of cooperation and competition. In *The experimental analysis of behavior,* T. Verhave, ed. New York: Appleton-Century-Crofts. Pp. 470-501.

Lovaas, O. I., Freitag, G., Kinder, M. I., Rubenstein, B. D., Schaeffer, B., and Simmons, J. Q. 1966. Establishment of social reinforcers in two schizophrenic children on the basis of food. *Journal of Experimental Child Psychology* 4: 109-25.

Riessman, F. 1962. *The culturally deprived child.* New York: Harper & Row.

Risley, T. and Wolf, M. M. Establishing functional speech in echolalic children. *Behaviour Research and Therapy* 5: 73-88.

Wahler, R. G., Winkel, G. H., Peterson, R. F., and Morrison, D. C. 1965. Mothers as behavior therapists for their own children. *Behaviour Research and Therapy* 3: 113-24.

Weikart, D. P. 1966. Results of preschool intervention programs. Paper presented at the symposium on the Education of Culturally Disadvantaged Children, University of Kansas.

Wolf, M. M., Giles, D. K., and Hall, R. V. 1968. Experiments with token reinforcement in a remedial classroom. *Behaviour Research and Therapy* 6: 51-64.

Wolf, M. M., Risley, T. R., and Mees, H. L. 1964. Application of operant conditioning procedures to the behavior problems of an autistic child. *Behaviour Research and Therapy* 1: 305-12.

Zimmerman, Elaine H., and Zimmerman, J. 1962. The alteration of behavior in a special classroom situation. *Journal of the Experimental Analysis of Behavior* 5: 59-60.

15 / Production and Elimination of Disruptive Classroom Behavior by Systematically Varying Teacher's Behavior

DON R. THOMAS, WESLEY C. BECKER, AND
MARIANNE ARMSTRONG

This study gets to the heart of what many teachers have described as their main problem in the classroom—techniques for handling disruptive behavior. The findings are striking because they indicate that as the teacher's disapproval increases, so does disruptive behavior. And as praise for appropriate behavior increases, so does appropriate behavior. The implications are that the old classroom maxim for the beginning teacher—"Don't smile until after Thanksgiving"—may be just what a teacher ought not do.

The effects of teacher behaviors on the classroom behaviors of children were investigated by systematically varying approving (praise, smiles, contacts, etc.) and disapproving (verbal reprimands, physical restraint, etc.) classes of teacher behavior. Measures were taken on both teacher and child behaviors. Each day a sample of 10 children was observed.

Source: Don R. Thomas, Wesley C. Becker, and Marianne Armstrong, "Production and Elimination of Disruptive Classroom Behavior by Systematically Varying Teacher's Behavior," *Journal of Applied Behavior Analysis* 1 (Spring 1968): 35–45. Copyright © 1968 by the Society for the Experimental Analysis of Behavior, Inc. Reprinted by permission of the authors and the *Journal of Applied Behavior Analysis.*

The subject pool was a class of 28 well-behaved children in a middle-primary public school class. The results demonstrated that approving teacher responses served a positive reinforcing function in maintaining appropriate classroom behaviors. Disruptive behaviors increased each time approving teacher behavior was withdrawn. When the teacher's disapproving behaviors were tripled, increases appeared most markedly in the gross motor and noise-making categories of disruptive behavior. The findings emphasize again the important role of the teacher in producing, maintaining, and eliminating disruptive as well as pro-social classroom behavior. [1]

Teachers are sometimes unaware of the effects of their actions on the behavior of their students. Many teachers assume that if a child performs disruptive acts in the classroom then the child must have a problem at home, or at the very least, must not have reached a stage of sufficient maturity to function adequately in the school situation. However, an increasing body of evidence indicates that many of the behaviors which teachers find disruptive are actually within their control. A teacher can modify and control the behavior of her students by controlling her own responses.

Contingent use of social reinforcement has been shown to control such motor behaviors as walking, standing, and running (Bijou and Baer, 1963), talking and crying (Kerr, Meyerson, and Michael, 1965; Hart, Allen, Buell, Harris, and Wolf, 1964), and classroom conduct (Becker, Madsen, Arnold, and Thomas, 1967; Zimmerman and Zimmerman, 1962).

Becker et al. (1967) worked in public schools with teachers who had problem children in their classes. Behaviors exhibited by the students were observed and the frequency of these behaviors was estimated for each child. Each teacher was taught to use praise, smiles, etc., to reinforce good behavior. The rate of appropriate classroom behaviors increased in most cases as soon as teacher approval and recognition were made contingent on such behavior.

The present study evolved from prior research showing the importance of social reinforcement, and Becker's work, which suggests that specific procedures, or definable classes of teacher behaviors can be used by the teacher to increase appropriate classroom behaviors. In order to provide more convincing data on the role of different teacher

[1] The authors wish to thank Urbana School District #116 and the principal of Thomas Paine School, Mr. Richard Sturgeon, for their cooperation. The observers (Loretta Nielson, Barbara Goldberg, Marilyn Goldberg, and Darlene Zientarski) deserve thanks for their conscientious work. This research was supported, in part, by National Institute of Child Health and Human Development Grant HD-00881-05. Reprints may be obtained from Wesley C. Becker, Bureau of Educational Research, University of Illinois, Urbana, Illinois 61801.

behaviors, the present study was designed to produce and remove problem behavior in students by systematically varying teacher behaviors in an initially well-behaved class.

Method

SUBJECTS

Students. A class of 28 elementary students at the middle-primary level was selected. According to the teacher her class was "a good class, with an above-average distribution of ability and no 'bad' kids." Most of the children were from upper-middle- and middle-income-range families. Ages at the beginning of the study ranged from 6 years, 11 months to 7 years, 11 months; I.Q. range (group test) was from 99 to 134.

Teacher. The teacher, age 23, obtained her student teaching experience with a class of "maladjusted" children. In addition, she had one year's experience with a class of "slow learners." Preliminary observations indicated that she rarely attended in an approving manner to children who behaved inappropriately, and rarely reprimanded children who were performing their assigned tasks. She volunteered to participate in the study because of its potential contribution to teacher training in the future.

OBSERVATION PROCEDURES

The basic data for the study consisted of the relative frequency of occurrence of classes of child behaviors in relation to classes of teacher behaviors utilizing rating schedules to be described. One to three observers were placed in the classroom each morning from approximately 9:15 to 10:00 a.m. while the students were completing reading and reading workbook assignments. To insure obtaining a daily sample of both child and teacher behaviors during this 45-min work period, a 20-min observation time was decided on for both child and teacher observations. Thus, even if only one observer was present, the relevant information could be obtained. This time restriction limited the number of children who could be observed each day. Ten children were selected for observation each morning by drawing numbers from a hat. During Baseline$_1$ and the first No-Praise condition a no-replacement procedure was used so that all children had to be observed before a child's number could be drawn a second time. At the start of Baseline$_2$ this restriction was removed. Through the use of a numbered seating chart, the observers recorded the behaviors of selected children in the order in which they were chosen. Five extra numbers were drawn each day to provide observation targets in case one or more of the first 10 subjects drawn were not available for observation. Target children were observed for 2 minutes each. Each minute was divided into six 10-second intervals. Observers were trained to record classes of behavior which occurred in a given interval. Recordings were made during the first five intervals of each minute. During the sixth 10-second interval the observers made notes, checked for synchronization, and/or prepared to switch to a new child. Thus, the daily child observation sample consisted of ten 10-second observation intervals on each of 10 children.

Teacher behaviors were recorded on a similar schedule, the only difference being that for teacher behaviors each occurrence of a response in a specified class was recorded (frequency measure), whereas for child behaviors a given class of behavior could be rated only once in a 10-second interval. This difference in procedure was necessitated by the greater difficulty in separating child behaviors into discrete reponse units. Observers used a clipboard, stopwatch, and a recording sheet which had spaces for 100 observation intervals, guides for computing reliability, and a place for comments.

Undergraduate university students were hired and trained to collect the data. Each observer memorized the definitions of classes of child and teacher behaviors. Pre-baseline training in recording of behavior was carried out in the experimental classroom to allow the children to become accustomed to the presence of the observers. The children were already well adapted to the classroom before observer training was started. Observers were instructed to avoid all interactions with the students and teacher while in the class or on the school grounds. At the scheduled time they would enter the class, walk directly to chairs provided for them, sit down, and begin the observations. A hand signal was used to insure synchronization of observation times. Initially two observers were scheduled to observe on Monday, Wednesday, and Friday, and two on Tuesday and Thursday. When a systematic difference developed between the two sets of observers, one of the Tuesday-Thursday observers was placed on a three-day-a-week schedule to tie the two sets of observations together with reliability checks. Thus, on some days there were as many as three observers in the classroom. The number of observers in the classroom varied from one to three. Due to illness or the need to obtain observations in other classrooms, there were times when only one observer was available. Observers were not informed of changes in experimental conditions.

CLASSES OF TEACHER BEHAVIORS: THE INDEPENDENT VARIABLE

The behaviors emitted by the teacher were defined as belonging to three general classes: (1) Disapproving Behavior, (2) Approving Behavior, and (3) Instructional Behavior. Disapproving and Approving Behaviors were rated only when they immediately followed discriminable child behaviors falling into inappropriate or appropriate classes (see below).[2] Listings were made of the teacher behaviors that could occur within each class.

The general class of Disapproving Behaviors included Physical Contact, Verbal, and Facial subclasses. The subclasses of Physical behaviors included forcibly holding a child, grabbing, hitting, spanking, shaking, slapping, or pushing a child into position. The Verbal subclass of Disapproving Behaviors included yelling, scolding, raising voice, belittling, or making fun of the child, and threats. Threats included "if-then" statements of loss of privilege or punishment at some future time. For example, the teacher might say to the class, "If you don't remain quiet, you will have to stay in from recess." The Facial subclass of Disapproving Behaviors included frowning, grimacing, side-to-side head shaking, gesturing, etc.

The general class of Approving Behaviors also included Physical Contact, Verbal, and Facial subclasses. Approving Physical Contacts included embracing, kissing, patting, holding hand or arm of child, or holding the child in the teacher's lap. Approving Verbal comments included statements of affection, approval, or praise. Approving Facial response was rated whenever the teacher smiled, winked, or nodded at one or more of the children.

The general class of Instructional Behavior included any response from teacher to children which involved giving instructions, information, or indicating correct responses.

In addition to recording the above classes of teacher behavior, note was taken of those times when the teacher terminated social interaction by turning out lights and saying nothing, turning her back on the class and waiting for silence, or stopping talking and waiting for quiet.

As noted earlier, the observers recorded every teacher response falling in a given class. Thus, the measures of teacher behaviors are frequency counts.

CHILD BEHAVIORS: THE DEPENDENT VARIABLE

The classes of child behaviors were developed by categorization of behaviors occurring with some frequency in the repertoire of problem children (Becker et al., 1967). It was assumed that certain behaviors, because of their common topography, could be grouped together. Five classes of Disruptive Behavior (Gross Motor, Noise Making, Orienting, Verbalizations, and Aggression) and one class of Appropriate Behavior

---

[2] As it turned out, approval following inappropriate behavior occurred only three times and disapproval following appropriate behavior did not occur. Also, this teacher did not make non-response-contingent approval or disapproval comments. Thus, we were dealing essentially with two response-contingent classes of teacher behavior.

(Relevant) were defined. Behaviors not specifically defined were rated in a separate category (Other Task). Disruptive Behaviors were essentially behaviors apparently incompatible with good classroom learning conditions.

Included in the category of behaviors labeled as Gross Motor activities were: getting out of seat, standing up, walking around, running, hopping, skipping, jumping, rocking chair, moving chair, sitting with chair in aisle, kneeling in chair, arm flailing, and rocking body without moving chair.

The category of Noise Making was rated with the stipulation that the observers must hear the noise as well as see the noise-making action, and included tapping feet, clapping, rattling papers, tearing papers, throwing books or other objects onto desks, slamming desk top, tapping objects on desk, kicking desk or chair, and scooting desk or chair.

The Verbalization category was rated only when the observer could hear the response. Lip movements alone were not rated. Carrying on conversations with other children, calling out teacher's name to get her attention, crying, screaming, singing, whistling, laughing, and coughing were included in the category.

The Orienting class of behaviors required that the child be seated. Turning of head or head and body toward another person, showing objects to another child, and looking at another child were rated. Looking behaviors of less than 4-second duration were not rated except for any turn of more than 90 degrees from the desk. When an Orienting response overlapped two rating intervals, and could not be rated in the first interval because it began too late in the interval to meet the 4-second criterion, it was rated in the second interval.

Aggression was defined as hitting, pushing, shoving, pinching, slapping, striking with objects, poking with objects, grabbing objects or work belonging to another, knocking neighbor's property off desk, destroying another's property, throwing objects. No judgments of intent were made.

Appropriate behaviors were labeled Relevant and were made more easily identifiable by restricting the observations to a period in the morning when all of the children were preparing reading and workbook assignments. Specific Relevant Behaviors were: looking at the teacher when she was speaking to the entire class or to the child being observed, answering questions of the teacher, raising hand and waiting for teacher to respond, writing answers to workbook questions, looking at pages of text in which reading was assigned. It was required that the entire 10-second interval be filled with on-task behavior before the Relevant rating was made.

When a child being observed performed a response not defined by one of the categories of Disruptive Behaviors or by Relevant Behavior, a rating of Other Task was made. The Other Task rating was incompatible with Relevent, but could be recorded in the same interval as any or all of the categories of Disruptive Behavior.

When rating the children, the observers were instructed to record each class of behaviors which appeared in an interval regardless of how many other classes had already been recorded in that interval. All five categories of Disruptive Behaviors and the Other Task category were compatible with each other. Relevant Behavior was incompatible with the other categories. No category of behavior was rated more than once in an interval. If a child was conversing with his neighbor, and he made two verbal responses in one interval, this class of behaviors was recorded only once. Thus, each child-behavior measure was a record of intervals in which the response occurred, rather than a count of the number of discrete responses as in the recording of teacher's behavior.

The overall level of Disruptive Behaviors was defined as the percentage of intervals in which one or more Disruptive Behaviors occurred.

RELIABILITY

Two types of reliability were calculated. Reliability I reflects simply the degree to which two observers obtained the same score for each category of behavior during a 20-minute observation period. The smaller score is divided by the larger. Reliability I most appropriately applies to the data as reported in Figure 1, since these are averages for an observation period. Random errors tend to cancel each other out when a score is based on a series of observations and a reliability measure should reflect the gain in accuracy obtained by averaging. For training purposes, and for greater confidence in the accuracy of the observation procedure, a second type of reliability was also calculated (Reliability II). Reliability II required that the same behavior category be recorded in the same interval by each observer to define an agreement. Reliability II was calculated by dividing the number of agreements by the number of agreements plus disagreements.

During the pre-baseline observer training, reliability checks were required for every observation. Before baseline observations were started, consistent reliabilities (Type II) above 80% were required. Reliability I data based on a weighted average of the reliabilities of the child-behavior codes are reported in Figure 1, as are the average reliabilities by conditions for teacher behaviors. Comparable Reliability II data averaged 82.6% for child behaviors and 83.2% for teacher behaviors. Reliabilities for individual categories are well represented by these averages.

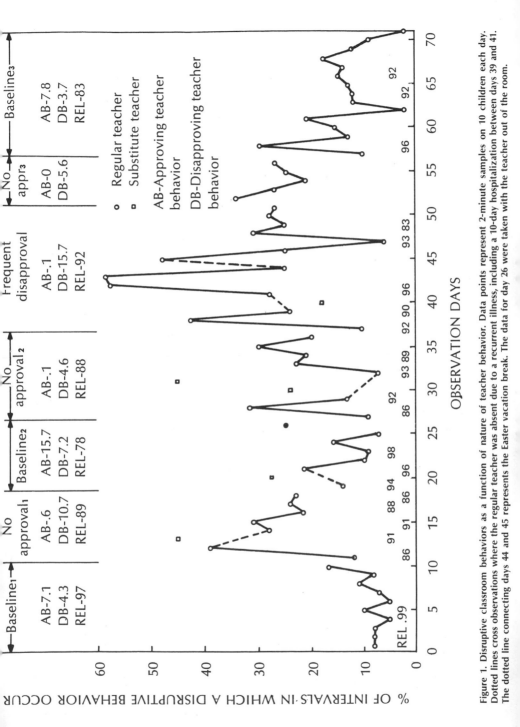

Figure 1. Disruptive classroom behaviors as a function of nature of teacher behavior. Data points represent 2-minute samples on 10 children each day. Dotted lines cross observations where the regular teacher was absent due to a recurrent illness, including a 10-day hospitalization between days 39 and 41. The data for day 26 were taken with the teacher out of the room. The dotted line connecting days 44 and 45 represents the Easter vacation break.

173

The first phase of the study (Baseline$_1$) consisted of measuring both teacher and child behaviors. No attempt was made to manipulate teacher behavior.

The second phase (No Approval$_1$) was defined by the absence of Approval Behaviors. The teacher discontinued the use of praise statements and used only contingent Disapproving Behaviors to control the children.

These phases were then repeated (Baseline$_2$, No Approval$_2$). At the beginning of No Approval$_2$ and throughout the rest of the study, the teacher carried a small "supermarket" adding machine with her to count the frequency of Disapproval Behaviors so that she could better monitor her behavior.

The fifth phase of the study, Frequent Disapproval, involved increasing the level of Disapproving Behaviors to approximately three times that given during Baseline$_1$ while continuing to withhold Approving Behaviors.

Phase 6 returned to the lower level of Disapproval (No Approval$_3$) and Phase 7 again returned to the baseline conditions (Baseline$_3$).

The teacher was instructed to maintain experimental conditions throughout the day, not just during the observation period. During the periods when praise was withheld beginning with No Approval$_2$, checks of the daily counts of Disapproving Responses obtained by the teacher with her counter corresponded closely to those which would have been predicted by extrapolation from the observation periods.

Results

The relationships of greatest interest are the effects of presence and absence of Approval Behaviors on Relevant Behaviors and the effects of levels of Disapproval Behaviors on Disruptive Behaviors. Because of a systematic rater bias which entered into the data for Other Task Behavior (discussed later), and therefore also affected Relevant Behaviors incompatible with Other Task, greater emphasis is given to the analysis of Disruptive Behaviors in presenting the results.

AVERAGE LEVEL OF DISRUPTIVE BEHAVIOR

In Baseline$_1$ Disruptive Behaviors occurred in an average of 8.7% of the intervals observed. When Approving Behaviors were discontinued (No Approval$_1$), Disruptive Behavior increased to an average of 25.5% (Fig. 1).

Approving Behaviors were again provided (Baseline$_2$) and Disruptive Behavior dropped to an average of 12.9%. In order to show more conclusively that the changes in Disruptive Behavior were related to the changes in teacher behavior, Approving Behaviors were again discontinued (No Approval$_2$) and the level of Disruptive Behaviors stabilized near the same level as in No Approval$_1$ condition (average 19.4%). When the Disapproving Behaviors (critical comments) were tripled (Frequent Disapproval), while Approving Behaviors were still withheld, Disruptive Behavior increased to an average of 31.2% with high points far above any observed before. The behavior stabilized, however, near the level at which the two previous No Approval phases had stabilized. When the rate of disapproval was lowered (No Approval$_3$), no great reduction in Disruptive Behavior occurred. The average level of Disruptive Behaviors over No Approval$_2$, Frequent Disapproval, and No Approval$_3$ was 25.9%. At the end of No Approval$_3$, Approval was again added to the low level of Disapproving Behaviors, and Disruptive Behavior dropped to an average of 13.2%, with the trend indicating a level far below this average.[3]

ANALYSIS OF CLASSES OF BEHAVIOR

Discontinuation of approving behaviors. In reviewing the changes in the individual categories of behavior through the first two withdrawals of Approving Behavior, the majority of the increase in Disruptive Behaviors could be attributed to changes in Verbalization and Orienting categories (Table 1). The mean of Verbalization in No Approval$_1$ was 22.6% due to one extremely high observation on the second day of the condition; however, these behaviors stabilized between 9% and 17% (Figure 2). Orienting showed a slight decrease across No Approval$_1$ (Figure 2). The second time Approval was discontinued, Orienting increased across the condition while Verbalization remained relatively stable except for two high observations. Gross Motor behaviors followed the same pattern as Orienting and Verbalization through No Approval (1 and 2), increasing each time Approving Behavior was discontinued and decreasing when Approving Behaviors were present (Figure 2).

Noise Making and Aggression followed a pattern through No Approval$_1$ and $_2$ which was distinctly different from the other categories

---

[3] A conservative statistical analysis was performed (*F* test) to compare those three conditions where approval responses were available with those two conditions where approval responses were withdrawn. For this test the Frequent Disapproval and No Approval^{2+3} conditions were collapsed into one condition. In order to insure independence of observations, the average values within each condition were used, thus providing four degrees of freedom. Significant differences were found for Relevant Behavior ($p < 0.01$), Noise Making ($p < 0.05$), Gross Motor ($p < 0.025$), and for the overall level of Disruptive Behavior ($p < 0.01$).

of disruptive behavior. Both of these categories of behavior were already occurring at a low frequency in the Baseline condition (Table 1), but they occurred even less often when only Disapproving Behavior was given.

Increase of disapproving behaviors. In the Frequent Disapproval condition, Noise Making, Gross Motor, and Orienting all increased (Table 1). Verbalizations showed a decline over this condition and continued to decline through the rest of the study.

Table 1   Average Percentages for Specific Behavior Classes for Each Experimental Phase

Behavior classes	Baseline$_1$	No Approval$_1$	Baseline$_2$	No Approval$_2$	Frequent Disapproval	No Approval$_3$	Baseline$_3$
Disruptive Behaviors[a]	8.7	25.5	12.9	19.4	31.2	26.8	13.2
Gross motor	2.7	6.7	2.0	4.8	12.3	10.4	2.4
Noise	0.9	0.1	0.7	0.09	4.1	4.4	0.9
Verbalization	4.6	22.6	7.7	9.6	7.9	6.0	3.9
Orienting	1.4	6.5	4.1	7.1	11.5	10.2	7.6
Aggression	0.25	0.01	0.2	0.01	0.04	0.04	0.1
Other task	7.0	10.4	5.9	10.7	5.9	4.2	1.2
Relevant	84.1	65.3	83.9	72.1	64.3	69.4	85.6

[a] The addition of percentages for the five classes of Disruptive Behaviors will usually lead to a sum higher than that reported as percentage of Disruptive Behaviors, since the latter does not reflect the occurrence of more than one subclass of Disruptive Behaviors in a given 10-second interval.

Changing from a high level of Disapproving Behaviors to a lower level did not markedly change the frequency of the various categories of Disruptive Behaviors relative to their terminal level under the Frequent Disapproval condition.

When Approving Behaviors were again used by the teacher (Baseline$_3$), the frequency of Gross Motor, Noise Making, and Orienting behaviors decreased noticeably (Figure 2). Verbalization continued to show the steady decrease in frequency which had started in the Frequent Disapproval condition. In Baseline$_3$ Aggression again occurred, but rarely. All Disruptive Behaviors except Orienting dropped to the level of the initial Baseline (or below) during the final Baseline.

Relevant behavior. Appropriate behaviors were initially high in the classroom (Figure 2). Behaviors such as getting out of seat to move to a reading group or to check a completed workbook assignment were rated in the Gross Motor category. The requirements for such behaviors, however, remained constant through all conditions so changes in the level of Relevant Behaviors cannot be attributed to changes in classroom requirements. Relevant Behavior decreased each time Approving Behavior was discontinued and increased each time the Approval was reinstated. Relevant Behavior was at a slightly higher level during the final Baseline than during the initial Baseline.

Other task: Behavior not specifically defined. As indicated earlier,

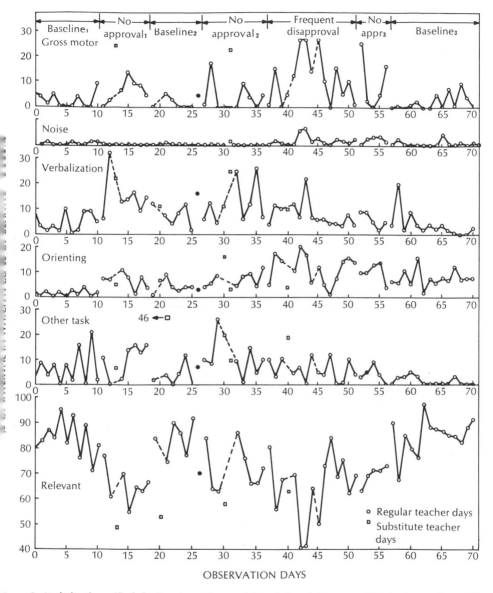

Figure 2. Analysis of specific behavior classes by condition. Data points represent 2-minute samples on 10 children each day. See notes under Figure 1.

a systematic rater difference was encountered early in the study in rating Other Task behaviors. In Figure 2 this bias can be seen by contrasting data collected on Days 2, 4, 6, 8, and 10 from one set of observers with the collected on Days 1, 3, 5, 7, and 9 by another set of observers. While an attempt was made to correct this bias by interlocking reliability checks, it is apparent that the bias continued to some extent throughout the study. Since Other Task is by definition incompatible with Relevant Behavior, Relevant Behavior shows the same bias. By looking at Disruptive Behavior, defined so as to exclude Other Task behaviors, the systematic bias was largely eliminated from the data presented in Figure 1.

TEACHER BEHAVIORS

The behavior of the teacher remained under good control throughout the study. Averages by conditions for Approving and Disapproving Behaviors are given in the upper part of Figure 1. As the conditions were changed, little difficulty was found in withholding behaviors in the Approving category. Some difficulty was reported by the teacher in regulating the frequency of Disapproving Behaviors while withholding Approving Behaviors, but a partial solution to this problem was found. The teacher found that by carrying a small hand-counter (mentioned earlier) she could more accurately judge the frequency of her critical comments. In the Frequent Disapproval Phase there were days when the children were not emitting enough Disruptive Behaviors for critical comments to be appropriate at the programmed frequency. Rather than make inappropriate comments, the rate of Disapproving comments was adjusted to the frequency of the Disruptive Behaviors. When enough Disruptive Behaviors were available, Disapproving Behaviors were dispensed at a maximum rate of one per minute throughout the day; thus, many of the responses of the children were reprimanded very quickly.

General frequency of instructional comments did not change appreciably across conditions. However, the teacher did increase the frequency with which she would say in a neutral tone whether responses were correct or incorrect in the phases where Approval was not given.

The behaviors characterized as Terminating Social Interaction occurred only twice during the study and were, therefore, not subject to further analysis.

Substitute teachers. Observations taken on the days when a substitute teacher was in charge of the classroom appear in four conditions of the study. The frequency of Disruptive Behaviors increased in the presence of a temporary teacher as long as the regular teacher was in either Baseline or No Approving Behavior phases. When the Disapproving Behavior was being dispensed at a high rate, however, the level of Disruptive Behaviors decreased in the presence of a temporary teacher (Figure 1).

Day 26. The data for this day were taken while the teacher was out of the room. Since the experimental conditions were not operative, this point should have been omitted altogether.

Discussion

The results indicate that some aspects of the behaviors included in the category of Approving Behaviors were reinforcing for task-appropriate behaviors. The frequency of Relevant Behaviors was high whenever approving Behaviors followed Relevant child Behavior, and decreased whenever Approving Behaviors were discontinued.

In each change of conditions that involved discontinuation of Approving Behaviors, there appeared a reliable transition effect (observation Days 11 and 27). This effect may be an example of the typical increase in rate found when a positive reinforcer is removed. In support of this explanation, the teacher reported, "When I stop praising the children, and make only negative comments, they behave very nicely for three or four hours. However, by the middle of the afternoon the whole classroom is chaotic." Since observations were taken during a study period in the morning, the periods of good behavior show up in the data each time a condition was changed. A similar low deviant behavior point occurred at the transition to Frequent Disapproving Behaviors (Day 37), but it is not clearly explained. "The children seemed stunned."

Reviewing the individual classes of Disruptive Behaviors brings out certain similarities and differences among the classes. During the first alternations of Baseline with discontinuation of Approving Behaviors, Gross Motor, Orienting, and Verbalization Behaviors increased with discontinuation of Approval, while Noise Making and Aggressive Behaviors remained at their already low frequency. The increases are interpreted as suggesting that some responses in the disruptive classes may be reinforced by peer attention or other environmental circumstances when control through approving teacher responses to incompatible behaviors is withdrawn. For example, Orienting behaviors, such as looking around the room or out the window may be reinforced by seeing other children playing, by observing a custodian cleaning up the schoolyard, or by seeing any of numerous events which have no relationship to the classroom. Observational evidence for this inference was clearest in the Frequent Disapproval phase (below). It is also possible to attribute the increases in Disruptive Behaviors during No Approval$_1$ to the increase in use of Disapproval. However, the data for No Approval$_2$, where Disapproval was held to the Baseline level, would argue that the effect was primarily related to the withdrawal of approval.

Increasing Disapproving Behaviors to a high level produced four days where Disruptive Behaviors were above 40%. Several individual categories of behavior also showed marked changes. The increase in Gross Motor Behaviors was related to an increase in interactions with other students. During the Frequent Disapproval condition, two or three children would make alternate trips to check their workbooks at a table provided for that purpose. Only one child was permitted at the table at a time. During Baseline and No Approval phases, it was rare to see a child make more than one trip to the table; in the Frequent Disapproval phase, some of the children would check their papers several times. Others responded by pushing their papers off of their desks and then getting up to get them. There was a noticeable "pairing off" with two or more children exhibiting the same behaviors.

Another consequence of the Frequent Disapproval phase was a marked increase in the noise level in the room. A majority of the noises during this period were created by children scooting their desks and chairs. One observer reported, "I waited for a few minutes after the regular observation period was over and counted the noises. During one 40-second period, I counted 17 separate chair scraping noises. They came in bursts of two or three at a time. It looked as though the kids were trying to irritate the teacher." The noises in "bursts of two or three" seemed similar to the "pairing off" of children noted with the Gross Motor behaviors, and strengthens an hypothesis that reinforcement from peers is one of the elements which accounts for the increase in Disruptive Behaviors during this time. Peer attention cannot be the only element affecting the behavior of the children, however, because the Verbalization category of behaviors showed a constant decrease throughout the Frequent Disapproval condition. The inhibition of Verbalization could be due to interfering emotional responses being elicited by the high level of critical comments by the teacher. More probable, however, is that the children simply talked more quietly to avoid being caught by the teacher. Observers' reports indicate that a substantial number of verbalizations would have been recorded during the Frequent Disapproving Behaviors condition if there had been no requirement that the responses be heard by the observers. The children could be seen to turn their heads, and lip movements could be seen frequently, but the verbalizations could not be heard.

Work by Lovaas, Freitag, Kinder, Rubenstein, Schaeffer, and Simmons (1964) suggests that for some children any adult attention may be reinforcing. Some of the present findings under the Disapproval conditions could also be interpreted as indicating that teacher behavior of the Disapproving variety was positively reinforcing. The level of Disruptive Behaviors during each of the conditions when only Disapproving and Instructional attentions were available does appear to vary with the level of Disapproving Behaviors dispensed by the teacher. Unfortunately, the illness-caused absences and Easter break make the results less clear than hoped. It should be apparent that the effect of Frequent Disapproval on the behavior of the children is not subject to a simple interpretation. Some criticized behaviors decreased, some increased, and several possible controlling stimuli could have been operating with contradictory effects on behavior. It is obviously difficult in a field-experimental study of this complexity to maintain control of all the possibly relevant variables at once.

Another limitation of the present design should be noted. Because of a shortage of observation time under the desired classroom conditions, a sample of 10 children was observed daily. A procedure which included all children each day would have provided a stronger basis for analysis of effects on individuals. A rough analysis of individuals with the present data confirms, however, that an average of 76% of the students made changes in the same direction as the group changes. From Baseline, to No Approval, 81% of the students showed increases in Disruptive Behavior. When Approving Behavior became available, 75% of the students improved within two weeks. Discontinuing Approving Behavior a second time resulted in 78% of the students being more disruptive, while the final addition of Approving Behavior showed an increase in appropriate behavior for 71% of the children. Across condition changes, 5% of the children showed no change on the average, and 19% showed change (usually minor) in an opposite direction. Procedures which permitted specifications of which children were praised or criticized for which behaviors would be needed to clarify fully individual effects. It is quite possible that the children who changed opposite to the group trend were being responded to differently. Of course, there are many ways one can speculate here. In an as yet unpublished study we have shown that praising some children but not others leads to changes in the behavior only for the children who are praised. Results of this sort emphasize the importance of looking at individual contingencies.

Brief mention should be made of the possible ethical considerations involved in producing Disruptive Behaviors. One needs to weigh the potential gains in knowledge against the short-term or long-term deleterious effects on the children or teacher. On the basis of prior research and the return to Baseline after the first No Approving Behaviors condition, the teacher and the experimenters were confident that appropriate behaviors could be readily reinstated at any time it was felt necessary. It may also be reassuring to know that this accelerated middle primary class did achieve well academically during the year. The children completed all second and third grade work and were all performing on a fourth grade level by the end of the year.

Implications

This further demonstration of the importance of specific teacher behaviors in influencing classroom behavior has a double implication. First, the teacher who uses her Approving Behaviors as immediate consequences for good behavior should find that the frequency and duration of appropriate behaviors increase in her classroom (at least for most children). On the other hand, the teacher who coddles the miscreant, tries pleasantly to get a child to stop behaving disruptively, talks with a child so that he "understands" what he was doing wrong, or who pleasantly suggests an alternative activity to a child who has been performing inappropriately, is likely to find an increase in the very behaviors she had hoped to reduce. This view of the functional importance of teacher's behavior in creating, maintaining, or reducing classroom behavior problems contrasts sharply with that generated by psychodynamic models of problem behaviors and what to do about them. Work of this sort also suggests a need to re-evaluate the popular cliche about the importance of the interaction of the "personality" of the teacher with that of the child in looking at classroom management procedures.

The suggestive evidence that peer reinforcement (among other stimuli) takes over when social reinforcement is not provided by teacher is given support by the recent work of Wahler (1967). Wahler has shown how preschool children can systematically control the behavior of their peers by differential use of social reinforcement. The more general implication for the teacher is this: unless an effort is made to support desirable classroom behaviors with appropriate consequences, the children's behavior will be controlled by others in ways likely to interfere with the teacher's objectives.

Finally, the possibility that critical comments may actually function to increase some behaviors upon which they are contingent cannot be overlooked. A recent study (Madsen, Becker, Thomas, Koser, and Plager, 1967), gives clear evidence that some forms of critical comment do function to strengthen behavior. The more often a teacher told first graders to "sit down," the more often they stood up. Only praising sitting seemed to increase sitting behavior.

References

Becker, W. C., Madsen, C. H., Jr., Arnold, Carole R., and Thomas, D. R. 1967. The contingent use of teacher attention and praise in reducing classroom behavior problems. *Journal of Special Education* 1: 287–307.

Bijou, S. W., and Baer, D. M. 1963. Some methodological contributions from a functional analysis of child development. In *Advances in child development and behavior,* ed. L. P. Lipsitt and C. S. Spiker. New York: Academic Press. Pp. 197–231.

Hart, Betty M., Allen, K. Eileen, Buell, Joan S., Harris, Florence R., and Wolf, M. M. 1964. Effects of social reinforcement on operant crying. *Journal of Experimental Child Psychology* 1: 145–53.

Kerr, Nancy; Meyerson, L., and Michael, J. 1965. A procedure for shaping vocalizations in a mute child. In *Case studies in behavior modification,* eds. L. P. Ullmann and L. Krasner. New York: Holt, Rinehart, & Winston, Inc. Pp. 366–70.

Lovaas, O. I., Freitag, G., Kinder, M. I., Rubenstein, D. B., Schaeffer, B., and Simmons, J. B. 1964. Experimental studies in childhood schizophrenia—Establishment of social reinforcers. Paper delivered at Western Psychological Association, Portland, April, 1964.

Madsen, C. H., Jr., Becker, W. C., Thomas, D. R., Koser, Linda, and Plager, Elaine. 1968. An analysis of the reinforcing function of "sit down" commands. In *Readings in educational psychology,* ed. R. K. Parker. Boston: Allyn and Bacon.

Wahler, R. G. 1967. Child-child interactions in free field settings: Some experimental analyses. *Journal of Experimental Child Psychology* 5: 278–93.

Zimmerman, Elaine H., and Zimmerman, J. 1962. The alteration of behavior in a special classroom situation. *Journal of the Experimental Analysis of Behavior* 5: 59–60.

16 / Acceleration of Academic Progress Through the Manipulation of Peer Influence

GARY W. EVANS AND GAYLON L. OSWALT

Every teacher has several students in each class who are not perform-ing at the desired level. Verbal exhortations often fail. In this study, the underachieving students were identified by the teacher and baseline measures were taken of their performance. Then, contin-gent upon their performance, these underachievers were put in the position of helping the class get things that they and their class-mates wanted. Under these conditions of peer approval-disapproval, the problem children were significantly more successful than students not under the conditions.

Behavior-modification techniques have been successfully applied to a variety of behavior problems associated with the classroom, e.g., hyper-activity (Homme, et al., 1963; Patterson, et al., 1965), peer isolation (Allen, et al., 1965; Patterson & Brodsky, 1966), and school phobia (Patterson, 1965). In spite of the successes in these areas, few attempts to manipu-

Source: Gary W. Evans and Gaylon L. Oswalt, "Acceleration of Academic Progress Through the Manipulation of Peer Influence," *Working Paper* No. 155 (Kansas City: Bureau of Child Research Laboratory, University of Kansas Medical Center, 1967). Reprinted by permission of the authors and the Bureau of Child Research. This study was conducted and supported under NICHHD (National Institute of Child Health and Human Development) Grant No. 00870-04. The authors wish to thank Mrs. Joella Ragan, Mrs. Linda Ney, Mrs. Nancy Thompson, and Mr. Gordon Huggins and the Parsons, Kansas, Public School System for their cooper-ation during the course of this study.

late academic achievement have been reported. Zimmerman and Zimmerman (1964) reported a case study of academic progress obtained by selective teacher-approval of correctly spelled words. The study by Patterson, et al. (1965), indicates that peer influence is helpful in reducing hyperactivity in the classroom, but its effect on academic achievement was not investigated.

This paper reports an attempt to accelerate academic progress of selected individuals by arranging contingencies in such a manner that peer influence is brough to bear on the subjects' academic performance. The specific procedures used in the following experiments resulted from the assumptions that (a) most grade-school children will approve of behavior which leads to a story period or early dismissal from class, (b) peer approval has reinforcing properties for the underachieving child.

Experiment 1

Subjects: The Ss were 22 students from a fourth-grade spelling class. Two experimental Ss (S_1 and S_2) were selected by the classroom teacher and the other 20 students served as control Ss. Experimental Ss were students who were, according to the teacher, "capable of doing considerably better work than they are presently doing."

Procedure: This experiment was conducted over a 13-week period. On the final day of each school week during this period, the teacher constructed and administered a ten-word spelling test covering words that had been presented during that school week.

The first four weeks (Phase 1) was a baseline period in which weekly test scores were recorded but no treatment was introduced. During weeks five through nine (Phase 2), the teacher announced daily, five minutes prior to the morning recess, that the class would be dismissed for recess immediately if S_1 could correctly spell a specified word (or words). The teacher then presented a word for S_1 to attempt to spell (the word was selected from those covered during the preceding period). If S_1 spelled the word correctly, the class was dismissed immediately. If his spelling of the word was incorrect, class work was continued until the customary dismissal time. During weeks ten through thirteen (Phase 3), the procedure was identical to that of Phase 2, with the exception that early dismissal was made contingent on S_2's responses rather than S_1's. No questions were asked of S_1 in Phase 3.

Results: The results are illustrated in Figure 1. The results clearly show that the test performance of both S_1 and S_2 showed considerable improvement when the experimental treatment was in effect. Once the experimental condition was discontinued however, S_1's performance declined to its previous level relative to the control Ss. The control Ss

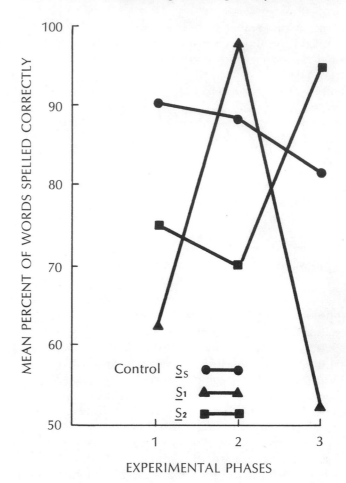

Figure 1. Mean percent of correctly spelled words on weekly tests under phase 1 (baseline), phase 2 (experimental treatment applied to S_2), and phase 3 (experimental treatment applied to S_3).

showed a slight decline in test performance throughout the experiment. Whatever the reason for this decline (e.g., more difficult tests, spring weather), it does serve to illustrate that the improvement manifested by S_1 and S_2 during the experimental phases was not due to the presence of elements common to the class as a whole.

Experiment 2

Subjects: The Ss were 20 students from a fourth-grade arithmetic class. Two experimental Ss (S_3 and S_4) were selected by the classroom teacher (the teacher of this class also taught the spelling class described in Experiment 1). Again, the two experimental Ss were students who the teacher believed were performing below their capabilities. The remaining 18 students in the class served as control Ss.

Procedure: This experiment was conducted over a 14-week period. On the final day of each school week during this period, the teacher constructed and administered a ten-problem arithmetic examination covering material that had been presented during the school week.

Again, the first four weeks (Phase 1) was a baseline period in which weekly test scores were recorded but no treatment was introduced. During weeks five through nine (Phase 2), the teacher announced daily, five minutes before the class was scheduled to be terminated, that she (the teacher) would read a story to the class for the remainder of the period if S_3 could solve a specified arithmetic problem. The teacher then presented a problem, selected from material presented during the period, for S_3 to attempt to solve. If S_3's solution were correct, the teacher read aloud to the class for the remainder of the period. If S_3's solution were incorrect, normal classwork was continued until the end of the period. During weeks ten through fourteen (Phase 3), story reading was made contingent on S_4's responses, rather than S_3's. Daily questions were asked of S_3 in Phase 3, but no experimental consequences were associated with her answers.

Results: The results are illustrated in Figure 2. Again, the results clearly show that the experimental Ss showed considerable improvement when placed under the experimental condition. Notice, however, that S_3's performance did not deteriorate in Phase 3 when the treatment was discontinued. This finding differs from that of Experiment 1 where S_1 failed to maintain his improved performance when the treatment was discontinued. The control Ss' test performance remained quite stable over the three phases of the experiment, illustrating that improvement manifested by S_3 and S_4 was not due to the presence to the class as a whole.

Experiment 3

Subjects: The Ss were 24 students from a sixth-grade social-science class. One experimental $S(S_5)$ was selected by the teacher on the basis that he had not been doing as well as he should have been doing in his classwork. The remaining 23 students served as control Ss.

Procedure: This experiment was conducted over a ten-week period. On the final day of each week, the teacher administered a ten-item test covering material presented during the week.

Again the first four weeks (Phase 1) was a baseline period in

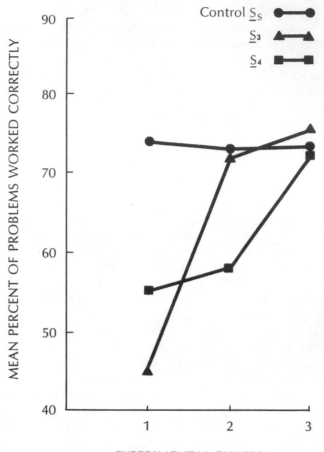

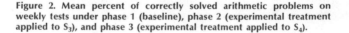

Figure 2. Mean percent of correctly solved arithmetic problems on weekly tests under phase 1 (baseline), phase 2 (experimental treatment applied to S_3), and phase 3 (experimental treatment applied to S_4).

which weekly test scores were recorded but a treatment was not introduced. During weeks five through ten (Phase 2), the teacher announced daily, five minutes prior to the customary noon dismissal time, that the class would be dismissed five minutes early if S_5 could correctly answer a question over material covered during the class period. The teacher then asked S_5 a question and, if he responded correctly, the class was dismissed. If he responded inappropriately to the question, classwork was continued until the customary dismissal time.

 Results: The results are illustrated in Figure 3. The results show that S_5 showed some improvement relative to the control Ss, but the

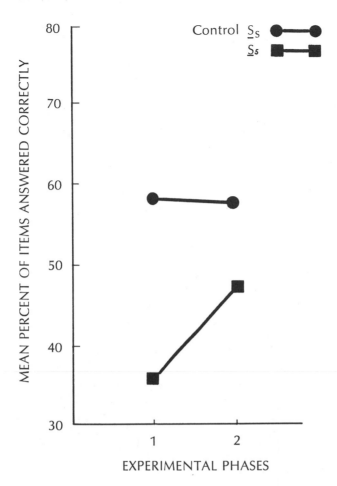

Figure 3. Mean percent of correctly answered items on weekly social science tests under phase 1 (baseline) and phase 2 (experimental treatment applied to S_5).

extent of the improvement was considerably less than that manifested by experimental Ss in the first two experiments.

Experiment 4

Subjects: The Ss were 24 students from a sixth-grade general-science class. An experimental $S(S_6)$ was selected by the teacher (the teacher of this class also taught the social-science class described in Experiment 3). Again, the experimental S was a student who the teacher believed should be doing better work than he was currently doing. The remaining 23 students served as control Ss.

Procedure: The procedure and time periods were identical to those employed in Experiment 3 with the exception that dismissal time was contingent on a correct response from S_6 five minutes prior to afternoon recess, rather than noon hour.

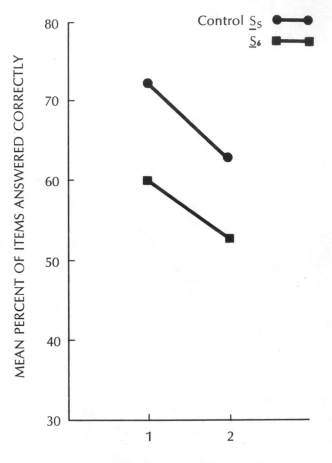

Figure 4. Mean percent of correctly answered items on weekly science tests under phase 1 (baseline) and phase 2 (experimental treatment applied to S_6).

Results: Figure 4 illustrates that the test performance of both S_6 and the control group declined during Phase 2. Since there was little change in S_6's standing relative to the control group, the decline was probably due to an environmental element (such as more difficult examinations) other than the experimental treatment.

Analysis of Results

A mean change score was obtained for each experimental S by subtracting his mean test score during the preceding baseline phase(s) from his mean test score during the treatment phase. Thus, the mean change score for S_1 was his mean test score in Phase 2, minus his mean test score in Phase 1. The mean change score for S_2 was his mean test score in Phase 3, minus his mean test score in Phases 1 and 2 combined. Mean change scores were also obtained for the control groups so that mean change scores for each experimental S could be compared with an appropriate group change score.

The difference between each experimental S's change score and the change score of the appropriate control group was obtained. These six difference scores were analyzed statistically by means of the paired t-test. The mean difference was found to be statistically significant beyond the .02 level of confidence ($t = 3.678$; $df = 5$). Whereas the experimental Ss showed a mean gain of 1.73 items per test (17.3%) under the treatment conditions, the control Ss showed a mean loss of .37 items per test (3.7%) under these conditions.

Discussion

The results of these experiments demonstrate that the procedures described can accelerate the academic performance of underachieving grade-school children. The lack of uniformity of results may have been due to:

1. Age or educational differences between fourth-grade and sixth-grade children.
2. Teacher differences in attitude toward or execution of the program.
3. Subject matter differences.
4. Individual differences among subjects.

The question of the relative effects of these different variables cannot be answered by the data obtained in these experiments. A confounding of effects is present due to the fact that one teacher taught both fourth-grade classes and the other teacher taught both sixth-grade classes. The difference in responsiveness to the treatment may have been due to certain attitudinal differences between the teachers, or the fact that the program was more effective with fourth-grade Ss than with sixth-grade Ss may have led to attitudinal differences between the teachers.

Anecdotal reports by the teachers indicate there was a difference in the manner in which the fourth-grade and sixth-grade children reacted to the program. The fourth-grade teacher reported several attempts by peers to influence the experimental Ss' success (e.g., urging S to study his material and offering assistance). No such attempts by peers were noticed by the sixth-grade teacher. Both teachers reported, however, that their classes were pleased when early dismissal occurred. Differences in teacher attitudes toward the program were indicated by their verbal reports. The fourth-grade teacher spoke very favorably of the program, while the sixth-grade teacher was unimpressed. Further experimentation to isolate teacher, grade, and subject matter differences is planned.

Experimentation is also planned to identify procedures which will prevent relapses after the treatment is discontinued, such as the one exhibited by S_1. At least two possibilities suggest themselves. One possibility is to continue to ask the child questions but eliminate the consequences of his answer. This treatment was applied to S_3 in Phase 3 (Experiment 2) and her performance did not deteriorate. A second possible preventative of severe deterioration after the treatment condition is removed is to gradually decrease the treatment frequency until the desired behavior comes under the control of positive natural consequences.

A comment on the generalization of learned behavior seems appropriate at this point. Note that the dependent variable employed in this study, weekly test performance, was not the behavior that was actually reinforced. The finding that reinforcing daily performance will affect behavior on weekly tests which is not reinforced, though not particularly surprising, demonstrates that behavioral generalization does occur under the conditions of these experiments.

Acquisition of control over an individual's behavior by making a class-reinforcer contingent on the behavior of the individual is a treatment technique that lends itself to a variety of behavior and learning problems in the classroom. In addition to its versatility, the technique has the advantage of requiring very little of the teacher's time or energy. Tests and records are necessary only to evaluate the effectiveness of the procedure. Once the conditions under which the procedure is effective are established, tests and records are not a necessary part of the program. Hopefully, these features will serve to make the technique both effective and practical for general use in the classroom situation.

References

Allen, K. E., Hart, B. M., Buell, J. A., Harris, F. R., and Wolf, M. M. 1965. Effects of social reinforcement on isolate behavior of a nursery school child. In *Case studies in behavior modification*, eds. L. P. Ullmann and L. Krasner. New York: Holt, Rinehart, & Winston. Pp. 307–12.

Homme, L. E., De Bacca, P. C., Devine, T. V., Steinhorst, R., and Richert, E. J. 1963. Use of the Premack principle in controlling the behavior of nursery school children. *J. Exp. Analyses Behav.* 6: 544.

Patterson, G. R., and Brodsky, G. In press. A behavior modification program for a child with multiple problem behaviors. *J. Child Psychol. Psychiat.*

Patterson, G. R., Jones, J. W., Whittier, J., and Wright, M. A. 1965. A behavior modification technique for the hyperactive child. *Behav. Res. & Therapy* 2: 217–26.

Zimmerman, E. H., and Zimmerman, T. 1962. The alteration of behavior in a special classroom situation. *J. Exp. Analyses Behav.* 5: 59–60.

17 / Rules, Praise, and Ignoring: Elements of Elementary Classroom Control

CHARLES H. MADSEN. JR., WESLEY C. BECKER, AND
DON R. THOMAS

"This . . . study . . . adds further confidence to the assertion that teachers can be taught systematic procedures and can use them to gain more effective behaviors from their students." So state the authors in the latter part of their paper. Their optimistic view is strongly supported by their data from children's behavior, but a perhaps more important finding is that the teachers in the study were successful and were consequently reinforced for their understanding and effective use of behavioral principles.

An attempt was made to vary systematically the behavior of two elementary school teachers to determine the effects on classroom behavior of Rules, Ignoring Inappropriate Behaviors, and showing Approval for Appropriate Behavior. Behaviors of two children in one class and one child in the other class were recorded by observers, as were samples of the teachers' behavior. Following baseline recordings, Rules, Ignoring, and Approval conditions were introduced one at a time. In one class a reversal of conditions was carried out. The main conclusions were

Source: Charles H. Madsen, Jr., Wesley C. Becker, and Don R. Thomas, "Rules, Praise, and Ignoring: Elements of Elementary Classroom Control," *Journal of Applied Behavior Analysis* 1 (Summer 1968): 139–50. Copyright © 1968 by the Society for the Experimental Analysis of Behavior, Inc. Reprinted by permission of the authors and the *Journal of Applied Behavior Analysis*.

that (a) Rules alone exerted little effect on classroom behavior, (b) Ignoring Inappropriate Behavior and showing Approval for Appropriate Behavior (in combination) were very effective in achieving better classroom behavior, and (c) showing Approval for Appropriate Behaviors is probably the key to effective classroom management.[1]

Modern learning theory is slowly but surely increasing its potential for impact upon social problems. As problems in social development and interaction are more closely examined through the methods of experimental analysis, the importance of learning principles in everyday life becomes clearer. The potential contribution of these developments to childrearing and education appears to be especially significant. This report is a part of a series of studies aimed at demonstrating what the teacher can do to achieve a "happier," more effective classroom through the systematic use of learning principles. The study grows out of a body of laboratory and field research demonstrating the importance of social reinforcers (smiles, praise, contact, nearness, attention) in establishing and maintaining effective behaviors in children. Extensive field studies in experimental nursery schools by Wolf, Bijou, Baer, and their students (e.g., Hart, Reynolds, Baer, Brawley, and Harris, 1968; Allen, Hart, Buell, Harris, and Wolf, 1965; Bijou and Baer, 1963) provided a background for the extension of their work by the present authors to special and typical elementary classrooms. In general, we have found to date that teachers with various "personalities" and backgrounds can be trained systematically to control their own behavior in ways which will improve the behavior of the children they are teaching (Becker, Madsen, Arnold, and Thomas, 1967). We have also found that teachers can "create" problem behaviors in the classroom by controlling the ways in which they respond to their pupils (Thomas, Becker, and Armstrong, 1968; Madsen, Becker, Thomas, Koser, and Plager, 1968). It is hoped that field studies of this sort will contribute to more effective teacher training.

The present study is a refinement of an earlier study of Becker et al. (1967), in which the behavior of two children in each of five classrooms was recorded and related to experimentally controlled changes in teacher behaviors. The teachers were instructed and guided to follow a program which involved making classroom rules explicit, ignoring dis-

[1] We wish to express our appreciation to the teachers involved, Mrs. Barbara L. Weed and Mrs. Margaret Larson, for their cooperation in a study which involved using and applying procedures which at times made their teaching duties very difficult. Gratitude is expressed to the Director of Elementary Education, Unit District #116, Urbana, Illinois, Dr. Lowell M. Johnson, and to the principals of Thomas Paine and Prairie Schools, Richard Sturgeon and Donald Holste. This study was supported by Grant HD-00881-05 from the National Institutes of Health. Reprints may be obtained from Wesley C. Becker, Bureau of Educational Research, 284 B Education Bldg., University of Illinois, Urbana, Illinois 61801.

ruptive behaviors unless someone was getting hurt, and praising appropriate classroom behaviors. Under this program, most of the severe problem children under study showed remarkable improvements in classroom behavior. However, that study lacked certain controls which the present study sought to correct. First, the teachers in the earlier study were in a seminar on behavior theory and practice during baseline conditions. Some target children improved during baseline, apparently because some teachers were beginning to apply what they were learning even though they had been requested not to do so. Second, public relations and time considerations did not make it possible to introduce the components of the experimental program one at a time (rules, ignoring, and praise) to better study their individual contributions. Third, a reversal of teacher behavior was not attempted. Such a reversal would more conclusively show the importance of teacher's behavior in producing the obtained changes. Fourth, extensive recordings of teacher behavior under all experimental conditions were not undertaken in the earlier study. The present study attempted to deal with each of these problems.

Method

PROCEDURES

Teachers in a public elementary school volunteered to participate in the study. After consultation with teachers and observation of the children in the classroom, two children with a high frequency of problem behavior were selected for study in each class. Previously developed behavioral categories (Becker et al., 1967) were modified for use with these particular children and baseline recordings were made to determine the frequency of problem behaviors. At the end of the baseline period the teachers entered a workshop on applications of behavioral principles in the classroom which provided them with the rationale and principles behind the procedures being introduced in their classes. Various experimental procedures were then introduced, one at a time, and the effects on the target children's behaviors observed. The experiments were begun in late November and continued to the end of the school year.

SUBJECTS

Classroom A. There were 29 children in Mrs. A's middle-primary (second grade) room who ranged in school progress from mid-first-grade level to early-third-grade level. Cliff and Frank were chosen as the target children.

Cliff was chosen because he displayed no interest in school. In

Mrs. A's words, "He would sit throughout entire work periods fiddling with objects in his desk, talking, doing nothing, or misbehaving by bothering others and walking around the room. Lately he has started hitting others for no apparent reason. When Cliff was required to stay in at recess to do his work, he would complete the work in a short time and it was usually completely accurate. I was unable to motivate him into working on any task during the regular work periods." Cliff is the son of a university professor who was born in Europe and immigrated when Cliff was 5-yr old. Cliff scored 91 on an early (CA 5-3) intelligence test. This score was discounted by the examiner because of language problems. His group IQ scores rose steadily (CA 5-9, IQ 103; CA 6-2, IQ 119; CA 7-1, IQ 123). His achievement scores indicated a low second-grade level at the beginning of the present study. Cliff was seen by the school social worker throughout the entire first grade and throughout this entire study.

Cliff was observed early in the year and it was noted that he did not respond once to teacher's questions. He played with his fingers, scratched himself repeatedly, played in his desk, paid no attention to the assignment and had to stay in at recess to finish his work. Almost continually he made blowing sounds and talked to himself. On occasions he was out of his seat making noises and talking. He would leave the room without permission. Before the study began the observers made the following notes: "What a silly kid, writing on the bottom of his shoes, writing on his arms, blowing kisses at the girls. He was vying for the attention of the girl behind him, but she ignored him. . . . Poor Cliff! he acts so silly for his age. He tried to talk to the other kids, but none of them would pay attention to him. . . . Cliff seems concerned with the little girl behind him (girl behind him last week). He has a sign on his desk which reads, 'Do you love me?'. . . ."

Frank was described by his teacher as a likeable child. He had a record of misbehavior in the classroom and intense fighting on the playground. He was often out of his seat talking to other children and did not respond to "discipline." If someone was reprimanded for doing something, Frank would often do the same thing. Test scores indicated an IQ of 106 (Stanford-Binet) and achievement level just under beginning second grade at the start of school (average California Achievement Test scores 1.6 grades). The school psychologist noted that Frank's mother was a person "who willingly permitted others to make decisions for her and did not seem able to discipline Frank." Father was absent from the home during the entire year in the Air Force.

Classroom B. Twenty children were assigned to Mrs. B's kindergarten room. Two children were observed initially; one moved from the community shortly after baseline was taken, leaving only Stan for the study.

Stan was described as coming from a truly pathetic home environment. The mother was not married and the family of four children subsisted on state aid. One older brother was enrolled in a special class for the educable retarded. At the beginning of the year, Stan's behavior was characterized by the teacher as "wild." She reported that, "Stan would push and hit and grab at objects and at children. He had no respect for authority and apparently didn't even hear directions. He knew how to swear profusely, and I would have to check his pockets so I would know he wasn't taking home school equipment. He would wander around the room and it was difficult to get him to engage in constructive work. He would frequently destroy any work he did rather than take it home."

The difficult home situation was made manifest during the month of March. Stan had been absent for two weeks and it was reported that his mother was taking her children out of public school and placing them in a local parochial school. Investigation by school personnel indicated that Stan's mother had moved the children into a relative's home and had gone to the hospital to have another illegitimate baby. A truancy notice was filed for all four children including Stan. Following legal notice the children were returned to school.

RATING OF CHILD BEHAVIOR

The same rating schedule was used in both classrooms except that Isolate Play was added to the list of Inappropriate Behaviors for the kindergarten. Since the children were expected to be involved in structured group activities during observation periods, going off by oneself to play with the many toys or materials in the room was considered inappropriate by the kindergarten teacher. Inappropriate Behavior was defined as the occurrence of one or more of the behaviors listed under Inappropriate Behavior in Table 1 during any observation interval.

Observers were trained in the reliable use of the rating schedule before baseline recordings began. Training consisted of practice in use of the rating schedule in the classroom. Two observers would each rate the same child for 20 min and then return to the research office to compare their ratings and discuss their differences with their supervisor. Training was continued until reliability was above 80% on each behavior code. Training lasted approximately two weeks. Reliability was determined periodically throughout the study by dividing the number of agreements by the number of agreements plus disagreements. An agreement was defined as a rating of the same behavior class in the same observation interval. Average reliability over children, behavior classes, and days for the 69 occasions (out of 238) on which it was checked was

81%. Single day reliabilities ranged from 68% to 96%. Reliabilities were checked in each phase of the study.

Instructions to observers followed those used by Becker et al. (1967). In essence, the observers were not to respond to the children, but to fade into the background as much as possible. Teachers, as well as children, quickly learned not to respond to the observers, although early in the study one observer was attacked by a kindergarten child.

Table 1   Behavioral Coding Categories for Children

I. *Inappropriate Behaviors*

A. *Gross Motor.* Getting out of seat, standing up, running, hopping, skipping, jumping, walking around, moving chair, etc.

B. *Object Noise.* Tapping pencil or other objects, clapping, tapping feet, rattling or tearing paper, throwing book on desk, slamming desk. Be conservative, only rate if you can hear the noise when eyes are closed. Do *not* include accidental dropping of objects.

C. *Disturbance of Other's Property.* Grabbing objects or work, knocking neighbor's books off desk, destroying another's property, pushing with desk (only rate if someone is there). Throwing objects at another person without hitting him.

D. *Contact (high ·and low intensity).* Hitting, kicking, shoving, pinching, slapping, striking with object, throwing object which hits another person, poking with object, biting, pulling hair, touching, patting, etc. Any physical contact is rated.

E. *Verbalization.* Carrying on conversations with other children when it is not permitted. Answers teacher without raising hand or without being called on; making comments or calling out remarks when no questions have been asked; calling teacher's name to get her attention; crying, screaming, singing, whistling, laughing, coughing, or blowing loudly. These responses may be directed to teacher or children.

F. *Turning Around.* Turning head or head and body to look at another person, showing objects to another child, attending to another child. Must be of 4-sec duration, or more than 90 degrees using desk as a reference. Not rated unless seated. If this response overlaps two time intervals and cannot be rated in the first because it is less than 4-sec duration, then rate in the interval in which the end of the response occurs.

G. *Other Inappropriate Behavior.* Ignores teacher's question or command. Does something different from that directed to do, including minor motor behavior such as playing with pencil or eraser when supposed to be writing, coloring while the record is on, doing spelling during the arithmetic lesson, playing with objects. *The child involves himself in a task that is not appropriate.* Not rated when other Inappropriate Behaviors are rated. Must be time off task.

H. *Mouthing Objects.* Bringing thumb, fingers, pencils, or any object in contact with the mouth.

I. *Isolate Play. Limited to kindergarten* free-play period. Child must be farther than 3 ft from any person, neither initiates or responds to verbalizations with other people, engages in no interaction of a non-verbal nature with other children for the entire 10-sec period.

II. *Appropriate Behavior*

Time on task; e.g., answers question, listens, raises hand, works on assignment. Must include whole 10-sec interval except for Turning Around responses of less than 4-sec duration.

The observer did not respond to the behavior and it quickly disappeared. Experimental changes were initiated without informing observers in an attempt to control any observer bias. However, the changes were often dramatic enough that observer comments clearly reflected programmed changes in teacher's behavior.

The target children were observed for 20 min per day, three days a week. In the middle-primary class, observations were taken when the children were engaged in seat work or group instruction. In the kindergarten class, observations were made when structured activities, rather than free play, were expected. Each observer had a clipboard, stopwatch, and rating sheet. The observer would watch for 10 sec and use symbols to record the occurrence of behaviors. In each minute, ratings would be made in five consecutive 10-sec intervals and the final 10 sec would be used for recording comments. Each behavior category could be rated only once in a 10-sec interval.

The primary dependent variable was percentage of intervals in which an Inappropriate Behavior occurred. Since the varieties of Inappropriate Behavior permitted a more detailed analysis with the schedule used, the presentation of results is focused on them, even though functionally their converse (Appropriate Behavior) was the main behavior being manipulated.

RATINGS OF TEACHER BEHAVIOR

Ratings of teacher behavior were obtained to clarify relationships between changes in teacher behavior and changes in child behavior. Recordings of teacher behavior were also used by the experimenters to help the teachers learn the contingent use of Approval and Disapproval Behaviors. The teacher rating schedule is presented in Table 2. Teacher behaviors were recorded by subclasses in relation to child behaviors. That is, the record would show whether a teacher response followed Appropriate child classroom behavior or whether it followed one of the categories of Inappropriate Behavior. Responses to all children were rated. Teacher behavior was scored as the frequency of occurrence of a specified class of behavior during a 20-min interval. Teacher ratings were either recorded during one of the periods when a target child was being rated by another observer, or immediately thereafter when only one observer made both ratings. Teacher behavior was rated on the average of once a week, except during experimental transitions, when more frequent ratings were made. The number of days teacher behavior was rated under each condition is given in Table 3. Most recorded teacher behavior (about 85%) fell in the *Verbal* Approval or Disapproval categories. For this reason we have used the term *Praise* interchangeably

Table 2 Coding Definitions for Teacher Behaviors

Appropriate child behavior is defined by the child rating categories. The teacher's rules for classroom behavior must be considered when judging whether the child's behavior is Appropriate or Inappropriate.

I. Teacher Approval following Appropriate Child Behavior
  A. *Contact.* Positive physical contact such as embracing, kissing, patting, holding arm or hand, sitting on lap.
  B. *Praise.* Verbal comments indicating approval, commendation or achievement. Examples: that's good, you are doing right, you are studying well, I like you, thank you, you make me happy.
  C. *Facial attention.* Smiling at child.
II. Teacher Approval following Inappropriate Child Behavior
  Same codes as under I.
III. Teacher Disapproval following Appropriate Child Behavior
  A. *Holding the child.* Forcibly holding the child, putting child out in the hall, grabbing, hitting, spanking, slapping, shaking the child.
  B. *Criticism.* Critical comments of high or low intensity, yelling, scolding, raising voice. Examples: that's wrong, don't do that, stop talking, did I call on you, you are wasting your time, don't laugh, you know what you are supposed to do.
  C. *Threats.* Consequences mentioned by the teacher to be used at a later time. If _____ then _____ comments.
  D. *Facial attention.* Frowning or grimacing at a child.
IV. Teacher Disapproval following Inappropriate Child Behavior
  Same codes as under III.
V. "Timeout" Procedures[a]
  A. The teacher turns out the lights and says nothing.
  B. The teacher turns her back and waits for silence.
  C. The teacher stops talking and waits for quiet.
  D. Keeping in for recess.
  E. Sending child to office.
  F. Depriving child in the classroom of some privilege.
VI. Academic Recognition
  Calling on a child for an answer. Giving "feedback" for academic correctness.

[a] These are procedural definitions of teacher behaviors possibly involving the withdrawal of reinforcers as a consequence of disruptive behaviors which teacher could not ignore.

with Approval Behaviors and *Criticism* interchangeably with Disapproval Behaviors.

Reliability of measures of teacher behavior were checked approximately every other rating day (21 of 42 occasions for the two teachers) by dividing the agreements as to time interval and behavior codes by the agreements plus disagreements. Average reliability over behavior classes, teachers, and days was 84% with a range from 70% to 96% for individual day measures.

EXPERIMENTAL CONDITIONS

In the middle-primary class (Class A) the experimental conditions may be summarized as consisting of *Baseline;* introduction of *Rules; Rules* plus *Ignoring* deviant behavior; *Rules* plus *Ignoring* plus *Praise* for appropriate behavior; return to Baseline; and finally reinstatement of *Rules, Ignoring,* and *Praise.* In the kindergarten class (Class B) the experimental conditions consisted of *Baseline;* introduction of *Rules; Ignoring* Inappropriate Behavior (without continuing to emphasize rules); and the combination of *Rules, Ignoring,* and *Praise.*

The various experimental procedures were to be used by the teachers for the classroom as a whole throughout the day, not just for the children whose behavior was being recorded, and not just when observers were present.

Baseline. During the Baseline period the teachers conducted their classes in their typical way. No attempt was made to influence their behavior.

Rules. Many people would argue that just telling children what is expected should have considerable effect on their behavior. We wished to explore this question empirically. Teachers were instructed individually and given written instructions as follows:

The first phase of your participation in the use of behavioral principles to modify classroom behaviors is to specify explicit rules of classroom conduct. When this is done, there is no doubt as to what is expected of the children in your classroom. However, do not expect a dramatic shift in classroom control, as we all know that knowing the prohibitions does not always keep people from "sin." This is the first phase in the program and inappropriate behavior should be reduced, but perhaps not eliminated. The rules should be formulated with the class and posted in a conspicuous location (a chart in front of the room or a special place on the chalkboard where they will not be erased). Go over the rules three or four times asking the class to repeat them back to you when they are initially formulated and use the following guidelines:

(a) Make the rules short and to the point so they can be easily memorized.

(b) Five or six rules are adequate. Special instructions for specific occasions are best given when the occasion arises. Children will not remember long lists of rules.

(c) Where possible phrase the rules in a positive not a negative manner (for example, "Sit quietly while working," rather than, "Don't talk to your neighbors"). We want to emphasize positive actions.

(d) Keep a sheet on your desk and record the number of times you review the rules with the class (strive for at least four to six repetitions per day). Remember that young children do not have the retention span of an adult and frequent reminders are necessary. Let the children recite the rules as you ask them, rather than always enumerating them yourself.

(e) Remind the class of the rules at times other than when someone has misbehaved.

(f) Try to change no other aspects of your classroom conduct except for the presentation of the rules at appropriate times.

Teacher tally sheets indicated that these instructions were followed quite explicitly. The average number of presentations of rules was 5.2 per day.

Ignoring Inappropriate Behavior. The second experimental phase involved Ignoring Inappropriate Behavior. In Class A, repetition of rules was also continued. Individual conferences to explain written instructions were given both teachers. Both teachers were given the following instructions:

> The first aspect of the study was to make expectations explicit. This you have been doing over the past few weeks. During the next phase of the study you should learn to *ignore* (do not attend to) behaviors which interfere with learning or teaching, unless of course, a child is being hurt by another, in which case use a punishment which seems appropriate, preferably withdrawal of some positive reinforcement. Learning to ignore is rather difficult. Most of us pay attention to the violations. For example, instead of ignoring we often say such things as the following: "Johnny, you know you are supposed to be working"; "Sue, will you stop bothering your neighbors"; "Henrietta, you have been at that window for a long time;" "Jack, can you keep your hands off Bill"; "Susie, will you please sit down"; "Alex, stop running around and do your work"; "Jane, will you please stop rocking on your chair."
>
> Behaviors which are to be ignored include motor behaviors such as getting out of seat, standing up, running, walking around the room, moving chairs, or sitting in a contorted manner. Any verbal comment or noise not connected with the assignments should also be ignored, such as: carrying on conversations with other children when it is not permitted, answering questions without raising hands or being called on, making remarks when no questions have been asked, calling your name to get attention, and extraneous noises such as crying, whistling, laughing loudly, blowing nose, or coughing. An additional important group of behaviors to be ignored are those which the student engages in when he is supposed to be doing other things, e.g., when the child ignores your instructions you are to ignore him. Any noises made with objects, playing with pencils or other materials should be ignored, as well as taking things from or disturbing another student by turning around and touching or grabbing him.
>
> The reason for this phase of the experiment is to test the possibility that attention to Inappropriate Behavior may serve to strengthen the very behavior that the attention is intended to diminish. Inappropriate Behavior may be strengthened by paying attention to it even though you may think that you are punishing the behavior.

Praise for Appropriate Behavior. The third phase of the experiment included individual contacts with teachers to encourage and train Praising of Appropriate Behavior. The Praise instructions to the teachers were as follows:

> The first phase included specifying explicit rules, writing them on the board and reviewing them 4–6 times per day. The second phase was designed to reduce the amount of attention paid to behaviors which were unwanted by ignoring them. This third phase is primarily directed toward *increasing*

Appropriate Behaviors through praise and other forms of approval. Teachers are inclined to take good behavior for granted and pay attention only when a child acts up or misbehaves. We are now asking you to try something different. This procedure is characterized as "catching the child being good" and making a comment designed to reward the child for good behavior. Give praise, attention, or smile when the child is doing what is expected during the particular class period in question. Inappropriate Behavior would not be a problem if all children were engaging in a great deal of study and school behavior; therefore, it is necessary to apply what you have learned in the workshop. Shape by successive approximations the behavior desired by using praise and attention. Start "small" by giving praise and attention at the first sign of Appropriate Behavior and work toward greater goals. Pay close attention to those children who normally engage in a great deal of misbehavior. Watch carefully and when the child begins to behave appropriately, make a comment such as, "You're doing a fine job, (name)." It is very important during the first few days to catch as many good behaviors as possible. Even though a child has just thrown an eraser at the teacher (one minute ago) and is now studying, you should praise the study behavior. (It might also decrease the rate of eraser throwing.) We are assuming that your commendation and praise are important to the child. This is generally the case, but sometimes it takes a while for praise to become effective. Persistence in catching children being good and delivering praise and attention should eventually pay off in a better behaved classroom.

Some examples of praise comments are as follows:

I like the way you're doing your work quietly (name).

That's the way I like to see you work _____ .

That's a very good job _____ .

You're doing fine _____ .

You got two right _____ , that's very good (if he generally gets no answers right).

In general, give praise for achievement, prosocial behavior, and following the group rules. Specifically, you can praise for concentrating on individual work, raising hand when appropriate, responding to questions, paying attention to directions and following through, sitting in desk and studying, sitting quietly if noise has been a problem. Try to use variety and expression in your comments. Stay away from sarcasm. Attempt to become spontaneous in your praise and smile when delivering praise. At first you will probably get the feeling that you are praising a great deal and it sounds a little phony to your ears. This is a typical reaction and it becomes more natural with the passage of time. Spread your praise and attention around. If comments sometimes might interfere with the ongoing class activities then use facial attention and smiles. Walk around the room during study time and pat or place your hand on the back of a child who is doing a good job. Praise quietly spoken to the children has been found effective in combination with some physical sign of approval.

General Rule: Give *praise* and *attention* to behaviors which facilitate learning. Tell the child what he is being praised for. Try to reinforce behaviors incompatible with those you wish to decrease.

The teachers were also instructed to continue to ignore deviant behavior and to repeat the rules several times a day.

Additional training given teachers consisted of: (a) discussion of problems with suggested solutions during weekly seminars on behavior analysis, and (b) specific suggestions from the experimenter on possible alternative responses in specific situations based on the experimenter's observations of the teachers during experimental transitions, or based on observer data and notes at other times when the data showed that the teachers were not on program.

Additional cues were provided to implement the program. Cards were placed on the teachers' desks containing the instructions for the experimental phase in which they were engaged.

Reversal. In Class A the final experimental conditions involved an attempt to return to Baseline, followed by a reinstatement of the *Rules, Praise,* and *Ignore* condition. On the basis of the earlier observations of Teacher A, we were able to specify to her how frequently she made disapproving and approving comments. The success of this procedure can be judged from the data.

Results

Percentage of observation intervals in which Inappropriate Behaviors occurred as a function of conditions is graphed in Fig. 1 and 2. Major changes in Inappropriate Behaviors occurred only when Praise or Approval for Appropriate Behaviors was emphasized in the experimental

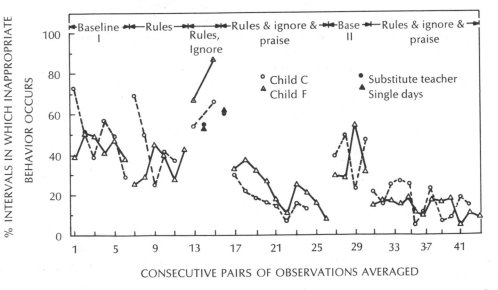

Figure 1. Inappropriate behavior of two problem children in Classroom A as a function of experimental conditions.

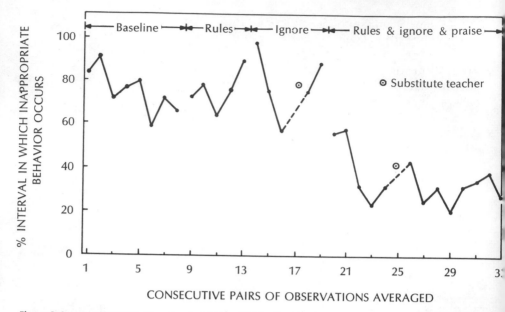

Figure 2. Inappropriate behavior of one problem child in Classroom B as a function of experimental conditions.

procedures. A *t* test, comparing average Inappropriate Behavior in conditions where Praise was emphasized with those where Praise was not emphasized, was significant at the 0.05 level ($df = 2$).

Before examining the results more closely, it is necessary to inspect the data on teacher behavior. Table 3 gives the frequency of classes of teacher behaviors averaged within experimental conditions. Since day-to-day variability of teacher behavior was low for the measures used, these averages fairly reflect what went on.

Introduction of Rules into the classroom had no appreciable effect on Inappropriate Behavior.

Ignoring Inappropriate Behaviors produced inconsistent results. In Class A the children clearly became worse under this condition; in Class B little change was apparent. Both teachers had a difficult time adhering to this condition, and Teacher A found this phase of the experiment very unpleasant. Table 3 shows that Teacher A was only able to reduce critical comments from an average of one per 1 min to an average of three in 4 min. Teacher B cut her critical comments in half. In view of these difficulties, the present results cannot be taken as a clear test of the effects of responding with Disapproval to Inappropriate Behaviors.

The failure to eliminate Disapproval Reactions to Inappropriate Behaviors in Phase Three of the experiment adds some ambiguities to the interpretation of the Phase Four data for Teacher A. The Rules,

Table 3 Teacher Behavior—Averages for Experimental Conditions (Frequency per 20-min Observation)

Teacher A Behavior Classes	Baseline I	Rules	Rules + Ignore	Rules + Ignore + Praise I	Baseline II	Rules + Ignore + Praise II
				Experimental Conditions		
Approval to Appropriate	1.2	2.0	0.0	18.2	2.5	12.5
Approval to Inappropriate	8.7	0.8	2.0	1.2	4.0	5.1
Disapproval to Inappropriate	18.5	20.5	15.7	4.1	9.8	3.5
Disapproval to Appropriate	0.9	0.7	1.0	0.3	0.9	0.0
Timeout	3.3	1.4	1.7	0.4	0.0	0.1
Academic Recognition	26.5	23.6	46.3	52.4	45.4	45.6
Days observed	15	8	3	11	4	9

Teacher B Behavior Classes	Baseline	Rules	Ignore	Rules + Ignore + Praise
Approval to Appropriate	19.2	14.1	19.3	35.2
Approval to Inappropriate	1.9	0.9	0.3	0.0
Disapproval to Inappropriate	16.9	22.1	10.6	10.8
Disapproval to Appropriate	0.0	0.0	0.0	0.0
Timeout	1.5	1.5	0.3	0.4
Academic Recognition	14.5	5.1	6.5	35.6
Days observed	8	6	6	10

Ignore, and Praise condition for Teacher A involved both a reduction in critical comments (Ignoring) as well as a marked increase in Praise. As demonstrated previously (Becker et al., 1967), this combination of procedures is very effective in reducing inappropriate classroom behaviors, but we still lack a clear isolation of effects. The data for Teacher B are not confounded with a simultaneous shift in frequency of Disapproval and Approval Reactions, but they are made less interpretable by a marked shift in Academic Recognition (defined in Table 2) which occurred when the shift in Praise was made. Since Academic Recognition does not show any systematic relations to level of Appropriate Behaviors elsewhere in the study, we are not inclined to interpret this change as showing a causal effect. A best guess is that the effective use of Praise gave the teacher more time to focus on academic skills.

The reversal operation for Teacher A quite clearly shows that the combination of Praising and Ignoring exerts a strong control over Appropriate Behaviors.

As with Academic Recognition, no attempt was made to control how frequently the teacher used procedures labeled "Timeout" (defined in Table 2). The frequency data reported in Table 4 indicates that during Baseline, Teacher A, especially, used "Timeout" procedures to try to establish control (usually turning off the lights until the children were quiet). The changes in the frequency of use of "Timeout" procedures are not systematically related to the behavior changes graphed in Fig. 1 and 2.

Table 4 Percentage of Intervals in which Behaviors Occur: Averages for Two Children in Classroom A by Experimental Conditions

Behavior Classes[1]	Experimental Conditions					
	Baseline I	Rules	Rules + Ignore	Rules + Ignore + Praise I	Baseline II	Rules + Ignore + Praise II
Inappropriate Behavior[2]	46.8	39.8	68.5	20.5	37.6	15.1
Gross Motor	13.9	11.3	32.7	5.9	15.5	4.1
Object Noise	3.5	1.4	1.3	0.5	1.9	0.8
Disturbing Others' Property	3.3	1.8	1.9	0.7	0.7	0.3
Turning Around	21.6	9.9	11.4	9.1	12.8	7.6
Verbalizations	12.0	16.8	21.8	6.5	8.0	3.5
Other Inappropriate Behavior	10.9	7.8	16.5	3.9	7.8	2.6
Mouthing Objects	5.5	2.9	3.5	0.7	0.2	0.1

[1] Contact occurred less than 1% of the time and is not tabulated here.
[2] The sum of the separate problem behaviors will exceed that for Inappropriate Behavior, since the latter measure does not reflect the possibility that more than one class of problem behaviors may occur in an interval.

In summary, the main results indicate: (a) that Rules alone had little effect in improving classroom behavior, (b) the functional status of Ignoring Inappropriate Behavior needs further clarification, (c) the combination of Ignoring and Praising was very effective in achieving better classroom behavior, and (d) Praise for Appropriate Behaviors was probably the key teacher behavior in achieving effective classroom management.

The effects of the experimental procedures on individual classes of behavior for the two children in Class A are presented in Table 4. The data in Table 4 illustrate that with a few exceptions the effects on individual classes of behavior are similar to those for Inappropriate Behavior as a whole.

Discussion

TECHNICAL CONSIDERATIONS

The problems of gaining good data and maintaining adequate experimental control in an ongoing classroom in a public school have not all been recognized as yet, much less solved. The greatest difficulty encountered was that of maintaining stable control over some important variables while others were being changed. When these variables involve aspects of teacher behavior, the problem becomes one of helping the teacher maintain discriminative control over her own behavior. Daily feedback from the experimenter, based on the observer ratings, can help in this task (i.e., show the teacher the up-to-date graph of her behavior). Also, providing the teacher with a small counter to help monitor her own behavior can be helpful (Thomas, et al., 1968). Most difficult to control in the present study was teacher's Disapproving Reactions to Inappropriate Behaviors during the Ignore Phase of the experiment. Teacher A became very "upset" as her classroom became worse. One solution to this problem might be a pre-study in which the teacher is trained in effective management techniques, and then taken through a series of short periods where both Approval and Disapproval are eliminated and one or the other reinstated. The teacher would then have confidence that she can effectively handle her class and be better able to tolerate short periods of chaos (if such periods did occur). She would also have had sufficient training in monitoring her own behavior to permit more effective control.

No attempt was made to program the frequency of various classes of Academic Recognition behaviors. Since such behavior may be important in interpreting results, and was found to vary with some experimental conditions, future work should strive to hold this behavior constant also.

The present study emphasized the importance of contingencies between student and teacher behaviors, but did not measure them directly. While producing similar effects on two children in the same classroom and one child in another classroom, and showing correlated changes in teacher behaviors (including a reversal operation), more powerful data are potentially obtainable with a different technology. Video-tape recordings could enable the use of present coding techniques to obtain contingency data on all classroom members over longer observation periods. Just as the children adapted to the presence of observers, a class could be adapted to the presence of a TV camera man. Costs could be trimmed by saving only some sample tapes and reusing others after reliability ratings are obtained. The current observation procedures (short of having an observer for each child) cannot readily be extended to include simultaneous coding of teacher and child behavior without over-taxing the observers. The present findings, and related studies in this series, are sufficiently promising to warrant an investment in more powerful recording equipment.

TEACHER REACTIONS

Teacher A. Initially, Mrs. A generally maintained control through scolding and loud critical comments. There were frequent periods of chaos, which she handled by various threats.

When praise was finally added to the program, Mrs. A had these reactions: "I was amazed at the difference the procedure made in the atmosphere of the classroom and even my own personal feelings. I realized that in praising the well-behaved children and ignoring the bad, I was finding myself looking for the good in the children. It was indeed rewarding to see the good rather than always criticizing. . . . I became convinced that a positive approach to discipline was the answer."

Teacher B. During Baseline Mrs. B was dispensing a great deal of praise and approval to her classroom, but it was not always contingent on Appropriate Behavior. Her timing was wrong and inconsistencies were apparent. For example, on one occasion two children were fighting with scissors. The instigator was placed under a table away from the rest of the class and left there for 3 min. After 3 min Mrs. B. took the child in her arms and brought her back to the group even though she was still emitting occasional loud screams. Mrs. B would also ignore behavior for a period of time and then would revert to responding to Inappropriate Behavior with a negative comment; she occasionally gave Approval for Inappropriate Behavior. The training given in seminar and discussions with the experimenter led to an effective use of contingencies. Teacher B was also able to use this training to provide instructions and training for her aide to eliminate problems which arose in the final phase of study when the aide was continuing to respond to Disruptive Behaviors.

CHANGES IN THE CHILDREN

Cliff showed little change until Mrs. A started praising Appropriate Behavior, except to get worse during the Ignore phase. He was often doing no academic work, talking to peers, and just fiddling away his time. It took considerable effort by Mrs. A to catch Cliff showing praiseworthy behavior. As the use of praise continued, Cliff worked harder on his assigned tasks, learned to ignore other children who were misbehaving, and would raise his hand to get teacher's attention. He participated more in class discussions. He was moved up to the fastest arithmetic group.

Frank showed little change in his "hyperactive" and "inattentive" behaviors until praise was introduced. Frank responded rapidly to praise. After just two days in the "praise" phase, Frank was observed to clean his desk quietly and quickly after completing a handwriting assignment. He was able to finish a task and study on his own until the teacher initiated a new activity. He began to ask for extra assignments and volunteered to do things to help his teacher. He had learned to sit quietly (when appropriate), to listen, and to raise his hand to participate in class discussion, the latter occurring quite frequently.

Stan slowly improved after contingent praise was instituted, but some of the gains made by Mrs. B were in part undone by the teacher aide. The aide was described as playing policeman and it took special efforts by the teacher to get her to follow the program. Mrs. B summarized the changes in Stan as follows: "Stan has changed from a sullen, morose, muttering, angry individual into a boy whose smile seems to cover his whole face." He became very responsive to teacher praise and learned to follow classroom rules, to pay attention to teacher-directed activities for long periods of time, and to interact with his peers in a more friendly way.

IMPLICATIONS

This replication and refinement of an earlier study by Becker, et al. (1967) adds further confidence to the assertion that teachers can be taught systematic procedures and can use them to gain more effective behaviors from their students. Unless teachers are effective in getting children "ready to learn," their technical teaching skills are likely to be wasted. Knowledge of differential social reinforcement procedures, as well as other behavioral principles, can greatly enhance teachers' enjoyment of the profession and their contribution to effective development of the students.

The reader should note that while we formally recorded the behavior of a few target children, teacher and observer comments indicated dramatic changes in the whole "atmosphere" of the classroom and in the teachers' enjoyment of their classes.

References

Allen, K. E., Hart, B. M., Buell, J. S., Harris, F. R., and Wolf, M. M. 1965. Effects of social reinforcement on isolate behavior of a nursery school child. In *Case studies in behavior modification*, ed. L. P. Ullmann and L. Krasner. New York: Holt, Rinehart & Winston. Pp. 307–12.
Becker, W. C., Madsen, C. H., Jr., Arnold, Carole R., and Thomas, D. R. 1967.

The contingent use of teacher attention and praise in reducing classroom behavior problems. *Journal of Special Education* 1: 287–307.

Bijou, S. W. and Baer, D. M. 1963. Some methodological contributions from a functional analysis of child development. In *Advances in child development and behavior,* ed. L. P. Lipsitt and C. S. Spiker. New York: Academic Press. Pp. 197–231.

Hart, Betty M., Reynolds, Nancy, J., Baer, Donald M., Brawley, Eleanor R., and Harris, Florence R. 1968. Effect of contingent and non-contingent social reinforcement on the cooperative play of a preschool child. *Journal of Applied Behavior Analysis* 1: 73–76.

Thomas, D. R., Becker, W. C., and Armstrong, Marianne. 1968. Production and elimination of disruptive classroom behavior by systematically varying teacher's behavior. *Journal of Applied Behavior Analysis* 1: 35–45.

Madsen, C. H., Jr., Becker, W. C., Thomas, D. R., Koser, Linda, and Plager, Elaine. (In press.) An analysis of the reinforcing function of "Sit Down" Commands. In *Readings in educational psychology,* ed. R. K. Parker. Boston: Allyn and Bacon.

18 / Daily Arithmetic Performance Compared with Teacher Ratings, I.Q., and Achievement Tests

NANCY J. ANN JOHNSON

This study is of singular importance because it implies that the usual ways of evaluating students are not similar to daily performance measures and that the teacher's rating of children is affected more by I.Q. and achievement tests than by daily performance.

Robert Rosenthal in his provocative book Pygmalion in the Classroom (New York: Holt, Rinehart & Winston, Inc., 1968) found somewhat the same thing. When psychologists told teachers that certain of their students were potential "spurters," those students later scored significantly better on a post-test I.Q. measure. The teachers did not know that the "spurters" had been selected at random.

Source: Nancy J. Ann Johnson, "Daily Arithmetic Performance Compared with Teacher Ratings, I.Q., and Achievement Tests," *Research Training Paper* No. 8 (Kansas City: Bureau of Child Research Laboratory, University of Kansas Medical Center, 1967). Reprinted by permission of the author and the Bureau of Child Research.

This article was written while the author was a graduate student in the School of Education at the University of Kansas and research trainee in the Bureau of Child Research, University of Kansas. The research was supported by training grant, MH 8262, to the Bureau of Child Research, University of Kansas, from the National Institute of Mental Health.

The author would like to express her deep gratitude to the classroom teacher and the pupils involved in this study for their participation and coopera-

Introduction

In the existing body of literature, there are many and various definitions, lists of characteristics, and methods of identifying the gifted child. The consensus of opinion is that the gifted child is superior in some ability and that his performance is consistently remarkable in an area potentially beneficial to society. The majority of these children are identified as intellectually gifted or academically talented because of superior performance in an academic setting. One aspect of their superior performance is the ability to use words, to comprehend their meanings, and to read and write effectively. A second aspect of superiority is revealed in mathematical ability; that is, rapid and accurate computation (DeHaan and Havighurst, 1961).

Until recently, questions regarding speed and accuracy of the gifted have been answered rather imprecisely due to the lack of a sensitive, direct, and continuous measurement of classroom performance. Superiority of performance, more often than not, is described by a test score or some subjective criteria established by parent, teacher, or society. The daily classroom performance of the academically talented pupil has been overshadowed by his test performance. Extensive test batteries have been developed to measure his level of intelligence and achievement, the underlying assumption being that the pupil's response to the test is the same as his response to daily classroom assignments.

Purpose

The purposes of this study were (1) to determine the practicality of collecting daily arithmetic performance scores, (2) to compare the arithmetic performance of pupils rated as superior with the performance of those rated as average and below average, and (3) to compare the daily arithmetic performance with scores on a standardized arithmetic test and a measure of the pupils' I.Q.

Procedure

Fourth graders in an elementary school located in a suburb of a large metropolitan area were the pupils in this study. The classroom teacher

tion. Moreover, without the support, generosity, and encouragement of Thomas E. Caldwell, this study could never have been completed. The author is also deeply indebted to Dr. Ogden R. Lindsley for his many suggestions, corrections, and infinite patience in helping with the analysis of the data and the writing of this paper.

selected and rated four pupils, each of superior, average, and below-average ability. Her selection and rating criteria were daily arithmetic scores, the number of times it was necessary to rework corrections, and the amount of help that was required on daily assignments by individual students. She also used scores from general and achievement tests. Each pupil's I.Q. was obtained from his score on the SRA Primary Mental Abilities Test (ages 7–11).

Daily performance records of each pupil's arithmetic assignments were collected for a period of five weeks. The three daily performance measures used were (1) rate of correct problems, (2) rate of incorrect problems, and (3) per cent of correct problems. Rate scores (problems per minute) were obtained by dividing the number of correct and the number of incorrect problems by the total amount of time it took the child to complete his assignment. After the five-week period the pupils were given a standardized arithmetic achievement test. Rate correct, rate incorrect, and per cent correct were computed for the test in the same manner as for the daily performance.

Results

Figure 1 presents raw data obtained during the five-week period and test day for pupils having the highest, middle, and lowest median performance rate. The remaining figures rank the pupils along the horizontal axis in ascending order, according to their median daily rate of correct problems per minute. Figure 2 shows that the median rate of correct problems for all 12 pupils in daily performance is .50 problems per minute. The median rate of correct problems for their achievement test performance jumps to 1.25 problems per minute. The increase is 150 per cent or .75 problems per minute when they are tested. Four of the pupils had a higher rate correct on the achievement test than at any time during their daily work.

Figure 3 shows an increase in the group median rate from .11 problems per minute in daily performance to .58 incorrect problems per minute on the achievement test, an increase of .47 problems per minute or 300 per cent. Eight pupils (66 per cent) had a higher rate of incorrect problems on the achievement test than on any day in their classroom performance.

Figure 4 shows a decrease of 12 per cent from the group median daily performance of 84 per cent to 72 per cent correct on the achievement test. Two pupils went below their lowest point per cent correct for daily work.

On all measures, a t test of means shows that the differences between the means for daily and achievement test performance is sig-

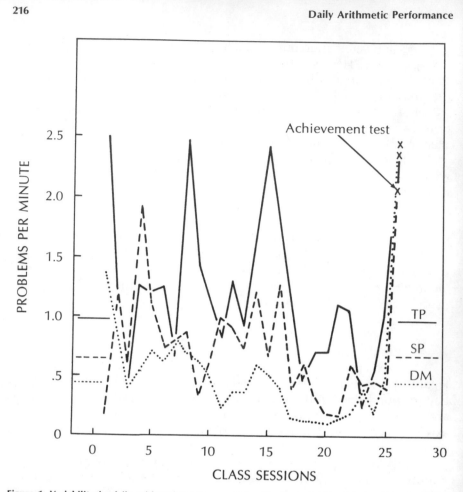

Figure 1. Variability in daily arithmetic performance for the three pupils with the highest, middle, and lowest median performance rate. Horizontal lines with pupils' initials indicate their median daily performance and X's indicate their achievement test performance.

nificant beyond the .001 level. A test of association, the Kendall coefficient of correlation (*tau*), was run to determine the correlation of I.Q. with daily performance and achievement test rate (correct and incorrect problems per minute) and daily performance and achievement test per cent of correct problems. I.Q. correlates with rate correct and per cent correct both on daily and achievement test performance, but not with rate incorrect. Achievement test rate correct and per cent correct correlate with I.Q. ten points higher than daily rate and per cent correct (see Table 1). The teacher's rating of four superior pupils is associated only with I.Q. as obtained from the SRA Test of Primary Abilities (see Fig. 5).

In Table 1, the Kendall coefficient of correlation (*tau*) shows SRA Primary Abilities Test I.Q. positively correlates with rate correct and per

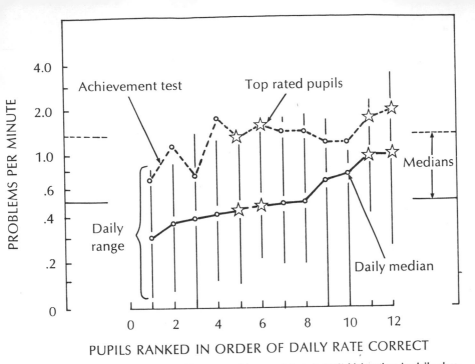

Figure 2. Rate of correct arithmetic problems on achievement tests is 150% higher than in daily class-work. Two of the top four pupils (starred in figure) rated by teacher are only in the middle of the group on daily rate correct.

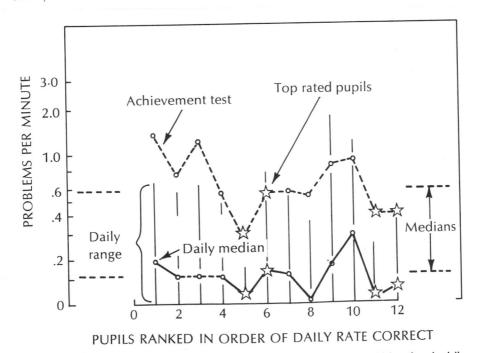

Figure 3. Rate of incorrect arithmetic problems on achievement tests is 300% higher than in daily classwork. Starred points represent top four pupils rated by classroom teacher.

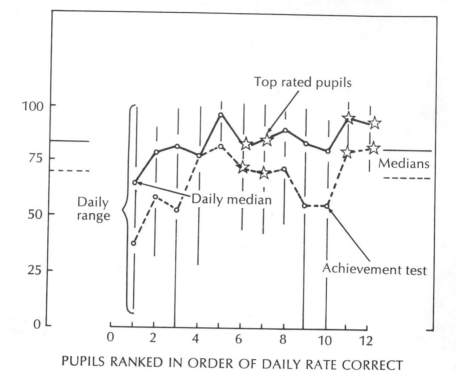

PUPILS RANKED IN ORDER OF DAILY RATE CORRECT

Figure 4. Per cent of correct problems on achievement tests is 12% lower than in daily classwork. Two of top four pupils (starred in figure) selected by teacher fall in the middle of the group.

cent correct but not with rate incorrect. Also I.Q. correlates higher with achievement test performance than with daily performance.

Discussion

These results, showing the measurement bias introduced by tests, are important since test results receive so much emphasis in current achieve-

Table 1

I.Q. Correlated With:	Tau	P
Rate Correct: Daily	+.41	.05
Rate Correct: Achievement Test	+.53	.02
Rate Incorrect: Daily	+.06	.10
Rate Incorrect: Achievement Test	−.27	.10
Per Cent Correct: Daily	+.43	.04
Per Cent Correct: Achievement Test	+.56	.01

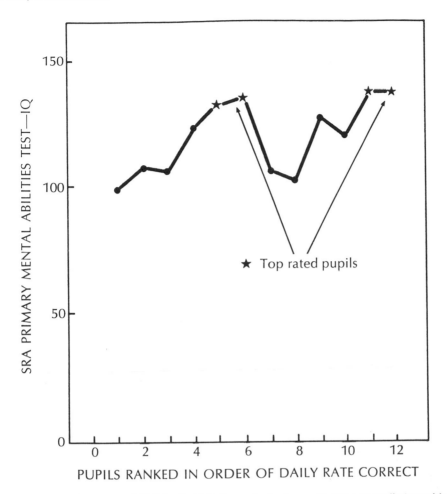

Figure 5. SRA Primary Mental Abilities Test I.Q. Scores for twelve pupils. Top four pupils (starred in figure) rated by teacher had the top four I.Q. scores. I.Q. scores were used by teacher in her ratings.

ment evaluations. Similar lack of correlation between standardized testing and actual performance was also shown by Haughton, 1966. The most serious damage is not to the person who administers the test and makes use of its results, but to the pupil whose academic life is arranged by and evaluated by test results. The pupil who achieves at a high level in daily classwork, but who is unfairly evaluated or remains unidentified due to poor test performance, is being cheated. Or perhaps more seriously, the pupil who is allowed to get by with relatively poor daily work because of high level test performance remains a source of untapped potential. In both cases, the pupils are denied challenging and rewarding educational experiences. Direct and continuous recording of classroom performance should be emphasized more and tests and other indirect measures less.

Continuous and direct recording of individual academic performance rates has proved useful in regular and special classrooms (Cox and Caldwell, 1966; Davis and Johnson, 1966; Dobbs and Holzschuh, 1966; Haughton and Ericson, 1965). Performance rate (Haughton, 1966) is more sensitive, more reliable, and more direct than per cent correct. Daily performance measured in terms of per cent correct gives the teacher and pupil only a summary number concerning the pupil's accuracy of response. Another limiting factor in the use of per cent correct is that it transforms information into 100 units, with 100 as the ceiling of the scale. Pupils working at the upper end of the per cent scale are denied information concerning the improvement of their performance (Caldwell, 1966).

On the other hand, rate is more sensitive because it includes two dimensions of each pupil's performance—number (how many problems completed) and time (how long it took the child to complete the problems). In contrast to per cent correct, rate does not have a limited ceiling.

Total rate (speed of doing work) can be refined further into a rate of correct problems which combines the components of speed and inaccuracy. Most important of all, rate measures provide both the teacher and child with precise and reliable records of each pupil's daily academic performance.

Conclusions

This study indicates that pupils do not perform the same on an achievement test as they do in their daily arithmetic assignments. In fact, it demonstrates that distortions occur in the very performance the test is attempting to measure. On the test, the increased rate correct is purchased at the expense of a greater increase in rate of incorrect problems: that is, the pupil works faster but is far more inaccurate. These data clearly show that the teacher was more influenced in her rating of superior students by I.Q. and achievement test performance than by their daily performance.

References

Caldwell, T. Comparison of classroom measures: per cent, number, and rate. Unpublished manuscript, 1966.
Cox, Lois, and Caldwell, T. Personal communication, 1966.

Davis, Jacqueline, and Johnson, Nancy. Personal communication, 1966.

DeHaan, R. F., and Havighurst, R. J. *Education of gifted children.* Chicago: University of Chicago Press, 1961.

French, J. R., ed. *Educating the gifted.* New York: Holt, Rinehart & Winston, Inc., 1964.

Haughton, E. Teachers and educational psychology: grounds for divorce? Paper read at Midwest. Psychol. Ass., Chicago, May, 1966.

Haughton, E., and Ericson, Colleen T. Why blame education? or how we learned to live with P. I. and still teach. *Prog. Inst.*, 1965, 5:2:1–8.

Lindsley, O. R. Direct measurement and prosthesis of retarded behavior. *J. Educ.*, 1964, 147, 62–81.

Walker, Helen M., and Lev, J. *Statistical inference.* New York: Holt, Rinehart & Winston, Inc., 1953.

Wilcoxon, F., and Wilcox, Roberta A. *Some rapid approximate statistical procedures.* Pearl River, New York: Lederle Laboratories, 1964.

19 / Good-Bye, Teacher . . .

FRED S. KELLER

Critics of education have pointed out for years that the great bastion of resistance to change has been undergraduate and graduate education. Indeed, classes today have an unusual similarity to what they have been for decades.

Keller offers an attractive alternative for an undergraduate, introductory course. It is particularly noteworthy because of the results: students know the material and seem to have enjoyed learning it.

As one involved in the system of higher education, imagine as you read that you were about to take this course designed by Keller.

When I was a boy, and school "let out" for the summer, we used to celebrate our freedom from educational control by chanting:

> Good-bye scholars, good-bye school;
> Good-bye teacher, darned old fool!

We really didn't think of our teacher as deficient in judgment, or as a

Source: Fred S. Keller, " 'Good-Bye, Teacher . . . ,' " *Journal of Applied Behavior Analysis* 1 (Spring 1968): 79–88. Copyright © 1968 by the Society for the Experimental Analysis of Behavior, Inc. Reprinted by permission of the author and the *Journal of Applied Behavior Analysis.* Originally the President's Invited Address, Division 2, American Psychological Association, Washington, D. C., September, 1967.

clown or jester. We were simply escaping from restraint, dinner pail in one hand and shoes in the other, with all the delights of summer before us. At that moment, we might even have been well disposed toward our teacher and might have felt a touch of compassion as we completed the rhyme.

"Teacher" was usually a woman, not always young and not always pretty. She was frequently demanding and sometimes sharp of tongue, ever ready to pounce when we got out of line. But, occasionally, if one did especially well in homework or in recitation, he could detect a flicker of approval or affection that made the hour in class worthwhile. At such times, we loved our teacher and felt that school was fun.

It was not fun enough, however, to keep me there when I grew older. Then I turned to another kind of education, in which the reinforcements were sometimes just as scarce as in the schoolroom. I became a Western Union messenger boy and, between deliveries of telegrams, I learned Morse code by memorizing dots and dashes from a sheet of paper and listening to a relay on the wall. As I look back on those days, I conclude that I am the only living reinforcement theorist who ever learned Morse code in the absence of reinforcement.

It was a long, frustrating job. It taught me that drop-out learning could be just as difficult as in-school learning and it led me to wonder about easier possible ways of mastering a skill. Years later, after returning to school and finishing my formal education, I came back to this classical learning problem, with the aim of making International Morse code less painful for beginners than American Morse had been for me (Keller, 1943).

During World War II, with the aid of a number of students and colleagues, I tried to apply the principle of immediate reinforcement to the early training of Signal Corps personnel in the reception of Morse-code signals. At the same time, I had a chance to observe, at close hand and for many months, the operation of a military training center. I learned something from both experiences, but I should have learned more. I should have seen many things that I didn't see at all, or saw very dimly.

I could have noted, for example, that instruction in such a center was highly individualized, in spite of large classes, sometimes permitting students to advance at their own speed throughout a course of study. I could have seen the clear specification of terminal skills for each course, together with the carefully graded steps leading to this end. I could have seen the demand for perfection at every level of training and for every student; the employment of classroom instructors who were little more than the successful graduates of earlier classes; the minimizing of the lecture as a teaching device and the maximizing of student participation.

I could have seen, especially, an interesting division of labor in the educational process, wherein the non-commissioned classroom teacher was restricted to duties of guiding, clarifying, demonstrating, testing, grading, and the like, while the commissioned teacher, the training officer, dealt with matters of course logistics, the interpretation of training manuals, the construction of lesson plans and guides, the evaluation of student progress, the selection of non-commissioned cadre, and the writing of reports for his superior.

I did see these things, of course, in a sense, but they were embedded deeply within a special context, one of "training" rather than "education." I did not then appreciate that a set of reinforcement contingencies which were useful in building simple skills like those of the radio operator might also be useful in developing the verbal repertories, the conceptual behaviors, and the laboratory techniques of university education. It was not until a long time later, by a very different route, that I came to such a realization.

That story began in 1962, with the attempt on the part of two Brazilian and two North American psychologists to establish a Department of Psychology at the University of Brasilia. The question of teaching method arose from the very practical problem of getting a first course ready by a certain date for a certain number of students in the new university. We had almost complete freedom of action; we were dissatisfied with the conventional approaches; and we knew something about programmed instruction. We were also of the same theoretical persuasion. It was quite natural, I suppose, that we should look for fresh applications of reinforcement thinking to the teaching process (Keller, 1966).

The method that resulted from this collaborative effort was first used in a short-term laboratory course[1] at Columbia University in the winter of 1963, and the basic procedure of this pilot study was employed at Brasilia during the following year, by Professors Rodolfo Azzi and Carolina Martuscelli Bori, with 50 students in a one-term introductory course. Professor Azzi's report on this, at the 1965 meetings of the American Psychological Association and in personal correspondence, indicated a highly satisfactory outcome. The new procedure was received enthusiastically by the students and by the university administration. Mastery of the course material was judged excellent for all who completed the course. Objections were minor, centering around the relative absence of opportunity for discussion between students and staff.

Unfortunately, the Brasilia venture came to an abrupt end during the second semester of its operation, due to a general upheaval

[1] With the aid of (Dr.) Lanny Fields and the members of a senior seminar at Columbia College, during the fall term of 1963–64.

within the university that involved the resignation or dismissal of more than 200 teachers. Members of the original psychology staff have since taken positions elsewhere, and have reportedly begun to use the new method again, but I am unable at this time report in detail on their efforts.

Concurrently with the early Brazilian development, Professor J. G. Sherman and I, in the spring of 1965, began a series of more or less independent applications of the same general method at Arizona State University. With various minor changes, this work has now been tried through five semesters with an increasing number of students per term (Keller, in press (a), in press (b), 1967; Sherman, 1967). The results have been more gratifying with each successive class, and there has been as yet no thought of a return to more conventional procedures. In addition, we have had the satisfaction of seeing our system used by a few other colleagues, in other courses and at other institutions.[2]

In describing this method to you, I will start with a quotation (Keller, 1967). It is from a hand-out given to all the students enrolled in the first-semester course in General Psychology (one of two introductions offered at Arizona State University) during the past year, and it describes the teaching method to which they will be exposed unless they elect to withdraw from the course.

This is a course through which you may move, from start to finish, at your own pace. You will not be held back by other students or forced to go ahead until you are ready. At best, you may meet all the course requirements in less than one semester; at worst, you may not complete the job within that time. How fast you go is up to you.

The work of this course will be divided into 30 units of content, which correspond roughly to a series of homework assignments and laboratory exercises. These units will come in a definite numerical order, and you must show your mastery of each unit (by passing a "readiness" test or carrying out an experiment) before moving on to the next.

A good share of your reading for this course may be done in the classroom, at those times when no lectures, demonstrations, or other activities are taking place. Your classroom, that is, will sometimes be a study hall.

The lectures and demonstrations in this course will have a different relation to the rest of your work than is usually the rule. They will be provided only when you have demonstrated your readiness to appreciate them; no examination will be based upon them; and you need not attend them if you do not wish. When a certain percentage of the class has reached a certain point in the course, a lecture or demonstration will be available at a stated time, but it will not be compulsory.

The teaching staff of your course will include proctors, assistants, and an instructor. A proctor is an undergraduate who has been chosen for his

---

[2] For example, by J. L. Michael with high-school juniors on a National Science Foundation project at Grinnell College (Iowa), in 1965; and by J. Farmer and B. Cole at Queens College (New York) in a course similar to the one described here.

mastery of the course content and orientation, for his maturity of judgment, for his understanding of the special problems that confront you as a beginner, and for his willingness to assist. He will provide you with all your study materials except your textbooks. He will pass upon your readiness tests as satisfactory or unsatisfactory. His judgment will ordinarily be law, but if he is ever in serious doubt, he can appeal to the classroom assistant, or even the instructor, for a ruling. Failure to pass a test on the first try, the second, the third, or even later, will not be held against you. It is better that you get too much testing than not enough, if your final success in the course is to be assured.

Your work in the laboratory will be carried out under the direct supervision of a graduate laboratory assistant, whose detailed duties cannot be listed here. There will also be a graduate classroom assistant, upon whom your proctor will depend for various course materials (assignments, study questions, special readings, and so on), and who will keep up to date all progress records for course members. The classroom assistant will confer with the instructor daily, aid the proctors on occasion, and act in a variety of ways to further the smooth operation of the course machinery.

The instructor will have as his principal responsibilities: (a) the selection of all study material used in the course; (b) the organization and the mode of presenting this material; (c) the construction of tests and examinations; and (d) the final evaluation of each student's progress. It will be his duty, also, to provide lectures, demonstrations, and discussion opportunities for all students who have earned the privilege; to act as a clearing-house for requests and complaints; and to arbitrate in any case of disagreement between students and proctors or assistants. . . .

All students in the course are expected to take a final examination, in which the entire term's work will be represented. With certain exceptions, this examination will come at the same time for all students, at the end of the term. . . . The examination will consist of questions which, in large part, you have already answered on your readiness tests. Twenty-five percent of your course grade will be based on this examination; the remaining 75% will be based on the number of units of reading and laboratory work that you have successfully completed during the term.

(In my own sections of the course, these percentages were altered during the last term, to a 30% weighting of the final examination, a 20% weighting of the 10 laboratory exercises, and a 50% weighting of the reading units.)

A picture of the way this method operates can best be obtained, perhaps, by sampling the activities of a hypothetical average student as he moves through the course. John Pilgrim is a freshman, drawn from the upper 75% of his high-school class. He has enrolled in PY 112 for unknown reasons and has been assigned to a section of about 100 students, men and women, most of whom are also in their beginning year. The class is scheduled to meet on Tuesdays and Thursdays, from 9:15 to 10:30 a.m., with a laboratory session to be arranged.

Together with the description from which I quoted a moment ago, John receives a few mimeographed instructions and some words of advice from his professor. He is told that he should cover two units of laboratory work or reading per week in order to be sure of taking an A-grade into his final examination; that he should withdraw from the course if he doesn't pass at least one readiness test within the first two weeks; and that a grade of Incomplete will not be given except in special cases. He is also advised that, in addition to the regular classroom hours on Tuesday and Thursday, readiness tests may be taken on Saturday forenoons and Wednesday afternoons of each week—periods in which he can catch up with, or move ahead of, the rest of the class.

He then receives his first assignment: an introductory chapter from a standard textbook and two "sets" from a programmed version of similar material. With this assignment, he receives a mimeographed list of "study questions," about 30 in number. He is told to seek out the answers to these questions in his reading, so as to prepare himself for the questions he will be asked in his readiness tests. He is free to study wherever he pleases, but he is strongly encouraged to use the study hall for at least part of the time. Conditions for work are optimal there, with other students doing the same thing and with an assistant or proctor on hand to clarify a confusing passage or a difficult concept.

This is on Tuesday. On Thursday, John comes to class again, having gone through the sets of programmed material and having decided to finish the study in the classroom, where he cannot but feel that the instructor really expects him. An assistant is in charge, about half the class is there, and some late registrants are reading the course description. John tries to study his regular text, but finds it difficult to concentrate and ends by deciding to work in his room. The assistant pays no attention when he leaves.

On the following Tuesday, he appears in study hall again, ready for testing, but anxious, since a whole week of the course has passed. He reports to the assistant, who sends him across the hall, without his books and notes, to the testing room, where the proctor in charge gives him a blue-book and one of the test forms for Unit 1. He takes a seat among about 20 other students and starts work. The test is composed of 10 fill-in questions and one short-answer essay question. It doesn't seem particularly difficult and, in about 10 min John returns his question sheet and is sent, with his blue-book, to the proctor's room for grading.

In the proctor's room, in one of 10 small cubicles, John finds his special proctor, Anne Merit. Anne is a psychology major who passed the same course earlier with a grade of A. She receives two points of credit for about 4 hr of proctoring per week, 2 hr of required attendance at a weekly proctors' meeting, and occasional extra duty in the study hall or test room. She has nine other students besides John to look after, so she will not as a rule be able to spend much more than 5 or 10 min of class time with each.

Anne runs through John's answers quickly, checking two of them as incorrect and placing a question mark after his answer to the essay question. Then she asks him why he answered these three as he did. His replies show two misinterpretations of the question and one failure in written expression. A restatement of the fill-in questions and some probing with respect to the essay leads Anne to write an O.K. alongside each challenged answer. She congratulates John upon his performance and warns him that later units may be a little harder to master than the first.

John's success is then recorded on the wall-chart in the proctors' room, he is given his next assignment and set of study questions, and sent happily on his way. The blue-book remains with Anne, to be given later to the assistant or the instructor for inspection, and used again when John is ready for testing on Unit 2. As he leaves the room, John notices the announcement of a 20-min lecture by his instructor, for all students who have passed Unit 3 by the following Friday, and he resolves that he will be there.

If John had failed in the defense of one or two of his answers, he would have been sent back for a minimal period of 30 min for further study, with advice as to material most needing attention. If he had made more than four errors on his test, the answers would not have been considered individually; he would simply have been told that he was not ready for examination. And, if he had made no errors at all, he would probably have been asked to explain one or two of his correct answers, as a way of getting acquainted and to make sure that he was the one who had really done the work.

John did fail his first test on Unit 2, and his first two tests on Unit 4 (which gave trouble to nearly everyone). He missed the first lecture, too, but qualified for the second. (There were seven such "shows" during the term, each attended by perhaps half of the students entitled to be there.) After getting through his first five units, he failed on one review test before earning the right to move on to Unit 6. On the average, for the remainder of the course, he required nearly two readiness tests per unit. Failing a test, of course, was not an unmixed evil, since it permitted more discussion with the proctor and often served to sharpen the concepts involved.

In spite of more than a week's absence from school, John was able, by using the Wednesday and Saturday testing sessions, to complete his course units successfully about a week before the final examination. Because of his cramming for other courses during this last week, he did not review for his psychology and received only a B on his final examination. His A for the course was not affected by this, but his pride was hurt.

Sometime before the term ended, John was asked to comment on certain aspects of the course, without revealing his identity. (Remember, John is a mythical figure.) Among other things, he said that, in comparison with courses taught more conventionally, this one demanded a much greater mastery of the work assignments, it required greater memorization of detail and much greater understanding of basic concepts, it generated a greater feeling of achievement, it gave much greater recognition of the student as a person, and it was enjoyed to a much greater extent (Keller, in press).

He mentioned also that his study habits had improved during the term, that his attitude towards testing had become more positive, that his worry about final grades had diminished, and that there had been an increase in his desire to hear lectures (this in spite of the fact that he attended only half of those for which he was qualified). When asked specifically about the use of proctors, he said that the discussions with his proctors had been very helpful, but the proctor's non-academic, personal relation was also important to him, and that the use of proctors generally in grading and discussing tests was highly desirable.

Anne Merit, when asked to comment on her own reactions to the system, had many things to say, mostly positive. She referred especially to the satisfaction of having the respect of her proctees, of seeing them do well, and of cementing the material of the course for herself. She noted that the method was one of "mutual reinforcement" for student, proctor, assistant, and instructor. She suggested that it ought to be used in other courses and at other levels of instruction. She wondered why it would not be possible for a student to enroll in a second course immediately upon completion of the first, if it were taught by the same method. She also listed several changes that might improve the efficiency of the course machinery, especially in the area of testing and grading, where delay may sometimes occur.

In an earlier account of this teaching method (Keller, 1967), I summarized those features which seem to distinguish it most clearly from conventional teaching procedures. They include the following:

(1) *The go-at-your-own-pace feature,* which permits a student to move through the course at a speed commensurate with his ability and other demands upon his time.

(2) *The unit-perfection requirement for advance,* which lets the student go ahead to new material only after demonstrating mastery of that which preceded.

(3) *The use of lectures and demonstrations as vehicles of motivation,* rather than sources of critical information.

(4) The related *stress upon the written word* in teacher-student communication; and, finally:

(5) *The use of proctors,* which permits repeated testing, immediate scoring, almost unavoidable tutoring, and a marked enhancement of the personal-social aspect of the educational process.

The similarity of our learning paradigm to that provided in the field of programmed instruction is obvious. There is the same stress upon analysis of the task, the same concern with terminal performance, the same opportunity for individualized progression, and so on. But the sphere of action here is different. The principal steps of advance are not "frames" in a "set," but are more like the conventional homework assignment or laboratory exercise. "The 'response' is not simply the completion of a prepared statement through the insertion of a word or phrase. Rather, it may be thought of as the resultant of many such responses, better described as the understanding of a principle, a formula, or a concept, or the ability to use an experimental technique. Advance within the program depends on something more than the appearance of a confirming word or the presentation of a new frame; it involves a personal interaction between a student and his peer, or his better, in what may be a lively verbal interchange, of interest and importance to each participant. The use of a programmed text, a teaching machine, or some sort of computer aid within such a course is entirely possible and may be quite desirable, but it is not to be equated with the course itself." (Keller, 1967.)

Failure to recognize that our teaching units are not as simple as the response words in a programmed text, or the letter reactions to Morse-code signals, or other comparable atoms of behavior, can lead to confusion concerning our procedure. A well-known critic of education in America, after reading an account of our method, sent me a note confessing to "a grave apprehension about the effect of breaking up the subject matter into little packages." "I should suppose," he said, "it would prevent all but the strongest minds from ever possessing a synoptic view of a field, and I imagine that the coaching, and testing, and passing in bits would amount to efficient training rather than effectual teaching."

Out "little packages" or "bits" are no smaller than the basic conceptions of a science of behavior and cannot be delivered all at once in one large synoptic parcel. As for the teaching-training distinction, one needs only to note that it is always the instructor who decides what is to be taught, and to what degree, thus determining whether he will be called a trainer or a teacher. The method he uses, the basic reinforcement contingencies he employs, may be turned to either purpose.

Many things occur, some of them rather strange, when a student is taught by a method such as ours. With respect to everyday student behavior, even a casual visit to a class will provide some novel items. For example, all the students seated in the study hall may be seen studying, undistracted by the presence or movements of others. In the test room, a student will rarely be seen chewing on his pencil, looking at a neighbor's blue-book, or staring out the window. In the crowded proctors' room, 10 pairs of students can be found concurrently engaged in academic interaction, with no couple bothered by the conversation of another, no matter how close by. Upon passing his assistant or instructor, in the corridors or elsewhere, a student will typically be seen to react in a friendly and respectful manner—enough to excite a mild alarm.

More interesting than this is the fact that a student may be tested 40 or 50 times in the course of one semester, often standing in line for the privilege, without a complaint. In one extreme instance, a student required nearly two terms to complete the work of one (after which he applied for, and got, permission to serve as a proctor for the following year).

Another unusual feature of our testing and grading is the opportunity given to defend an "incorrect" answer. This defense, as I noted earlier, may sometimes produce changes in the proctor's evaluation, changes that are regularly checked by the assistant or the instructor. Occasionally, a proctor's O.K. will be rejected, compelling the student to take another test, and sensitizing the proctor to the dangers of leniency; more often, it produces a note of warning, a correction, or a query written by the instructor in the student's blue-book; but always it provides the instructor with feedback on the adequacy of the question he has constructed.

Especially important, in a course taught by such a method, is the fact that any differences in social, economic, cultural, and ethnic background are completely and repeatedly subordinated to a friendly intellectual relationship between two human beings throughout a period of 15 weeks or more. Also, in such a course, a lonesome, ill-favored underprivileged, badly schooled, or otherwise handicapped boy or girl can be assured at least a modicum of individual attention, approval, encouragement, and a chance to succeed. The only prerequisite for such treatment is a well-defined amount and quality of academic achievement.

Another oddity of the system is the production of a grade distribution that is upside down. In Fig. 1 are the results from a class of 208 students at Arizona State University during the past semester. Note the diminishing relative frequency as one moves from A to D. The category of E, indicating failure, is swollen by the presence of 18 students who failed to take up their option of W (withdrawal from the course). Grades of C and D were due to the failure of students to complete all the units of reading or laboratory before going into the final examination.

Figure 2 shows data from the class 1 yr earlier. Essentially the same distribution holds, except for the category of Incomplete, which was then too easily obtainable. Discouraging the use of the Incomplete,

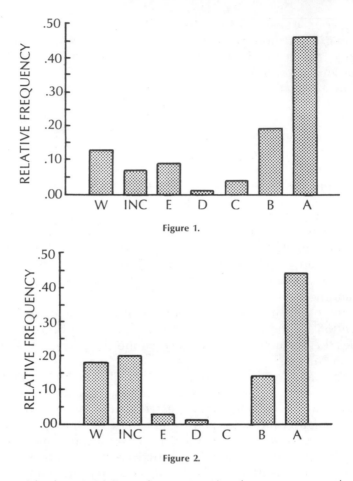

Figure 1.

Figure 2.

together with the provision of more testing hours, apparently has the effects of regularizing study habits and equalizing the number of tests taken per week throughout the term.

In Fig. 3 (filled bars), the grade distribution is for a section of 25 students in an introductory course at Queens College (N. Y.) during the second semester of the past school year. The same method of teaching was employed as at Arizona State, but the work requirement was somewhat greater in amount. The distinctive feature here is the relative infrequency of low grades. Only four students received less than a B rating. Professor John Farmer, who provided me with these data, reports that the two students receiving F had dropped out of the course, for unknown reasons, after seven and eight units respectively.

With this teaching method, students who are presumably inferior may show up better upon examination than presumably superior students taught by more conventional procedures. Figure 4 shows two distributions of grades on a mid-term examination. The empty bars represent the achievement of 161 students of an Ivy League College, mainly sophomores, in the first semester of a one-year lecture-and-laboratory course in elementary psychology. The filled bars represent the achievement of 66 Arizona State University students, mainly freshmen, on an unannounced mid-term quiz prepared by the Ivy League instructor and from which 13% of the questions had to be eliminated on the grounds of differential course coverage.

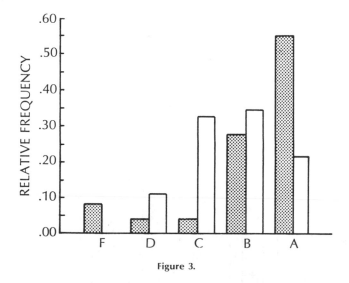

Figure 3.

Relevant to this comparison is that pictured in Fig. 3. The grade distribution obtained by Professor Farmer (and his associate, Brett Cole) is here compared with one obtained from a section of 46 students in the same course, taught in the conventional manner by a colleague who is described as "a very good instructor". The filled bars show the Farmer-Cole results; the empty ones are those from Professor Brandex.

Such comparisons are of some interest and may relieve the tedium of a lecture, but they raise many questions of interpretation, and their importance should not be overemphasized. The kind of change needed in education today is not one that will be evaluated in terms of the percentage of A's in a grade distribution or of differences at the 0.01 (or 0.001) level of confidence. It is one that will produce a reinforcing state of affairs for everyone involved—a state of affairs that has heretofore been reached so rarely as to be the subject of eulogy in the world's literature, and which, unfortunately, has led to the mystique of the "great teacher" rather than a sober analysis of the critical contingencies in operation.

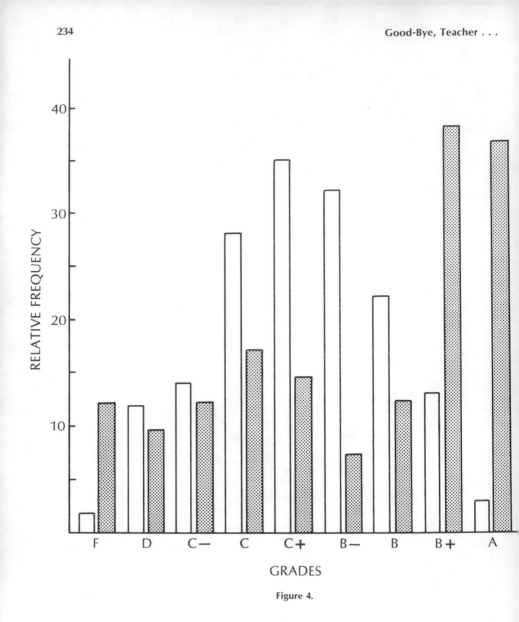

Figure 4.

Our method has not yet required a grant-in-aid to keep it going. On one occasion we tried to get such help, in order to pay for mimeograph paper, the services of a clerk, and one or two additional assistants. Our request was rejected, quite properly, on the grounds that our project was "purely operational." Almost any member of a present-day fundgranting agency can recognize "research" when he sees it. I do think, however, that one should be freed, as I was, from other university demands while introducing a system like ours. And he should not be asked to teach more than two such courses regularly, each serving 100 students or less, unless he has highly qualified assistants upon whom he can depend.

Neither does the method require equipment and supplies that are not already availabe to almost every teacher in the country. Teaching machines, tape recorders, and computers could readily be fitted into the picture. Moving pictures and television could also be used in one or two ways without detriment to the basic educational process. But these are luxuries, based on only partial recognition of our problem, and they could divert us from more important considerations. (Proctors, like computers, may go wrong or break down, but they can often be repaired and they are easily replaced, at very little expense.)

The need for individualized instruction is widely recognized, and the most commonly suggested way of filling this need is automation. I think that this solution is incomplete, especially when applied to the young; and I'd like to mention a personal experience that bears upon the matter.

In the summer of 1966, I made numerous visits to a center for the care and treatment of autistic children.[3] One day, as I stood at the door of a classroom, I saw a boy get up from his chair at the end of a class period and give a soft pat to the object on the desk in front of him. At the same time, he said, with a slight smile, "Good-bye, Teaching Machine!"

This pseudo-social behavior in this fundamentally asocial child amused me at the time. It reminded me of Professor Moore's description of the three-year-old who became irritated when his "talking typewriter" made a mistake, called the device a "big bambam," requested its name, and ended by asking, "Who is your mother?" Today, however, I am not so sure that this is funny. It does suggest that affection may be generated within a child for an electro-mechanical instrument that has been essential to educational reinforcement. Unfortunately, such a machine, in its present form, is unlikely to generalize with human beings in the boy's world, giving to them a highly desirable reinforcing property. In fact, the growth of this type of student-machine relation, if it were the only one, would be a poor substitute for a directly social interaction.

In an earlier report upon our method, I mentioned that it had been anticipated, partially or *in toto,* in earlier studies and I described one of these in some detail. As for current developments by other workers in our field, I have not made any systematic attempt to examine the offerings, even those that deal with college or university instruction. However, I have been impressed by several of them which seem to have points in common with ours, which have met with some success, and which will probably be increasingly heard from in the future.

[3] At the Linwood Children's Center, Ellicott City, Maryland.

One of these is the Audio-Tutorial Approach to the teaching of botany, developed by S. N. Postlethwait at Purdue University (Postlethwait and Novak, 1967). Another is the Socratic-Type Programming of general psychology by Harry C. Mahan (1967) and his associates at Palomar College, in California; and a third is the Interview Technique recently applied by C. B. Ferster and M. C. Perrott (1968) in teaching principles of behavior to graduate students in education at the University of Maryland.

Professor Postlethwait's method places great emphasis upon "independent study sessions" in which students carry out each individual work assignment in the course at their own pace, by means of extensive use of tapes and films. Teaching assistants provide for oral quizzing on major concepts and help the students with difficult assignments. Weekly "small assembly sessions" are used primarily for recitation and the discussion of problems or small research projects; and "general assembly sessions" deal mainly with motivational materials. Postlethwait reports high student interest and greatly improved performance with the use of this technique. "Grades have risen from 6% A's under the conventional system to as high as 25% A's in some semesters. Failures have decreased from 20% in the conventional system to as few as 4%."

"Socratic-Type Programming" is described by Professor Mahan as "a philosophy and technology of instruction which emphasizes student response rather than presentations by the teacher. Its basic media consist of exercises made up of questions and short answers covering the content of a standard text, the text itself, tapes for recording the questions in the exercises, a classroom tape recorder for administering tests, tape duplicating facilities, a listening center in the college library, and student-owned tape recorders for home use whenever possible. Classroom time is devoted largely to the discussion of points covered by the questions. All examinations are the short-answer type and are presented aurally on tape." Students must pass three periodic tests with a score of 85% or better before they are permitted to take a comprehensive final examination. The method does not yet permit "multiple exit" from the course, but Mahan says it is "tending very much in that direction." (1967.)

The Interview Technique, as described by Ferster and Perrott, does permit students to complete the course at different times, and it also approximates the student-and-proctor feature. Progress through the course is possible by verbalizing successive units of course content in a lengthy series of short interviews. The interviews are conducted mainly between students currently enrolled in the course, and any student is free to leave the course when all of his reading assignments have been adequately covered. The interviewer may sometimes be a staff member, as at the beginning of the course, but generally he is a student who has already been interviewed by someone else on the topic in question. The interviews are highly formalized, with the interviewer playing the role of the listener, checker, appraiser, and summarizer. Each interview is an open-book affair, but of such short and sharply defined duration (10 min, as a rule) that the student can do no more than cue himself by reference to the printed page.

The goal of this method is nothing less than fluency with respect to each main feature of the course. Lectures, group discussions, and demonstrations are available at certain times, contingent upon a given stage of advance. Inadequate interviews are rejected, in whole or part, without prejudice, and with suggestions for further study. A product of high quality is guaranteed through staff participation at critical points. A modification of this procedure, which is to include written tests and the employment of advanced-student proctors, is planned by Professor Ferster for the introductory course in psychology at Georgetown University during the coming semester.

In systems like these, and in the one I have centered on, the work of a teacher is at variance with that which has predominated in our time. His public appearances as classroom entertainer, expositor, critic, and debater no longer seem important. His principal job, as Frank Finger (1962) once defined it, is truly "the facilitation of learning in others." He becomes an educational engineer, a contingency manager, with the responsibility of serving the great majority, rather than the small minority, of young men and women who come to him for schooling in the area of his competence. The teacher of tomorrow will not, I think, continue to be satisfied with a 10% efficiency (at best) which makes him an object of contempt by some, commiseration by others, indifference by many, and love by a few. No longer will he need to hold his position by the exercise of functions that neither transmit culture, dignify his status, nor encourage respect for learning in others. No longer will he need to live, like Ichabod Crane, in a world that increasingly begrudges providing him room and lodging for a doubtful service to its young. A new kind of teacher is in the making. To the old kind, I, for one, will be glad to say, "Good-bye!"

I started this paper on a personal note and I would like to end it on one. Twenty-odd years ago, when white rats were first used as laboratory subjects in the introductory course, a student would sometimes complain about his animal's behavior. The beast couldn't learn, he was asleep, he wasn't hungry, he was sick, and so forth. With a little time and a handful of pellets, we could usually show that this was wrong. All that one needed to do was follow the rules. "The rat," we used to say, "is always right."

My days of teaching are over. After what I have said about efficiency, I cannot lay claim to any great success, but my schedule of rewards was enough to maintain my behavior, and I learned one very important thing: *the student is always right.* He is not asleep, not unmotivated, not sick, and he can learn a great deal if we provide the right contingencies of reinforcement. But if we don't provide them, and provide them soon, he too may be inspired to say, "Good-bye!" to formal education.

20 / Administration and Precision Teaching

ERIC HAUGHTON

This article was included for the value it may have for future administrators interested in innovation. The thesis here is the necessity
for precise data in the decision-making process. Too often, argues
the author, educational decisions are made on the basis of intuitive,
biased, impressionistic, anecdotal data, which are especially inadequate when the decision involves the lives of children. This article
raises a number of questions about present-day practices and considers redesigning the current decision-making process.

*Educational decisions have wide-reaching effects on personnel and pupils.
Therefore precise information is required (a) as the basis for change and
(b) to record the effects of administrative changes. Direct records of
classroom behavior, taken by the teacher, charted by the youngsters
themselves, and analyzed by the teacher and advisers can improve the*

Source: Eric Haughton, "Administration and Precision Teaching," *Research
Training Paper* No. 5 (Kansas City: Bureau of Child Research Laboratory, University of Kansas Medical Center, 1967). Reprinted by permission of the author
and the Bureau of Child Research. This research was supported by the United
States Office of Education and the National Institute of Neurological Diseases
and Blindness when the author was a trainee with the Bureau of Child Research
(Grant NB-05362-06). This paper was submitted in partial fulfillment of the
requirements for Education 371 (Spring 1966), under the guidance of Dr. J. O.
Smith. The author thanks Dr. Smith and the members of the seminar for their
contributions to this paper. The author is now a specialist in precision teaching
with the Eugene School District No. 4J, Eugene, Oregon.

efficiency of educational planning. Examples of those records inlcuded in this paper indicate the crucial part such records can play in improving education by wise administrative recommendations and suggestions.

Precise Language

Educational administrators have to make decisions that involve the economy and the efficiency of school systems. These decisions often have implications at various levels. The administrator's responsibilities can be broken into three components: Stimuli, Responses, and Consequences.[1] The S-R-C components of a principal's behavior would look like this:

Stimuli	*Responses*	*Consequences*
State Dept.	Meet requirements	"OK"?
School Board	Run school	Salary, "O.K." ?
Superintendent	Direct	"OK," well-run school
Department Head	Direct	"OK," well-run school
Parents	{ Activate interest	Parent participation
	Offer educational alternatives	
Teachers	{ Supervise	Quality teaching
	Advise	Effective management
Pupils	{ Activate	Qualified graduates
	Discipline	
	Expanded opportunities	

This listing is incomplete, as I have limited the stimuli analyzed to some of the *people* a principal has above or below him in the typical administrative situation.

Mention of the typically pyramidal hierarchy raises the topic of administrative structure. Several writers have gone into the issue of reorganizing the structure of education (Carlson, et. al., 1965; Griffiths, 1959; Meals, 1967). This major problem has brought about a variety of proposals. An alternative is that an efficient educational system based on precise language and methods of data collection is possible for the contemporary educational system. Listing different aspects under the S-R-C simplifies the analysis of shared and dissimilar components. The degree to which components are shared often determines the outcome of administrative decisions.

---

[1] This equation was developed by Ogden R. Lindsley, Ph.D., Professor of Education, University of Kansas. It is identified as IS-DOES and was developed in some detail by Lindsley (1964). The equation has been refined considerably and is now available in an updated form through the Curriculum Bulletin Series, School of Education, University of Oregon, Eugene, Oregon.

Behavior Management: Stimuli

For example, a teacher may report that a child is disturbing the classroom by talking out without permission. In such a situation the teacher's equation would be:

(1) (Teacher) S_1 Pupil talks out R_1"Be quiet."   C?
                  occasionally.

or, as the problem becomes more serious:

(2) (Teacher) S_1 High rate of R_1"BE QUIET!"   C?
                  talking out.

                                     R_2 Complains to   C?
                                         principal.

When the teacher doesn't have a rate record of the target behavior (talking-out), the principal hears only the teacher's anecdotal, highly impressionistic report of the pupil's disruptive target behavior. He cannot tell if this really is a problem, or if the teacher is oversensitive or possibly dislikes the pupil. The principal's components in this situation are:

(3) (Principal) S_2 Complaining R_2"Not really a   C?
                  teacher.   problem."
                                        $_3$ "She is just over-   C?
                                            sensitive."
                                        $_4$ "She dislikes the   C?
                                            pupil."

None of the principal's responses are acting on the problem. Therefore the consequences are difficult to specify. On the other hand, suppose the teacher took a frequency count of the disruptive behavior and plotted the rate. Then the teacher's components would appear:

(4) (Teacher) S_1 Pupil talks out. R_1 "BE QUIET."   C?
                                         $_2$ Takes frequency   C?
                                            count.
                                         $_3$ Plots data. C_{graph}

If the teacher takes the graph to the principal, the formula then becomes:

(5) (Principal) S_1 Graph of dis- R_1 Evaluate rate. C_1 Sees problem
                  ruptive behavior. $_2$ Advise remedia-   clearly.
                                            tion or remove C_2 Helps teacher
                                            pupil from class.   (by reduction in
                                                                      target behav-
                                                                      ior's rate).

The teacher can present data designed to clarify certain aspects of classroom problems for the principal. Moreover, teachers can refine and expand these data and show academic performance rate on the target child, as well as the entire class, indicating the academic deceleration produced by the disruptive behavior. By having such precise, objective information at hand, the principal can act decisively.

These five brief precise formulations of this "talk-out" project do not guarantee innovation, nor do they guarantee remediation. However, the stimulus analysis suggests that the principal will act very differently when presented graphical data instead of anecdotal information. Charted classroom data focus attention on a specific problem and reduce inappropriate social and interpersonal behavior. Presenting graphs to parents also demonstrates the effects of teaching or new procedures more clearly than mere verbal description.

CLASSROOM MANAGEMENT

Gerry is a second-grade pupil. His case will demonstrate the techniques described so far and illustrate the foregoing points. Gerry used to hit his peers several times a day. When the teacher began to count, the frequency of hitting ranged between 15 and 30 hits a day. He hit in lines, at lunch, during classroom activities, and on the schoolyard. To record Gerry's hitting rate, teachers involved in each activity used a wrist counter to record these events. His regular teacher, Carole, and others who supervised Gerry counted each hit. They also continued to handle the problems as they had in the past. After a few days of precise recording and rate computation, we devised an individualized program. The teacher, after checking with the parents to insure their cooperation, began to call the parents after each school session to report the number of hits that occurred during the day. Within five days Gerry stopped hitting. Follow-up records show no return of hitting nor the development of any other inappropriate behavior. The working chart is presented in Figure 1 and also indicates the exact probability of the change occurring by chance. This rate deceleration could have occurred by chance only once in 1,000 times. The equation for this project was:

(1) (Teacher)	S_1 Gerry hits.	R_1 Record and chart.	C_1 Chart of project.
		R_2 Call parents.	C_2 ?
(2) (Gerry)	S_1 Peers.	R_1 Plays.	C_1 Teacher reports appropriate acts.
		R_2 Hits.	C_2 Teacher reports hitting frequency.

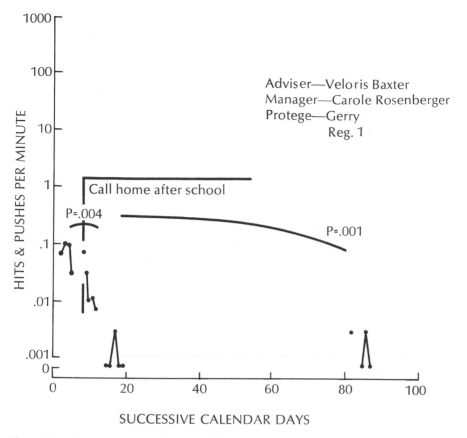

Figure 1. Rapid and permanent deceleration of hitting peers after the teacher phoned the count home each day after school.

One other function of this project included changing the principal's opinion of Carole. Gerry had been so disruptive that questions were raised as to her classroom management capabilities. Concrete and objective information from this project helped Carole demonstrate her management skills. The equations for the principal and teacher might be like this:

Before Project:

(1) (Principal)	S_1 Teacher with problem child.	R_1 "I wonder if she knows how to teach."	C_1 ?"I have to make *some* decision."
(2) (Teacher)	S_1 Gerry hitting.	R_1 Tries to manage. $_2$ Worries about problem.	C_1 No effect. $_2$?

After project:

(1) (Principal) S_1 Teacher has solved problem. R_1 "This teacher knows how to teach." C_1 Revised estimate of teacher.

            $_2$ Gerry doesn't hit.

(2) (Teacher) S_1 Gerry doesn't hit. R_1 Reports appropriate acts to parents. C_1 Better peer relationships.

            $_2$ Acknowledgment of good teaching from principal. $_2$ Continues good work. $_2$ Improvement in students and fair evaluation.

INNOVATION THROUGH PRECISION

The preceding projects were analyzed using IS-DOES equation s. A different symbol represents each behavioral component for each person in the analysis. This type of analytic tool is useful to describe complex interactions and aids the interpretation of available data. I have referred to the type of data that complements an IS-DOES analysis and will describe how to collect these data in the next section.

Exactly what does the analytic tool IS-DOES contribute to our understanding of innovation? In the talk-out project, I placed emphasis on the analysis of stimuli available to a principal and teacher. When a typical educational system is broken into major administrative or managerial units, their relations as stimuli become clear.

Table 1

	Superintendent	Director	Principal	Teacher
STIMULI	Number of administrative units above:			
State level	░	░	░	░
Superintendent		░	░	░
Director of special education			░	░
Principal				░
Parents				░
Teacher				
Pupil (data source)				

Perhaps innovation from upper levels is difficult because stimuli have to sift down through so many people. Conversely, if the teacher should attempt to innovate looking upward through the maze of S-R-C equations, she may be completely decelerated. The teacher can try to introduce change by going up through the administrative maze, but this structure may not accelerate a teacher's innovative behavior.

RESPONSES

The teacher may report disruptive behavior quantitatively or anecdotally. A charted quantitative record will be accepted while unsubstantiated whining or bitching about a pupil may be interpreted as a teacher's "personality deficit." If the teacher's response to the pupil who has been disruptive in the class includes precise performance-rate data on the other children showing marked rate of deceleration in academic areas, the administrator's response will be rapid. He will move to decelerate the disturbance and to accelerate the other pupils' performance rate.

CONSEQUENCES

In the classroom management example, accurate and precise stimuli—charted records of behavior—elicited effective administrative behavior. These stimuli also clarified and enhanced the consequences. Note that consequences could not be specified in several equations. Our ignorance of consequences is a major block to innovation. Consequences are not necessarily shared by those at different educational levels, but increasing the number of shared stimuli and responses increases the number of shared consequences.

Consequences are recognized as an important issue in administrative innovation. Griffiths (1959) refers to anticipated and unanticipated consequences of administrative decisions. Urwick (1957) treats the problem of motivation in detail. None of these writers, however, executes a precise or functional analysis of consequences that follow responses and either accelerate desired reponses or decelerate undesired responses.

Direct Recording

Precise data collection is a major issue in education today. The main component in our system—the pupil—is not adequately or precisely represented. There are no continuous and direct daily records of pupil performance so the effects of various procedures and modification attempts exist only as the impressionistic accounts of pupil behavior. In other production areas accurate records are kept daily. For example, industrial administrators clarify their targets, stimuli, and behaviors through precise, quantitative records. When production begins to lag, the shop manager does not rely on the foreman's impressions. He goes to the production record. Unfortunately, there is no such appeal to *daily* and *accurate* quantitative records in most of today's classrooms.

Over three fourths of the books on school administration I read covered such topics as "clarifying the problem." Although Griffiths (1959; in Miles, 1964) writes about operationism and observational methods, he makes no specific recommendations on appropriate class-room direct-recording techniques. Therefore, educational and particu-larly classroom information tends to be impressionistic, vague, and, consequently, highly personal. Our usual classroom information is a mixture of teacher-pupil behavior rather than a precise, quantitative, and fair representation of pupil behavior.

In fact, no reports (including over fifteen articles and over eight books) I read referred to or employed directly recorded data. Many studies used attitudinal scales (Kendall's report in Miles, 1964). Some studies reported final grades. Several studies used check lists and similar evaluations of pupils by teachers or administrators.

Curriculum Modification

Supervisors often locate new educational materials and wish to have them implemented. While the supervisor's formula or equation is simple:

(6) (Supervisor) S_1 New materials. R_1 Buy. C_1?
                                                      $_2$ Give to teacher. $_2$ Improve
                                                                                                          instruction.

the equation for the teacher is not:

(7) (Teacher) S_1 New materials. R_1 Read instruc- C_1 ?
                                                             tions.
                                                      $_2$ Learn new pro- $_2$?
                                                            cedures.
                                                      $_3$ Implement: $_3$ Better learning.
                                                            a) schedule
                                                            b) introduce to
                                                                the class.

Here is a shared stimulus, i.e., the new materials. Yet there is little or no response required from the supervisor. On the other hand, the teacher must well be prepared before introducing the material to the class, so her response requirements are maximal while the supervisor's are minimal.

In addition, the teacher and supervisor face the usual "post-mortem" testing problem. Achievement tests are given when it is *too late* to do anything about a deficient teaching sequence. Continuous, daily-performance-rate records provide a day-to-day record of how each child is progressing with the new materials. By this method, materials can be continuously evaluated *while* they are being used. Moreover, ineffective materials can be eliminated more rapidly than if just a haphazard guess were being made as to their effectiveness.

CLASSROOM DIRECT-RECORDING

Two major types of academic recording are in use at present. Perhaps the easiest method of recording performances rate is to set a fixed period of five or ten minutes' duration. The pupils are then given more problems than can be completed in this period. This procedure yields total number of problems completed, total number correct, and, by dividing, $\frac{\text{total correct}}{\text{total time}}$ = the rate of problems correct. For example, a child may complete 85 correct problems in 10 minutes or $\frac{85}{10}$ = 8.5 correct per minute. Each day's classroom information is plotted on separate charts for individual pupils. We have found it easier to analyze effects when rate correct and error rates are charted separately, with one chart for each rate. Two examples of these records comprise Figure 2 and 3.

Figure 2 is the arithmetic performance rate (correct rate) of a sixth-grade pupil. Figure 3 is pegboard rate for a child in a preschool classroom for disturbed children. Figure 4 shows that a publicly displayed graph showing rate increases above the previous mid-rate. Thus public display of gains helped accelerate Lewie's multiplication facts. Lewie was one of eleven pupils identified during full classroom record-

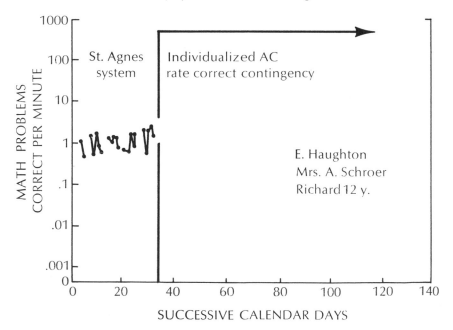

Figure 2. **Individualized consequence accelerates arithmetic rate correct in a regular classroom.**

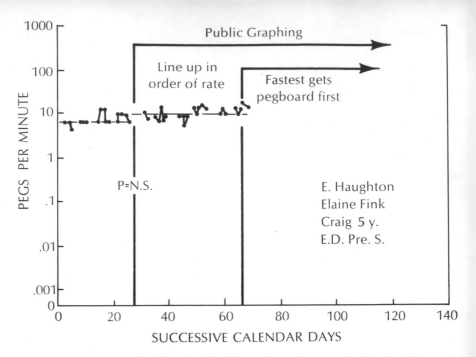

Figure 3. Acceleration of peg-board rate using a classroom natural consequence.

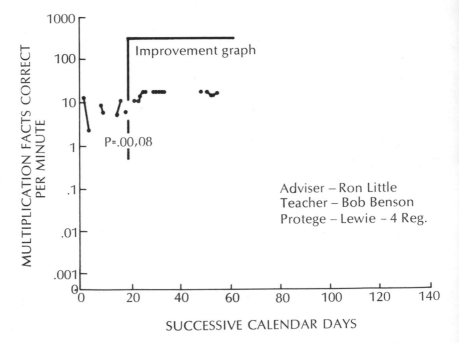

Figure 4. Rate correct on basic multiplication facts accelerates after introducing a public improvement graph.

248

ing of basic multiplication fact performance rates. The improvement graph helped accelerate all protégé rates except Connie's. Figure 5 shows that she remained at her usual correct rate of about three facts per minute. Connie required another administrative decision. We decided to try individual tutoring. Ray tutored Connie and produced a marked performance acceleration within five days. This change would have occurred by chance three times out of a trillion.

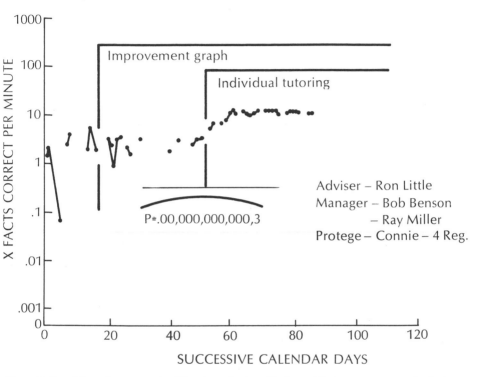

Figure 5. Connie's performance rate did not accelerate with the public improvement graph. Contacts with a tutor accelerated and maintained her performance rate.

A second recording procedure requires continuous monitoring all of the time. However, this complicates the computation because the division changes all the time. Using 1, 10, 100, 1,000 minutes simplifies rate computation since you simply move the decimal point. The alternative procedure requires recording the exact time a pupil starts and stops assignments. The previous record is referred to as a time sample whereas this is a continuous, daily record. This procedure requires close supervision if the teacher makes the entries, however, pupil recording simplifies the collection of these data no matter which technique you choose. Performance rate is computed as before, $\frac{\text{total correct}}{\text{total time}}$ = rate correct.

These records are made of the pupil's behavior, often in a worksheet or in a workbook. Therefore, because they are written and objectively scored, they are not contaminated by observer bias. Precise records such as these give the teacher accurate information.

Summary

Educational innovation is in more demand than ever before. Pressures come from an exploding population, rapidly expanding amounts of information, and rising expectations of education's contribution to our society. At the same time that the quantity of education is increasing there is greater emphasis on quality work, the development of mastery, and the production of well-qualified graduates.

Traditionally, educators have spoken in global terms. Our literature is full of nonspecific terms such as "understanding," "comprehension," "concept formation," "task orientation," and "perception." Today these terms are being replaced by specific component descriptions and fully developed equations (IS-DOES) describing specific student behavior so a precise definition often prescribes the type of teaching and may in part define educational materials. Precise description of administrator's responses, what he does, also leads us away from global generalities and into a careful, functional analysis. Therefore, administrative decisions can become more and more practical and effectively attained.

Although we may conduct precise and refined analyses of administrative decisions and educational sequences, we still lack accurate criterion data. These data must come from pupils and must be sensitive enough to pick up behavioral changes produced by our management and advising procedures. In the past, educational experimenters often attempted to measure effects on pupils by analyzing questionnaires given to pupils and teachers. However, direct recording of the pupil's behavior introduces precise and accurate data, thus reducing teacher bias and impressionistic evaluations. While information such as that plotted in Figure 1 aids classroom remediation of daily pupil performance rates, Figures 2 and 3 let the pupil tell us immediately and directly of classroom changes in his performance.

General and special education needs precision. Perhaps the need is greater in general education than in other educational settings for prevention of educational problems.

Our responsibility is to educate pupils economically and efficiently. Therefore, we need the most precise behavior specifications and records available. If we believe that the child is always right, then we must have sensitive, valid records of target behaviors. A complete IS-DOES equation consists of the functional description, whereas continuous direct recording will aid the functional analysis of classroom behaviors. Precise teaching that is the product of combining IS-DOES and direct recording gives the administrator the information he needs for making or changing decisions.

Accurate continuous data are a firm base for the evaluation of innovations. Since the pupil's performance rate is an accurate, sensitive summary of his work, we have unbiased records of the effects of educational variables. Armed with accurate information based on precision teaching procedures, the educational innovator can substantiate his decisions on data from the ultimate educational arbiter, the pupil.

References

Carlson, R. O., et al. 1965. *Change processes in the public schools.* Eugene, Oregon: University of Oregon Press.

Griffiths, D. C. 1959. *Administrative theory.* New York: Appleton-Century Crofts.

Lindsley, O. R. 1964. Direct measurement and prosthesis of retarded behavior. *J. Educ.,* 62–81.

Meals, D. W. 1967. Heuristic models for systems planning. *Phi Delta Kappan* 48: 199–203.

Miles, M. B. 1964. *Innovation in education.* New York: Teachers College, Columbia University.

Urwick, L. F. 1965. *The Pattern of Management.* Minneapolis: University of Minnesota Press.

21 / Effects of Group Contingent Events upon Classroom Noise

GILBERT W. SCHMIDT AND ROGER E. ULRICH

If there is any one problem that gets under the skin of most beginning teachers (and some not-so-beginning teachers), it is that of
classroom discipline. These studies by Gilbert Schmidt and Roger
Ulrich were conducted in an actual classroom. They demonstrate that
student's behavior can be effectively changed by means of relatively
minor changes such as adding time to the much-desired gym period.
It is another example of the teacher's discovering what the students
will work for and using that knowledge to achieve classroom goals—
a principle applicable in all educational environments.

*The first study investigated a group control procedure for suppression
of excessive sound-intensity levels in a regular public school classroom.
Reinforcement consisted of a 2-min addition to the class gym period
and a 2-min break after maintenance of an unbroken 10-min quiet
period as monitored on a decibel meter. Transgressions of the sound
limit (42 decibels) resulted in a delay of reinforcement by the resetting
of the timer to the full 10-min interval. The results indicated that these*

Source: Gilbert W. Schmidt and Roger E. Ulrich, "Effects of Group Contingent
Events upon Classroom Noise," *Journal of Applied Behavior Analysis* 2 (1969):
171–79. Copyright © 1969 by the Society for the Experimental Analysis of Behavior, Inc. Reprinted by permission of the authors and publisher.

procedures were highly effective in suppression and control of sound intensities. The second experiment utilized a similar procedure coupled with a procedure of eliminating out-of-seat behavior. Experiment III studied the effects of Exp. II procedures on a single student's out-of-seat behavior rate. All procedures were found effective.[1]

A number of studies clearly indicate that the systematic application of operant conditioning techniques has been highly effective in modifying a variety of behavioral problems (Ullmann and Krasner, 1965; Krasner and Ullmann, 1965; Ulrich, Stachnik, and Mabry, 1966). Thus far, the application of these techniques has been used primarily within special educational settings and with individuals rather than groups. The present study investigated the utilization of operant principles in a regular public school classroom using the combined behavior of a group of persons as the dependent variable.

Experiment I: Control of Pupil-Produced Noise

The first experiment investigated a group control procedure designed to suppress excessive classroom sound. The class was allowed a 2-min addition to the gym period and a 2-min break contingent upon maintaining an unbroken 10-min quiet period as monitored on a decibel meter. Direct contingencies were not placed on other classroom behaviors.

METHOD

Subjects. A class of 29 fourth-grade elementary students, 14 boys and 15 girls, was selected because of excessive noise during their free-study period. This was a regular public school class with most of the children coming from lower-middle- and middle-class backgrounds.

Apparatus. The experiment was conducted in a typical classroom equipped with desks and facilities for 29 students. A General Radio

[1] This paper is a report of a study conducted jointly by The Behavior Research Laboratory at Western Michigan University and the Kalamazoo Valley Intermediate School District, Albert Bradfield, Superintendent. In addition to the above-named institutions the project received support from several other sources: (1) The Extramural Research Fund, State Department of Mental Health, Lansing, Michigan, and (2) Kalamazoo County Mental Health Board. We are especially grateful for the encouragement of Marland Bluhm, Director, Special Education, Kalamazoo Valley Intermediate School District, and Ken Otis, Superintendent, Vicksburg Public Schools and the Vicksburg School Board, who not only allowed but encouraged us to attempt this project within their district. Finally, a very special thanks to Mrs. Smink, Principal of the Indian Lake School, and teachers Pat Mahaney and Donnal Newell Wood, whose cooperation made this possible. Reprints are available from Roger Ulrich, Department of Psychology, Western Michigan University, Kalamazoo, Michigan.

Corporation model 710-A sound-level meter was used to measure the sound intensities during all phases of the experiment. An SRA electric timer with a buzzer was used to signal the time periods. A whistle was used as a signal to the pupils when they had exceeded the sound intensity limits. A stopwatch attached to the clipboard, which held the data sheets, indicated the time intervals used in recording the data.

Observation procedures. The basic data for the study consisted of the decibel (db) readings from the dial of the sound-level meter. The observer recorded the data from a position in the rear center of the room. Recording was done on sheets of paper attached to a clipboard. Readings were taken every 3 min on the minute during the baseline phase and every 1 min on the minute during the experimental and reversal phases. The change to 1-min interval recordings was to increase the sensitivity of measurement during the experimental, reversal, and follow-up phases. Frequent reliability checks were accomplished by having two observers simultaneously record individual sessions. Reliability, in this case, reflected the degree to which two observers obtained the same average decibel reading during 20-min observation periods. The smaller score was divided by the larger score. The interobserver reliability was found to exceed 95% in all cases.

Procedure. The study was conducted during a free-study period that occurred daily, Monday through Friday, sometime between 9:00 A.M. and 11:00 A.M. It was during these periods that the class had been noted to be excessively noisy. The sessions recorded ranged in duration from 40 to 60 min, depending upon completion of the morning's activities.

For purposes of this study, the entire class of 29 students was treated as a single responding organism. The decibel intensity readings are a total of the noise produced by the entire class.

After the 10-day baseline period recordings and before the first experimental phase, the teacher informed the pupils of the procedures by which they, as a group, would earn extra gym time.

They were told the following:

A timer will be set at ten minutes and be allowed to run to zero, at which time a buzzer will sound. Each time the buzzer sounds, you (the class) will receive two extra minutes added to your gym period, and a two-minute break to talk, ask questions, sharpen pencils, or whatever before beginning the next ten-minute period. If, however, you become too noisy at any time during the ten-minute period, Mr. _____ will blow a whistle to let you know and reset the timer back to ten minutes regardless of how many minutes have gone by.

During the reversal phase, the students were told simply that the previous conditions were not in effect. Data were taken without explanation to the students during the follow-up.

It was arbitrarily decided that the noise-level limit be set at
42 db. Thus, the experimenter constantly maintaining the sound meter
dial would sound the whistle and reset the timer for each class-produced
noise that exceeded 42 db. A 42-db limit proved reasonable since the
room without students registered between 36 and 37 db. Sound levels
near 42 db were found to be generally acceptable to the teaching staff.

RESULTS

The data for all phases of the experiment are presented in Figure 1. Each
point on the graph represents the average sound-level reading for one
session and the vertical lines denote the mean deviation of the sound.
The ordinate indicates the sound-level reading in decibels of sound
intensity and the abscissa denotes the session with the vertical lines
separating the various phases of the experiment. The first phase represents data collected before any contingencies were placed on the classroom sound level, the first experimental phase shows the results of
Phase I conditions, the reversal phase is the return to noncontingent
conditions, and the second experimental phase is the reinstatement of
sound contingencies.

Evidence of the degree of suppression of sound intensity can
be seen by comparing the average sound-level readings of the baseline,
experimental, reversal, and second experimental phase of the study. The
mean readings of the 10 sessions of baseline data in decibels were
52, 52, 52, 50, 55.5, 50.5, 52, 50, 55.5, and 52. The first session of the
experimental phase shows an immediate drop from the preceding mean

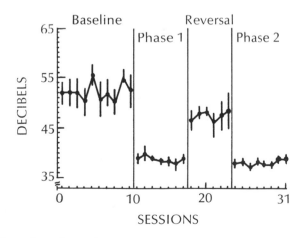

Figure 1. The effects of sound control procedures on the classroom noise level. Each point represents
the average sound-level reading for one session with vertical lines denoting the mean deviation.

baseline reading of 52.5 to a mean of 39 db, a drop of 13.5 db in sound intensity. The mean 39-db reading indicates that the students were producing little extraneous noise, since the classroom without the students present registered a sound level between 36 and 37 db. The other readings during Phase I averaged 40, 39, 38.5, 38.5, 38, and 39 db per session. During the reversal period, when the baseline conditions were again put into effect, there was an immediate increase in sound intensity per session and averages of 46.5, 48, 48.5, 46, 47.5, and 48.5 db occurred. Although intermediate to the baseline and experimental phases, these readings more closely approximate baseline. During Phase II, when the sound contingencies were again in effect, the sound level lowered to averages of 38, 38.5, 37.5, 38.5, 38, 38, 39, and 39 db per session. As was true in Phase I, this drop was immediate with no apparent transition or gradual reduction of sound level during the first or subsequent sessions.

Figure 2 provides examples of readings taken during individual sessions. The top portion of the figure represents readings taken every 3 min during Sessions, 1, 4, 7, and 10 (baseline). Phase I of Figure 2 shows the recordings taken each minute during Sessions 11, 13, 15, and 17 while Sessions 18, 20, 21, and 23 represent samples of the reversal phase. Sessions 24, 26, 29, and 31 show recordings taken from the second experimental phase. These sessions are typical of each phase and show that the sound levels were uniform throughout each session as well as throughout each session within the phase. The sessions shown in Figure 2 are the first session, two intermediate sessions, and the last session of each phase.

DISCUSSION

The results of Exp. I show that, under certain specific circumstances, control and suppression of sound-intensity levels can be accomplished in a regular elementary school classroom. The immediate increase of sound intensity during the reversal and its immediate suppression with reinstatement of reinforcement contingencies strongly indicate that the contingencies, in effect, were the crucial variable. While the additional gym time, as well as the 2-min breaks, may have been reinforcing for most students, it need not have necessarily been so for all. Peer consequences in the form of threatening gestures, arm moving, and facial expression were observed being directed at more noisy members of the class. These expressions were also directed at special teachers and the school nurse who were observed entering the room during the quiet periods. Such behaviors on the part of certain students may have had some effect on maintaining quiet.

Quay, Werry, McQueen, and Sprague (1966) pointed out that

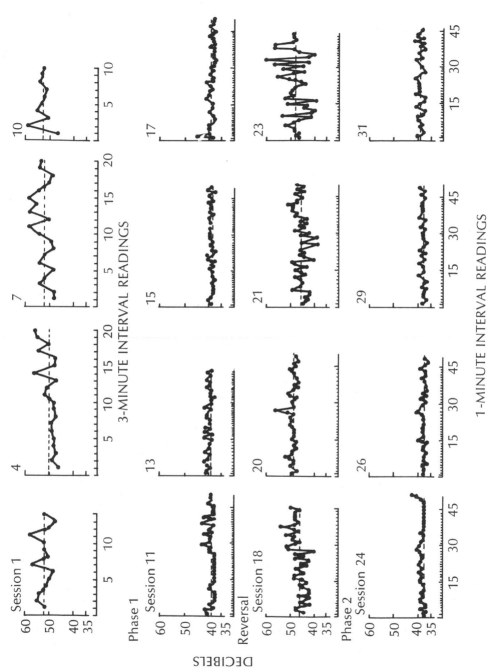

Figure 2. Typical examples of sound-level readings taken during individual sessions of all four phases. Dotted horizontal lines indicate mean reading for each session.

the economics of public schools require the development of group techniques that will allow children to be handled by as few adults as possible. They further point out that it is crucial at this stage that the techniques developed on an individual basis be extended to group situations. The present experiment provided an example of a technique that allows for handling a group as an individual responding organism. In developing methods that are both economically feasible and practical for application to the entire classroom, group procedures such as described here probably hold the most promise of success and acceptance by concerned teachers.

The apparent effectiveness of this technique in suppressing out-of-seat behavior and disturbing antics further suggests its application in the control of individual behavior problems. It may also be helpful in promoting increased learning because studying is generally quite compatible with quietness.

Experiment II: Control of Noise and Out-of-Seat Behavior and Its Effect upon Teacher Reprimands

In the previous experiment, the teacher noted that the children seemed to be better behaved in relation to their out-of-seat behavior. In this study, data were collected not only on sound level, but on out-of-seat behavior and teacher reprimands as well. During Phase I, contingencies were placed on sound level only with 2-min additional gym period allowed for each unbroken 5-min quiet period. No breaks between quiet periods were allowed. During Phase II, special contingencies of a 5-min loss of gym time were levied on individuals who exceeded the sound level or were found inappropriately out of their seats. Teacher reprimands were recorded throughout all phases. Follow-up phase data were recorded the following school year.

METHOD

Subjects. A class of 28 second-grade elementary students, 13 boys and 15 girls, was selected for this experiment, again due to excessive noise and other behaviors conflicting with ongoing small reading groups. The children were from the same locale and background and attended the same school as the subjects of Exp. I.

Apparatus. This experiment was conducted in a regular classroom very similar to that described in Exp. I. The apparatus for Phase I was the same as that used in Exp. I.

In Phase II, a common household interval timer with a bell signal was used to control out-of-seat behavior.

Observation procedures. Sound-level data were recorded by an observer in the rear center of the classroom monitoring the decibel readings dial as in Exp. I. Sound intensities were recorded every minute on the minute throughout all phases.

In addition, every minute on the half minute, the observer recorded the number of students inappropriately out of their seats at that moment. Inappropriate out-of-seat behavior included any student found out of his seat and not directly enroute to or from the reading materials table.

Every teacher-initiated reprimand to the class at large was indicated by an X recorded beneath the 10-sec interval space in which it occurred. The teacher was unaware that reprimand was defined as any statement such as "Sit down" or "Be quiet, it's too noisy in here" when not directed at one individual as the recipient. Points at which reinforcement or punishment for sound level occurred were similarly indicated on the data sheets. A "D" was used to indicate the point at which the out-of-seat bell sounded and the number of those punished indicated by the number following it.

Interobserver reliability checks were made on the sound-level data by having two observers record readings from the sound meter dial for 20 min. Reliability was calculated by dividing the largest mean reading into the smallest. These checks yielded interobserver reliabilities in excess of 99%. Reliability checks were performed for teacher reprimands by having two observers record the number of reprimands occurring over a 30-min period. The larger number was then divided into the smaller number, yielding interobserver reliabilities of 100%. Interobserver reliabilities were also 100% for out-of-seat tallies by a similar procedure. Two observers recorded the number of students out of their seat every minute on the half minute for 20 min. These tallies were totaled and the largest total was divided into the smallest total.

Procedure. This experiment had five phases. All phases, including the follow-up phase, were conducted during a morning reading class from approximately 8:30 to 9:30 A.M., Monday, Tuesday, Thursday, and Friday. The teacher reported that the excessive noise and the problem of keeping the students at their respective desks without giving each of them her full attention made this particular period especially troublesome to her.

During these periods, small groups of students attended 20-min teacher-led reading sessions held in the rear corner of the classroom. The corner in which these groups were held was partitioned off on one side by a cardboard divider, with the end facing the class left open. If the teacher's voice was loud enough to register on the sound-intensity meter, the minute reading was taken when she paused or terminated her speech. This seldom occurred.

During the 13 baseline sessions, the data were recorded as previously indicated. There were no direct experimenter-induced contingencies in effect throughout this phase.

Phase I: Directly before the first session of Phase I, the teacher read the following message to the class:

> The class has been too noisy and disruptive during the time that I am working with the reading groups, so we are going to let you earn extra time in the gym by being extra quiet. Mr. _____ will set the timer clock for five minutes. Each time the five minutes are up, a buzzer will sound and you will have two minutes extra added to your gym period. The room captain will put marks on the board to show how many extra minutes you have earned. If you become too noisy, Mr. _____ will blow the harmonica and set the timer back to the start of the five minutes without the buzzer ringing.

These procedures were adhered to throughout Phase I without contingencies being placed directly on out-of-seat behavior. The sound-intensity limit used was arbitrarily set at 42 db as in Exp. I. Thus, the harmonica was blown and the timer reset for sound intensities exceeding the 42-db limit, except when reading groups were changing. During these interludes, readings were not taken because of necessary noise created by moving chairs.

Phase II. Directly before the first session of Experimental Phase II, the teacher informed the class of the following procedure and changes. They were informed that they would now have to earn all of their gym period by the method used in Phase I. Under the Phase II conditions, however, the class was allowed to earn 3 min for every unbroken five-min quiet interval. Further, individual pupils who alone created noise in excess of the 42-db limit, such as by yelling across the room or slamming a door, were required to write their names on the blackboard. For each such infraction, they lost 5 min of their individual gym time.

To control out-of-seat behavior, an interval timer with a bell device was continuously set at varied intervals. Each time the timer bell rang, any students discovered out of their seat and not enroute to or from the reading material were also required to place their names on the blackboard and forfeit 5 min of their gym time. During the first sessions, the timer interval averaged approximately 5 min. This interval was lengthened, reducing the number of bells per session, until it was phased out by the last four Phase II sessions.

During the reversal phase, all conditions were returned to baseline with no contingencies placed upon either the classroom as a whole or upon individuals. The gym period was again established as 15 min in length with no extra time available.

The follow-up data were recorded over five sessions during

October and November of the following school year. Conditions were
the same as those of baseline, the only major difference being a different teacher.

RESULTS

Figure 3 (top graph) presents the sound-intensity data for all phases of
the experiment. As in Exp. I, the class as a whole was treated as a single
responding organism with each point on the graph representing the

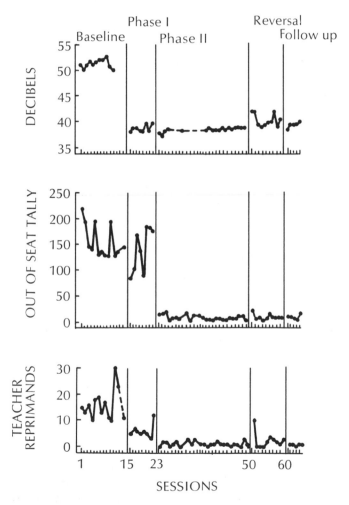

Figure 3. Top: each point represents average sound-level reading for one session. Middle: each point
represents cumulative tally of out-of-seat behavior per 45-min session. Bottom: each point indicates
the number of teacher reprimands directly to the class per 45-min session. Dotted lines without
points represent equipment malfunction.

average sound-level reading for one session. The vertical axis indicates the sound-level readings in decibels and the horizontal axis denotes the session with vertical lines separating phases of the experiment. The dotted lines indicate the sessions during which the sound meter was malfunctioning. During these sessions, conditions did not change because the experimenter estimated sound level and acted accordingly.

The degree of suppression of classroom sound level is evidenced by a comparison of the baseline sound-level with those of the sound-level mean during Phases I and II and reversal phase of the experiment. It can be seen that this was an immediate drop of 12 db. The level during reversal tended to be slightly higher. The number of timer resets that occurred during Phase I averaged 13 per 45-min session, while during Phase II, only 3.86 punishments were levied per session.

Figure 3 (middle graph) represents the cumulative out-of-seat tallies recorded every minute on the half minute. Each point on the graph represents the cumulative tally per 45-min period. The ordinate represents the accumulated tally for each 45-min session and the abscissa denotes the session. Each point represents the summation of these tallies for the first 45 min of each session. Sessions 30 and 34 were omitted because they were less than 45 min in duration. Figure 3 (middle graph) shows that many of the students were out of their seats during the baseline period with little change occurring during the Phase I condition. During Phase II, an immediate and very substantial drop is noted in out-of-seat behavior. This level was maintained throughout the Phase II and reversal sessions. Individual sound-level readings for Phases I and II are similar to those shown for Exp. I. Figure 3 (bottom graph) shows teacher behavior in terms of number of reprimands directed to the class at large per 45-min session. The ordinate represents the actual number of reprimands per session and the abscissa denotes the session number. As can be seen in Fig. 3 (bottom graph), teacher reprimands were highest during baseline with a considerable reduction during Phase I. Phase II data show drastic reduction over the baseline level. A slight increase was noted during reversal, especially the first reversal session. Again, Sessions 30 and 34 were eliminated because they were less than 45 min.

DISCUSSION

The results of Exp. II, consonant with the results of Exp. I, again clearly indicate that under certain specific circumstances, control and suppression of sound-intensity levels can be demonstrated in the elementary school classroom, in this instance, even with younger second graders. Although the data indicate substantial sound-level reduction in Phase I, the average number of timer resettings, relative to the average number of resettings in Phase II (13 to fewer than three) indicates that greater numbers of infractions were occurring, usually between decibel recordings. This may in part have been due largely to less disciplined individuals rather than the group as a whole, since these occurrences largely dropped out with the institution of added individualized contingencies in Phase II. The sound data further indicate that the method is feasible without allowing timeout periods as frequently or of the unstructured type used in Exp. II. This finding suggests that the longer-term reinforcer of accrued gym time in itself may be sufficient to maintain more quiet behaviors.

The technique used here for control of out-of-seat behavior is a simple one that a teacher alone could easily operate or could allow another student to operate. Its effectiveness with these relatively young students implies possible wide application. The present data further suggests that it can be gradually discontinued without loss in effectiveness. This may be because behaviors incompatible with being out of one's seat have been sufficiently strengthened.

The reversal phase, while showing some increase in unwanted behaviors, was still relatively stable at low levels. This may be related to the length of the experimental control phases. The 10 reversal sessions were taken over the last three weeks of school.

During the follow-up phase the next school year, the class was being taught by the same teacher who had previously had them as first graders. It was her opinion that they were very much improved in conduct, particularly in regard to noisiness and being out of their seats. Her impression was supported by the follow-up data. Thus, it appeared that the changes effected in the previous school year were lasting, at least over the summer and following fall.

It is unlikely that the observer's presence influenced the class's behavior during the follow-up phase, since he appeared to be able to enter any classroom at the school without arousing the students' interest or attention. Further, the teacher's impression was that the class did not behave any differently when the observer was not present. Without reliability data, these subjective opinions must be presented in a guarded manner.

The teacher during the follow-up phase, however, had had two years' experience and had been enrolled in the in-service training course in behavior modification for teachers, and thus may have inadvertently been able to exercise increased controls over the class's behavior. She was not yet, however, using any defined behavioral control techniques for this class during or before the follow-up.

While the effects of the changes in procedure in Phase II were effective in gaining control of the classroom noise level and out-of-seat behavior, the fact that both the revised sound-control contingencies and institution of the timer for control of out-of-seat behavior were simultaneous makes the assessment of the effect of each move difficult. Changing these conditions at different times would allow a cleaner analysis of the effects of each condition.

Experiment III: Affecting an Individual's Out-of-Seat Behavior during Group Control Procedures

This experiment followed the behavior of one individual student through all phases of Exp. II. Emphasis was placed on the student's excessive out-of-seat behavior, which was her only noted problem. The behavior was greatly reduced with the institution of a variable-interval timer and bell. Whenever the bell rang, every student inappropriately out of his seat lost 5 min of his gym period.

METHOD

Subject. The subject of this study was a 7-yr-old girl in the second-grade class used in Exp. II. She was chosen for her excessive out-of-seat behaviors which were deemed a problem by the classroom teacher. Other undesirable behaviors, such as talking, etc., were minimal.

Procedure. Data for all phases of this study were collected simultaneously with Exp. II data. The subject's data were very discrete and easily observable, since out-of-seat was defined as any occurring whenever she was not in contact with the seat portion of her chair. A reliability check indicated reliability of 100% between two observers over a 20-min period. Recordings were taken on a 10-sec interval basis. At the end of any 10-sec interval, the observer marked a box on the sheet divided into six boxes per minute (one per 10-sec interval) and 5 min per line. An O was placed in each box if the subject left her seat at any time during that 10-sec interval. A line was placed in the box if she was seated in any manner or permissibly out of her seat (teacher permission for leaving seat or going to and from reading materials).

The observation sessions varied in length, with the shortest being 20 min. Most were near 30 min. Observations were omitted while she attended her reading group. The procedures and apparatus are those described in Exp. II.

RESULTS

Figure 4 indicates the per cent of time the subject was inappropriately out of her seat during the observation period. The baseline data indicate a relatively high and consistent rate of out-of-seat behavior (compared to other students). During Phase I, this rate of out-of-seat behavior increased. During the first session of Phase II, the subject was discovered out of her seat on one occasion and for the remainder of the session remained seated. The subject's out-of-seat behavior was virtually eliminated. As indicated by the reversal, it maintained itself at an even lower rate after the contingencies were removed. The follow-up data indicate that the change had been maintained.

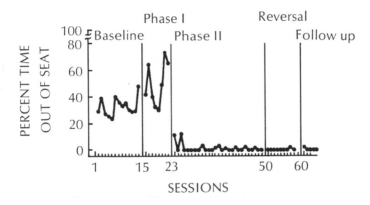

Figure 4. Each point indicates the per cent of time the subject was inappropriately out of her seat during the observation period.

DISCUSSION

This study represents the behavior of one individual within the class under varied experimental and baseline conditions. The experimenters' somewhat subjective impression suggests that the high degree of suppression of undesirable behavior was probably not as marked in many of the other more deviantly behaving individuals.

At present, the experimenters can offer not explanation for the rise in out-of-seat behavior in Phase I, since the low rate of talking was not significantly altered throughout the experiment. The rapid and highly effective suppression noted in Phase II strongly suggests that the specific interval timer contingencies were responsible for the behavior change.

The maintenance of this low rate of out-of-seat behavior may have in part been the result of reinforcement of the incompatible behaviors required in completion of work. The teacher reported a higher rate of work completed by the student. Praise and better grades (sometimes leading to further reinforcement) followed this.

General Discussion

Perhaps the most valuable contribution of the tactics of behavior control utilized in this study is in terms of preventing the occurrence of problem behavior. With an understanding of the variables which, when manipulated, can eliminate nonadaptive classroom behavior, teachers will be in a position to program their classrooms so that the probability of such behavior occurring is minimized by the strengthening of more desirable behaviors compatible with educational goals and good adjustment. In cases where maladaptive behaviors do arise, they could often be dealt with before they were allowed to reach critical proportions.

Further, such tactics used effectively in eliminating and controlling behavior problems may have the added advantage of freeing the teacher so that he might have more time to do a better job of teaching. In order to accomplish this successfully, these tactics must be more often applied to students as a group, rather than as individuals. These studies show that group control procedures are possible in terms of economic feasibility and practicability.

References

Krasner, L., and Ullmann, L. 1965. *Research in behavior modification.* New York: Holt, Rinehart & Winston, Inc.

Quay, H. C., Werry, J. S., McQueen, M., and Sprague, R. L. 1966. Remediation of the conduct problem child in the special class setting. *Exceptional Child* 31: 509–15.

Ullmann, L., and Krasner, L. 1965. *Case studies in behavior modification.* New York: Holt, Rinehart & Winston, Inc.

Ulrich, R. Stachnik, T., and Mabry, J. 1966. *Control of human behavior.* Glenview, Ill.: Scott, Foresman and Company.

22 / Self-Application of Behavior Modification Techniques by Teenagers

ANN DELL DUNCAN

There is something about the following article that is just plain fun. In effect, it says that you can modify your own behavior if you follow a set of simple principles.

On reading this study, a psychology professor (who shall remain anonymous) decided it was time he lost a little weight. Using a counter (see p. 386) to establish the rate of between-meal snacking, he first established a baseline. As a demonstration of progress, he brought a scale into his class (Principles of Behavior Modification, no less) and once a week there was a public weigh-in. Figures 1 and 2 show frequency of between-meal intake and weight over the five-week period.

Curiously, the technique works for persons other than teen-agers.

Source: Ann Dell Duncan, "Self-Application of Behavior Modification Techniques by Teenagers," *Research Training Paper* No. 11 (Kansas City: Bureau of Child Research Laboratory, University of Kansas Medical Center, 1968). Reprinted by permission of the author and the Bureau of Child Research. This project was supported in part by the National Institute of Neurological Diseases and Blindness (NB-05362-05) and by grants from the National Institute of Child Health and Human Development (HD-00870-05) to the Bureau of Child Research. Appreciation is extended to the administration and faculty of Shawnee Mission North High School and especially to Mr. David Roberts, psychology instructor, who initiated this project. Charlie Galloway led one of the groups and gave willingly of his time and efforts to make this project a success. To the young adults whose enthusiasm and interest were the sparks of this project goes the author's deepest appreciation, for without their behavior this study would not have been possible. To Dr. Ogden R. Lindsley, mentor extraordinary, go the author's thanks for stimulating her towards this research boulevard and for his perceptive assistance in all phases of this project.

267

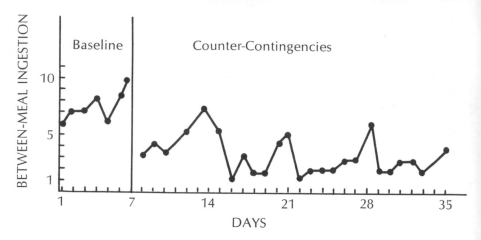

Figure 1. Number of between-meal snacks for a five-week period.

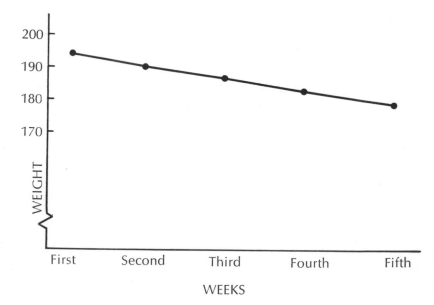

Figure 2. Weight loss during the five-week experimental period.

Would you like to lose weight? Stop swearing and being sarcastic? Have beautiful fingernails? Teen-agers reported in this study wanted to, and did. They found by applying precise behavior management techniques to specific problems they could experience that elusive phenomenon called self-control.

      Definitions of self-control vary with the researcher. For Kanfer (1966), self-control is the behavior which occurs in the presence of conflicting response tendencies. Goldiamond (1965) prefers to discuss the functional relationship between the individual's behavior and the environment. Ferster et al. (1962) refer to self-control as "some specific performances which will lower the disposition to emit the behavior to be controlled (p. 88)."

The elusiveness of self-control may be in the lack of a precise definition. For the moralists among us, self-control is doing what is right. For the psychodynamically oriented, it is achieved by controlling the inner forces and redirecting them towards more constructive patterns. For this researcher, self-control is *procedurally* defined as the self-selection and application of behavior modification techniques.

Teachers (Lindsley, 1966), parents of children with retarded behaviors (Sebastian, 1967), and a community agency (Holzschuh, 1968) have successfully applied precise behavior-management techniques. These adults were given brief instructions in behavior analysis and sent out to record one or more behaviors (Lindsley, 1967a). Teen-agers in this study learned to analyze their selected behavior targets by recording and plotting daily rates of occurrence. They precisely measured the effects of altering their environments with contingent consequences. They found that the more precise the measurement, the more successful the management.

Method

PARTICIPANTS

Fifty-five high-school seniors (enrolled in a psychology class at a suburban high school) volunteered to participate in this project. Their previous exposure to behavior modification consisted of reading ten pages of an introductory psychology text section about Skinner and pigeon operant conditioning. The median age was 17. There were 28 girls and 17 boys. These were not deviant young adults, just normal teen-agers finishing up the last semester of their high-school careers.

PROCEDURES

The psychology instructor asked the volunteers to sign up for one of three meeting nights. The author met with two groups; one at the high school, the other at the medical center. The third group met with another graduate student at his apartment. Each group met for approximately two hours once a week for eight weeks. They presented their projects to the other group members. There were no formal lectures.

The teen-agers learned behavior modification in three steps: pinpointing their behavior targets, daily recording and plotting the rate of occurrence, and altering the environment. The target behaviors were self-selected, the movement rates self-recorded, and alterations self-selected and self-applied. Contingencies were set for attendance at every group meeting. For example, in order to come to the second meeting, each was required to record six days of data.

EQUIPMENT

The only equipment provided was tally sheets and six-cycle semi-logarithmic graph paper which has been standardized to facilitate across behavior comparisons (Lindsley, 1967a). Three alternative types of counters were suggested. The Domatic Wrist Counter (Lindsley, 1968), a less expensive, plastic golf-score caddy, or a knitting stitch counter which fits over the end of a pencil. The majority of the students used the plastic golf-score caddy which may be purchased from local sporting goods stores for about $.85.

Results

Thirty-three of the 55 enrollees turned in reports of successful behavior modification projects. Ninety-three percent of the 33 projects were deceleration targets. The six projects selected for detailed presentation include one each of the four most common deceleration targets. Figure 3 summarizes the median emission rates of the deceleration targets before modification. The ranges of these phase-one medians and the median of that distribution are reported. The six-cycle semi-logarithmic plot facilitates comparisons across behavior topography. It is interesting to note that with an equal number of projects, nail-biting rates cover four log-cycles (from five per day to once a minute), whereas face touching only covers one-half of one log-cycle (from four to eight times every 100 minutes).

FOOD REACHES

Teen-age girls select losing weight as a target more frequently than boys. Ferster's (1962) obese women attempted to decelerate their weight and caloric intake. If decelerating weight on the body is the target, then the measure should not be the bathroom scale. Rather, the more precise measure would be the behavior which puts pounds on in the first place —that is, food reaches, snacks, or chews per minute.

Debbie recorded her rate of eating snacks between meals (Figure 4). During phase one, her median snack rate was .007 per minute. In other words, she ate seven snacks during 16½ hours. After it was

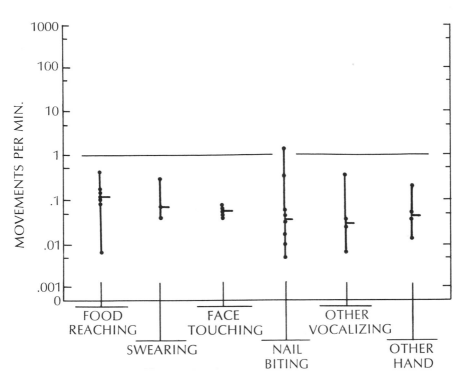

Figure 3. Phase One behavior rates. Deceleration target rates before treatment all occur less frequently than two per minute.

mutually agreed by Debbie and her group members that she had sufficiently stable premodification data, the group suggested alternative decelerating consequences. Since it was close to Senior Prom time, Debbie wanted to lose weight and decelerate her snacks fairly rapidly.

From the suggested alternatives, she chose to shock herself after every snack. She located a "joke" cigarette pack which contains a small battery and coil. When the top is removed, the metal binding on the case completes the circuit and shock is administered. She required herself to hold the shock pack for ten seconds. At the next meeting when she presented her graphed data, it was evident that the shock after she ate the food significantly decelerated snacking between meals to a median of five a day.

She then tried shocking herself as she reached for food. In the presence of food, every time she reached, she self-applied ten seconds of shock. The between-meals food reaching decelerated to only once a day. This resulted in such a weight loss that she was able to fit into the formal she wanted to wear to the prom. The significant differences in snacking were computed using the Lindsley Mid-Median test (1967b).

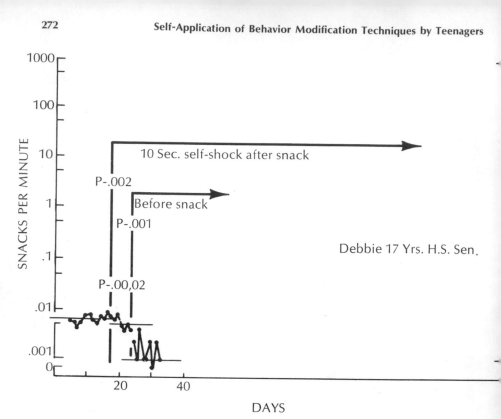

Figure 4. Decelerating snacking. Self-application of shock after (consequence) each snack decelerated snacking between meals. Then self-application of shock before (stimulus) each snack further decelerated snacking.

The exact probability level of the difference between phase one and three was p = .00,02.

SWEARING

Dave said at the first meeting what he really wanted to get rid of was all his swearing. Swearing embarrassed him especially on dates. Dave counted his swearing rate on the Domatic wrist counter. He tried using the smaller, plastic golf-score caddy but his rate was so high that he could not operate the smaller counter as fast as he swore during an outburst. He recorded all day long.

His median rate during the pre-modification phase was .4 per minute or four swear words every ten minutes. Dave selected the consequence of placing a surgical gauze mask over his face, wearing it for three minutes, and not allowing himself to talk to anyone while wearing it. He immediately placed the mask over his mouth every time he swore regardless of where he was. After the first week of phase two, Dave reported that he had masked himself twice at a local student hang-out, once on a date, and once at home. As indicated in Figure 5, the rate markedly decelerated. Using the Lindsley Mid-Median test, this difference was highly significant (p = 00,000,000,000,1).

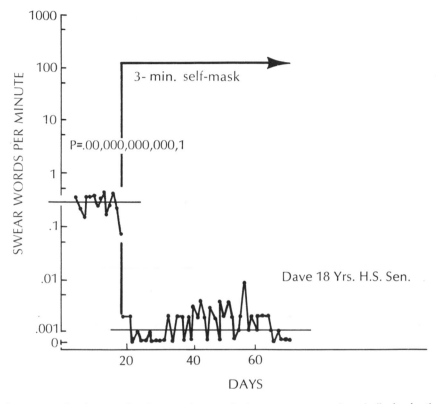

Figure 5. Decelerating swearing. Dave put on a mask after every swear word, markedly decelerating his swearing rate.

FACE TOUCHING

Of the completed behavior modification projects currently on file (total of 650), we find that about one out of 20 behaviors simply decelerate by recording its frequency (Lindsley, 1967a). This may be an example of a multiple-functioning event. The self-recording may serve both as a decelerating stimulus and a decelerating consequence. Betty decided she was going simply to record the behavior after collecting six days of premodification data and noted the rate was going down. The first large rate deceleration occurred on the day of the second group meeting.

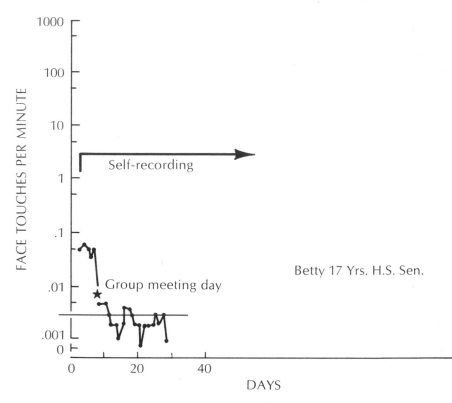

Figure 6. Decelerating face touching. Counting and plotting her daily rate decelerated Betty's face touching. The first marked deceleration occurred on the day of the second group meeting.

NAIL BITING

Emma reported she had bitten her nails ever since she was two years old. She recorded 11 days of premodification rates which indicated she bit or picked at her nails a little over once every minute of her waking day (median rate). With some assistance from her group members, she selected wearing gloves as her consequence. For every bite or pick she wore a glove on the nail-bitten hand for five minutes.

For the first five days of phase two, she wore a pair of winter gloves. At the end of the fifth day when Emma got home from school, her mother presented her with a pair of huge, flaming red mittens which she had made. Emma did not bite or pick her nails for three days. After seventeen days of the contingency-consequence of red mittens, Emma went on a week-end trip with the high-school band. She left her mittens at home but took her counter. Nail biting and picking immediately accelerated, although not to the former rate. She then reapplied the con-

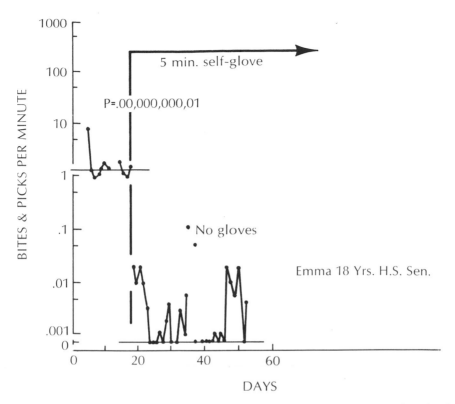

Figure 7. Decelerating nail biting. Effect of contingent self-application of gloves decelerated nail biting and picking. Note the faster rate of biting and picking during the two days without the glove contingency.

tingency and the rate again decelerated. Changes in the behavior were highly significant across phases one through four (p = .00,000,000,01).

KNUCKLE CRACKING

Patty cracked her knuckles at a median rate of once every five minutes. She stated it was interfering with her dating but she wasn't sure of what kind of a consequence to select. Her little brother suggested she wear his "monster hand" every time she cracked her knuckles. However, she had another set of knuckles needing a consequence. Her little brother offered to loan her one of his much prized boxing gloves. Patty wore both the glove and the hand and her knuckle cracking rate dropped to .03 per minute or once every 35 minutes. After three days, she withdrew the contingency and consequence, whereupon the behavior decelerated even further. This was an excellent example of an event which could decelerate upon presentation as well as upon removal—a double-barreled

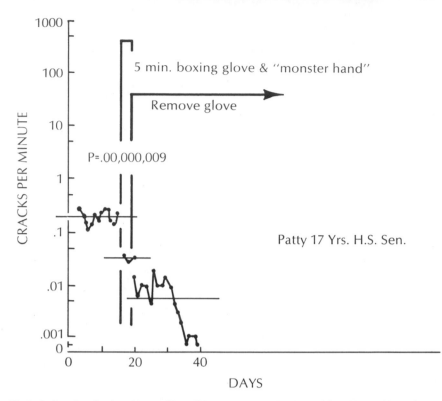

Figure 8. Decelerating knuckle cracking. This consequence decelerated knuckle cracking when presented and when withdrawn (pDCw).

variable. The differences across phases was highly significant (phase one: three $p = .00,000,009$).

SARCASMS

Bev defined sarcasms as any "put-down" comment which may or may not hurt someone. She made a list of ones commonly in her repertoire and added to them as she became more skillful in the assessment of her own behavior. Two days after starting the project, she was in a minor automobile accident which decelerated the behavior but did not eliminate it. For phase one, she was sarcastic a median rate of three times every two hours. Bev decided to apply a surgical gauze mask immediately after every sarcastic remark and keep it on for five minutes. Sarcasms decreased to four a day. The Senior Prom was the next week-end and she did not want to take the mask with her to the dance. She removed the contingency for the week-end and the behavior did not accelerate (both she and her boy friend counted over the week-end).

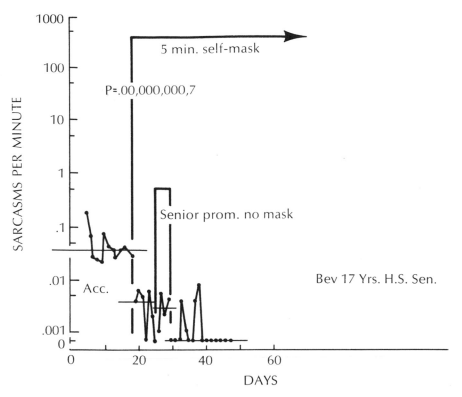

Figure 9. Decelerating sarcasms. Self-masking decelerated sarcastic comments. No increase in rate occurred during the Senior Prom when this procedure was temporarily suspended.

She reapplied the contingent mask wearing and the behavior decelerated even further. The exact probability level between phase one and four was $p = .00,000,000,7$.

Discussion

Teen-agers can control their own behavior by self-applying behavior-modification techniques. Given minimal instructions, a tally sheet, graph paper, and some assistance in pinpointing target behaviors, they can effectively and efficiently change behaviors their parents had complained about for years. One mother told me that she hadn't seen her daughter so happy since before junior high school. The girl had never lost her "baby fat" but had continually gained weight instead. When she recorded her food-reaching rate, applied a decelerating consequence, and lost weight, her social world brightened up. Now the mother and daughter plot food-reach records and keep an eye on each other's graphs.

One of our concerns before this project started was the self-recording. The opportunity for hedging or fabrication was there. None of the 33 successfully completed projects were fabricated. Since these young adults had volunteered for the program and their grade in psychology was not contingent on successful performance, we tend to believe that hedging was at a minimum. Currently, our belief is backed by a certification requirement. Teen-agers are randomly assigned to each other to certify the projects as having correct computations and being valid.

A randomly selected number of projects were followed up. For example, Dave had started to swear again but this time only in the fraternity house. For others, the target behaviors remained decelerated. Possibly, the natural consequences in the environment took over and helped maintain the change brought about by synthetic programming.

Thus, teen-agers can select behaviors they wish to decelerate or accelerate, maintain recording the rates over an extended period of time, and effectively alter their environment with contingent consequences.

Skinner (1959) states "A science of man . . . supplies striking support for the working faith that men can build a better world and, through it, better men." It also seems likely that better men could build a better world.

References

Ferster, C. B., Nurnberger, J. I., Levitt, E. B. 1962. The control of eating. *Journal of Mathetics* 1: 87–109.

Goldiamond, I. 1965. Self-control procedures in personal behavior problems. *Psychological Reports* 17: 851–68.

Holzschuh, R. D. 1968. Annual report of the Big Brothers Association of Greater Kansas City.

Kanfer, F. H. 1966. Influence of age and incentive conditions on children's self-rewards. *Psychological Reports* 19: 263–74.

Lindsley, O. R. 1966. Teaching teachers to teach. Paper presented at the annual meeting of American Psychological Association, New York City, 1966.

Lindsley, O. R. 1967a. Lecture presented to Education 115 University of Kansas, fall semester, 1967.

Lindsley, O. R. 1967b. The mid-median test for assigning exact probabilities to precision teaching products. Unpublished manuscript.

Lindsley, O. R. 1968 (in press). A reliable wrist counter for recording behavior rates. *Journal of Applied Behavioral Analysis* 1: 77–78.

Sebastian, E. 1967. Fathers groups for behavior modification of retarded children. Paper presented at *American Association of Mental Deficiency*, Denver Colo., 1967.

Skinner, B. F. 1959. Freedom and the control of men. In *Cumulative Record*. New York: Appleton-Century-Crofts, 1959.

23 / The Role of Social and Material Reinforcers in Increasing Talking of a Disadvantaged Preschool Child

NANCY J. REYNOLDS AND TODD R. RISLEY

Previous research reported here has shown that attention from the teacher contingent upon desired behavior is a strong shaping agent. This study extends that finding into the area of speaking. A four-year-old spoke infrequently. Since vocalization—talking—is an important part of communication, it was decided that this child needed to develop the skill beyond what she had displayed. To help her increase talking, it was decided to permit her to have play-school materials contingent upon asking for them (mands). If the child did not ask, no material was forthcoming; but if the child asked, and responded to the teacher's questions about the material, it was made available. In addition, the child's speaking was followed by other forms of attention such as smiling, verbal responses, and touching.

Contrast this technique to the more usual, where the teacher pays a great deal of attention to nonverbal behavior in coaxing a child to talk. Unfortunately, attention to nonverbal behavior often builds in nonverbal behavior, and the shy child becomes more shy.

Adult social reinforcement and access to materials in the preschool were made contingent on the verbalizations of a 4-yr-old Negro girl with an extremely low frequency of talking. Though the teachers' social attention was always given immediately for all spontaneous speech, if the child's spontaneous verbalizations were requests for materials, those materials were withheld until she had responded to the teachers' questions about those materials. When she was silent, the teachers withheld their attention and the materials. A high frequency of verbal behavior was quickly established. When both teacher attention and materials were provided only when the child was not verbalizing, the child's frequency of talking immediately decreased. When social attention and materials were again made contingent upon spontaneous speech and answering questions, the child's frequency of talking quickly increased to its previous high level. The content of the child's verbal behavior which increased was primarily a repetition of requests to the teachers with little change noted in the non-request verbalizations, or verbalizations to other children. A further experimental analysis demonstrated the social interaction per se was not the reinforcer which maintained the increased verbalization; rather, for this child, the material reinforcers which accompanied the social interaction appeared to be the effective components of teacher attention.[1]

Children in an economically deprived area lack many skills which would enable them to function effectively in the public schools or in the middle-class society, of which public schools are an integral part. The most damaging deficiency appears to be a lack of verbal and language skills (Bereiter and Engelmann, 1966), whereby the child learns what the school has to teach and communicates what he has, or has not, learned. Consequently, most people interested in remediating the effects of cultural deprivation are concerned with increasing the language skills of these children. In view of this concern with the value of verbal skills

[1] This study is based upon a thesis submitted by the senior author to the Department of Human Development in partial fulfillment of the requirements for the Master of Arts degree. The authors express appreciation to Dianetta Coates, Maxine Preuitt, and especially, Betty Hart for their able assistance in all aspects of the study. This research was supported by Grants (HD 03144) from the National Institute of Child Health and Human Development and (CG-8474) from the office of Economic Opportunity, Headstart Research and Demonstration to the Bureau of Child Research and the Department of Human Development at the University of Kansas. Reprints may be obtained from Todd Risley, Juniper Garden Children's Project, 3rd and Stewart, Kansas City, Kansas 66101.

Source: Nancy J. Reynolds and Todd R. Risley, "The Role of Social and Material Reinforcers in Increasing Talking of a Disadvantaged Preschool Child," *Journal of Applied Behavior Analysis* 1 (Fall 1968): 253–62. Copyright © 1968 by the Society for the Experimental Analysis of Behavior, Inc. Reprinted by permission of the authors and the *Journal of Applied Behavior Analysis*.

for economically deprived children, it was felt that an especially low frequency of verbal behavior by one such preschool child should be altered. Previous studies utilizing operant conditioning procedures have demonstrated how a manipulation of this nature could be undertaken. The pioneering studies from the University of Washington Preschool have investigated the applicability of operant principles to changing the problem behavior of normal children in naturally occurring situations (summarized in Harris, Wolf, and Baer, 1964). These studies, which investigated the relationship between the behaviors of teachers and the behaviors of preschool children, have indicated that the "attention" of the teacher can function as a strong reinforcer to establish, modify, and maintain the behavior of preschool children.

This development has provided information about principles of behavior and how these principles affect human behavior. It has also provided a technology for therapeutic intervention in human problems and for increasingly more sophisticated analyses of human behavior. The present study was undertaken to increase the frequency of verbalization of a child in a preschool setting and subsequently to analyze the controlling components of the teacher-child interaction in producing the behavior increase, as well as to assess some of the changes in the content of verbalizations in relation to changes in the frequency of verbalizations.

Method

SUBJECT AND SETTING

The study was conducted at the Turner House preschool of the Juniper Gardens Children's Project in Kansas City, Kansas. The subject was a 4-yr-old girl who exhibited a low frequency of verbal behavior well after the period considered normal for adaptation to the preschool routine and setting. She was one of 15 children, all Negroes from a lower-class community, selected from large families with extremely low incomes. The subject's Peabody Picture Vocabulary Test I.Q. was 59, slightly below the average (79) of the group, but she did not appear retarded. She gave appropriate answers in structured teaching situations if the teacher could get her to speak loud enough to be heard. She was particularly skilled in motor activities, and despite her non-verbal method of obtaining play materials from other children ("grabbing"), appeared well-liked by the other children.

The preschool ran from 8:30 to 11:30 a.m. five days a week. During the first 45 min of the morning, special training programs and individual tasks for the children were combined with breakfast. The remainder of the morning consisted of an approximately 45-min period of free play inside, a 30-min snack and instruction time, a 45-min period of free play outside, and a story time inside just before going home.

During free-play periods, the children could move from one to another of the unstructured activities usually found in preschool programs such as a block area, a doll area, a painting area, or a sand box. Some materials such as blocks were available to the children, and others such as paint were dispensed by the teachers. During the free-play periods, the three teachers always attended to, talked to, and interacted with the children and occasionally provided snacks (fruit, cookies, crackers, etc.) contingent upon generally appropriate play behavior.

Procedures and Results

RECORDING

Three observers recorded data during the morning free-play periods, and although present in the preschool room and yard with the children, did not interact with or respond to them. Observations of the subject were made at sample intervals only during free-play periods. During these periods the child's speech was sampled using two different recording procedures, one recording how often she spoke and one recording what she said.

Frequency of verbalization. Verbal frequency data were collected simultaneously by all three observers. They carried data sheets similar to those described by Allen, Hart, Buell, Harris, and Wolf (1964) and Hall, Lund, and Jackson (1968). Each row of the data sheet contained 30 squares representing a 10-sec interval per square or, 5 min per row. Two adjacent rows were used for each 5-min observation. The top row was used to record talking or verbalization by the child. Whenever the child verbalized during a 10-sec interval a (T) was written in the square corresponding to that interval. Only one (T) was marked in any interval during which the child verbalized irrespective of the amount of talking that occurred in that 10-sec period. If the child's verbalization began in one 10-sec interval and extended into the next, a (T) was noted in both intervals. Frequency of verbalization was therefore recorded as the per cent of 10-sec intervals of the sample during which verbalization occurred. The bottom row was used to record teacher attention by placing the initial of the attending teacher in the square corresponding to the 10-sec interval in which teacher attention occurred. Teacher attention was counted in the same way as verbalizations by the child.

Starting at the same time, using stopwatches, the three observers simultaneously but independently recorded the frequency of the child's verbalizations for 5-min periods. Usually, three such 5-min samples were taken each day during the two free-play periods: two during the first free-play period and one during the second, although occasionally only one or two 5-min samples were taken during a day.

Verbalizations were defined as any speech from the child heard by the observers, except random noises such as shrieking, humming, or laughing. During rate samples, speech which was too low for the observers to understand fully was counted, though this was not true of the content samples. Teacher attention was counted as any time a teacher spoke to, gave equipment to, or touched the child.

The correspondence between the three observers' data on frequency of verbalization is shown in Fig. 1, where the top line represents the highest rate and the bottom line the lowest rate obtained by an observer on a given sample. The product-moment correlation coefficients between the frequency data of the three observers on all observations throughout the year were:

> 0.97 for observers A and B (64 samples)
> 0.96 for observers A and C (59 samples)
> 0.99 for observers B and C (59 samples).

The product-moment correlation coefficients between the teacher attention data over the same samples were:

0.85	for	observers	A	and	B	(64	samples)
0.90	for	observers	A	and	C	(59	samples)
0.97	for	observers	B	and	C	(59	samples).

Content of verbalization. The content of verbalization samples were collected over the same portions of the year as the frequency of verbalization samples, but not necessarily on the same days. The verbal content samples were recorded during free play by one of three observers, who wrote down in longhand "everything" that the child said while following her from one activity to another during a 15-min period. Twenty-nine such samples were taken on different days during the baseline condition (Days 1 to 29), 7 by observer A, 13 by observer B, and 9 by observer C. During the experimental conditions (Days 130 to 164) observer A recorded all 30 verbal content samples, with observer B simultaneously recording on two occasions (Days 157 and 162). These verbalization records were then transcribed and content was categorized and counted from the transcribed phrases by one teacher. As observers recorded the data, they also put a check in one column if the verbalization was directed toward a child, and a check in a second column if it was directed toward a teacher (immediately following a recorded verbalization). General grammatical rules were used to categorize roughly the content of the verbalizations. As the nouns and verbs were counted, the first appearance of a noun or a verb was added to the count of *different* nouns and verbs. Each subsequent time the child said that noun or verb in the same content sample, it was counted as a repetition. The phrases were also defined as sentences if they included a subject (or implied subject) and a verb. These sentences were then categorized as *mand,* generally a request, demand, or question which specified the reinforcer (Skinner, 1957), or *non-mand* sentences. Sixteen of these verbalization records (randomly selected but including at least two from each condition) were independently categorized and counted by the second teacher.

The averages of the content measures from each observer's records during the baseline period are compared in Table 1. The correspondence between the measures taken from the three observers

Table 1 Comparison Between the Three Observers' Records of the Content of the Child's Speech during Baseline (Average Frequency per Sample)

	Observer		
	A	B	C
Nouns and Verbs:			
Total	10.0	8.6	12.3
Different	4.6	5.5	6.9
Verbalizations:			
To teacher	3.8	2.8	5.3
To child	4.8	11.0	5.8
Verbalizations:			
Mands	6.6	3.6	5.4
Non-mands	0.02	3.4	1.0

records indicates the reliability of the low frequencies of the content measures between different observers on different days. On the two occasions of simultaneous recording, observer A recorded 12 different nouns and verbs with 37 repetitions and observer B recorded 11 different and 22 repetitions on Day 157; observer A recorded 16 different and 58 repetitions and observer B recorded 14 different and 43 repetitions on Day 162. On the 16 samples categorized by the second teacher, the product-movement correlation coefficients between the scores of the two raters were 0.99 for nouns and verbs, and *mand* sentences and 0.95 for *non-mand* sentences.

EXPERIMENTAL CONDITIONS

The following contingencies and experimental manipulations were in effect throughout the entire free-play periods, which usually totaled close to 1.5 hr each day:

A. Baseline.	(Days 1 to 129)
B. Teacher attention contingent on verbalization.	(Days 130 to 142)
C. Teacher attention contingent on non-verbalization; differential reinforcement of other behavior (DRO).	(Days 143 to 148)
B. Teacher attention contingent on verbalization.	(Days 149 to 154)
D. Modified teacher attention contingent on verbalization.	(Days 155 to 161)
B. Teacher attention contingent on verbalization.	(Days 162 to 163)

A. Baseline. During the first 129 days that the child was in school, verbalizations occurred during an average of 11% of the 10-sec intervals of each sample, ranging between 1% and 32% on individual samples. Teacher attention during that time ranged between 0% and 36% with an average of 11%. Data between Days 31 to 45, 65 to 78, and 119 to 129 are shown in Condition A of Fig. 1.

B. Teacher attention contingent upon verbalization. From Day 130 through 142, the teachers' attention to the child was contingent upon her verbalizations and was maintained while she was talking. Teacher attention consisted of a variety of stimuli which included one or more of the following: praising the child, asking her questions, giving her equipment, assisting her, attending to, talking to, and providing a requested object or material. The form of the teacher attention varied according to the context of the child's verbalizations and the nature of the situation. However, whenever the child's verbalization was in the form of a request for materials, the teacher would ask questions about the materials or the child's projected use of the materials. The material itself would only be given contingent upon the child's responding to one or more such questions. For example, if the child said that she wanted to paint, the teacher would praise her for saying what she wanted, and then ask her what she was going to paint or what other things she needed in order to paint, e.g., brush, paper. Again they praised her for any verbal responses she made and perhaps asked her another question. This was continued as long as the teacher could ask reasonable or logical questions concerning the situation; it usually ranged between one and three questions per request for materials, though occasionally no questions were asked. Thus, while teacher atten-

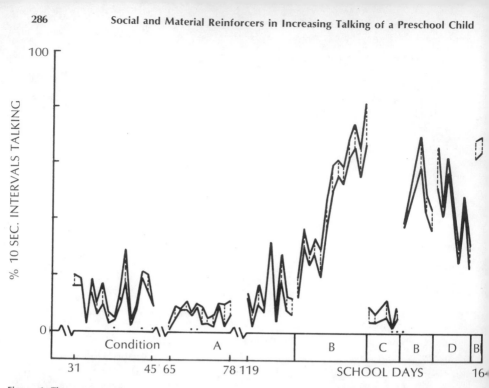

Figure 1. The per cent of 10-sec intervals during which talking occurred. The experimental conditions were
(A) Baseline. (B) Teacher attention contingent upon any verbalization (social interaction immediately con
tingent upon all verbalizations; access to materials contingent upon responding to variable number of question
whenever verbalizations were requests for materials). (C) Teacher attention contingent upon silence (DRO
(D) Teacher attention contingent upon any verbalization (social interaction immediately contingent upon a
verbalizations; materials immediately contingent upon requests). The two lines on the graph represent the
highest and lowest scores of the three observers. The dots in the lower portion of the graph mark those day
when observations were made by only two observers.

tion in the form of social interaction was given contingent upon each
instance of verbalization, whenever the verbalization was a request for
materials, teachers' interactions were in the form of asking questions
about the materials and the materials were dispensed on a small variable
ratio for answering questions. When possible, teachers required the child
to ask for materials by preventing her free access to them.

During the 13 days of these conditions, the frequency of the
child's verbalization increased rom 11% to 75% of the 10-sec intervals
(Condition B, Fig. 1). The number of nouns and verbs used increased
from an average of 15 (range 3 to 25) to an average of 46 (range 14
to 73) per 15-min content sample. The number of different nouns and
verbs used per sample increased from an average of seven to an average
of 16 while the frequency of repetitions increased nearly twice as much
from an average of seven to an average of 30 (Condition B, Fig. 2).

The number of verbalizations directed to a child remained approximately constant (changing from an average of 7.6 to 7.9) while the number of verbalizations directed to a teacher increased from an average of 4.2 to 26.8 during this period (Condition B, Fig. 3). The number of *non-mand* sentences remained approximately constant (changing from an average of 2.3 to 2.6) while the number of *mand* sentences increased from an average of 4.2 to 19.5 during this period (Condition B, Fig. 4).

In summary, the marked increases in frequency of verbalizations were almost entirely a function of an increase in the frequency of requests (*mands*) to the teacher (usually for materials). These increased requests involved the use of a slightly greater vocabulary than before but a proportionately greater increase in repetitions of the same words.

C. *Teacher attention contingent on non-verbalization (DRO)*. Since the frequency of teacher attention was now higher, it became necessary to investigate whether the increased instance of teacher attention, per se, or the contingency of presenting teacher attention immediately after the child verbalized was maintaining the verbal rate. It might be said that the child verbalized at a higher frequency simply because the teachers were attending and talking to her more, indicating

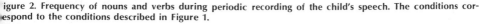

Figure 2. Frequency of nouns and verbs during periodic recording of the child's speech. The conditions correspond to the conditions described in Figure 1.

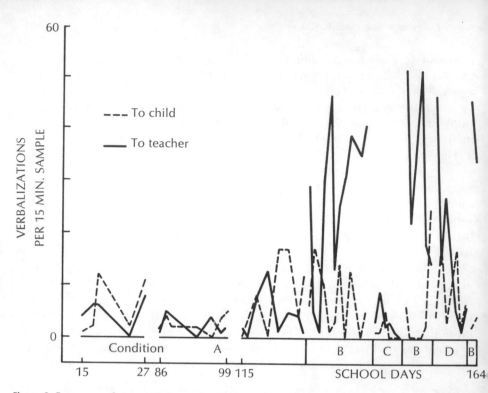

Figure 3. Frequency of statements to teachers and to other children during recording of the child's speech. The conditions correspond to the conditions described in Figure 1.

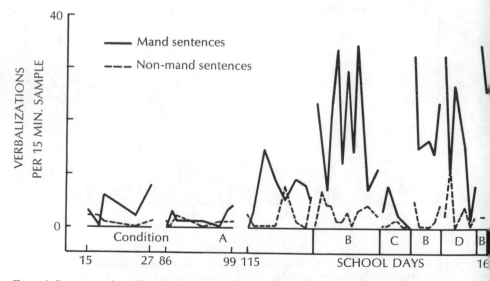

Figure 4. Frequency of **mand** and **non-mand** sentences during periodic recordings of the child's speech. The conditions correspond to the conditions described in Figure 1.

288

that the higher incidence of teacher attention rather than its contingency of following the child's verbalizations was maintaining this frequency. Therefore, the teacher attention was maintained at as high a rate but was now made contingent upon non-verbalization by the child. Typically the teachers would attend to the child, praising her and providing her with materials while she was silently engaged in activities. For example, if the children near the child were asking for water and she picked up a cup, the teacher would reinforce the child's behavior of not asking by pouring water into her cup and keeping it filled as long as she was silent, and praising her for pouring from her cup, working hard, and keeping busy. The teachers removed their attention and the supplying source of materials for 15 to 30 sec immediately following a verbalization by the child. (This procedure is often described as differential reinforcement of other behaviors, [DRO], since teacher attention is presented contingent upon any behavior except the behavior being measured, in this case talking.)

During six days of DRO, the rate of verbalization dropped from an average of 46% to 6% while the rate of teacher attention was maintained at an average of 67% (Condition C, Fig. 1 and 5). At this point, teacher attention was again given contingent upon verbalization by the

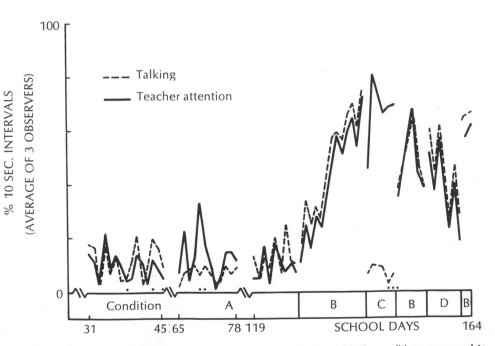

Figure 5. The relationship between teacher attention and talking by the child. The conditions correspond to those described in Figure 1.

child. Her frequency of verbalization immediately increased to an average of 51% during the four days of this condition, while the rate of teacher attention averaged 47% (Condition D, Fig. 1 and 5).

During DRO, several aspects of the child's verbal content dropped well below the baseline level. The number of total nouns and verbs used dropped to an average of four per day. The amount of talking decreased to the point that little verbalization was made to either teachers or children, though the amount of talking to teacher was higher at an average of three per day, but only one per day to children.

D. Modified teacher attention contingent on verbalizations. The DRO condition demonstrated the function of the gross category of teacher attention in maintaining the child's increased rate of verbalizations. However, the analysis of the content of the verbalizations, which revealed that the increase was primarily in repeated requests to the teachers for materials, indicated that the praise and social interaction components of the teachers' attention might not be functional. Therefore, a further manipulation was made to analyze experimentally the functions of the two components of teacher attention: the teachers' praise and social interaction, and the teachers' questioning the child and requiring additional verbalizations before providing a requested material.

After recovery from DRO, for six days social interaction with the teacher remained exclusively contingent upon verbalization, but questioning the child and requiring further verbalization before providing any requested material to the child was discontinued. Now she could immediately acquire materials by asking for them, rather than being required to respond verbally to questions in order to get them. Under these conditions, the child's frequency of verbalization gradually declined from 61% to 28% of the 10-sec intervals (Condition D, Fig. 1). Since teacher attention was given only after verbalization by the child, it too dropped along with the frequency of verbalization (Condition D, Fig. 5). Non-mand sentences, different nouns and verbs used and verbalizations to children remained relatively stable, while mand sentences, repetitions of nouns and verbs, and verbalizations to teachers decreased systematically (Condition D, Fig. 2, 3, and 4).

When the teachers again asked questions and required several responses from the child before providing her with requested materials during the following two days (the final two days of school), the rate of verbalization immediately increased from 29% on the last day of Condition D to an average of 67% (Fig. 1 and 5). The number of repetitions of nouns and verbs, verbalizations to teachers, and mands all increased to a level comparable to the previous periods in which these conditions were present (Fig. 2, 3, and 4).

Discussion

In the present study, a child's low frequency of verbal behavior was increased, utilizing the techniques of consequent teacher attention. This increase was reversed and recovered by altering the contingent relationship between teacher attention and verbalization. Thus, this study consisted in part of a replication of prior preschool studies showing that contingent teacher attention can effectively alter yet another behavior of the preschool child.

Teacher attention includes a variety of behaviors such as looking at, smiling at, talking to, touching, providing materials for, and assisting the children, only some of which may be functional in altering or maintaining the behavior of a child. In studies utilizing teacher attention as a consequence for children's behavior, the form of the teacher attention varies from instance to instance according to the activity in which the child is engaged and the content of the child's verbalizations. Therefore, to a large extent, the child's behavior determines the form of the teacher's attention. In the present study, the criterion behavior, verbalization, appeared primarily in the form of a request for materials. The teacher's attention, therefore, almost always included providing the child with materials.

Both the DRO procedures and the fact that the majority of the child's verbalizations were directed toward teachers indicated that the teachers were in fact controlling the relevant reinforcers. However, the fact that the majority of the child's verbalizations were *mands* (primarily, requests for materials) indicated that the strictly social interaction components of teacher attention were perhaps not the functional components. The DRO contingency provided no information on this question since social interactions, questions, and access to materials were simultaneously altered. The subsequent manipulation, in which access to materials no longer entailed answering a series of the teachers' questions, resulted in a steady decline in the child's frequency of verbalization. This decline occurred in spite of the fact that social interaction was still contingent upon each instance of the child's verbalization and materials were immediately contingent upon those verbalizations which were requests for materials. This demonstrated that the social interaction per se was not the reinforcing component of teacher attention that maintained the high rate of verbalization. The important component of teacher attention was questioning the child and requiring several verbal responses before allowing access to materials. Time did not permit a further experimental analysis to separate the two obvious aspects of this functional component of teacher attention: the questioning per se and the ratio scheduling of access to materials. However, the facts that the questioning occurred only when the child requested materials and the child usually responded to the questions by simply repeating her original request rather than "answering" the question, and that most of her increased verbalizations were *mands* indicate that the ratio scheduling of access to materials through the teacher was critical to establishing and maintaining a higher rate of verbal behavior. This child could get few materials or equipment without first obtaining the teachers' attention. Only when the teachers' attention "mediated" access to materials did it function as a reinforcer for this child's verbalization. A similar procedure (of allowing access to materials contingent upon certain forms of speech) but without the prompts or questions proved to be functional in altering the speech of the other children in the preschool (Hart and Risley, 1968).

In work with culturally deprived preschool children, the teachers have informally observed that these children's verbalizations contain relatively few descriptive or informative statements, but a large proportion of commands and requests. Bereiter and Engelmann (1966) have reported similar observations. The high frequency of requests may indicate that material reinforcers are disproportionately strong, or that social interaction with adults is a disproportionately weak reinforcer, and that adults may be important primarily as dispensers of material reinforcers. Such appeared to be the case for this child. However, since the previous studies utilizing adult attention as a reinforcer (summarized in Harris et al., 1964) did not analyze the components of attention which were functional in producing changes in the behavior of middle-class preschool children, material reinforcers may have, in fact, been the functional aspect of the teacher attention for those children as well.

In an analysis of the effect of a behavioral manipulation, usually the rate of only one aspect of the behavior is considered. A concurrent analysis of other aspects of the studied behavior allows a more detailed specification of the effect of the functional variables. In this study, as the frequency of the child's talking increased, the data on the content of verbalization revealed that the increase involved primarily an increase in verbalizations to teachers in the form of repetitions of the same nouns and verbs in *mand* sentences.

With additional time, access to materials might have been applied to alter the content of this child's speech. However, before considering differential reinforcement of the content of verbalization, it seems essential to obtain a high stable frequency of verbalization. The data indicated that the teachers could control the rate of verbal behavior. Once this high frequency was obtained, it would have been possible to provide access to materials differentially contingent upon *non-mands,* child-directed speech, or variety of nouns and verbs. The nature of such differential reinforcement procedures, their success or even their necessity, are questions for further investigation.

References

Allen, K. Eileen, Hart, Betty M., Buell, Joan S., Harris, Florence R., and Wolf, M. M. 1964. Effects of social reinforcement on isolate behavior of a nursery school child. *Child Development* 35: 511–18.
Allen, K. Eileen, Henke, Lydia B., Harris, Florence R., Baer, D. M., and Reynolds, Nancy J. 1967. Control of hyperactivity by social reinforcement of attending behavior. *Journal of Educational Psychology* 58: 231–37.
Bereiter, C. and Engelmann, S. 1966. *Teaching disadvantaged children in the preschool.* Englewood Cliffs: Prentice-Hall.
Hall, R. V., Lund, Diane, and Jackson, Delores. 1968. Effects of teacher attention on study behavior. *Journal of Applied Behavior Analysis* 1: 1–12.
Harris, Florence R., Johnston, Margaret K., Kelley, C. Susan, and Wolf, M. M. 1964. Effects of positive social reinforcement on regressed crawling of a nursery school child. *Journal of Educational Psychology* 55: 35–41.
Harris, Florence R., Wolf, M. M., and Baer, D. M. 1964. Effects of adult social reinforcement on child behavior. *Young Children* 20: 8–17.
Hart, Betty M., Allen, K. Eileen, Buell, Joan S., Harris, Florence R., and Wolf, M. M. 1964. Effects of social reinforcement on operant crying. *Journal of Experimental Child Psychology* 1: 145–53.
Hart, Betty M. and Risley, T. R. 1968. Establishing use of descriptive adjectives in the spontaneous speech of disadvantaged preschool children. *Journal of Applied Behavior Analysis* 1: 154–65.
Johnston, Margaret K., Kelley, C. Susan, Harris, Florence R., and Wolf, M. M. 1966. An application of reinforcement principles to development of motor skills of a young child. *Child Development* 37: 379–87.
Skinner, B. F. 1957. *Verbal behavior.* New York: Appleton-Century-Crofts.

24 / Effect of Contingent and Non-Contingent Social Reinforcement on the Cooperative Play of a Preschool Child

BETTY M. HART, NANCY J. REYNOLDS, DONALD M. BAER, ELEANOR R. BRAWLEY, AND FLORENCE R. HARRIS

For many teachers, cooperative behavior is to be desired over uncooperative. Such was the case with the investigaors in this study.

It is an important study because it demonstrates that indiscriminate attention ("Loving the children into learning") is less effective than attention based upon more appropriate behavior, in this case cooperation. The systematic changing of conditions from noncontingent reinforcement to reinforcement for cooperative play, to noncontingent reinforcement, and finally to reinforcement for cooperative play with a concomitant and predictable response for each condition indicates clearly the effect a teacher's behavior can have on children.

The effect of adult social reinforcement on the cooperative play of a five-year-old girl in a preschool setting was assessed under two conditions: (1) presented randomly throughout the school day, and (2) pre-

Source: Betty M. Hart, Nancy J. Reynolds, Donald M. Baer, Eleanor R. Brawley, and Florence R. Harris, "Effect of Contingent and Non-Contingent Social Reinforcement on the Cooperative Play of a Preschool Child," *Journal of Applied Behavior Analysis* 1 (Spring 1968): 73–76. Copyright © 1968 by the Society for the Experimental Analysis of Behavior, Inc. Reprinted by permission of the authors and the *Journal of Applied Behavior Analysis*.

sented contingent on cooperative play. Only in the latter condition was a significant change in cooperative play observed.[1]

A series of recent studies has shown that adult social stimulation, presented as a consequence of various behaviors of preschool children, successfully increased those behaviors (Allen et al., 1964, 1967; Harris, Johnston, Kelley, and Wolf, 1964; Baer and Wolf, 1968). In each case, the child's behavior was modified by making this teacher reinforcement both frequent and contingent upon the behavior, whereas previously reinforcement had been intermittent and non-contingent. In this study, a simple comparison was made of the separate roles of frequent reinforcement and contingent reinforcement in developing the cooperative play of a preschool child.

Method

SUBJECT

Martha, aged 5 yr 4 months, was enrolled in a group of 15 normal children in a university preschool. The group attended school five afternoons per week for approximately 2.5 hr each day. Most of Martha's time at school was spent in non-social tricycle-riding, sand play, swinging, "cooking," and playing with animal toys. Her contacts with other children, though frequent, tended to be brief and non-cooperative. Her refusals to play when invited, her taunts and competitive statements ("I can do that better than you"), and her foul language and rambling accounts of violent accidents perhaps made her aversive to other children. These behaviors, her frequent upsetting of materials, and her typical delay in fulfilling routines seemed to have a similar effect on teachers.

PROCEDURES

General procedures. The general play of study was built upon a "reversal" design incorporating two different contingencies of reinforcement. The baseline consisted of normal preschool practices, composed essentially of intermittent attention to Martha, in no particular contingency. The first type of reinforcement consisted of greatly increased and carefully non-contingent[2] social reinforcement from teachers. There then

[1] This research was supported by PHS grants MH-02208 and MH-11768, National Institute of Mental Health, entitled An Experimental Analysis of Social Motivation. Reprints may be obtained from Donald M. Baer, Department of Human Development, University of Kansas, Lawrence, Kansas 66044.

[2] In this report, the term "Non-contingent reinforcement" means reinforcement presented according to random intervals of time, without regard for what behavior might be occurring at those times. It is to be distinguished from the term DRO (differential reinforcement of other than cooperative behavior).

followed a period of decreased reinforcement presented contingent upon cooperative play or approximations to it. Following clear evidence of behavioral change, this condition was discontinued and a return to the prior condition, frequent non-contingent reinforcement, was instituted. This was done to demonstrate experimental control of the behavioral change, thus validating the functional nature of the contingent reinforcement used to bring it about, and again demonstrating the previously noted lack of function in frequent but non-contingent reinforcement. As soon as this was clear, decreased but contingent reinforcement was again instituted, and a more intermittent schedule was approached.

Approximations to cooperative play were reinforced when necessary in the first stages of shaping the behavior. These approximations were typically verbal responses to children who had been prompted by the teachers to approach Martha with an idea for play. Verbal response was a minor component of cooperative play (as defined below), but was judged a good behavioral route to the cooperative behaviors ultimately sought.

The major behavior observed and treated experimentally was cooperation between Martha and any other children. In' addition, a second class of behavior, Martha's proximity to other children, was observed and recorded. Proximity was studied in part because it is often taken as evidence of a social orientation in a child, and in part because it existed at a considerable rate in Martha from the outset, and could easily be mistaken for a cooperative social orientation when in fact it need not be.

Specific procedures. For 10 days, Martha's teachers maintained their ongoing pattern of responding to her intermittently and without regard for her immediately preceding behavior. Objective records were taken of Martha's rates of cooperative play and of maintaining simple proximity to other children. This constituted the baseline period of the study.

Cooperative play was defined specifically as any of the following activities: pulling a child or being pulled by a child in a wagon; handing an object to a child, or pouring into his hands or into a container held by him; helping a child by supporting him physically, or bringing, putting away, or building something verbalized as expressly for him; sharing something with a child by digging in the same hole, carrying the same object, painting on the same paper or from the same paint pot, or adding to the same structure or construction (such as a chain of manipulative toys, or a block house).

Proximity was defined as being within 3 ft of another child, indoors, and within 6 ft outdoors.

For the next seven days, the teachers displayed attention and approval to close proximity to Martha at random intervals throughout the school session, so that approximately 80% of each session involved such interaction. This constituted the first period of non-contingent reinforcement.

Teacher reinforcement consisted of remaining near Martha and attending closely to her activities, sometimes supplying her with equipment or materials, and sometimes smiling, laughing, conversing, and admiring her.

Subsequently, for a period of 12 days, Martha received the same teacher reinforcement only as a consequence of cooperative play or behavior conducive to cooperative play. This constituted the first reinforcement of cooperative play.

Since Martha emitted cooperative play at a very low rate initially, it was necessary to use priming and shaping procedures. Priming meant that other children were prompted to speak to Martha or initiate potentially cooperative situations with her. (No such promptings were ever given to Martha herself.) Shaping meant that Martha was initially reinforced for all responsive verbalizations in proximity to children, subsequently only for such verbalization in potentially cooperative situations, and finally (by the seventh day of this 12-day period) only for full-blown cooperative play.

After these 12 days, non-contingent stimulation was resumed for four days, the second non-contingent reinforcement period. Again, teachers interacted with Martha for approximately 80% of each school session.

Finally, over an eight-day period (the last eight days of the school year), the teachers again resumed contingent reinforcement of cooperative play, constituting the second reinforcement of cooperative play. During the last four days of this period, the teachers steadily decreased their rate of reinforcing cooperative play and correspondingly increased their attention to desirable behaviors other than cooperative play, to regain a more typical reinforcement schedule for the girl, and to see if the rate of cooperative play would be maintained nevertheless.

Recording. Data on Martha's behavior were recorded daily in consecutive 10-sec intervals by an observer. Observation was continuous during the school-day session, except for a teacher-structured group-activity period of 20 to 30 min daily. In recording Martha's behavior, the observer used the categories of proximity, cooperative play, and teacher reinforcement. The child's scores for any day were the percentages of the 10-sec intervals marked as involving proximity or cooperative play.

Observer reliability was checked on five separate days by having a second observer record Martha's behavior in the same fashion as the first. Comparison of total incidences of proximity, cooperative play, and teacher reinforcement yielded 92% or better agreement on each of the five days.

Results and Discussions

The percentage of each session involving proximity and cooperative play is graphed in Fig. 1. It can be seen that during the baseline period Martha was in proximity to children roughly 50% of the day; at the same time, her rate of cooperative play was 5% or less of the day, and on five of the 10 days, 0%. Teacher reinforcement averaged about 20% of the school day.

When Martha was then given continual, non-contingent teacher reinforcement for about 80% of each session (Days 11 through 17 in Fig. 1), her rate of proximity to children varied sporadically between about 40% and 90% of the day, the average rising to about 65%. Probably this was due in part to the attraction of other children to a situation in which a teacher was giving close and continual attention. The decline in the rate of proximity to children after Day 15 might indicate the adaptation of the other children to a teacher always being somewhere near Martha. Except for Day 14 (when Martha's favorite companion returned from four days of hospitalization and she spent some time pulling him in a wagon), there was no overall change in Martha's rate of cooperative play, which still averaged less than 5% of the day.

After the eighteenth day, when teacher reinforcement of Martha was made contingent on cooperative play or approximations to it, the rate of teacher reinforcement dropped to its baseline level, and frequently amounted to less than 20% of the day; yet at the same time Martha's rate of cooperative play increased from 4% of the day to almost 40%. In the course of developing this increase, teachers found that their verbalizations to Martha frequently drew her out of cooperative play with a child and into interaction with them; therefore, reinforcement was given with increasing frequency to the entire cooperating group rather than to Martha as an individual.

Figure 1 shows that during the period of reinforcement of cooperative play, Martha's proximity to children increased to about 75% of the day and was maintained at approximately that level. When Martha was again given almost continual non-contingent teacher reinforcement for any and all behavior (beginning on Day 30), both proximity to children and cooperative play dropped almost to their baseline levels. Martha again spent about 55% of the school day in proximity with children and only 5% in cooperation with them; yet teacher reinforcement had increased from near 20% of the day to about 80%. During this time cooperative play was not ignored; like any of the rest of Martha's be-

Martha's Behavior

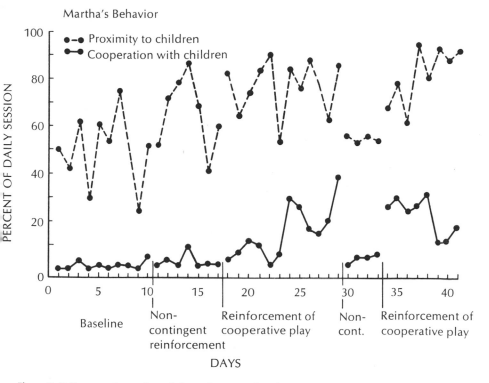

Figure 1. Daily percentages of proximity and cooperative play over sequential experimental conditions.

haviors, it might be reinforced if it occurred while a teacher was present. However, teachers during this period went to Martha immediately upon her arrival at school rather than waiting for a cooperative behavior to occur, and thus tended to reinforce behaviors sometimes incompatible with cooperative play at the start of each school day.

When teacher reinforcement was again made contingent upon cooperative play, a high rate of the behavior was immediately recovered, and was maintained for four days (Days 34 to 37) at 25% or more of the day. In this process, teacher reinforcement again decreased to about 20% of the day. Martha's proximity to children (not reinforced as such) rose again to a 75% average.

When teachers began on Day 38 to generalize reinforcement from specifically cooperative behaviors to broader categories of play, there were only four days of school remaining. As can be seen in Fig. 1, teacher reinforcement of cooperative behaviors was decreased too quickly during the first three days, and Martha's rate of cooperative play declined, though not to its baseline level. During this time, however, Martha was spending approximately 90% of the day in proximity to children. Her interactions with them appeared to be not only of much longer duration, but of a more positive nature than had characterized baseline interactions. Teachers judged that Martha had changed from an "obnoxious" girl to one who was "sometimes unpleasant." A high rate of "obnoxious" behavior could hardly co-exist with a high rate of cooperative play, of course, but many preschool children are capable of alternating between the two repertoires.

It can be seen in Fig. 1 that non-contingent reinforcement, whether continual or intermittent, did not appreciably develop cooperative play. Only when reinforcement was made contingent upon the behavior did any reliable change in rate appear. Hence, the data indicate that the behavior change was less a function of teacher attention (whether "a lot" or a "little") than it was a function of teacher attention made contingent on the behavior. Yet it is frequently assumed that children display hostile or angry (non-cooperative) behaviors as a result of too little positive attention from the adults in their environment. In this case, at least, abundant positive attention from all involved adults had no power to develop a cooperative replacement for Martha's unpleasant behaviors as long as it was presented as a non-contingent gift. Yet a much smaller amount of reinforcement could drastically alter her behavior, so long as it occurred in contingency with that behavior. Furthermore, it is to be noted that abundant but non-contingent attention could not maintain Martha's newly shaped cooperative repertoire, when contingent reinforcement was discontinued early in that development. It would seem, then, that to whatever extent Martha's behavior can serve as a guide, deliberate behavior modification is likely to proceed more effectively when it is based upon contingent, rather than abundant, stimulation.

References

Allen, K. Eileen, Hart, Betty M., Buell, Joan S., Harris, Florence R., and Wolf, M. M. 1964. Effects of social reinforcement on isolate behavior of a nursery school child. *Child Development* 35: 511–18.

Allen, K. Eileen, Henke, Lydia B., Harris, Florence R., Baer, D. M., and Reynolds, Nancy J. 1967. Control of hyperactivity by social reinforcement of attending behavior. *Journal of Educational Psychology* 58: 231–37.

Baer, D. M., and Wolf, M. M. 1968. The reinforcement contingency in preschool and remedial education. In *Early Education: current theory, research, and practice,* ed. R. D. Hess and Roberta M. Bear. Chicago: Aldine.

Harris, Florence R., Johnston, Margaret K., Kelley, C. Susan, and Wolf, M. M. 1964. Effects of positive social reinforcement on regressed crawling of a nursery school child. *Journal of Educational Psychology* 55: 35–41.

Hart, Betty M., Allen, K. Eileen, Buell, Joan S., Harris, Florence R., and Wolf, M. M. 1964. Effects of social reinforcement on operant crying. *Journal of Experimental Child Psychology* 1: 145–53.

25 / Token Reinforcement Systems in Regular Public School Classrooms

R. J. KARRAKER

The article you are about to read is not one but several accounts of
the use of behavior-modification techniques by regular classroom
teachers who were part-time students of the author.

The findings are important, and perhaps most important is
the discussion of settings in which the techniques did not work. All
too often, journals emphasize only the positive instances and neglect
the studies that for some reason do not work. But, curiously, a
research failure can often be as helpful in understanding a
phenomenon as can a success.

Another interesting aspect of this study is the discussion of
the teacher's inability to find reinforcers. Karraker's implicit conviction is that there is a host of positive reinforcing consequences in
the school setting. The examples mentioned in the article provide a
good starting point.

Token reinforcement systems have demonstrated their effectiveness in
controlling behavior in a variety of settings, including mental hospitals
(Ayllon and Azrin, 1965, Atthowe and Krasner, 1965; Gericke, 1965),

Source: R. J. Karraker, "Token Reinforcement in Regular Public School Classrooms," a revision of an address given at the annual meeting of the American
Educational Research Association, Chicago, February 1968. This is the first
publication. Students who collected the data reported in this paper are Janeese
Turney, Marilyn Rudell, Marian Hobbs, and Margaret Vondera.

hospitals for retarded (Girardeau and Spradlin, 1964; Birnbrauer, et al., 1965), a training school for delinquents, (Cohen, 1967), special education classes in public schools (O'Leary and Becker, 1966; Clark et al., 1967), and a remedial classroom (Wolf et al., 1966).

All of these experiments and demonstrations have in common the fact that the token reinforcement system has very much maintained a "research flavor." Most programs are characterized by (1) observers in addition to the behavioral managers, (2) close supervision and direction by individuals trained in an analysis of behavior, (3) research funds for consequences, (4) complete nonintervention from administrative personnel in their respective institutions, and (5) a relatively high degree of control of the environment.

Although virtually every published report of token reinforcement systems claims unqualified success in modifying behavior, the extent to which token systems can be employed by the regular public school classroom teacher without such supportive services and conditions has not been explored. It has been suggested (Baer, in press) that teachers not undertake behavior modification projects because of the unreliability of observation. However, the position taken by this author is that attempts to assess procedures objectively by systematic data collection, even in the absence of impressive reliability data, is appropriate if these techniques are to be incorporated in the mainstream of education.

The past year part-time graduate students who are also employed full time as teachers have been executing behavior modification projects based on principles of learning from an experimental analysis of behavior. Over the past year ten teachers chose to implement a token-reinforcement system in their classrooms. The teachers formulated their plan, and then consulted the author for advice before beginning the project. Each teacher evolved his own adaptation of a token-reinforcement system. The type and number of target behaviors, the length of baseline observations, the contingencies, the consequences presented or withdrawn, and the duration of the project varied in each project.

The students were informed, in order to reduce the probability of falsification of data, that their grade in the course was not contingent upon modifying the behavior. In addition, the author visited each project at least once, and sometimes more than once, during the semester.

Projects in Secondary Schools

INNER-CITY STUDY HALL

A thirty-minute study hall in a predominantly black school was reported to be a problem by the supervising teacher. In analyzing the behaviors that were disrupting the class, the pinpointed behaviors of talking without permission and being out of seat without permission were identified. In discussions with the teacher it became apparent that one condition that may have been functionally related to these behaviors was the observation that the students were not bringing to the study hall materials that would permit effective study behaviors. The teacher suggested that if each student brought to the class a pencil, a notebook (or paper), and a book, study behaviors *could* occur.

Premodification data on these three behaviors were collected for 11 successive class days: talking without permission, being out of seat without permission, and bringing study materials (book, pencil, and paper) to study hall.

The recording procedure was that the teacher would record each student who emitted the defined behaviors. It was suggested to the teacher that recording each instance of the talking out and out-of-seat behavior would be more sensitive to the consequence to be implemented, but she preferred to record just whether or not the student emitted the behavior as this would simplify her recording operations.[1]

Figure 1 presents the percent of the class which emitted each of the behaviors. Absentees were not counted in computing the percentages. The median percent of students who brought all three study materials to class was 50. For those who talked without permission the median percent was 64. Finally, the median percent of those who were out of seat without permission was 28.

In selection of a consequence to make contingent upon emission of the desired behaviors, the P-hypothesis (Premack, 1959, 1965) was invoked.[2] Briefly, the P-hypothesis states that any behavior that is higher in probability of occurrence (High Probability Behavior or HPB) than another (Low Probability Behavior or LPB) can be used as a reinforcer to increase the rate of the LPB. In observing the behavior of students in this study hall, talking to one another and reading comic books were HPBs, while emitting study behaviors were LPBs.

Therefore, the following contingency contract was presented to the students by the teacher. If the students displayed pencil, paper, and a book when they entered the study hall, and if during the first 20 minutes they did not talk or rise from their seats during the study hall, the last 10 minutes they would be permitted to sit by a peer and converse quietly or read comic books at their desks.

Figure 1 illustrates the effect of this procedure. The median percents during the 15 sessions the contingency contract was in effect were bringing study materials 90, talking out 25, and being out of seat 0. On

[1] This is an example of the compromise that often must be made in getting these techniques implemented by teachers in their classrooms. If the behavior is brought under control, teachers can subsequently be "shaped" into better applications of the procedures.

[2] For elaboration of the P-hypothesis and its application to human behavior, refer to Homme, 1965; Homme and Tosti, 1965.

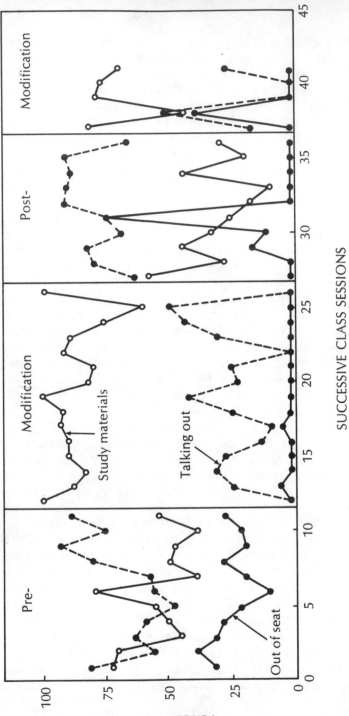

Figure 1. Percent of class bringing study materials, talking without permission, and being out of seat without permission during an inner-city study hall.

session 19, some calculators were placed at one end of the study hall. This was to be a temporary arrangement, but the teacher observed that this situation was likely to interrupt her control of the environment, so she added the consequence of five minutes' time on the calculators to the conversation-time and comic-book contingencies.[3]

On session 27 she told the students the contingency contract was no longer in effect. This return to premodification conditions resulted in median percents of 29 (materials), 81 (talking out), and 0 (out of seat) over a 10-day period. During this period the students were unhappy with the teacher for removing the contract, and most of the talking out consisted of questions to her regarding why the contingencies had been removed.

For five sessions the teacher reinstated the contingency contract and there was an immediate change in all three target behaviors. This condition would have been run longer but a school vacation interrupted data collection. The atypical behavior as shown in Figure 1 in session 38 was the result of a fight that had been precipitated prior to the study hall but continued at intervals during the period.

SUBURBAN BIOLOGY CLASS

A secondary biology teacher was concerned about the percent of her class which was earning grades of C or below on quizzes which were administered three times a week. The quizzes contained items that should have been easy for the students if they had read the assignment. There was an effort to keep each quiz reinforcing rather than punishing, and with this effort the label "progress check" (Homme, 1965) was employed to describe them. A major exam every two or three weeks was being administered in addition to the progress checks. Conventional letter grades were being given to the students prior to data collection.

Although the following contingency contract was made with the entire class, the data reported are on only 16 students who had an average grade of C or below before the contract was introduced. Prior to session 1 the students were told that grades would no longer be administered, but points would be awarded depending upon the percent correct on the progress checks: 90% or better = 3 points; 80 through 89% = 2 points; 70 through 79% = 1 point; and, below 70% = -1 point.

Five progress checks were given to the students with no other consequence attached to the points.

Figure 2 indicates that under the point system with no further contingencies, the 16 students had a median of 60% correct on five

[3] This is an example of the many events that often terminate these projects.

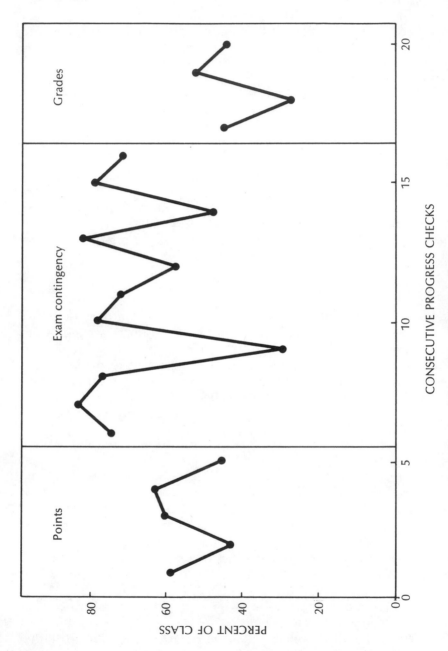

CONSECUTIVE PROGRESS CHECKS

Figure 2. Median percent correct on biology progress checks of 16 low-achieving students.

progress checks. On session 5, the following announcement was made: "We will now have a major exam every other Friday. You can avoid taking this exam by cashing in 10 points. You may use the points you have accumulated during this past two-week period."

The teacher's rationale for selection of this particular consequence was that if the students had 10 points available, they were acquiring the skills on a daily basis (an average of 80% through 89%) and a major exam would not be necessary to assure acquisition of the material. During 11 progress checks of this contract the 16 low-achieving students had a median percent correct of 74.

On session 16 the teacher announced the point system was being abandoned, and the class would return to the conventional grade system on the next progress check. Performance of the 16 pupils decelerated to a median of 46% correct over the next 4 progress checks. This is a lower percent than before the exam contingency was introduced.

One interesting side effect of this project was that several of the students who were maintaining a B or better average prior to the project began comparing their accumulated points, and competition in regard to total points earned was evidenced. Some of these students would not cash in their points to avoid the exam in order to "hoard" their points.

Projects in Elementary Schools

SECOND-GRADE CLASS

A second-grade teacher was concerned about the rate of her class talking without permission. The teacher recorded each instance of a student talking without permission on a golf counter attached to her wrist (Lindsley, 1968). Data were collected during the 210 minutes daily that the pupils were under the teacher's direct tutorage (minus lunch, recess, and classes taught by other teachers).

Premodification data revealed a median rate of .19 talkings out per minute over an 8-day period (See Figure 3). The consequence the teacher selected was a 15-minute story time at the end of each day. The teacher placed in front of the room a chart with each pupil's name written on one side. The first time a pupil talked without permission, the teacher walked to the chart and placed a cover over his name. She also advanced her golf counter and did so after each succeeding response. This procedure did reduce the talking out initially, but the pupils soon learned that the consequences were attached to the first response only. The data show an initial decrease the first day of this procedure, but the next four days resulted in a steady increase in the behavior with a median rate of .14.

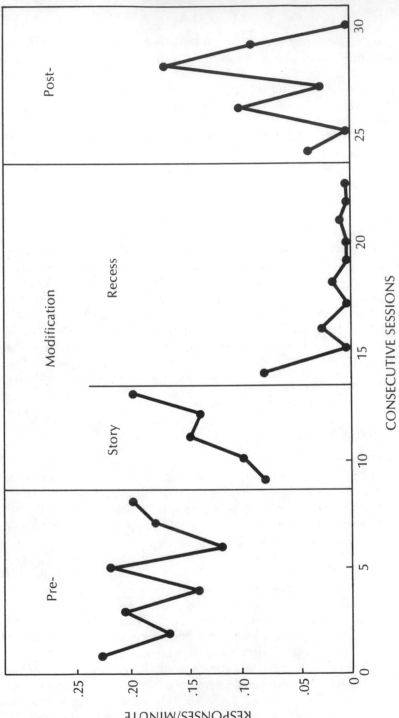

Figure 3. Rate of talking without permission in a second-grade class.

The teacher observed that it would be necessary to select a consequence that would be responsive to every talking out that occurred, so she began assessing one minute loss of recess time for every response. She kept a cumulative record of the talking out on the chalkboard, and also continued her recording on the wrist counter. The first day of this contingency there were 17 talk-outs in the 210 minutes. Over the next nine days the talking out was reduced drastically, with six days of less than three responses occurring. Removal of the contingency resulted in the behavior returning to within the premodification level with a median rate of .07 talkings out per minute.

FIFTH-GRADE SPELLING

A fifth-grade teacher was concerned that a boy in her class was consistently close to the bottom of his class on spelling tests. This performance was in contrast to his level of achievement in other subject-matter areas. In addition, the pupil's scores on standardized achievement tests led the teacher to state that he was performing well below expectations considering these scores.

The teacher had expressed her intention earlier to acquire permission from her principal to make the majority of recess time contingent upon academic performance. The principal agreed to the arrangement, and the teacher checked her gradebook and figured percent correct on spelling tests for the first five weeks of school. The median percent for the class was 70 and the median percent for the subject was 40. It can be observed from Figure 4 that test premodification data revealed the subject never had the lowest percent correct in the class, but was below the class median on each test.

The consequence implemented was one minute of afternoon recess for each word spelled correctly. During premodification the number of words on each test varied between 12 and 20, but beginning on the sixth week the number of words presented was 20 on each test.

Figure 4 illustrates the effect of this procedure. The subject's percent correct jumped from the premodification median of 40 to 100, while the class median also rose from a median of 70 to 90. The variability of performance of the class also indicates the effectiveness of the procedure.

Prior to the test on week 12 the pupils were informed recess would no longer be contingent, and the behavior decelerated for both the subject and the class. The median for the class during the nine weeks of post-modification was 76, while the subject's median was 39.

The teacher managed this arrangement by controlling when the pupils left the classroom at the time recess was made available. Those students who had spelled all 120 words correctly left the room imme-

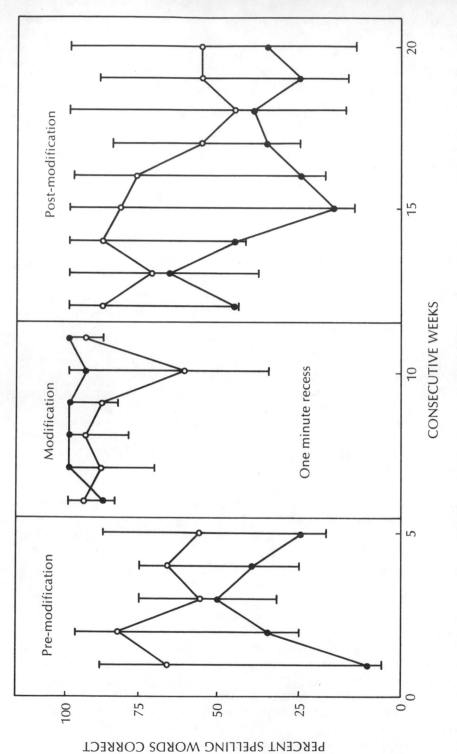

Figure 4. Percent correct spelling performance of a fifth-grade pupil and his class. The pupil's percents are the solid data points, and the class medians are the open circles. The lines through the data points indicate the range of class performance.

diately. Other pupils were permitted to leave contingent upon the number of corresponding minutes they had earned on their spelling test.

Problems in the Application of Token Reinforcement Systems

RECORDING THE BEHAVIOR

Most behaviors in classrooms are of such low frequency that a rate measure in terms of minutes is often meaningless to teachers. For example, reporting a rate of behavior at .07 per minute has quite different effects on teachers than saying a behavior occurred twice in a thirty-minute class. Therefore, rates utilizing behavior over longer units of time (such as class period) communicates more clearly to teachers. Perhaps rates under one per minute could be employed for those persons with experience in looking at data, but for feedback to classroom teachers, frequency or cumulative response measure may be preferable.

A second observation is that recording duration of behavior is difficult for teachers. For some behaviors, it is the fact that the behavior is initiated, rather than the duration of the behavior once initiated, that is significant. For instance, a child who talks out in a study hall interrupts the study behavior of others, and whether the behavior occurs for five seconds or one minute may be less important than the fact that he did talk out. Also, recording on a time-sampling technique is difficult when other teaching behaviors are being emitted simultaneously.

If observers are available, more continuous recording rechniques (such as recording the behavior in ten-second intervals) would provide data more sensitive to procedures. However, most classroom teachers simpy do not have access to observers.

FINDING CONSEQUENCES

Most teachers who have information about token reinforcement systems and have been exposed to Homme's application of the Premack Principle (Homme, 1965; Addison and Homme, 1966) still have difficulty identifying consequences to employ. Such obvious consequences as recess time, access to library books, magazines, art activities, story time, class monitor, opportunity to tutor others, early lunches, teacher proximity on specified occasions, parties, nonrequired school supplies, trips, films, preferred school subjects, and other individualized high-probability behaviors are at times difficult for teachers to identify. Of forty-two graduate students who employed behavior-modification projects last semester, 46% indicated deciding on a consequence was their biggest problem. Deciding on a behavior to modify was mentioned by 19%, recording the behavior by 13%, and deciding on a principle of learning on which to base the modification procedure by 9%. There were miscellaneous problems which accounted for 1%.

AVERSIVE CONTROL

In the beginning it was almost demanded of the students that they arrange their modifications to avoid any form of aversive control. Justification for this demand was easy to document (Skinner, 1961; 1965). However, some teachers began using a point-loss component in their systems anyway, and the dire consequences that have been predicted to result from aversive control were not observed.

SPECIFIC FAILURES

Three such systems were classified by either the teacher or the author as failures.

Teacher A. This teacher implemented a token system in a fourth-grade class with four target behaviors. Students earned tokens for scoring 80% or better on exams and turning in assignments on time. Tokens were lost by talking out without permission and not being seated within one minute after each bell sounded. Tokens were backed up with choice of activity in free time, opportunity to tutor other children, and extra recess time. Tokens were exchanged for the consequence at the end of the day, and it was planned to extend gradually the number of days per payoff.

Three problems contributed to the failure of the tokens to modify behavior. (1) The teacher reported the introduction of the system to the pupils went "badly." Her instructions were not taped, so it is impossible to recapture exactly what she said. She attempted to explain verbally how the system would operate instead of just demonstrating the contingencies. This tactic generated many questions and confusion regarding target behaviors, contingencies, etc. (2) All four target behaviors were augmented at once, which contributed to the reported confusion. (3) The consequences, while high-probability behaviors for many individuals, may not have been effective for the class, as the class voted on what consequence would be available at the end of the day. In retrospect, this teacher either did not have a consequence that was reinforcing to the entire class, or she was poorly organized at the beginning and set up too many target behaviors.

Teacher B. This teacher set up a token system to decelerate disruptive behaviors in a fifth-grade class—hitting, pinching, or tripping others. After one week of modification the teacher reported the behaviors were not decelerating. The class was observed, and on one occasion reliability of the teacher's observations was found to be less than 40% agreement.

It was discovered that the teacher did a lot of individualized teaching and was often physically not in a position to accurately record the behavior. She has now implemented a system with such target behaviors as turning in work on time, 80% or better correct on exams, and pages completed in arithmetic workbooks, all of which result in a permanent record on the environment.

Teacher C. This seventh-grade teacher increased the frequency of work turned in on time with a token system backed up by an RE menu (Addison & Homme, 1966), which included availability of comic books for fifteen minutes every Friday. She failed to change the RE menu frequently, and lost control when the students read all of the available comic books.

REPERCUSSIONS IN SCHOOLS

When the abstract for this paper was written, two events had occurred that were quite alarming. One elementary principal had told a teacher that "behavior modifications" sounded too Orwellian, and he did not intend to have any "brainwashing" going on in his school. The second incident was a school psychologist's recommendation to a principal that "psychology was in too much of a state of flux" to begin implementing such systems. Apparently some administrators should be desensitized to the term "behavior modification" before teachers announce what they are doing.

This past semester teachers were encouraged just to begin their work and if questioned about it by fellow teachers or administrators to show them the data. Challenges such as these are best met by objective data and observation of the system in operation.

Many pupils who have been exposed to token-reinforcement systems have requested other teachers to implement such systems in their classrooms, and some parents have volunteered feedback to the teacher that their child seemed quite enthusiastic about the new procedure in school.

Conclusions

The teachers who have implemented token-reinforcement systems have all indicated initial enthusiasm for the projects. Even the teachers whose systems were reported as failures are either currently planning or conducting other token arrangements. In every project the system is being adapted to situations encountered on the initial trial.

The behavior-modification projects have proven to be a very useful teaching technique. Students report their motivation to increase as a result of the project, and part of the class discussion centers around the data class members are collecting. At the end of the course, students consistently report they consider the behavior-modification project the most useful part of the class.

References

Addison, R. M., and Homme, L. E. 1966. The reinforcing event (RE) menu. *National Society for Programed Instruction Journal* 4: 8–9.

Atthowe, J. and Krasner, L. 1965. The systematic application of contingent reinforcement procedures (token economy) in a large social setting: A psychiatric ward. Paper read at American Psychological Association, Chicago, 1965.

Ayllon, T., and Azrin, N. H. 1965. Measurement and reinforcement of behavior of psychotics. *J. exp. anal. Behav.* 8: 357–83.

Baer, D. M. In press. Recent examples of behavior modification in preschool settings. In Neuringer, C., and Michael, J. L. *Behavior Modification in Clinical Psychology,* ed. C. Neuringer and J. L. Michael. New York: Appleton-Century-Crofts.

Birnbrauer, J. S., Wolf, M. M., Kidder, J. D., and Tague, C. E. 1965. Classroom behavior of retarded pupils with token reinforcement. *J. exp. Child Psych.* 2: 219–35.

Clark, Marilyn, Lackowicz, J., and Wolf, M. M. 1967. A pilot basic education program for school dropouts incorporating a token reinforcement system. Unpublished manuscript, Bureau of Child Research, University of Kansas.

Cohen, H. L. 1967. Motivationally oriented designs for an ecology of learning. A paper presented at the American Educational Research Association, New York, 1967.

Gericke, L. L. 1965. Practical use of operant conditioning procedures in a mental hospital. *Psychiatric Studies and Projects* 3: June.

Girardeau, F. L., and Spradlin, J. E. 1964. Token rewards in a cottage program. *Ment. Retard.* 2: 345–51.

Homme, L. E., and Tosti, D. T. 1965. Contingency management and motivation. *National Society for Programed Instruction Journal* 4: 14–16.

Homme, L. E. 1966. Human motivation and environment. In *The learning environment: Relationship to behavior modification and implications for special education,* ed. N. G. Haring and R. J. Whelan. Lawrence, Kansas: *Kansas Students in Education,* pp. 30–39.

O'Leary, K. P., and Becker, W. C. 1966. Behavior modification of an adjustment class: A token reinforcement program. Unpublished manuscript, Urbana, University of Illinois.

Skinner, B. F. 1961. Why we need teaching machines. *Harvard Educational Review* 31: 377–98.

Skinner, B. F. 1965. Why teachers fail. *Saturday Review,* October 16, pp. 80 ff.

IV / HARDWARE AND
  SOFTWARE

The previous three parts have tried to make the point that human
learning is based upon certain principles and that when these
principles are applied carefully the learning process is greatly
enhanced. To this point emphasis has been placed upon change
agents such as attention, tokens, verbal praise, money, earning
privileges, incentives, and peer approval, all mediated by others as
reinforcers, which, by definition, increase the probability of
specific, desired behaviors.

The concept of reinforcers and reinforcement can become
automated, as the first three articles of this part outline. With
automated reinforcement the agent of reinforcement is mediated by
a mechanical-electronic-chemical feedback device that partially
relieves the teacher's burden and facilitates the student's
opportunity to pace his own rate of learning.

The first article in this part, by Edward B. Fry, discusses
programming and the varieties of ways material can be and has
been programmed. It is important information. Programmed material
is becoming more and more a part of the educational scene, because
it works. The second article, "Write and See," is a review of a new
technique for teaching handwriting developed by B. F. Skinner. The
third article is a résumé of the significant work of O. K. Moore, who

has designed what he calls a "responsive environment" for learning. Moore's teaching device is hardly applicable to the classroom, primarily because of cost, but it demonstrates how learning principles can be used to produce what anyone would agree are unusual effects.

The last two articles are technical notes on pieces of hardware that have proved helpful for persons involved in behavior modification. They can be important additions to a teacher's methods for gathering data.

26 / Programmed Instruction: An Introduction

EDWARD B. FRY

One of the principle problems apparent to you, the perceptive
reader, as you set out to use reinforcement theory is that of
serving twenty-five to thirty-five different children in a
classroom. Obviously, you cannot respond to each child with the
frequency that the theory demands. Programmed learning is
designed to help fill that void and answer some of the logistic
problems of omnipresence. This article is an
introduction to a technique to which, in all probability,
you have already been exposed as a student, because programmed
material is already standard operating procedure in many
schools. In the following selection Edward Fry makes
several references to other parts of his book Teaching
Machines and Programmed Instruction, which the interested
reader may wish to follow up.

The technique of programming is designed for those
students who are reinforced by correct answers to interesting
problems, which is a way of saying it does not work for
everyone. Nonetheless, the notion of programmed learning is an
important contribution to education and one about which every
teacher should be knowledgeable.

Learning is such an omnipresent factor in human life that we often overlook its presence in our everyday affairs and think of it chiefly in connection with formal academic education. Yet the worker who is assigned to a new machine in his factory, the family which moves to a new neighborhood, the new army recruit, indeed anyone faced with the need to acquire new or different knowledge, has a learning problem. In some few cases, learning must proceed without assistance; the worker may simply be taken to the new machine and left to his own devices. But it is usually recognized that this is a most inefficient method of learning; more often the worker is provided with a "teacher," in the form of a supervisor sent along to explain how the machine works, or of a book of instructions. *Both* the supervisor and the set of instructions are "teachers." This is a most important point. Although learning usually involves both a student and a teacher, the teacher need not be physically present in order to teach. Books, instruction pamphlets, moving pictures, television lecturers, phonograph records, or color slides may all be classified as teachers since they are able to impart knowledge. In fact they are often much more efficient at the task than is the live teacher.

Obviously, both the student and the teacher are vitally concerned with the question: What is the most rapid and efficient means of acquiring new information, or of learning? Though a final solution to this problem is beyond our present means, various teaching techniques have been developed and tested, and some have produced better results than others. One of the oldest of teaching techniques, and one of the most useful, is the practice of breaking down a body of subject matter into its constituent elements or steps and requiring the student to master one step before moving on to the next. Commonplace examples of the practice are found in arithmetic, or in the study of music, where lengthy items are broken into segments and mastered separately. The technique is at least as old as Plato and is the object of a number of hoary maxims. Modern research has sharpened and refined this procedure into a powerful and efficient teaching tool.

Programming

In the past few years teaching machines and programmed learning materials have attracted the attention and interest of teachers, school administrators, and training directors. The reason is that programmed learning materials have been shown to be surprisingly effective. Fre-

Source: Edward B. Fry, *Teaching Machines and Programmed Instruction* (New York: McGraw-Hill Book Company, 1963), pp. 1–13. Copyright © 1963 by McGraw-Hill, Inc. Reprinted by permission of McGraw-Hill Book Company.

quently they can teach as well as a human teacher, and sometimes even better. Often they can do the same teaching job in less time.

Although there is something less than unanimous agreement on the psychological principles involved in a programmed instruction situation, here are some which are most agreed upon:

1. The subject matter is broken up into small units called frames. In actual practice, these frames usually vary in size from several sentences to several small paragraphs.

2. At least part of the frame requires some type of response from the student. He must answer a question or fill in a blank. Active participation on the part of the student is required. Generally, it is desired that the activity also demonstrate understanding of the material.

3. The student is provided immediate feedback reinforcement. He is told the correctness of his answer, which has the advantage of immediately reinforcing the activity or immediately correcting a misunderstanding. Since many programs are written in such a way that the student is right a high percentage of the time, the act of telling the student that he is correct becomes a reward or reinforcement. Thus programs have a much higher amount of reward or reinforcement than most ordinary teaching situations.

4. The units are arranged in careful sequence. Because the subject matter is broken into small bits, the author must think carefully about the learning steps involved, and the result is a much better sequence of presentation. Careful sequence also embodies the notion of *shaping* or gradually leading the student toward the desired goals by rewarding him for activity that more and more closely approximates those goals.

5. Programs are aimed at specific goals. This has the desirable effect of making those involved in training evaluate their goals much more carefully and specifically.

6. Revisions are based on student responses. Because the student's behavior can be recorded for each frame, a knowledge of his understanding of each part of the lesson can be easily obtained. Thus if a student is making many errors on one section, the program obviously is not teaching well and must be revised. Here, then, is another cardinal principle of programming; namely, that the student is the final authority in determining whether or not the program is good. In traditional curriculum materials an "expert" often determines the final presentation, but in programming, the approach is more student-centered. Programs are also more carefully aimed at a particular ability level of student based on experimentation, not on opinion.

7. The student is usually free to vary his own rate of learning. A student may work through a program rapidly or slowly. He is completely independent of others in the class. Traditional methods such as lectures or motion pictures force every student to proceed at the same rate, which might be too fast for some and too slow for others.

These and many more learning principles are involved in programmed instruction. . . . If it has done nothing else, the programmed instruction movement has caused educators to rethink many of their teaching procedures and to revise them in the light of the theories and experiments of the field of psychology.

Types of Programs

Programs are usually divided into two main types, depending on the kind of response demanded of the student. The *constructed-response* type of program requires the student to write an answer to a question put before him by the programmer. The *multiple-choice* type of program requires the student to select one of a number of alternate answers to a given question. The constructed-response program asks the student to frame his own answer to an "open-ended" question; the multiple-choice program asks for a choice among alternate answers. The former clearly depends more upon the student's ability to *recall* data; the latter, on the ability to *recognize* it.

There are two major techniques for programming sequences that are currently widely used. In one case, the material is arranged in a single ordered sequence and every student must proceed from the first through the last item. This is known as *linear* programming. In other cases, more than one sequence or route through the material is arranged, and the student follows the sequence determined by his own answers. For example, a correct response to one question may lead down a route that skips several questions, while an incorrect reply produces a route on which each of these questions must be answered. This practice of providing alternate routes through the program is called *branching*. Since the student's responses determine the route followed, this type of programming is also called *intrinsic*. Both techniques are mentioned frequently throughout the text.

CONSTRUCTED-RESPONSE PROGRAM

The constructed-response program is associated chiefly with the work of psychologist B. F. Skinner at Harvard University, and his associates, including James Holland. The identifying features of a constructed-response program (often called a "small-step" or "Skinnerian" program) are:

    1. Use of small bits or units (or frames), averaging perhaps two sentences in length
    2. Forced student responses, usually in the form of a short written answer, following each item or frame
    3. The use of small, easily grasped steps in the presentation of the information (shaping)
    4. The use, generally, of linear arrangement

Skinner and Holland tend to program in such a way that the number of student errors is reduced to a low figure; hence, the small steps. They believe that the absence of errors contributes to more efficient learning, as a correct answer is in effect a "reward" or "reinforcement" for the student; that is, knowledge that he has answered correctly is stimulating and rewarding to the student, and an incentive to greater effort or continued effort. Holland attempts to maintain an error rate below 10 percent (or incorrect replies from fewer than 10 percent of the students responding to a given question); other programmers who accept this principle believe that the error rate should be less than 5 percent. . . .

The constructed-response program is not concerned with error rates alone, of course. Other considerations, discussed fully below, are the number of responses required of the student, the type of item included in the program (differentiated into those which convey information, those which review, those which test, etc.), and the techniques of programming actually employed.

MULTIPLE-CHOICE PROGRAM

The multiple-choice program offers the student a number of alternative answers to the question posed at the end of each frame, requiring him to choose one of them. Usually, multiple-choice programs are arranged in branches; the actual branch taken by the student is determined by his answer to any particular question. As already mentioned, this is often referred to as an "intrinsic" program, since each reply leads the student into a different route. One of the most widely known illustrations of this type of program is the so-called "scrambled-book system," developed by Norman Crowder. Here a correct response leads into a new body of material; an incorrect response leads through a corrective branch, then back again to the main body of the program. . . .

In an intrinsic or branching program, the item usually tends to be larger than the item used in the Holland-Skinner constructed-response program and normally requires a multiple-choice response. A typical item consists of one or two short paragraphs to be read by the student, followed by the multiple-choice question. An obvious advantage of this type of program is its capacity for explaining "why" a response is either correct or incorrect. Since the program always moves according to the predetermined pattern set for a particular response, it is possible to determine the cause of most errors and to prepare an appropriate explanation and remedial branch for insertion into the program at any point. The student who answers incorrectly can be forced into this remedial program before he is allowed to proceed with the regular program material.

Similarly, when a certain response indicates a need for review, the student choosing this response can be directed back to an earlier part of the program and asked to review its contents before continuing.

Since the program provides this built-in method for handling student errors, the rate at which errors are committed causes much less concern than in the Skinner-Holland program. In fact, it might even be argued that a few errors will provide the student with a more clearly defined understanding of the points explained by the program.

OTHER TYPES OF PROGRAMS

There are a number of variations on these two basic program types, depending in some degree on the material to be taught by the program and on the type of student for whom the program is intended. These variations include combinations of the various types of programming (branching and linear used together) as well as combinations of narrative writing and programmed sections, either linear or branching, or combinations of both. Obviously, a program intended for skilled adult workmen who require small amounts of specialized training directly related to their own work experience will differ markedly from a program intended to teach simple arithmetic to backward students. But most of the principles of programming can be demonstrated in terms of the two basic program types, constructed-response programs and multiple-choice programs.

Presenting a Program to the Student

The term *program* refers only to the material that is arranged in the sequence just described. There remains, then, the problem of selecting a vehicle for presenting this programmed material to the student. In general, programmed information is available in book form or in forms that may be used with a wide range of devices, popularly called "teaching machines" (see further on in this chapter, under Teaching Machines). In some cases, a single program may be available in a variety of forms.

BOOK OR MACHINE?

When a teacher leads her class through a particular problem one step at a time, explaining each step as it arises and questioning the class after each step to make certain that the lesson is being grasped, something very close to programmed learning is taking place. One might say that the teacher is presenting a "programmed" lecture. At present, most programs are available in a form that does not require the presence of a teacher, though the teacher may add materially to the value of a programmed exercise. The student is able to work through the program without assistance. Originally, programs are designed for use with teaching machines, but a number of programs have now appeared in book form and have been well received. Which type of program should be preferred or chosen? The question is at present being earnestly debated by those who are well informed about programming. . . . For the moment, there appear to be no sufficient grounds for always preferring one form to the other.

PROGRAMMED BOOKS

Programs available in book form, for use without a teaching machine, are usually in the form of a "programmed text" or a "scrambled book." A programmed text makes use of a small-step, constructed-response program. In a book with a horizontal format each item is printed on a page separate from the correct answer, which is usually given on the back of the page or at the beginning of the next page. The student reads the programmed item or frame, responds to the question posed for him, then turns the page to learn the correct answer. . . .

Recently the vertical format has become popular in programmed books. In this design, the correct answer is presented either beside or below the frame. This format allows the programmer to vary the frame size and also to present narrative material, such as introductions and summaries. This design does not require the constant turning of pages necessitated by the horizontal format, but does require that the student voluntarily cover the answers with a piece of paper or simple masking device. Many users of this format like the advantage of being able easily to review previous frames. This design is rapidly gaining popularity while other variations are being tried experimentally. An example of this format is given in Fig. 1.

Some authorities in programming depreciate the programmed-text format because it permits the student to cheat by looking ahead to learn the correct answer without properly answering the question, or even properly reading the question. Others feel that this type of cheating is irrelevant; they claim that since the student *does* learn the correct response, the object of teaching is fulfilled. As long as the student has a clear grasp of the question, this principle may be sound; if he skips over the question, it is questionable whether the answer he learns by cheating has much meaning for him. Student motivation is especially important in the use of programmed books.

A scrambled book unlike the programmed text, does not have its frames printed sequentially. Instead, they are scattered at random throughout the book. The student begins with one frame, and the response he gives to the multiple-choice question at the end of the frame determines the next frame to be done. This is always printed on a different page. When the student turns to the indicated page, he learns whether or not

FIGURE 1. Vertical Format*

Lesson 14. The Sampling Distribution

Most of our discussion of probability so far has made use of coin-tossing experiments as examples, because these experiments furnish convenient examples for learning the fundamental rules of probability. For the next step, however, coin-tossing is an inadequate example. There are only two kinds of potential events in coin-tossing experiments, and ideas developed around the coin-tossing examples can be used only with data which have been classified into two categories. This limitation is particularly handicapping when the outcome of an experiment may vary in degree or *amount*. A coin cannot turn up "partly heads" or "heads-to-some-extent," but in the "new drug" experiment, for example, the difference between a pair of matched "new drug" and "neutral drug" patients might vary in size.

The procedure suitable for coin-tossing experiments can be applied to all those cases in which outcomes fall into two distinct classes. Lesson 13 illustrated these applications and gave the procedure a name—the "sign test." It is now time to study how information about the amount of difference can be taken into account, and how the significance of a particular amount of difference can be evaluated.

Section 1. Difference Scores

1. In the drug example as described so far, things were arranged in such a way that the psychiatrist had to make a very simple judgment: either that the one patient had im-

---

his answer is correct and finds also the next frame in his branch or route through the program. . . .

TEACHING MACHINES

Although teaching machines were developed before programs (partly as devices for testing), the close relation between machines and programs is readily apparent when one compares the basic characteristics of a teaching machine with the basic characteristics of a program. Most teaching machines are so designed that they:

1. Present subject matter in small units, usually consisting of a few sentences or a paragraph

proved more, or that his partner had improved more. Each pair of patients was like a single coin: the number of potential events for the pair was _____ , and it was assumed according to the null hypothesis that the probability of each potential event was _____ .

2

½

2. Instead of this simple arrangement, the psychiatrist might have been asked to assign a rating or score to each patient, indicating the *amount* of improvement. Then, for each pair of patients, a *difference score* could be calculated: the "new drug" patient's score minus the "neutral drug" patient's score. The difference score for the pair might have a _____ or a _____ sign, and it might have any one of several different _____ .

positive; negative

magnitudes, sizes

3. With 10 pairs of patients in this experiment, there would be _____ difference scores. With 100 pairs of patients, there would be _____ difference scores. The number of difference scores is equal to the number of***.

10

100

pairs of patients

4. The sign test could be applied to these difference scores. The scores could be divided into two categories: _____ and_____ .

positive;

negative

* The student covers the responses with a card while he reads the item.

Source: A Programmed Introduction to Statistical Concepts in Psychology and the Social Sciences, McCollough and Van Atta, McGraw-Hill Book Company, Inc., 1963.

2. Require the student to respond to each of these items by pushing a button or writing a word

3. Inform the student of the correctness of the response as soon as it is completed, either by showing the correct answer or by moving forward to the next frame when a question has been answered correctly

Most teaching machines present a linear program, though a few have been constructed so that branching may take place. In some of the complex electronic machines now available, branching of a very complex sort is possible. Clearly, it is mechanically easier to construct a machine that moves in serial order from one item to the next; if all the items are printed on a roll of tape or paper, for example, the paper need only be pulled through an exposure opening, manually or by machinery, to carry out the essentials of programming. Recently, the whole area of teaching machines has grown formidable and complex, particularly with the adaptation of electronic computers to programming techniques. . . .

AUTOMATION AND EDUCATION

One problem that everyone in education and training must face in these days of rapidly mushrooming technologic advance is the attitude that should be adopted toward the appearance of such devices as teaching machines and programs in the classroom. We have grown accustomed to the use of "visual aids" and other mechanical or electronic devices as auxiliaries to classroom teaching, just as we have adjusted to the impact of technology on other aspects of our lives. Formal educational institutions were, on the whole, fairly slow to adopt and use many of the new mass-communication techniques, such as motion pictures, educational television, tape recorders, etc., partly, no doubt, because of the considerable expense involved, and partly because of the difficulties encountered when new equipment and new techniques are adapted to traditional classroom patterns. Each year, however, there is an increased recognition of the new world of sounds, sights, and ideas that such tools can bring into the classroom.

Programmed instruction and teaching machines seem also to offer great promise as aids to instruction, although they are still new and in some respects untried. Many basic features of programs are unique. Whereas motion pictures and other means of communication are suited, generally, for mass training, teaching machines are intended for individuals. They offer a range of flexibility that may well make it possible, in an age of large classes and limited time for individual instruction, to achieve the great educational ideal of allowing each student to proceed at his own best pace; this is a boon not to be lightly thrust aside. The teaching machine, if sufficiently complex, can interact with the student to a surprising degree, varying with his responses, changing to meet changes in his rate of progress or in the complexity of the material being studied. Even the simpler machines produce an element of interaction with the student if they are well designed and carefully programmed. There are machines, in fact, which allow the student to question, to ask for further information, to demand review, to demand explanation. It is this individualizing aspect of teaching machines and programs which distinguishes them most sharply, perhaps, from more conventional teaching devices. This characteristic broadens their application, rendering them suitable, or even desirable, for the solution of educational problems that cannot be solved by books alone.

MACHINE VS. TEACHER?

Under no circumstances should the preceding remarks be taken to mean that the program and teaching machine can, in some mysterious way, "replace" the teacher, any more than educational television relegates the classroom lecturer to oblivion or books eliminate the need for lecturers. Quite to the contrary, the program and teaching machine constitute one of the greatest benefits to the teacher to appear on the educational horizon in years. To the harassed and overworked teacher, burdened with large classes and endless time spent in supervising what is essentially rote learning or presenting facts to be memorized, the program and teaching machine may prove a bonanza. They make possible, and practical, the regulation of the student's progress by his own ability, and offer an opportunity to banish much of the drudgery of teaching, leaving ample time for the individual teaching that every teacher wants to provide. The need for the teacher, to inspire and motivate, to guide and correct and criticize, is in no way diminished by the development of teaching machines. What is offered is the possibility that the teacher will be able to spend more time on the all-important task of teaching.

THE VALUE OF TEACHING MACHINES AND PROGRAMS

One of the most interesting and rewarding developments in the introduction of teaching machines and programmed learning has been the acceptance of the students who have used them. But this is dwarfed at times by the exciting possibility that individual achievement can be extended more efficiently than is possible with conventional instruction techniques. For research studies indicate that both training time and teaching time can be materially reduced by the use of programmed learning. Teaching machines and programs *do* work, and work well, for the gifted, for the average student, and for those who are below average.

Of course, it must be remembered that many aspects of programmed instruction have yet to be fully and carefully investigated. Perhaps this is one reason why teachers and administrators have thus far shown only a limited interest in its use. Some of the current findings in programming research are included in the material that follows, even though the work has been carried out on a small scale. Already, enough evidence is available to indicate that many of the problems which are inherent in the more traditional forms of education and which educational psychologists have already thoroughly investigated are identical to those encountered in programming. It may, in fact, soon be found that there is a wealth of information already available that can be used to improve and stabilize the techniques of programming and the design of teaching machines.

In this respect, it is significant that the development of teaching machines and programs is due primarily to the work of educational and research psychologists. Pressey at Ohio State University, B. F. Skinner at Harvard, and others similarly engaged in research pioneered the development of this new technique. For them, it offered the opportunity to apply the learning principles observed in the laboratory to instruction in the classroom and to do so in a consistent manner. Programming, in these terms, is a technique for applying the fruits of painstaking research in learning to individual study, in a way that will make study more interesting, more individualistic, and more fruitful.

27 / Using Operant Techniques to Teach Handwriting

TRUDY VILLARS

The preceding article dealt with the rationale of programmed instruction. This article is an introduction to a programmed set of instructional materials to teach handwriting. It is unique in that it uses a special pen with chemically treated paper to feed back appropriate responses.

The task of training a child to write is usually time-consuming and often as frustrating for the teacher as it is for the student. This method promises to take some of the strain out by providing, through increasingly difficult steps, immediate confirmation or correction of the child's efforts.

Though there is much that is unknown about human learning, there are some principles for which there is considerable empirical support. One of these deals with feedback during the learning process. The return "messages"—be they correct answers, neurological-kinesthetic feedback, or nods of approval from a teacher—are an important ingredient in teaching-learning. Moreover, the sooner feedback comes after the correct or appropriate response, the more that behavior has a chance to become built in or learned.

Source: This is the first publication of "Using Operant Techniques to Teach Handwriting," written especially for this volume.

One of the forerunners in the application of the principle of immediate feedback was B. F. Skinner. Programmed learning, where the student's answer can be quickly compared to the correct answer, is so well known that it hardly needs description here, for that student who has not used programmed material of some sort is indeed rare. Recently, Skinner has elaborated on the principle of programming to teach handwriting with a set of materials entitled *Handwriting with Write and See*.[1]

Write and See is one of a number of programmed instructional aids which are being adapted to all grade levels. This method is used to teach a wide range of subjects including languages, mathematics, grammar, and social sciences, and it makes available to the classroom the techniques of operant conditioning, a demonstrably effective means of teaching.

Programmed learning breaks the subject matter into very small steps, which gradually explain the material. Each step is designed to follow the preceding one logically and to provide for the user a minimum of difficulty. Thus the subject matter is presented in a way that maximizes the probability of success and consequently the probability of satisfaction with results.

Handwriting is, in this case, learned by means of a chemically prepared book and pen, similar to the children's water-color books where water alone turns the sections of the picture a variety of colors. In *Write and See* if the student forms a stroke or letter properly, the pen writes with a gray color. If a stroke is not correct, only a pale yellow will appear. Thus the child sees a mistake immediately and can correct it, or, conversely, the dark line reinforces his correct response. See figure 1.

The program consists of four books, which develop in programmed steps printing and then cursive writing to the point where the child writes paragraphs and answers questions about correct handwriting. The guidance of the special pen is gradually withdrawn. Much as training wheels on a bicycle, initially the special materials allow the student confidence as he is learning, but by the time he has completed the fourth book he is independent of the "training lines" and has developed his own handwriting.

The major reinforcement of this learning program is within the program. It is designed so that the successful completion of each step may serve as a reinforcer. The ability to form a letter completely in gray, with no stray yellow, is the goal and is usually rewarding each time it is accomplished.

Not only does the reinforcement affect behavior but the frequency

---

[1] B. F. Skinner, with the assistance of Sue Ann Krakower, *Handwriting with Write and See* (Chicago: Lyons and Carnahan, Inc., 1968). Reproduction of material from *Write and See* is by permission of the authors and publishers.

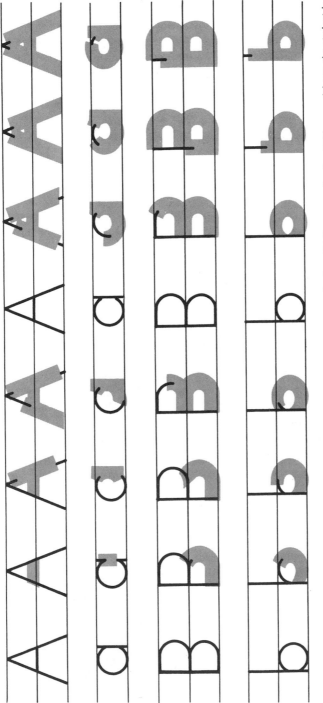

Figure 1. An example of student material from Book I of Write and See. The student has only the solid lines as a stimulus. With a special pen the student is to make the incomplete letters look like the completed models. The gray areas here indicate that part of the paper treated with an invisible chemical. When the pen and chemical interact, a dark gray line results; when the pen marks outside the invisible gray area, a pale yellow mark is made.

with which the reinforcement of a behavior is given greatly affects how quickly the behavior is learned. If a child is reinforced every time he does his homework, he very quickly begins completing his homework every night. On the other hand, if reinforcement is rare for completing homework, he will take longer to learn. Speed of learning is related to the frequency of reinforcement.

Likewise, the frequency of reinforcement often affects the drop-out quality of learning. Although constant reinforcement develops the behavior more quickly, it also allows the behavior to extinguish or drop out more quickly. If conduct marks are the sole reinforcement for good behavior in the classroom and they are suddenly removed without replacement by other reinforcers, the behavior in the classroom will rapidly change. If, however, reinforcement begins with constant reinforcement and is shifted to some variable schedule, where the behavior is reinforced randomly, that behavior usually continues much longer after the reinforcement is removed.

The most effective method of training is initially to reward the behavior constantly until it is established and to taper the reinforcement off gradually. Initially in *Write and See* the child needs to see when he is correct, to establish his skill. After the student is confident, he can continue without guidance of the special pen and paper. For a while the occasional check and reinforcement of the formal handwriting class will be helpful, but by the end of the program his style will be firmly established.

The most valuable aspect of the program is that it is designed to allow each student to progress at his own rate. This individualized instruction has many advantages, not the least of which is that the teacher is freed to assist students on an individual basis. The slow student is not lost but can be encouraged and assisted. The quicker student is allowed to progress more quickly and is not bored. This is an ideal situation for instruction to avoid both boredom and frustration.

In addition to rather straightforward training exercises *Write and See* has a number of games involving writing. Figure 2 is an example of such an activity once the children have learned the rudiments of cursive writing.

Another activity in the middle part of the series is designed to train students in spacing as well as correct letter formation. Figure 3 is a sample page.

Finally, the special pen is no longer used and the children are asked to write with pencil. The training immediately prior has defined specific criteria for what the authors believe constitutes good hand-writing. Note in figure 4 that, on the basis of these criteria, the students criticize their own handwriting.

All the lower-case letters of the alphabet are hidden in this picture. Find and write them.

a b c d e f g
h i j k l m n
o p q r s t u
v w x y z

Figure 2. An example of one of the writing games in <u>Write and See</u>. Again, as in Figure 1, the gray areas are invisible in the student's book.

Write the words that are missing from this story. They are at the end of each line.

Little Bear	
One day ~~*Little*~~ *Bear*	*Little*
went ~~*for*~~ *a walk.*	*for*
"Stay ~~*away*~~ *from*	*away*
the ~~*bee*~~ *tree," his*	*bee*
mother ~~*said*~~ *to him.*	*said*
Little Bear ~~*did*~~ *not*	*did*
listen. ~~*He*~~ *ran right*	*He*
to the bee ~~*tree*~~*. He*	*tree*
dipped in his ~~*paw*~~	*paw*
and ~~*began*~~ *to eat*	*began*
the sweet ~~*honey*~~*.*	*honey*

Figure 3. An example of training in spacing.

Write a short paragraph about your handwriting.

Consider each of these points:

beginning strokes	upper loops	size and slant
ending strokes	tracing	spacing
lower loops	capital letters	letters on base line

_____

_____

_____

_____

_____

_____

_____

_____

_____

_____

_____

_____

_____

_____

Look at your paragraph. How has your handwriting improved?

☐ correct beginning strokes   ☐ good capital letters

☐ correct ending strokes   ☐ correct size

☐ correct lower loops   ☐ correct slant

☐ correct upper loops   ☐ good spacing

☐ correct tracing   ☐ letters rest on base line

Figure 4. The final activity of the last book in the series. The students have now discarded the special pen for pencils.

Write and See has been in the commercial market for only a short time and has yet to undergo use by large groups of children. Indeed, there may be flaws in it, but the prospects are good for success as a teaching-learning aid because of its foundation in learning principles.

28 / Autotelic Responsive Environments and Exceptional Children

OMAR KHAYYAM MOORE

O. K. Moore created quite a stir among behavioral scientists and educators when he first introduced his "talking typewriter." In effect, he demonstrated that he could teach two- and three-year-old children to (a) use a typewriter, (b) spell words correctly, and (c) compose respectable poetry and prose. It was quite a shock to an educational tradition that had assumed a child was not "ready" for such sophisticated activity until school age. Moreover, Moore's children seemed to be happy and, between sessions, eager to get back to the typewriter.

This, one of the longest articles reprinted here, describes in careful detail Moore's rationale, his equipment, students' responses, and various phases of the training. This article is important not just because of Moore's technique but because it demonstrates that children are ready for structured learning experiences long before most people realize.

In every society there are those who fail to learn the things which are held to be essential for carrying out the role of a competent adult, or who learn so slowly that they are generally out of phase with the age-

Source: O. J. Harvey, ed., *Experience, Structure, and Adaptability* (New York: Springer Publishing Company, Inc., 1966), pp. 169–216. Reprinted by permission of Omar Khayyam Moore, O. J. Harvey, and the publisher.

graded societal demands imposed upon them. Slow learners are apt to be problems to themselves and to their friends. It is recognized, in scientific circles at least, that there are many and diverse causes for failure to learn at the socially prescribed rate: brain damage, emotional disturbance, social-cultural deprivation, and the like.[1]

What is not perhaps so generally recognized is that prodigies are sometimes out of phase with societal demands also; they tend to make people as uncomfortable as retarded children do. Both retarded children and prodigies unwittingly violate social expectations—they need help if they are to reach their full potential. Both the ultrarapid and the ultraslow are *exceptional* children. The main topic of this paper is to describe some methods whereby the acquisition of complex skills can be accelerated, for both ultraslow and ultrarapid learners.

For a number of years my staff and I have been conducting studies of early learning in prenursery, nursery, kindergarten and first grades, where children are in the process of acquiring complex symbolic skills. In the course of this work I formulated the notion of a responsive environment and decided to act on the assumption that an *autotelic responsive environment* is optimal for acquiring such skills (Moore, 1961). I will now try to make clear just what this assumption means.

I have defined a *responsive environment* as one which satifies the following conditions:

1. It permits the learner to explore freely.
2. It informs the learner immediately about the consequences of his actions.
3. It is self-pacing; i.e., events happen within the environment at a rate determined by the learner.
4. It permits the learner to make full use of his capacity for discovering relations of various kinds.
5. Its structure is such that the learner is likely to make a series of interconnected discoveries about the physical, cultural or social world.

My colleague, Alan Ross Anderson, and I have defined an activity as *autotelic* if engaging in it is done for its own sake rather than for obtaining rewards or avoiding punishments that have no inherent connection with the activity itself (Anderson and Moore, 1959). The distinction between autotelic and nonautotelic activities is somewhat vague, but it can be applied in some cases without difficulty. Consider tennis playing as an example: we cannot play tennis without getting exercise,

[1] At present there is no way to measure the basic capacities of human beings independently of their experiences. Also, there undoubtedly are interactional effects between *capacities* and *experiences*. It is not assumed here that the retarded child is necessarily wanting in "basic capacity." The use here of such terms as "gifted" and "retarded" is simply intended to be consonant with standard usage in the field.
For acknowledgements see the end of this chapter.

playing at all is a sufficient condition for exercising—so if we play for this reason, among others, this is an intrinsic reward. However, if we play for money, then the activity is not autotelic, since tennis and money need not go together—witness, amateur players.

In general, setting up a system of extrinsic rewards and punishments for engaging in an activity makes the learning environment more complex. As an illustration, consider a child who is learning to read aloud a list of words such as "fat" and "fate," "mat" and "mate," and "rat" and "rate," etc.; pretend also that an experimenter rewards or punishes the learner depending upon success or failure. Imagine that the reward is candy and that the punishment is mild electric shock.

Under these circumstances, the child not only has the task of learning to read and pronounce these words, but also that of figuring out the relation between candy and electric shock, on the one hand, and his own efforts, on the other. There is no intrinsic relation between the words to be learned or between the letters of the words and the pronunciation, or between candy and the sensation of being shocked. It should be easy to see that learning to read and to pronounce words *and also* to anticipate the candy or the shock introduces irrelevancies which may distract or confuse the learner. It is not irrelevant, however, that after the child masters the words "fat" and "fate," he may be able to generalize to the words "mat" and "mate," or that he may be able to decipher new words not on the list such as "tin" and "tine." Children are pleased, and some become ecstatic, when they make discoveries of this kind. Pleasure thus derived, unlike the pleasure of eating candy, is inherently related to the internal structure of the task (and more broadly to the structure of the spoken and written language)—it is *not* a pleasure arbitrarily associated with the task by the experimenter acting in accord with his own ad hoc rule. Of course, sophisticated adults manage to disentangle nonautotelic irrelevancies from the essential features of many tasks; but we hold that this is not an optimal situation for learning difficult things.

The distinction between autotelic and nonautotelic activities is sometimes confounded with the issue as to whether rewards and punishments are either necessary or sufficient for learning to occur at all. Our objection to the use of extrinsic rewards and punishments is that they make learning situations unnecessarily complex. In effect, they add relations to be learned. However, to grant that, generally, there are intrinsic rewards and punishments associated with learning is not to prejudge the questions as to whether learning could take place without them.

As a theoretical matter it is very difficult to see how a learning experiment could be designed which would be in any way meaningful to the learner, and in point of fact, we assume (for the sake of conceptual clarity vis-à-vis the making of a distinction between learning and performance, i.e., practicing what has been learned) that rewards and punishments, whether intrinsic or extrinsic, are neither necessary nor sufficient for the occurrence of learning. But of course no one would want to deny that they are highly relevant to the willingness of the learner to continue to learn more and to his desire to practice what he has learned.

From what has been said above it is undoubtedly clear that not all responsive environments are autotelic, nor are all autotelic activities carried out within the context of responsive environments. It is the purpose of this chapter to describe an environment which is *both* autotelic and responsive. I feel that I have been able to contrive an environment of this kind, which takes the form of a research laboratory, for young children. Some aspects of the autotelic "responsive environments laboratory" to be described here are novel; for example, the children play with a "talking typewriter." But in order to interpret the behavior of children within this environment, it is well to keep the system as a whole steadily in view—to see it as a social as well as a mechanical system. For this reason, a physical description of the laboratory is followed by a description of the norms under which the laboratory is operated. A cultural characterization of what is to be learned is counterbalanced by a description of equipment and procedures which facilitate the learning. No one aspect of the environment should be thought of as constituting its essence; the laboratory was designed to fulfill all the conditions of an autotelic responsive environment. The techniques of operation are intricate and presuppose careful planning. And since the description of an environment without some reference to the behavior of its denizens is incomplete, at the end of this chapter information is given about the background and laboratory behavior of five children: two "educable retardates," one child on the borderline between the "educable retardate" and the "dull normal" one who is on the borderline between the "very bright" and the "gifted," and one "gifted" child (to use standard terminology).

The emphasis in this paper on exceptional children should not be construed as a lack of interest in those who are within the normal range. As a matter of fact, most of my work has been with normal children. However, extreme cases are sometimes illuminating. I hope that this is true here.

To return to the problems of those who do not meet the age-graded demands imposed upon them, the relevance of the research reported here on retarded youngsters is patent: anything which may help them become more competent is of educational interest. On the other hand, it is not at all obvious that accelerating prodigies is a socially useful thing to do; society seems to be organized so as to slow them down, if anything. However, a case can be made for the acceleration of prodigies. Indications will be given as to how prodigies can develop some of their own potentialities while helping other children in the development of theirs.

Laboratory—Physical Description[2]

The Responsive Environments Laboratory is located at Hamden Hall Country Day School, Hamden, Connecticut, a few yards from the Hamden Hall preschool classrooms. It consists of two adjoining prefabricated metal sheds, each 20' × 40', set on concrete foundations. One shed is windowless and the other has windows only in a small office area; they are centrally heated and air conditioned. The sheds are as simple as modern construction permits; they are made up of one-foot modular sections, have exposed ceiling and wall beams, and so on. In Shed 1 are five portable soundproofed booths, 7' × 7' × 7', lined along two 40' walls, leaving a middle aisle as well as small aisles between booths for observation through windows with one-way glass. Through a face and by-pass system the booths are separately air conditioned. One booth has camera ports and built-in lighting equipment so that sound motion pictures can be made on a semi-automatic basis. Shed 1 also contains a desk, a conference table and a secretary's desk.

A central two-way communication system permits the staff to speak or listen at the main console or at the booths themselves.

The interior of Shed 1 gives an impression of psychological warmth despite its spartan construction. Perhaps this is because the booths, which are its most prominent feature, have a natural wood finish. (Booth interiors are finished with off-white, sound-absorbent tiles.)

Shed 2 is divided into three areas separated by natural wood partitions: a small classroom, an office-conference room which also contains a booth for testing, and a bathroom. From the standpoint of construction the 16' × 20' classroom is an over-sized booth. Like the booths it is soundproofed, air conditioned, equipped with one-way glass, finished in natural wood (exterior) and natural wood and sound-absorbent tile (interior). Again there is provision for the making of motion pictures on a semi-automatic basis. Shed 2, like Shed 1, is warm and pleasant in emotional tone; together they form one functional unit.

[2] The Responsive Environments Laboratory described here served as the model for four other laboratories. Two of the laboratories operate under my personal direction —the others work cooperatively with me.

In order to avoid confusion, everything that is said here pertains to the Hamden Hall laboratory although the children discussed in the section (below) "Children in a Responsive Environment" did not necessarily come to this laboratory.

This laboratory was designed in accord with one overriding objective, that of making it conducive to carrying out autotelic activities by young children: it is simple, distinct, and separate: (a) simple in the sense that a game board or a playing field is devoid of irrelevancies, (b) distinct in the sense that a playing field has clear-cut boundary lines, and (c) separate in the sense that a grandstand sets barriers between participants and spectators.

The parts of the laboratory used by children are windowless; windows are an open invitation to digress. The absence of windows also increases the children's sense of privacy. . . . The booth interiors are free of the attention-grabbing patterns and whirligigs so typical of nursery and elementary classrooms. The soundproofing muffles irrelevant noises and further enhances a sense of privacy. The buildings are air conditioned in order to produce a constant comfortable environment; it makes no difference whether it is raining or snowing, sunny or cloudy, the general laboratory atmosphere is invariant. One-way windows, camera ports, semi-automatic motion-picture controls, and the like make it possible to observe and document children's behavior without intruding upon them.

It is important to note that children spend only a small fraction of their day in this laboratory. It is not suggested here that gay designs and intriguing novelties are not appropriate in many other contexts.

Laboratory-Autotelic Operational Norms

Behavioral scientists take it for granted that human organizations function within the context of sets of interlocking social norms; this is certainly true of the Responsive Environments Laboratory as a social organization. By *operational norms* I mean the social rules which govern the relations between laboratory activities, on the one hand, and the school, the parents, and children, on the other.

One problem with which I have been concerned in constructing a new environment is that of being explicit about its normative aspects. A fundamental part of the task of creating a special environment for carrying on activities autotelically is to differentiate these activities from other important aspects of children's lives.

It is worth noting that, in addition to the educational problems mentioned at the outset, all, or nearly all, human societies make provision for engaging in autotelic activities. This is not only a matter of specifying times and places for these activities—the basketball court at game time, the theater at 8:40—but it is also a matter of creating and observing norms which safeguard these activities as autotelic. For example, one is not supposed to bribe a basketball player to shave points.

The general public reacts with moral indignation whenever it is discovered that a norm of this kind has been violated. A distinction should be drawn between the norms which surround or protect an activity in its autotelic status and the rules of the activity itself. For example in bridge, onlookers are forbidden to *kibitz,* but this injunction is not a rule of the *game* of bridge. More generally, it is always possible to relax the norms which make an activity autotelic while leaving the rules of the "game" intact. Conversely, autotelic conventions can remain invariant while the rules of the game are changed.

With respect to the Responsive Environments Laboratory, every effort is made to maintain a setting in which "kibitzing" by parents and friends of the children is virtually impossible (there is a rule against their visiting[3] and the physical arrangement ensures privacy vis-à-vis the "significant persons" in the child's life—more technically, the "significant others," in the sense of Mead [1934], are excluded).

The staff seeks to make the laboratory a child-centered milieu. Even the introduction of a child to the laboratory is done by another child rather than an adult. A child guide takes the newcomer through the laboratory (equipment is turned off; the introduction to its operation is made later). Sometimes three introductory visits are needed before a newcomer seems to be at ease, although one visit is sufficient for most children. The guide also explains some of the relevant rules: (1) that he need not come to the laboratory unless he wants to, (2) that he can leave whenever he wishes, (3) that he must leave when his time is up (30 minutes maximum stay), (4) that he need not explain his coming or going, (5) that he go to the booth to which he is assigned for the day, (6) that if he says he wants to leave, or starts to leave, he can come back again the next day (but not the same day). Newcomers have the opportunity to explore every nook and corner of the laboratory. The guide watches this activity but does not interfere. After a while newcomers seem to feel satisfied that they have seen everything and are ready to leave.

It should be obvious that the role of the guide requires the ability to communicate clearly and to exercise self-restraint. The task of being a guide is assigned to gifted children; this is but one of many special tasks which they are given.

The laboratory staff is carefully instructed about treating the children. The import of the rules is that we want children to initiate activities. The staff is to respond to them rather than to teach them. Those who are in daily interaction with the children are not permitted

---

[3] As a matter of practice, parents are allowed one visit per school year. The visit is arranged so that they do not see their own child in a booth and the child does not see his parents in the laboratory. However, the laboratory has many visitors—roughly 600 in the past three years. Most visitors are either scientists or professional educators.

to see the background information gathered by the project's professional staff; for example, the operating personnel do not know I.Q. test scores. Operating personnel are randomly assigned to booths every day. (There are two kinds of booths, automated and nonautomated. In nonautomated booths an adult is with the child. Since adults do not teach, we prefer to call them "booth assistants."[4] The members of the staff who. are professional teachers[5] serve as supervisors of the laboratory as a whole, as well as booths.) No booth assistant should be uniquely associated with any given booth and its equipment, or with any particular child. (Children as well as booth assistants, are randomly assigned to booths each day.[6]) The conduct of the operating staff is monitored by a supervisor who can talk directly to the booth assistant without interrupting a child. This is especially important in training new booth assistants. (The foregoing remarks are applicable to nonautomated booths. At present there is one fully automated booth, which requires no adult in the booth with the child; further details about automation appear below.)

The Hamden Hall children leave their classrooms (nursery, kindergarten and first grade) to come to the laboratory every school day. When it is a child's turn to come, his classroom teacher[7] lets him know. He then either accepts or rejects his turn for the day. If he decides to come he takes his "pass" and goes by himself the few yards to the

---

[4] Booth assistants generally have been the wives of graduate students. (This means we have to train new assistants quite frequently because their husbands graduate.) One of the qualifications for the job of booth assistant is a strong aesthetic sense. Teacher training is not necessary. The importance assigned to aesthetics is perhaps a prejudice on my part. I assume that those who are artistically inclined are likely to find the subtle workings of children's minds to be of continuing interest, and that they are not apt to impose their views on children. This assumption may be unwarranted but it has resulted in the selection of remarkably emphatic, nondirective and patient booth assistants.

[5] It has been my experience that professional teachers who work out well as laboratory supervisors have both the ability to empathize with children and to organize efficiently. The role of laboratory supervisor is a critical one for the successful employment of the methods we are considering. It is in this role that the teacher, as a professional, can use her training and experience to good advantage. The seasoned professional teacher can draw on her years of experience to do such things as spot the child who is ill and should be home, or to analyze the hitches which arise in the process of performing a task which requires nicely coordinated effort on the part of the staff.

[6] Of the 102 children that I have studied there have been a few who, at times, have responded so much better to a particular booth assistant, or to the nonautomated equipment, or to the automated instrumentation than they did to the other conditions, that the laboratory departed from the usual procedure of random assignment until these children were able to play with pleasure wherever they found themselves. It will be made clear in the section "Children in a Responsive Environment" that it is important to take individual variability into account.

[7] The regular classroom teacher, like the laboratory supervisor, is important to the successful employment of these methods in the context of a school. She must be flexible enough to organize her own classroom activities so that the short individual trips to the laboratory do not unsettle the general routine. Her attitudes toward early learning are also important.

laboratory where he is checked in and goes to the booth assistant to whom he has been assigned. One of the most remarkable things about this environment is that, day in and day out, children elect to come to it. Sometimes several months go by without one child of the current group (which numbers 60) refusing his turn. However, it frequently happens that a child does not want to leave when his time is up, in which case he is gently picked up and told that another child is waiting.

From what has been said it should be clear that the adults the child encounters in the laboratory are *not* the significant adults in his life—they are *not* his mother, father, grandmother, etc. Those significant adults who ordinarily are in the best position to reward or punish him have no way of knowing how he spends his time in the laboratory on a day-to-day basis. It is therefore unlike Little League Baseball, with relatives and friends observing from the sidelines; the laboratory time represents 30 minutes *away from* the significant persons in his life.

To "cut off" 30 minutes from the rest of the day in this fashion does not necessarily mean that the experience is without consequences for the remainder of the child's day. Just as most autotelic activities make use of cultural objects (Anderson and Moore, 1957; Moore, 1958; Moore and Anderson, 1963; Moore and Lewis, 1963), which are formally isomorphic with significant features of many serious activities (as Anderson and I have argued before [Moore and Anderson, 1962]: (a) puzzles, (b) games of chance, (c) games of strategy, and (d) aesthetic objects are formally similar to (a) puzzling situations, (b) the aleatory features of experience, (c) cooperative and competitive undertakings, and (d) the affective side of living) so, too, it is possible to design autotelic responsive environments in which a child can play with cultural objects, which though not ordinarily treated autotelically, are still structurally isomorphic with selected aspects of the world outside the laboratory.

General Description of the Curriculum

As remarked above, a responsive environment is so structured that the learner is likely to make a series of interconnected discoveries about the physical, cultural, or social world. A responsive environment may occur naturally, or it may be planned. In this chapter the main interest is in the latter; i.e., environments that are artificially contrived to achieve certain objectives. Therefore, it is essential to decide what the learners are to be exposed to in the way of a curriculum. It will be explained in the section, "Procedures and Equipment," that there is a wide range of subjects which can be learned in a responsive environments laboratory.

Recently, and for the past several years, attention has been focused on acquiring languages, especially languages in their written form. From the perspective of a cultural analysis, the topic is a natural language and the children's *task* is to learn how to handle it more effectively. It was taken for granted that the children would already be able to use their native tongue (to date, most of the work has been done with English). My objective, then, was to design an environment (within the microworld of the booths) in which children would learn another form of their language: its written form. This enterprise presupposes that, in the broadest sense, spoken English and written English are isomorphic. From this standpoint, we can think of written English as visible speech and spoken English as audible writing. It is true that written English is a very imperfect phonetic transcription of speech; nevertheless, in planning this environment, I decided to work on the assumption that the spoken and written forms of English are *sufficiently* isomorphic[8] to enable children to find for themselves some set of rules which would permit them to move back and forth between these two linguistic forms. Certainly, spoken and written English are more nearly isomorphic than are spoken English and written German or spoken Chinese and written Chinese.

One of the obvious differences between spoken and written English is that they are handled through two distinct sensory systems: auditory and visual. There are also social differences between the two linguistic forms in their appropriate occasions of use. But young children do not know this and perhaps by constructing an environment in which writing is on a par with speaking and reading with listening, it might be possible to avoid some of the more unfortunate consequences of our educational system, a system which tends to produce speakers who have difficulty in writing, and tongue-tied writers. There also are avid readers who find it almost impossible to write—and good listeners seem to be in short supply all the way around.

I should like to make it clear (once and for all, I might add) that the Responsive Environments Laboratory is *not* just a place where children learn to read: approximately equal emphasis is given to speaking, writing, listening and reading. The underlying rationale is not only to treat speaking and listening, on the one hand, and writing and reading, on the other, as correlative processes, nor is it only to treat these two pairs of correlatives as elements of a four-cell matrix of linguistic relations. It is also to develop higher-order symbolic skills which are superordinate to these relations.

Speaking and writing are active processes and listening and read-

---

[8] By an *isomorphism* I mean something like the vague, usual use of the word in mathematics. Two structures are said to be "isomorphic" if there is a one-to-one correspondence between their elements which "preserves order" in some appropriate sense, i.e., which preserves corresponding relations defined on each structure. In practice we have to define isomorphisms, one at a time, for each structure in which we are interested. But the idea is at least sufficiently clear so that we can usually tell when we have one.

ing are passive ones. An attempt is made to tie each of these four activities (or passivities) to the others, not only maintaining a balance between active and passive processes, but also avoiding the pitfalls of under-emphasizing or over-emphasizing any one of them at the expense of the others. The overall objective is to develop higher-order intellectual abilities which may be thought of as ranging over this complex of linguistic processes.

In order to determine whether such overall abilities are developing and, at the same time, to facilitate their development, it is necessary to set some task for the children which involves all four of the processes. There are many jobs which would do the work. The one which was chosen as a part of the laboratory curriculum was publishing a newspaper. The first-grade class publishes its own newspaper (there are also contributions by nursery and kindergarten children) and the four processes (speaking, writing, listening, and reading) are subordinate to the superordinate skill of *publishing a newspaper*. A child may begin a newspaper story by speaking into a microphone; later, he will type his own story from dictation—this means that he goes directly from the spoken word to the written word. After he has completed his transcription he may then read it critically before turning it over to one of the other children who is an editor. The editor first reads the typescript, perhaps reading it aloud to a fellow editor, and suggested changes are then discussed with the author. Next step: the children type the story on stencils along with other stories. Finally, they mimeograph, collate, staple and distribute the paper. If they wish to discuss the newspaper in their regular classroom, they may do so (with their teacher's permission). It is also permissible to take the newspaper home where it is sometimes subject to further discussion.

It can be seen, then, that publishing a paper, as the children do it, is an achievement which embraces speaking, writing, listening and reading. This activity provides guidelines on the basis of which the children set standards for spelling, punctuation, intelligibility, general relevance and interest. The emergence of such a higher-order skill helps give to reading and writing the same kind of direction and meaning that listening and speaking have by virtue of their ordinary social uses.

Publishing a newspaper is an activity which ordinarily would be beyond the ability of a first-grade class. Permitting the children themselves to set the standards for the newspaper seems like a risky educational practice; however, here again is another vital role for gifted children to play. They are capable of serving as editors and coordinating the efforts of the other children, which allows them to make extensive use of their intellectual abilities within the social context of their peer group.

By the time the laboratory children are able to publish a newspaper the subordinate skills have been learned well enough so that the *learning* problem has been replaced by the *practicing* problem. There are many intrinsic rewards and punishments associated with turning out a newspaper. To be sure, when the proud parents get copies there may be additional extrinsic rewards and punishments—but by this time it is too late for anyone to interfere with the learning of the subordinate skills.

The actual work of turning out the newspaper is done under the supervision of a teacher who introduces the children to the equipment (copy aid, mimeograph, Thermofax, etc.) and guides their first efforts. This takes place within the small classroom in the laboratory, already mentioned. This classroom is called the "transfer room." What this name connotes is the *transfer* of skills acquired individually within the privacy of the booths to social activities. Just as we make explicit provision for the introduction of children to the laboratory with the help of gifted child guides, we also make explicit provision for relating laboratory activities to outside interests through the help of our more precocious children who serve as editors. The children are very proud of their newspaper—everyone contributes in his own way and most importantly it really is *theirs*. Several articles taken from the fourth issue of the paper are included in order to give the reader some notion of the general level of competence of the children. (See Figure 1.)

In many schools the curriculum for the first six grades tends to treat reading and writing as separate subjects. Writing in the sense of composing original stories is yet another subject. Spelling and particularly punctuation are handled as special topics; and some punctuation marks (say), the ampersand, asterisk, colon, or semicolon, are entities whose appearance on the printed page remain a mystery to many even beyond the Ph.D. dissertation. The laboratory curriculum represents an attempt to deal with these skills and topics as part of an integrated complex of linguistic processes. In the next section we describe some procedures and equipment by which children can be led to such excellence.

Procedures and Equipment

Useful as the idea of an autotelic responsive environment proved to be in constructing the laboratory and in laying down guidelines for its operation, it still did not have a sharp enough cutting edge to be of much help in planning the procedures and equipment to be used by children within the microworld of laboratory booths. I found that it was worthwhile, as an aid to my thinking at least, to make additional assumptions of a psychological kind about personality and human learning processes in order to get a purchase on the problem of designing practical procedures and equipment. Fortunately, I had been working for a number of years on the more general problems of formulating a theory of social interaction. This theory is still in an unsatisfactory state; nonetheless, the procedures and equipment described here are an application of some of its fundamental ideas. It lies beyond the scope of this paper to present even as much of the theory as has been worked out, but for present purposes it probably will be sufficient to say that this theory builds on the work of George Herbert Mead (1934), or, more accurately, it builds upon his work as I understand it. It also takes some account of the subject matter of other important psychological and social psychological theories.

PHASE 1. FREE EXPLORATION

Let us turn our attention now to the interior of a booth and imagine that a child, already introduced to the laboratory in the manner previously explained, is ready for his first booth session. For convenience of exposition, pretend that he is to begin learning in an automated booth. . . . The booth assistant helps him get into the elevated chair (because some children do not like to sit in a *high chair,* in the laboratory we call it an "elevated chair"), turns one switch, tells the child to enjoy himself and to raise his hand if he wants anything. Without further comment the assistant leaves the booth, closes the booth door and then goes to a control panel mounted on the exterior wall of the booth, presses appropriate buttons and begins to watch the child through a one-way window located just below the control panel.

The child is alone in the booth confronted with what may appear to him to be a typewriter with colored keys. (Prior to entering the booth his fingernails have been painted with non-toxic water colors. There is a match between the nail colors and the colored typewriter keys so that striking keys with matching fingers constitutes correct fingering. Also, there is a noticeable difference in pressure between the left-hand and the right-hand keys to help the child orient his hands. Behind the keyboard is a Lucite housing which permits him to see everything in front of him, but which keeps his fingers out of the moving parts of the typewriter.) Whether or not he believes that the object in front of him is some kind of a typewriter, he is in fact in charge of much more than an electric typewriter—he is at the controls of a computer in-put and read-out device, three distinct memory systems, an audio-recording system, and two visual exhibition systems, all of which are integrated by a central electronic logic and control system.[9] Nevertheless, the operation of this complex instrument is under his management.

[9] E.R.E., the Edison Responsive Environment, is the product of a three-year collaborative effort with an engineering team of the Thomas A. Edison Research Laboratory of West Orange, New Jersey, a division of the McGraw-Edison Company.

FURRY AND NUTTY
by Venn Moore

Once upon a time there were two
squirrels named Furry and Nutty.
They were very cute squirrels; they
would scamper up and down the trees
to play. Also they would do cute
tricks on telephone wires. These
squirrels liked acorns, peanuts and
walnuts. At night they hunted for
food and dug a hole to store it in
a secret place. They lived in holes
in trees; sometimes they moved away
to build a different kind of home.
One spring they had a baby and
named it Bushy. The reason they
wanted to name it Bushy was that
they lived in bushy trees and they
had bushy tails.
One day when they were doing tricks
on the telephone wires, it was
stormy and it lighteninged. It
caught on to the wire, and Furry was
electrocuted. Poor Furry was dead!
Poor Bushy and Nutty were alone.
From that time Nutty and Bushy were
more careful than they used to be.

TWO FIRES
by Jeffrey Batter

Once when we were going to school,
there was a fire on Laurel Road.
When the fire started, the children
were already outside, and the mother
was badly hurt. On March 31, my
brother lit a fire beside the garage.
The firemen next door put it out.

THE FUNNY BUNNY
by Shirley Horne

If I were a bunny,
I'd be funny.
I'd earn money
By selling honey.
In the sunny
It would get all runny.
Isn't that funny?

THE PEABODY MUSEUM
by Mary Ellen Burns

During vacation I went to the
Peabody Museum with my Daddy
and my brother, Joseph. We saw
a big dinosaur, and it was so big
that Joseph had to look up. In the
same room we saw the largest turtle
in the whole wide world.

OUR TRIP TO BOSTON
by Lisa Whitcomb

We went to Boston and when we were
driving we had to stop to have
supper. We stayed with some friends.
When we got there, it was ten o'-
clock--way past our bedtime.
We woke up Mom and bothered her.
I mostly watched TV. Daddy watched
TV with me, and Mom talked with
Ellie Priess. When Daddy was not
watching TV, he was talking to Uncle
Al. We had fun!

MY LOOSE TOOTH
by Kathy Johnstone

I have a loose tooth and it is my
first one. When it come out I will
put it in a glass of water and in
the morning I will find a quarter
under my pillow.
The fairy will leave the money for
me. I may buy some groceries with
it for my mother.

THE WOODPECKER
by Tamara Plakins

I saw somebody peck
And did wreck,
But I never saw anybody smack
Someone in the back.

Figure 1. Selections from the "Lab Record."

The boys and girls in Kindergarten are one year younger than we are. They all made up their stories, and then they typed them for our newspaper. We showed them how to cut a stencil. "Lab Record" Editors.

THE ELEPHANT
by Spencer Taylor

Once upon a time in the far away land lived a little elephant named Timmy. He ran away. He almost got run over.

THE HAUNTED HOUSE
by Susan Connelly

The haunted house has ghosts and goblins and demons. It's scarey to go in, and you might get killed.

susan SQUIRTED ME
by Pam Malley

My friend Susan squirted me with water on my new dress. Susan had to put her head down.

MY BIRTHDAY
by Richard Wright

May 3 is my birthday. I will blow out the candles on my birthday cake. I want a fire engine.

MOTHER
by Helen Greenspan

Mother is well now. The cast is off her leg. Now she can drive me to school. I am glad.

GOLDTEID
by Jonathan Cahn

This is fun. We play combat soldiers. Davie and Stevie break through our team. We break through their team.

The Nursery school children just started to type their stories for the "Lab Record" and we helped them type the stencils. The Editors.

PAM
by Melanie Canadeo

Pam, you could be a nurse some-day. But when you be a nurse, you can not scream like you do now.

A MONKEY
by Brian Symmes

I saw a monkey feeding peanuts to lots of people.

I LIKE SCHOOL
by Carissa Whitcomb

I paint at Sharon's house. I like Ricky. I like God. He makes us healthy.

FISHING
by Larry Batter

I went fishing with my Father and my brother and we caught a goldfish and a whale!

PIRATES
by Charles Stainton

Larry and Charles are pirates. When my baby brother sleeps, my sister and I play outside.

KITES
by David Black

I went to the ball field and flew kites. We didn't get to stay long.

Figure 1 (continued)

Of course, not all of the abilities of the instrument are needed for the child's first session. The booth assistant has set E.R.E. in what is called Phase 1, Free Exploration, i.e., the instrument is set so that the child can explore the keyboard freely. Whenever a key is struck, E.R.E. types the letter (in large type) and pronounces the name of the character that has been typed. (The "reaction time" of E.R.E. to a key operation averages 1/10th of a second.) When a key has been depressed and released no key can be operated for about one second; this gives E.R.E. time to pronounce the name of the character. No two keys can be depressed simultaneously; this makes it impossible to jam keys or to garble pronunciations. The moment any given pronunciation is completed, the keyboard is automatically unlocked so that the child can go on exploring. The keyboard of E.R.E. is, essentially, a full standard one. (It has some additional keys which are needed for foreign languages —E.R.E. can be switched to any of six languages and special accent marks are provided—the extra keys are covered when not in use.) Because the standard keyboard has both upper and lower case, and the young child probably does not know this, there are small lights next to the upper and lower case keys to show which case is operative. If the child were to play by himself with an ordinary typewriter he might get "stuck" at the end of a line because he does not know about the carriage return. E.R.E. automatically returns the carriage at the end of a line even though there is a carriage return key whose function the child will catch on to sooner or later. His exploration will not be interrupted by using up a sheet of paper; E.R.E. has a fan-folded tape of paper several thousand feet long. It should also be mentioned that E.R.E. is rugged; it withstands the pounding it sometimes receives.

Returning to the hypothetical child, the intriguing question is: What will he do when he is alone at the keyboard of the "talking typewriter"? Until he strikes the first key he does not even know that the typewriter talks. (A motion picture was made of the first few minutes of a normal 2-year 7-month-old boy's initial exploration of a keyboard [Moore and Anderson, 1960]. This film shows nonautomated equipment with a booth assistant carrying out the various functions performed by E.R.E. This boy's behavior is typical of many normal children.) One thing we can say with near certainty about our hypothetical child is that he will not sit there for a half an hour simply looking at the instrument. Only one child out of the 102 children whom I have studied sat for as long as 10 minutes before striking a key. Most children begin immediately, using fingers, fists, elbows and an occasional nose—if the instrument were not jam-proof, the game would be halted in less than a minute, or if the keyboard were not locked during pronunciations, E.R.E. would babble. There are some children who proceed in a very thoughtful way; looking, listening, repeating what the instrument says, reflecting—in brief, they explore systematically. Some notice at once the relation between their colored fingernails and the colored keys and painstakingly match fingers to keys. If, at first, a finger is wayward, they use their other hand to guide it. Some children go on exploring for their full 30 minutes; others raise their hands and want to leave after a few minutes.

In order to guess what our hypothetical child is likely to do, it would be necessary to posit a great deal more about him. I will make one overall comment based on my experience with the laboratory children: he will like his first session and he will want to return to play with this fascinating "toy."

A daily record is kept of each child's performance in the laboratory. Some parts of this cumulative record are quite objective. E.R.E., for example, keeps track of the time the child spends in the booth and his stroke count, i.e., the number of times he depresses keys. Other aspects of the record are less objective, for instance, booth assistants' notes about a child's attitude. There is a daily staff conference at which each child's performance is reviewed. It is the laboratory supervisor's responsibility to decide when a child is beginning to lose interest in any given phase of the curriculum. There are children who will go on happily in Phase 1 for a number of weeks, whereas others' interest in this phase declines rapidly after as few as two sessions. Sooner or later every child's interest in Phase 1 will wane (at least every child the laboratory has encountered behaved this way) and before his interest completely disappears, he must be shifted to the next phase. If a child were permitted to completely exhaust his interest, he might very well not return to the laboratory. Quite clearly, the decision as to when to shift a child from one phase to another still is a matter of experience and judgment. In the very early days of this research I had to make this decision. Later, I trained supervisors who now are fully capable of performing this task. For the most part, the more objective indicators of declining interest are a sufficient basis for judgment; for example, a child's sessions become markedly shorter and his stroke count drops off. Sometimes a child will simply say that he is tired of what he is doing—his opinion counts. As a general rule, it is safer to err on the side of shifting the child too soon. It will be made clear below that explicit provision is made for regressing from advanced phases to more elementary ones, and since no significant persons in his life are there to see this regression, there is little stigma attached to it. All the children whom I have studied have regressed from time to time. The children call Phase 1 (Free Exploration) "plain typing." It is not unusual for even a gifted child to say with a little laugh, "Today I just want to plain type."

PHASE 2. SEARCH AND MATCH

When the laboratory supervisor makes the decision to shift a child from Phase 1 to the next phase, the learner receives no warning; he has to discover for himself that he is playing a new game with new rules. Phase 2 is called "Search and Match.". . .

. . . There is a picture [shown] on a rear-view projection screen. . . . To the left of the [picture] is an illuminated rectangular window (exhibitor cards can be inserted into this space through the open door on top). On the upper right side of E.R.E. is a triangular shaped open panel; this exposes controls for some of E.R.E.'s functions which are set by the booth assistant.

In Phase 2 the exhibitor system on which the picture . . . is projected is not used. The only new thing about this phase, in terms of visual display, is the use of the rectangular window. In this window characters can be exhibited in four different ways: (1) one character at a time with a red arrow pointing down to it, (2) a cumulative exhibit in which the red arrow points to a newly exposed character while all previously exposed characters on the same line remain visible, (3) all characters on one line are visible with the red arrow pointing to the one to be typed, and (4) all characters on the four lines in the rectangular window are exposed, again with the red arrow pointing to the one to be typed.

In Phase 2, unlike 1, E.R.E. takes the initiative in starting the game. All typewriter characters appear in the rectangular exhibitor window one at a time in random order. When a character appears with the red arrow pointing to it, E.R.E. automatically locks the keyboard with the exception of the appropriate matching key and pronounces the name of the character. If the child wants to get a response from E.R.E., he must find the right key. As soon as he strikes the matching key which causes the character to be typed, E.R.E. repronounces the character and then covers it up before exposing a new one. The game becomes a little more difficult when the new character is in a different case. Under this circumstance, E.R.E. first says "upper case" or "lower case" (as the case may be), the appropriate case light flickers, and the keyboard must be changed to the proper case (when this is done, E.R.E. again pronounces it) before the matching character is named by E.R.E. and can be struck by the child. It should be mentioned that if a child is fast enough at pressing the appropriate key, he can cause E.R.E. to speed up by omitting redundant pronunciations. If a child's attention has wandered so that he missed the first pronunciation, or if he has forgotten it, there is a repeat cycle which the booth assistant can start, using a delay appropriate for the given child. A dial can be set which will delay E.R.E.'s repronunciation in order to give the child a chance to speak first. E.R.E.

is not restricted to pronouncing the names of characters—it also can give phonetic values for them (or, for the linguistic purist, hints as to phonetic values).

What has just been described is the simplest version of Phase 2, Search and Match. As interest wanes in this first version of Phase 2, the booth assistant (following the laboratory supervisor's instructions) can make the game more challenging in many ways. For example, the assistant can cause (by pushing buttons or setting dials) E.R.E. to omit its first pronunciation of characters, or the second, or both. The window display can be changed to show characters cumulatively, one line at a time, or four lines at a time. A blank card can be used in the window so that the match is solely between pronunciations and keys.

I have found that adults, as well as children, like to play with E.R.E. in both Phase 1, Free Exploration, and the various versions of Phase 2, Search and Match. These activities are especially interesting to adults when E.R.E. is switched to a foreign language—one unfamiliar to the players. Of course, for children who are learning to read, the written form of English is a new language. Both children and adults discover that they always can succeed in finding the appropriate key in Search and Match by the simple-minded expedient of trying each key. This is a tedious and boring way to go at it on a continuing basis; both children and adults prefer to learn the characters.

PHASE 3. WORD CONSTRUCTION

When a child has eliminated nearly all of the "search" from the Search and Match game, it is time to shift to a new phase of the curriculum. Phase 3 is called "Word Construction." There are two forms of this game. One form leads to reading, the other to writing, i.e., writing in the sense of composing original stories. We will designate the former as "WC-R" (Word Construction-Reading) and the latter as "WC-W" (Word Construction-Writing). When a child has been shifted to Phase 3 he alternates in his booth sessions between these two forms of the game. Let us take up WC-R first.

Phase 3. WC-R / Up to this point, the child has been dealing exclusively with the building blocks, or primitive elements, of the written language (in this, punctuation marks have not been neglected). He has been exposed to and can discriminate among the basic set of elements from which all meaningful written expressions are formed. He is in a position to begin to get some sense of the formation rules of the written language. Now other of E.R.E.'s abilities can be brought into play.

Imagine that a child, who has become quick at finding individual characters, is confronted without notice with several of them at a time, isolated either by a margin and a space or by spaces. For instance, the first letters might be *b-a-r-n*. So, the child types *b-a-r-n*. E.R.E. pronounces these letters before and after each is struck and then, following the pronunciation of *n*, it calls for a space. A light flickers just under the space bar, and after the bar is pressed, E.R.E. says, "Space, *b-a-r-n*, barn." E.R.E. may also exhibit a barn on the projector. (As a matter of fact, pictures have been used very sparingly because they can be quite misleading in the early phases of learning to handle written symbols. The referent of many important words such as "if," "then," "either," "or," "some," etc., cannot be pictured in the same way that the referent of the word "barn" can be. Other words which are relational, but not obviously so, such as "mother," "father," "sister," etc., are not as easily denoted through pictures as some writers of children's primers seem to think. The use of pictures comes into its own when E.R.E. is "teaching" foreign languages or in Phase 4 where content, e.g., maps for geography, is important.)

From the standpoint of planning the curriculum, WC-R offers an infinitely large number of choices with respect to the selection of a beginning or basic vocabulary. The question is: What words should come first? There are a great many plausible criteria which have been offered by reading experts, linguists and others who have concerned themselves with this topic. For example, (1) word frequency, (2) letter frequency, (3) pronounceableness, (4) word length, (5) familiarity, (6) stimulus similarity, (7) grapheme-phoneme correspondence, etc. It is apparent that at least some of these are conflicting criteria; for instance, many familiar words are phonetically irregular. A sophisticated analysis could be carried through in which a vocabulary was selected in terms of a multidimensional weighting system based on the contribution various "dimensions" of words make to easy learning. I have no doubt that careful experimental studies would be of value in selecting an optimal basic vocabulary.

For my own part, faced with the problem of selection, I preferred a direct solution, namely, to choose those words which are constituents of interesting stories—that is, stories which have proved to be intriguing to children and adults over a long period of time, for example, *Aesop's Fables*.[10] Many children can be expected to have lost interest in WC-R long before they have mastered a vocabulary large enough to enable them to read a wide variety of stories. Therefore, it is essential to be able to shift them to at least some stories—this can be done only if they have mastered enough of the words to get started reading stories. If the stories are of some intellectual and aesthetic value, it is highly probable that the words out of which they are composed will offer a sufficient basis for

[10] I have also made use of word lists suggested by linguists and at times have combined these lists with those compiled from interesting stories.

making sound inferences about the relations between letters and sets of letters, on the one hand, and appropriate verbalizations, on the other.

The inventor Samuel Morse was faced with a similar problem when he was devising his code consisting of spaces, dots, and dashes. He wanted, in the interest of efficiency, to have the shorter symbols for the more frequently used letters, and the longer symbols for those less frequently used. If he had been like some contemporary investigators, he might have launched a rather extensive research project sampling the distribution of letters of the alphabet in various writings—but he did nothing of the sort. What he did instead was to count the number of types in the various compartments of a printer's type box. He assumed that printers would have discovered empirically the right proportions of letters to keep on hand in order to set type, and incidentally, this solution to his problem was within 15 percent of an optimal one.[11]

I assume that stories that have stood up over long periods of time use words in ways that are compatible with the intricate sets of relations holding between the spoken and the written forms of the language. I am not quite as sanguine about some of the concocted stories found in contemporary "basal" readers, although children can learn to read using basic vocabularies that are, in all likelihood, far from optimal.

Phase 3. WC-W / The WC-R form of the Word Construction game, explained above, is somewhat arbitrary from a child's standpoint. The experimenter has decided, in advance, what is good for him. It is especially important, from the point of view of sustaining children's interest, to let them take the initiative. It is also important to see to it that at times there is an almost perfect correspondence between their verbal skills and the written symbols with which they will be dealing. WC-W serves these purposes. The first step in this activity is to have the child go to the Transfer Room (the small classroom) where he is encouraged to talk—he may talk about anything he pleases—and everything that he says is recorded. Later, an analysis is made of his utterances and a list is compiled consisting of those words which are constituents of coherent statements on some topic in which he was engrossed. Sometimes it has taken weeks with a child to elicit such material. The next step is to program this word list in E.R.E. (E.R.E. is easily programed—it is not necessary to translate material into a machine language; hence, there are no technical difficulties to get in the way.) The child is virtually certain to find some of his own words meaningful.

An alternative version of WC-W involves the use of a standard recording-reproducing unit attached to E.R.E. or to an electric typewriter.

---

[11] The foregoing information about Morse is found in Pierce's valuable book on Information Theory (1961).

This version does not require programing. The child simply talks into a microphone and then takes his own dictation, word by word. In this version of the game, he responds to his own voice. (Interestingly enough, from a social-psychological perspective, some children reject their own voice, but will type other children's dictation.) A motion picture (Moore, 1960) was made of a girl 3 years 11 months old in which she first read a story—her voice was recorded—and then typed the story from listening only; she handled the dictation controls (start, stop, repeat) by herself.

This second version of WC-W eliminates the presentation of written symbols; the child goes directly from verbal utterances to the corresponding written symbols. Visitors who have watched this process are often surprised by children's ability to spell new words that are non-phonetic, or markedly irregular. Indeed, this is extraordinary! I have concluded that there must be some subtle lawfulness holding between the spoken and written forms of English, otherwise young children would not spell as well as they do in this version of WC-W. This should give pause to enthusiasts for spelling reform. In any case, this relation seems worthy of serious study.

PHASE 4. READING AND WRITING

Anyone who has followed children's progress from Free Exploration to Search and Match and on through Word Construction easily can see that the shift to Phase 4 comes very naturally. E.R.E. is at its best here. It can read a sentence, a paragraph, or tell a story before or after a child types, while at the same time it can continue to respond to individual characters and words. In sum, it can deal with reference to the earlier learning sequences.

E.R.E., of course, can ask questions, just as teachers do. The questions may pertain to what is visually exhibited in the rectangular window or on the projection screen. The questions may call for subtle interpretations. Answers can be either typed out or expressed verbally on E.R.E.'s own recording-reproducing unit.

The material programed for E.R.E. can be as banal as the dullest courses in school or it can be as stimulating as the best of new programs, for example, some in modern mathematics or science. (It should be noted that E.R.E. can handle many aspects of mathematics and of science programs—numbers and some arithmetic symbols are on the keyboard.)

Every effort is made to select materials which give children a chance to make imaginative interpretations. As a general principle, it seems advisable to select materials that permit several levels of interpretation. A good case in point is *Alice's Adventures in Wonderland*. Retarded, normal, and gifted children can all begin reading this story with enjoyment just because it starts off with a little girl and an extraordinary rabbit. Even though gifted children like the manifest content of Alice's adventures, at the same time they can begin to get glimpses of deeper meanings. A serious objection to many stories found in beginning readers is that they confine children to one interpretation since the manifest content of such stories is all there is to them.

It is in Phase 4 that the methodology presented in this chapter must come to terms with the traditional school curriculum.[12] The bridging mechanism between the laboratory booths and the school classroom is the Laboratory's Transfer Room. Here, children who have been working alone have an opportunity to engage in cooperative activities, for example, publishing a newspaper, under the guidance of a teacher. Discipline emerges from the interaction of the children with each other.

When children go to first grade, having reached Phase 4 in both reading and composing original stories, a new curriculum is needed. Most of the things which ordinarily are taught in first grade lie far behind them. (At the end of first grade, the Hamden Hall Country Day School children who had been in the E.R.E. program at least two years read, on the average, at the beginning sixth-grade level, according to the Metropolitan Achievement Test. Their competence in composing original stories can be judged by examining their newspaper (Figure 1). For second grade they again will require a totally new curriculum.) The half hour a day the children can spend in the laboratory is certainly not a substitute for the rest of the school day. Fortunately, at Hamden Hall there has been strong administrative support for curriculum revision.[13] However, an adequate curriculum is not the whole answer either. Competent teachers are equally necessary. Teachers find that they have independent students on their hands, students who are accustomed to solving problems on their own or in cooperation with their peers.

HANDWRITING

One of the five booths is reserved for learning to write by hand. The writing equipment in this booth is primitive. It consists of a lined blackboard, chalk, and eraser. On a random basis children spend about one tenth of their time in this booth after they have completed Phase 1. I

[12] There is a Phase 5, the Dialogue (Moore, 1961), which is not presented here for two reasons: 1) to keep this chapter within reasonable bounds, and 2) as yet, I have had no experience with children in this phase. Essentially, the Dialogue has to do with children's interpreting group interaction and taking what is said in dictation, adding the necessary punctuation and connecting commentary so as to create a plausible reconstruction of ongoing social situations in which they were participants. The Dialogue is of theoretical importance because of its connection with the Meadean concept of the "generalized other" (Mead, 1934).

[13] It is not within the scope of this chapter to present the school curriculum which is still being developed. However, in broad outline, the curriculum is based upon the notion of folk models (Anderson and Moore, 1959) and their scientific formalization.

assumed that after children had been exposed to the characters on the typewriter they would begin to reproduce them manually if they had the opportunity. Children begin by scribbling or drawing pictures on the board, but it appears that some would go on doing this indefinitely if they were not subtly guided by a patient booth assistant. The difficulty lies in the fact that the environment is not sufficiently responsive. (Automated equipment could be divised for facilitating the development of this skill.)

The children are exposed to cursive or manuscript writing, as opposed to printing, through the use of typewriters with cursive type. This serves to familiarize them with this form of writing. Even two- and three-year-olds, including retarded children, can learn to print and write in the cursive style. A motion picture has been made of the printing of a few preschool children in order to show what they can do (Moore and Anderson, 1960, 1960, 1960).

I promised at the beginning of this section to try to explain the various phases of the learning sequence in terms of the use of automated instrumentation. However, in the development of this program of research, work began with nonautomated equipment—modified electric typewriters, projectors, recording-reproducing units, and so on. The functional specifications for automated equipment were obtained by coding the activities of booth assistants using nonautomated devices.

In the nonautomated form of Phases 1 through 4, the booth assistant sits in a chair beside the child who is at a modified electric typewriter. The booth assistant has a switch which is used to control the typewriter in the same way that E.R.E.'s logic and control circuitry does. The booth assistant is instructed to be passive just as is E.R.E. Of course, not all booth assistants carry out this role perfectly day after day—some have a strong tendency to intrude upon children. It requires constant monitoring by the laboratory supervisor to keep booth assistants from teaching.

At present, four of the five laboratory booths are nonautomated, thus there is a human instructor with the child on an average of four sessions out of five. In time, all booths will be automated, but this does not mean that they always will be operated in a fully automated way —with no human being in the booth with the child. It is not known whether children would continue to come to the laboratory on a daily basis over a long period of time if they were interacting with automated equipment only. Even if they were able to go through all phases on automated equipment this might produce undesirable psychological or social-psychological side effects. No one knows now the optimal mixture of automated and nonautomated equipment. It is reasonably certain, however, that a one-to-four mix will work; at least it has worked with the children who have come to the laboratory.

One of the interesting consequences of having a fully automated booth has been its effect on assistants. Before such equipment was available, it was difficult to explain to new personnel what was expected of them. Also, some of them apparently did not believe that children would work out problems for themselves—so they tended to be too *helpful.* The automated equipment proved to be a good instructor for new booth assistants. With reference to this point, there is an illuminating film made of some laboratory children working on a prototype of E.R.E. In one sequence, a little girl (Moore 1962, last sequence), who was in Phase 4, forgot where the lower case key was. At first she seemed to be nonplused; finally, she regressed to a systematic trial of every key—the right key was almost the last to be tried. Many viewers of this search sequence said that they felt an almost irresistible urge to help her. She, unlike these viewers, was calm about the whole matter—confident in her ability to find her way. Like E.R.E., well-trained booth assistants do not intrude. In my opinion, in too many situations in everyday life adults rush to the aid of children, thus depriving them of the opportunity of making discoveries and consequently undermining their confidence in their own resourcefulness.

Children in a Responsive Environment

Before a child enters the Laboratory for his introductory session quite a bit is known about him. Each child is given a general physical examination, an eye examination, and a hearing test. A speech evaluation is made with special attention paid to a child's ability to produce utterances in conformity with the phonemic structure of the language. A clinical psychologist obtains a developmental history from the mother and gives the child an intelligence test as well as projective tests. A sociological analysis is made of the family in terms of socio-economic variables. In sum, an attempt is made to characterize the child's family with reference to its position in the broader society, to see the child within the context of his family, and to understand something about the child himself in the light of this developmental history. The various tests and observations are repeated on a semiannual or annual basis depending upon their nature; for example, I.Q. tests are given annually.

A daily record is kept of each child's behavior in the laboratory, and the child is examined periodically to determine his level of skill.

Let us now consider children who have gone through the phases presented in the preceding section. Some background information is given with each case. The first two children to be discussed are in the nebulous range between the normal and exceptional. The last three are clear-cut cases of exceptional children—two are educable retardates, the third is gifted.[14]

BILLY

Billy's mother enrolled him in an integrated public school kindergarten when he was five years old. After a few weeks his teacher reported to her supervisor that he was unable to follow directions and that he disrupted the classroom—for instance, he rolled on the tables and stubbornly refused to move. Nothing was done about her complaints until a month later when she delivered an ultimatum: "Either Billy goes or I go." At this point the school psychologist was called in and Billy was given a Stanford-Binet intelligence test with the result that he was classified as an educable retardate with an I.Q. of 65. It was recommended that he be placed in a nursery group for the mentally retarded. The mother, a former special-class student herself, was irate about this recommendation; she caused so much difficulty over it that the school, in self-defense, sent Billy to an outside expert who confirmed the prior evaluation. (This second examination was slightly more hopeful in that it placed him on the borderline between the educable retardate and the dull normal.) With great reluctance, Billy's mother acquiesced to his removal from public school at mid-term and to his placement in a nursery group for educable retardates.

When Billy was six years old, he came to the Laboratory under the auspices of a state agency. The Laboratory's initial evaluation of Billy's intelligence (I.Q. 72) agreed with the more promising of the two prior reports. However, it was obvious at once that there were at least two sides to Billy in terms of his ability to get along with adults; for example, the examiner commented, "In the testing situation, Billy was a pleasant child, friendly and responsive and anxious to please." This judgment says something about both Billy and the examiner. This examiner is very skillful in establishing rapport with children and it is a difficult child indeed who does not respond positively to her.

So we have Billy, age six, already out of the mainstream of education. He either could not or would not take directions; what is more, he was willing and able to cause disturbances.

Billy, a light-colored Negro, is always neatly dressed. His appear-

[14] Since it has been the policy of the Responsive Environments Project to protect the anonymity of children and their families, we have seen to it that there is not a one-to-one correspondence between children shown in pictures (either stills or motion pictures) and case history material. In addition, the children described here are drawn from several responsive environments centers located in five cities and three states. Background and personal data which would be sufficient to identify a particular child and his family have been changed so as to protect their privacy. Although I have personally worked with only 102 subjects on a day-to-day basis, there are over 250 children who have been part of the Project, taken as a whole.

ance is normal but his physical movements are somewhat clumsy although he has an alert manner. He always has been in excellent health; his vision and hearing are normal. However, his speech was very difficult to understand even at six; the speech evaluation showed, for instance, that he omitted most final consonants. Also, there were many repetitions and hesitations in his speech and his mother said that he, unlike her other children, did not talk until he was four. Whatever else, Billy had not done a very good job of mastering his native tongue—he had not developed the requisite verbal skills to express his needs or interests.

The eight members of Billy's family share five rooms in a low-income row house: a reasonably large living room (with a record player and a monstrous TV set), a large kitchen, and three bedrooms. There are three older boys in their middle teens and Billy and his younger brother and sister, ages 5 and 4. The family is crowded but the apartment is spotless and tastefully decorated. There is a large bookcase nearly full of books topped by a complete set of supermarket encyclopedias. At present, the family is wholly self-supporting, though off and on in the past it has been on welfare. Billy's father, a small, meek, self-effacing person, is an unskilled laborer who generally works in construction. A social worker, who has known the family for years, classifies the whole family as dull normal.

Billy's mother is the dominant figure around whom everything turns. She is a heavy-handed, strict disciplinarian who can wither her husband and children with a glance. In or out of the family, she is a formidable woman who is articulate about her ambitions for her children, but she lacks knowledge about how to advance them. She had hoped that the older boys would be able to go to college, but their academic records are so poor (she is forcing them to stay in school) that the guidance counselor has told her that college is out of the question. Though the older children are disappointing to her, she still has great hopes for her two youngest children who are developing more rapidly than any of the others did. Billy is the only child who has her worried. He was later than the others in standing, walking, talking and toilet training. Toilet training must be a nightmare for Billy, because as she says, "Whenever he goes in his pants, I whack him in front of everybody." (Billy still has accidents quite frequently). The other members of the family are very fond of Billy, baby him, and try to cover up his many mistakes before they are discovered by his mother. His mother says that Billy is not dumb, he is "stubborn and lazy." When Billy does something that really pleases her, she picks him up and enfolds him in her enormous arms while smothering him with kisses.

Billy's introductory session was calm. He quietly followed the guide around; he could not be drawn into conversation. Once in a while he smiled and in general was wide-eyed. In his second introductory session he explored some on his own but spent most of the time holding the guide's hand. By the end of this session he was becoming curious about the equipment and seemed quite relaxed, and so he was scheduled for the automated booth the following day. The third day he came in, noisy and confident, and permitted the booth assistant to help him into the elevated chair. He watched her leave and then turned his attention immediately to the keyboard. What happened next is best described as an attack upon the instrument. In 30 minutes he typed 1302 characters. The booth assistant had to turn off the instrument and lead him out of the booth when his time was up. For the next nine sessions he continued to "machine gun" the instrument at a gradually slowing pace. In his eleventh session there was a sharp drop in strokes; the booth assistant wrote, "He seems to be getting interested in looking at what he has typed." The laboratory supervisor shifted him from Phase 1, Free Exploration, to Phase 2, Search and Match. Billy was startled and angry—he put up his hand over and over to call the booth assistant in. Billy evidently thought the instrument was broken and that the assistant would not fix it. All previous sessions had lasted 30 minutes but Billy stopped this one after 9 minutes. He had made five matches by accident (he had not come up with a way of systematically trying all keys). The laboratory supervisor switched him back to Phase 1 for his next session and he was very pleased, although he proceeded more cautiously than he had before—looking, listening, and occasionally repeating what was said. After another five days his time dropped to 15 minutes and the supervisor again switched him to Phase 2 for the following session.

This time he was calmer about the change. After five minutes he was pressing every key with his thumb—he clapped his hands when he made a match. At the end of this 30-minute session he said he wanted to take the "typewriter" home. For the next 60 days he played Search and Match in its increasingly difficult versions. There seemed to be no diminution in his interest. This was the game for Billy—he made it more complex for himself by shutting his eyes while finding keys, by "dive bombing" the keyboard, by first using one hand and then the other. He was still not using the color coding of fingers to keys, however. The supervisor switched him to Phase 3, Word Construction, R and W, even though his interest had not waned. He could find the characters to make words but he did not want the words; he told the instrument to "shut up." His time dropped down to 3 minutes after five days. He was shifted back to Phase 2. In WC-W he had been nearly mute; he kept mumbling something about "it's not broken." Billy continued in Phase 2 for another 30 days, still eager and interested. His refusal to go on to words was perplexing because by this time he was very expert at finding all characters and was using the color-coding system. Also, he had learned to print all the characters in the handwriting booth (this included the ampersand which most booth assistants have to learn, too).

An interviewer was sent to Billy's home to find out if something unusual was going on there. His mother said that she had caught Billy "playing with himself," and that she had whipped him and told him he would hurt himself. This made it much clearer what Billy was mumbling about. In WC-W the assistant pointed to his penis when he said "it's not broken." She said the word "penis" and spelled it. It was put on the dictation equipment for him in a nonautomated booth. He typed the word "penis" twelve times with manifest enjoyment. In his next WC-W story-telling session he said, among other things, "When my dad took the prayers away, my mother got sick and died." The constituent words of this story were made into a word list for the next WC-W typing session. Billy liked these words and now was willing to accept word lists in WC-R.

Billy was shifted to Phase 4 in his 130th session. At the end of his laboratory experience (172 sessions) he was reading pre-primer and beginning first-grade stories, he could print nicely, and he could type 5 words a minute with correct fingering on the automated equipment. His typing was comparable to that exhibited by other children classifiable as educable retardates.

When Billy was transferred from public school to the nursery for educable retardates at mid-year, he established a satisfactory relation with the skillful teacher in charge of this group. However, he would not accept her assistant. The end-of-the-term report stated, "When he is helped or scolded by the assistant he becomes very belligerent and disrespectful." Billy began his laboratory sessions in late spring while still in this nursery class. Public school officials were invited to watch Billy in booth sessions. They were so impressed by his good manners and by his ability to concentrate that arrangements were made to re-admit him to public school kindergarten in the fall. Given this second chance he managed to get on with this new teacher, and at the end of the year she passed him to first grade.

Billy entered first grade with 172 laboratory sessions behind him as well as with the benefits of a constructive experience in the nursery group and kindergarten. The Laboratory, of course, was interested in following his progress even though he was no longer in its program.[15]

Billy was placed in a "combined" first grade, that is, a class with a reading readiness group and a first-grade group. He was assigned to the

---

[15] The project, taken as a whole, has conducted a number of pilot studies to determine whether it was feasible to work with various kinds of exceptional children. Billy was part of one such study (and an evaluation of its success or failure) and the establishment of long-term programs. Billy, his family, and the Project would have liked to have had him go on.

latter section on the basis of a reading-readiness test. His teacher wrote, "When we began our work, Billy was ahead of the other children. He could write and recognize his numbers to 10 and count up to 29. He knows his colors, alphabet, and his knowledge of phonics is very good in that he knows the sounds of each isolated consonant and can tell with what letter various words begin. What he needs now is to develop his comprehension not only in reading words but in picture interpretation. As you know, to get the idea of a story in the pre-primers and primers, the child should understand the picture. Billy's reasoning and associations are ofttimes far-fetched. I must ask him many questions before he gets the point of the picture. He finds it hard to follow directions, but he will ask many questions in order to get the directions correct. There are now children who have caught up to Billy but he still has an edge on them because he has a better background and the work I am doing now is not completely new to him. The proof of the pudding must wait until I begin to teach in completely new areas, for example, addition and subtraction."

Billy finished first grade successfully and will be in second grade next year. He did have trouble with arithmetic.

Billy was retested by the Laboratory at the end of first grade. His I.Q. score is now 79. The appraisal of his speech placed him in the normal range with respect to the making of phonemic discriminations in speech production; the repetitions and hesitations have disappeared. Billy now can express his needs and interests verbally in a much more adequate way and, as his teacher mentioned, he is able to ask many questions in order to understand directions. One year of first grade did not improve Billy's reading significantly—for all practical purposes, he was held back, though his skill at picture interpretation undoubtedly improved. It is my overall impression that Billy is still a vulnerable dependent child who will rebel if he is not skillfully handled. A second year in the Laboratory would have afforded him a good deal of protection. It would have been especially helpful if his introduction to arithmetic could have been carried out within the context of a responsive environment.

Billy's family is proud of him and now they let him work more things out for himself. His mother feels completely vindicated: all the psychologists, social workers, and teachers were wrong—Billy is not dumb, he is simply a "stubborn and lazy" child who needs a good whack.

EDWARD

Edward's mother was slim, attractive, and beautifully groomed. She graduated summa cum laude from a midwestern college at 20 and married immediately after graduation. The marriage ended in divorce three years later, with the husband keeping their two-year-old daughter. After a year she married Edward's father who was three years her junior and who was working as a tennis instructor at the time—he had completed only two years of college. A year after they were married, Edward was born; she went to work part time at a style shop to help pay for her husband's education (she also had an annual income from a trust fund), and voluntarily began what turned out to be three and a half years of psychotherapy.

Edward came to a Project laboratory at four years of age as a referral from a private psychiatric clinic. At three and a half years of age, he had developed food allergies and was having difficulty in sleeping through the night (he would wake up screaming). When Edward first came to the Laboratory his father was just leaving for another part of the country to take a good position in a large firm (by this time he had gotten his B.A. and an M.A. in business administration). Edward's mother did not think it advisable to break off her psychotherapy, so she and Edward did not go with him.

Edward and his mother lived alone, then, in an elegant apartment during the time in which he came to the Laboratory. His mother had stopped working and so she was free to make the daily trip to bring Edward.

Up to the age of four, Edward had spent most of his time with "sitters," except for the hours from 5 to 7 in the evening when the family had dinner and his mother devoted herself exclusively to him. His father had spent almost no time with the boy. Edward himself was the very opposite of an athlete. He was a thin, frail little boy who was afraid of almost everything physical—cats, dogs, playground equipment—but who was extremely verbal. His mother reported that he began saying words at one year of age, and she had used those daily two-hour devotionals to teach Edward all manner of things. Edward looked and acted like what many people think of as a prodigy. He enjoyed embarrassing children and adults by asking such questions as "How many planets does Saturn have?" and before an answer could be given he would add, "Stupid! It doesn't have planets, it has rings!" His mother said, "Edward could read at three . . . he picked it up entirely on his own, but now he will have nothing to do with books." She also said, "I really don't care whether Edward learns to read at the Laboratory so long as it is a creative experience for him." His increasingly negative attitude toward learning, his allergies, and his sleeping problem upset her a great deal.

Edward's laboratory experience almost ended before it began when his mother found out about the rule prohibiting parents from watching children. She had seen the film, *Early Reading and Writing* (Moore and Anderson, 1960, 1960, 1960), and was looking forward to watching Edward every day. She wanted to know what she could do with herself while he was having his session; it was annoying to her to have time on her hands. Arrangements were made for her to go to a library.

She had purchased a typewriter for Edward to use at home. In her first interview she wanted to know the color coding system so that she could duplicate it. The information was given to her, but as it turned out, Edward would not type at home until much later.

The Laboratory's evaluation of Edward was virtually a duplicate of the clinic's, including the analysis of his responses to projective material. Edward was an extremely tense child, impersonal in outlook, with excellent speech, and his I.Q. placed him on the borderline between very bright and gifted (I.Q. 139). He was difficult to test and free with insulting remarks. He was very much aware of his failures and he categorized difficult test items as "stupid." In fact, everybody was stupid but Edward, with the possible exception of his mother. Edward's mother felt that he should spend more time with children his own age, but there were no acceptable children in the apartment house. He played occasionally with a thirteen-year-old girl who sometimes filled in as an emergency sitter.

Edward greeted his child guide, a girl of four, with the statement, "You have an ugly face," followed by, "What are you doing here, I hate it!" The guide shot back, "Don't be ridiculous!" and took him by the hand. He followed meekly. When he went into a booth with a typewriter, he said, "My typewriter at home is better." He did not explore the Laboratory on his own. During his second visit, he was equally prickly and paced back and forth by himself. In his third introductory visit, he quizzed the guide and was taken aback to find that she knew "bigger" words than he did. He asked if she could type. When she said, "Yes," he said, "Show me!" The guide replied that she did not have to prove it. He shouted derisively, "You can't! You can't!" The guide laughed and Edward announced that he was going to "learn the typewriter" and that he would be much better than the guide. The supervisor scheduled him for his first booth session the next day.

Edward went willingly into a nonautomated booth. He was extremely serious. He painstakingly matched his fingers to keys, for, as he said, "My mother told me to look at my fingers and press the keys with the same colors." Edward did not explore the keyboard. Instead, he searched out the upper-case alphabet, avoiding all punctuation marks and numbers. After a while he was going through the upper-case letters in alphabetic order. After ten minutes of this, he asked for the pictures. He said, "At home my books have colored pictures," and before the booth assistant could say anything, he added, "I hate this stupid thing— I want to go." The assistant immediately turned off the equipment and lifted Edward from the elevated chair. He said, "I want to do it some more." When he was told that he could come back the next day, he cried, "I want to do it now!" Edward left the Laboratory complaining bitterly, but he greeted his mother with the statement, "Their typewriter is better than yours." For the next four sessions, Edward confined himself to the letters with which he was familiar and each day he tried to elicit punitive responses from the booth assistants.

In his 6th, 7th and 8th sessions, all less than 15 minutes in length, he stopped matching his fingers to keys and tried to get the booth assistants to say how good he was for knowing all the letters. His 9th session marked the first major change in Edward's behavior. Instead of sitting stiffly, he slumped down and began to pick away at the keyboard, spending most of his time on characters new to him. He noted that *period* was the same whether "up or down," he liked the end-of-the-line warning bell and the carriage return. For the first time he stayed 30 minutes and did not insult anyone. Edward's interest grew each day—he repeated aloud nearly every character after it was pronounced by the booth assistants.

The supervisor switched him to Phase 2, Search and Match, for his 15th session. He announced that he was tired of this game during his 21st session—he could match quickly and accurately.

Edward liked WC-R immediately. In free story telling for WC-W he told long complex stories about how he was going to be his father's partner in doubles tennis. He told about not having a ball of his own and that he was spanked for touching his father's tennis racquet . . . but the balls and racquets were gone now. Edward would not listen to his own voice in dictation. He wanted the little girl's voice (the guide's); he very happily typed her dictated word lists. For the next 30 sessions, Edward stayed in Phase 3. All of his typing was done with one finger of each hand and he became very pleasant to have in the Laboratory.

In Edward's 10th week, his mother asked for a conference about his behavior. She said that at home he had become very "sloppy," for example, he would not put his toys away. More importantly, he had become rude and disrespectful to her. He would not play with the typewriter at home, and, as far as she could see, he had *learned nothing*. He would not look at his books; he had told her that the "Lab" did not have pictures and that pictures were stupid. His allergies were worse, if anything, but he was sleeping a little better. She said she wanted to withdraw him from the program but that he looked forward to the trip every day. What she said she wished to discuss "at a theoretical level" was whether the program tended to make children self-centered.

She was told that it was her privilege to withdraw Edward, but that it would be advisable for her to take him to the referral clinic for a re-evaluation. She accepted this advice. The clinic reported to Edward's mother that he enjoyed his laboratory experience (a representative of the clinic came to the Laboratory to watch Edward for four sessions) and that it was unlikely his sessions were disturbing to him. On the contrary, he seemed to be a little less tense and apprehensive. The question as to whether Edward was learning to read or not was irrelevant from the clinic's standpoint, so long as he found pleasure in this activity. The clinic advised her to put the typewriter at home away until he asked for it. Also, the clinic reiterated the advice it gave when he was three and a half years old, namely, "Find some children of his own age for Edward to play with." The Laboratory staff re-examined Edward from the standpoint of assessing his emotional stability. The examiner did not find, or expect to find, any marked change, though Edward was friendlier. Edward's mother decided to keep him in the program and she also enrolled him in a nursery school for the mornings.

Edward liked the nursery school from the first day on. The experienced teacher slowly and skillfully got him to join in group activities. She also succeeded in getting Edward to play with the group's mascot, a puppy.

In Edward's 53rd session, he was shifted to Phase 4, Reading and Writing. He worked his way rapidly into *Alice's Adventures in Wonderland*. His mother bought the book and record set. He would listen to the records at home, though he would not touch the book.

Edward stayed in Phase 4, without regressing, from then on. At the end of his laboratory experience (93rd session), he passed a standardized reading test at the second-grade level.[16] His printing was poor, though legible (he never did get along with assistants in the handwriting booth). His typing was rapid but with two fingers only. He came to accept his own voice in dictation. His I.Q. had jumped to 152, his speech continued to be excellent. There were not detectable changes in his personality structure although he had learned more satisfactory ways of dealing with others. His food allergies continued—his mother reported that he was sleeping restfully almost every night. His mother stated that he now liked to go to the library with her to check out books and that he was looking forward to seeing his father.

The referral clinic made a similar assessment of Edward. The clinic's final report stated, in part, "The laboratory and the nursery were positive for Edward. His ability to cope with the demands of his mother is much improved. Edward needs the companionship of his father if he is to keep the gains that he has made."

---

[16] It should be noted that passing standardized reading tests calls for formal academic skills in addition to the ability to read meaningfully. Edward could read and answer questions about, for example, Alice's adventures, yet he passed the test only at the second-grade level.

Although Edward's mother had not planned to leave the area during the school year, she abruptly changed her mind in mid-February. She informed the clinic, the laboratory, and the nursery of her decision only one week prior to their departure.

BETTY AND JANE

Betty and Jane are physically sturdy, normal-appearing, identical Negro twins. They entered an integrated public school kindergarten at five, and after a month they were referred by their teacher and principal to the school psychologist for examination. During this month they had not spoken to anyone or actively participated in kindergarten activities. For the most part, they sat quietly, smiling irrelevantly from time to time. Children who knew them said that they did not talk but just made noises. When the children in kindergarten stood, Betty and Jane had to be taken by their hands and helped to their feet; when it was time to sit, the twins continued to stand until again they were taken by their hands and shown to their chairs. They constantly sucked their fingers or stuffed their whole hands into their mouths, with saliva flowing freely down their arms and over the fronts of their dresses.

They went willingly with the examiner to take intelligence tests. She reported, "They cannot understand or follow any directions, even when blocks were placed in their hands, they could not put them in tower formation. Their chronological age is 5 years 2 months, but they were unable to pass any test at the 2-year level or beyond." On the basis of the psychological tests and their behavior in kindergarten, it was decided that they were too limited in mental development to profit by kindergarten attendance. They were excluded immediately from school for one year and re-admittance was to be dependent upon the outcome of tests to be given the following year.

The question of re-admittance to public school did not arise the next fall because a social worker, who assisted the family, was able to get the twins into a state agency's class for retarded children. The twins started coming to the Laboratory in late spring after they had attended this special class for eight months. At the time they came to the Laboratory, according to the psychological examiner for the special class, Betty's I.Q. was 55 and Jane's was 56 as measured by the Stanford-Binet intelligence test. The children still drooled, and toilet training had not been completed.

The twins with their family live in a small, three-room apartment in a double-entrance, tumble-down brownstone complex. The back yard and front sidewalk are littered with scraps, glass and discarded beer cans. The apartment is cramped and dingy though not filthy. The furniture is in a terrible state of disrepair, plaster hangs from the walls and in places is simply missing. The door to the kitchen balances precariously on one hinge.

The family consists of two younger children, the twins, the mother, and a maternal grandmother. The grandmother seems to be the one who takes the initiative in holding the family together and she is doing her best to raise the children. The twins' mother, who may be thought of as a loving older sister, frequently plays with them on the floor in a childlike unrestrained manner. The grandmother exercises firm, though gentle, control over the twins by confining them, most of the time, to the apartment or to the back yard. It is her opinion that the twins cannot defend themselves in the streets where the neighborhood children play. The twins thus have had very limited experience with other children or adults. Also, city life is new to the family; only three years before, they had moved from the South where they had lived in an isolated area. Since coming North the family has been totally on welfare; there is no breadwinner.

The eight months the twins had spent in the special class before coming to the Laboratory served to widen their horizons. According to the teacher the children were extremely shy at first and did not speak to anyone. At the end of several months they began to whisper to each other and to the teacher. Within eight months they were able to "shout, scream and talk to the teacher, children, and any other person who enters the classroom." Their teacher reported that in strange situations they were still very shy. The twins enjoyed the class and felt comfortable with the teacher, assistants and other children. In social interaction Jane was the more dominant one, Betty seemed to be stronger in "intellectual" pursuits. However, the twins are so similar in appearance and behavior that even those who know them reasonably well frequently mistake one for the other. At six the twins had not yet learned to exploit, as most identical twins do, the social possibilities inherent in their identity.

The Laboratory's evaluation of the twins concurred with that of the psychologist for the special class with respect to their intellectual abilities. They were definitely in the category *educable retardate*. There was nothing wrong with their general health and eyes. It was not feasible to do initial speech and hearing analyses because of the difficulty of eliciting an adequate number of utterances. The twins were uniformly pleasant but nonresponsive. It was also difficult to determine much about the structure of their personalities. The finger-thumb-hand sucking, the inane smiling, the extreme shyness and so forth, all would have to be taken into account, of course, in any adequate analysis of their development.

The Laboratory had agreed in advance with the state officials that it would accept a small number of retarded children, free of charge, if the children were "certified" as retarded by the state's experts. When the twins were sent to the Laboratory, there was no way to have one be a control subject without violating the agreement to accept whatever children were assigned to the Laboratory. It would have been desirable for some scientific purposes to have worked with only one of the twins. Yet, if the laboratory experience proved to be a valuable one, this would have been unfair to the neglected twin and might have had untoward consequences for them in their close relationship to each other. Under these circumstances, I decided to think about the twins from the stand-point of assessing their identicalness. Just how identical are identical twins when each is faced with a new environment?

Betty and Jane were introduced to the Laboratory together for fear that they might be frightened alone. They accepted their guide passively, they asked no question—in fact, they did not say anything—they drooled and sucked their fingers. Nevertheless, they did not seem to be espe-cially fearful. Their guide was very gracious; she omitted spontaneously the discussion of the Laboratory rules and, instead, assured them over and over that they would like the "Lab." It was decided to have them go separately into nonautomated booths after one introductory visit because they might be passive for weeks.

Betty permitted herself to be seated in the elevated chair without comment. She sat up straight and appeared to be interested in the key-board. After about one minute she began to rapidly press keys with an odd sort of looping movement of her right hand using her middle finger. She continued to do this for the full period at a nearly constant rate. Her stroke count for the period was 2204. She struck 27 of the 52 keys. However, she concentrated heavily on three keys, the slant, the comma and the period (these keys are located next to each other on the right side of the bottom row). Forty-nine percent of the keys she struck were these three keys, and of these, the slant was most frequently struck—she produced 815 slants. At the end of her session she was led out of the booth and did not say anything.

Jane permitted herself to be seated and appeared to be interested in the keyboard. After about one minute she began to rapidly press keys with an odd sort of looping movement of her right hand using her middle finger. She continued to do this for the full period at a nearly constant rate. Her stroke count for the period was 3189. She struck 35 of the 52 keys. However, she concentrated heavily on three keys, the slant, the comma and the period. Forty-three percent of all the keys she struck were these three keys, and of these, the slant was most frequently struck —she produced 807 slants. At the end of her session she was led out of the booth and did not say anything.

In their 2nd through 5th sessions the twins continued to be very similar in their approach, but they never again were as identical as they were during their first booth session. At the end of five days, Betty's stroke count was 8571 and Jane's was 8724—a difference of 153 strokes. During the 2nd week they began to diverge; Jane became noticeably more active in the booths. Their graphs for stroke counts crossed after three weeks at 14,377 strokes for Betty and 14,202 for Jane. From then on Betty remained slightly more active than her sister. At the completion of 150 sessions, Betty had typed 10,109 more characters than had Jane. On a day-to-day basis, this means behaviorally that Betty did about a line and one half more typing—a very small difference but an observable one. The girls were more closely matched in booth time than in stroke count. Each almost always stayed the full period. (Their similarity in time is, in part, an artifact of the methods used in handling them. The girls would stay almost anywhere you put them until told to leave.)

The twins stayed in Phase 1 for 19 sessions. It was decided to shift them to Phase 2 in their 20th session because their stroke count was beginning to fall off rapidly.

They had no difficulty in adjusting to Phase 2, though they were slow in working out a systematic search pattern for finding the correct keys. Neither Betty nor Jane used the color-coding scheme. By their 70th session each was quick to find the appropriate keys. Betty was slightly more accurate.

They were shifted to Phase 3 in their 71st session. They would accept word lists in WC-R; but for five weeks they would not talk in WC-W; also, they would not respond to other children's dictation. Finally, Jane began to make a few disjointed comments during her 97th session in WC-W, Betty during her 100th session.

Leaving aside the WC-W recording sessions, the girls began to talk above a whisper during their 5th week at the Laboratory. They both have deep rich voices. It was hard to guess when they would speak up. Occasionally, they would make rather surprising remarks. For example, the first time Jane encountered the cursive typewriter she shouted, "Dig this crazy typewriter!"

Once the twins were speaking with some regularity in WC-W, it was feasible to do a speech analysis (recall that there were no speech and hearing evaluations because of the difficulty in eliciting utterances). Both were rated as having intelligible speech; Jane's speech was marked by a w/r substitution, Betty made the same w/r substitution and in addition had consonant blend substitutions. Their hearing was checked at this time and it turned out to be normal.

In Betty's 115th session and Jane's 120th, they were shifted to Phase 4. They clearly liked stories, although it was very difficult to tell how much they understood of the stories they typed. It was useless to quiz them about what they had typed because this tended to make them withdraw. Once in a while they would make a fairly incisive comment which indicated some understanding of the material.

The twins completed 150 sessions (see footnote 15). By this time they could print all upper- and lower-case letters as well as the punctuation marks and other symbols on the typewriter. On automated equipment they could type four words a minute. There was strong indirect evidence to indicate that they could handle first-grade stories if they would only speak freely. Drooling had almost ceased and they no longer wet their pants in the Laboratory.

With respect to their I.Q., Betty scored 64 on the Stanford-Binet and Jane scored 60. Both were weakest in the verbal language tasks. Betty successfully passed one item at the 6-year-old level; Jane passed none at this level.

Even though the twins had to be dropped from the laboratory program, as was mentioned before, a follow-up investigation was made one year later. The twins had been re-admitted to public school and assigned to a special class. Their teacher had visited the Laboratory the year before and had seen them at "work." She was favorably disposed toward the girls. She emphasized in her report that they were very different from the rest of the class. In her opinion it was their lack of social experience rather than low I.Q. which was holding them back. Their individual performances in class fluctuated so much that she felt that there was not a sufficient basis for determining which twin performed better. The teacher began to have them read books at the beginning of the spring term (until that time she felt that they were not ready for work at this level). She was uncertain about how much they had retained from their experience at the Laboratory, but she said that at the beginning of school the girls remembered letters and numbers though they apparently had forgotten sounds.

A Laboratory observer, who sat in on the class during a reading session in the second term, reported that the twins read aloud from the Ginn first pre-primer. Each read her own selection both accurately and quickly; the selection was unfamiliar though simple. The twins did not have reading every day. As the Laboratory observer arose from the reading session, Betty, half hiding behind her teacher's skirt, screeched, "Lab, Lab! I wanna go Lab!" The observer's report reads as follows: "I then completed my discussion with the teacher and went to speak to the girls. I had hoped that I would be able to talk to each one individually, but I found that impossible because Betty kept hovering over the table mooning at us. Rather than risk Jane 'turning off,' I let them talk with me together. They both recalled many details about the Lab; red building, white chalk, yellow station wagon and colors on their fingers. Jane kept babbling about the yellow station wagon. They both remembered typing, reading books, writing on the table and coloring their nails. Jane recalled they 'played games,' Betty remembered the talking typewriter for 'the story about the golden chicken.' (In all likelihood this

is the *Aesop Fable* 'The Goose that Laid the Golden Egg.') They both
agreed they had had fun playing at the Lab, and they obviously wanted
to come back again. Initially, I was leery about their enthusiasm because
the teacher had alerted me to the fact that their grandmother had a
record of prompting the girls. Nevertheless, Betty and Jane did recall a
lot about the Program that she (the grandmother) could not have known
about, and I didn't feel that they were sophisticated enough to show a
sustained and artificial enthusiasm, even prompted."

SANDRA

It is the general policy of the Laboratory to obtain children by working
with schools, clinics, government agencies, and so forth. In this way the
Laboratory gains the benefit of whatever information the relevant organization has about the children in question, and the Laboratory's findings
can be integrated with those of other organizations which serve children.
This policy also obviates the necessity of dealing on an ad hoc basis
with numerous families. Nevertheless, parents call the Laboratory; most
calls are about handicapped children and we suggest that they see their
pediatrician or other appropriate specialist.

There is one kind of telephone call which the Laboratory follows
up, in an informal way, whenever possible. For instance, a mother may
call and say that she has a three-year-old who can do extraordinary
things—that he is a mathematical prodigy or that he reads like a whiz.
Time permitting, an interviewer goes out to see the child in his home,
explaining that our concern is to better understand exceptional children.

One of the things that has impressed us about these visits is the
lack of information parents have about the achievements of children.
Parents are in the unfortunate position of having to judge the possibly
unusual achievements (i.e., accomplishments as opposed to the ability to
achieve as estimated by some standardized test) of their own child by
the standards derived from reading and personal experience. They may
conclude that they have a *wunderkind*.

There is also great vagueness about what constitutes reading. We
have been in some homes where a child is said to be reading brilliantly
when he can only identify a few words. Parents say, almost uniformly,
that whatever the child does, he learned all by himself. Yet even casual
inspection of the living room reveals flash cards, slates, or educational
toys directly related to the child's accomplishments. Questioning the
parents closely is generally sufficient to reveal the method of instruction
which the mother, father, grandmother, older sister, or neighbor used.
In a few cases, when parents stoutly maintained that the child has had
no instruction whatsoever in reading or numbers, we have said to them
that if their child, unaided, can discover so much, then perhaps he could

help at the University to decipher some heretofore untranslated hiero-
glyphics that had even the specialists wondering whether to start from
the right, left, top or bottom. At this point parents quickly volunteer that,
of course, they answered all the child's questions.

I do not wish to impugn the ability of these children to learn, or
to minimize their accomplishments in any way, or to make light of the
pride their parents take in them, or to discourage such parents. The plain
fact is that parents lack comparative information about children's accomplishments, and even if they were to search the relevant scientific literature, generally they would not receive very much help.[17] Behavioral
scientists, including myself, are pretty much in the dark about extraordinary
accomplishments. It is for this very reason that we are appreciative of
the opportunity to observe children who strike their parents as prodigious.

Sandra's mother called to ask questions about enrolling her four-
year-old daughter in a Laboratory program. She said that Sandra, an only
child, was beginning to learn to read by herself and that she did many
precocious things. A visit to the home was arranged.

Sandra lived with her parents in a rambling winterized beach
house which they had rented four years before when they moved to this
area. Sandra's father is an engineer and her mother is a painter who
occasionally accepts commercial assignments. The house was filled with
the accouterments of their work. One room was set aside for the father's
extensive files. Sandra was probably the only person who knew where
everything was.

Her parents were swimming when the Laboratory interviewer
arrived and Sandra introduced herself (she was waiting) and asked if he
wanted to see her photographic equipment. Her father had set up a
miniature studio for her with a dark room three months before. She explained in great detail the complete process of taking pictures and developing them. She also showed some of her work with a running
commentary on the quality of each picture. She explained that the current
project was to use mirrors in taking pictures. She distinguished clearly
between those things which she did by herself and those things which her
mother or father helped her with. Also, anything that might be dangerous
she would do only when a parent was present. There was no doubt in
the interviewer's mind that basically the studio was hers even though
she received a great deal of technical assistance.

In about half an hour her parents came in, wearing their beach
robes, and sent Sandra out to play. They reminded her to stay out of the
water and to stay within view—the interview took place on the porch
where Sandra could be watched. She took a pail, a shovel, a few toys,
and a camera with her. Her mother apologized for not being there when

[17] Terman's monumental study (1925, 1959) is a gold mine of factual information
for those who are interested in gifted children.

the interviewer arrived but said that she wanted him to visit with Sandra first.

Sandra's father was 40 and her mother 35. The father received his degree in engineering, the mother went to art school. They wanted to learn about the Laboratory program and also wanted to know whether the interviewer agreed with them that Sandra was some kind of prodigy. Their attitude seemed to be one of concern about what would be best for Sandra. They said she got along reasonably well with the neighborhood children; nevertheless, most of the time she preferred to pursue her own projects. She would have liked to have played more with some of the older children in the neighborhood, but she could not get them to stay in her studio long enough—besides, they messed things up. The parents had not intended for her to get so wrapped up in photography, but once started she had kept after them to tell her more and more about it. She had other hobbies: collecting shells, painting (trying to copy things) and currently she was tying her various hobbies together through photography. She had learned the alphabet while getting things for her father from his files and now she wanted to learn to read so that she could help her parents better and read instructions for herself, especially those related to photography.

Her parents, who were quite relaxed, were somewhat appalled by the thorough, relentless way in which she pursued her interests. They thought that though she was friendly and helpful, even affectionate, she was rapidly becoming more and more exclusive. The only way to get close to her was to become a part of her projects. The parents had great sympathy for the idea of a child pursuing interests independently, but they did not think it was healthy for her to become so absorbed in her own affairs.

The interviewer suggested that Sandra be sent to a clinic for a thorough examination and to see if the clinic felt that it was advisable that the Laboratory accept her. It was pointed out that the clinic probably would recommend that she go to nursery school in conjunction with the laboratory sessions. This recommendation would have to be followed. The parents agreed.

All during this conversation (approximately 45 minutes) Sandra played. When the interviewer was leaving they walked up to see what she was doing. She had made an elaborate sand castle decked out with toys which she was in the process of photographing.

Sandra came to the Laboratory in September and also started nursery school. She was an attractive child, big for her age, in good health, and had normal vision and hearing. Her speech was excellent and her I.Q. tested 160. Her general personality development was sound; she was without marked tensions or anxieties. The examiner commented that she seemed to be somewhat wanting in spontaneity and humor and thought that she needed the companionship of other superior children. The over-all assessment was that she was a gifted child in good psychological health. There was no evidence of coaching for the tests or academic pressure at home. She liked the examination and said she wanted to do it again sometime.

Sandra was intrigued by the Laboratory in her introductory visit. She noted the photographic equipment, she said she thought she would like the typing "studio," she got along beautifully with her guide and her main disappointment was that she had to wait till the next day to play with the equipment. The supervisor scheduled her for a nonautomated booth session the next day. When her fingers were painted she wanted to know why; she was told that she would find out. The moment she sat in the elevated chair and looked at the keyboard carefully she re-marked that now she knew—from the first she matched fingers to keys. Sandra's search pattern, even in free exploration, was deliberate; she tried every key row by row. When she encountered the lower-case key she started over again, trying each key both ways. She told the booth assistant that it was not necessary to say the letters that she already knew, that she would say them. Sandra stayed 30 minutes and was quite annoyed about having to leave though she controlled her temper. Her stroke count was 410. Her 2nd and 3rd sessions were spent in the same way. At the end of the 3rd session she said that she would like to do something else.

The supervisor switched her to Phase 2, Search and Match, for her 4th session even though she did not know the names of all of the keys. Her first reaction to the new game was to say that she understood it. She went quickly through the increasingly difficult forms of the game. At the end of her 13th session she knew the keyboard cold and con-tinued to use correct fingering. She asked when she could have a "really" new game. The supervisor gave her one the next day.

Sandra spent 18 weeks in Phase 3, Word Construction, R and W. In WC-W she talked freely and happily about her projects. She brought material from her studio to copy as well.

In her 103rd session she was shifted to Phase 4 because her stroke count and eager interest were falling off. With her ability to retain what-ever she was exposed to, she immediately began reading pre-primers, and two weeks later she was reading first-grade books. Occasionally she asked to go back and do some special word lists. At the end of spring term (170 sessions) the reading test showed she was at the second-grade eighth-month level. She could type eight words a minute on nonauto-mated equipment. She printed all typewriter characters with precision.

Sandra's experience in nursery school was not altogether satis-factory to her. She liked her teacher and a few of the children but she complained, in a ladylike way, that it was all too babyish. She attempted to mother the other children and some of the boys said that she was too "bossy." Unfortunately, at the time she came to the Laboratory there was no newspaper project to challenge her, nor was there any other common activity for laboratory children. As things stood, she was a leader *sans* followers.

A recheck of her I.Q. showed it to be 169. At home she added reading and writing to her other projects. She did very little in the way of creating original stories. Her favorite book, which she had just started to read, was *Tal*.

The personality assessment showed no basic change. However, her parents felt that she had changed significantly. She wanted to discuss the stories that she read and it was their opinion that this greater common area of interest was drawing her closer to them again. She continued to pursue her projects independently, but as her father put it, "She is running into ideas that cannot be captured in a photograph."

The family moved to a large city in another state when school was out. Sandra was enrolled in a special class for gifted children. Her parents write occasionally to keep the Laboratory posted. At present, she is in a class with an ungraded program. Thus far, this class has provided a challenge which she enjoys.

Concluding Comments

At the beginning of this chapter it was pointed out that slow learners are likely to be out of phase with the age-graded societal demands imposed upon them and that they are apt to be problems to themselves and to their friends. The three slow learners that we have considered, Billy, Betty, and Jane, are certainly cases in point. As soon as they appeared in school the duly constituted authorities decided that they were not "ready." In all likelihood, the authorities were correct—these children were not "ready" to be taught by conventional methods. Nevertheless, they could be reached and the procedures through which they learned did not depend upon a rescue by one of those rare marvelous teachers who, through empathy, insight, and intelligence, can reach the nearly unreachable.

It also was stated that ultrarapid learners, too, may create problems for themselves and others. Edward and Sandra, in very different ways, made people uncomfortable. Neither Edward nor Sandra had had the opportunity to take part in the full Laboratory program where they could have used their intellectual skills within the context of a meaningful group that was heterogeneous in ability.

The vignettes of the background and laboratory behavior of the five children just considered perhaps have served to clarify both the operation of the Laboratory and some of its effects upon exceptional children. It might have been more revealing to have presented some of the children who started coming to the Laboratory at two and three years of age and who are still in the program on a daily basis. Cases of this kind demand a more lengthy and systematic treatment. Also, in my opinion, very early exposure to a responsive environment produces deep personality changes, and it would be inappropriate to analyze children thus exposed outside the context of a theoretical interpretation of personality development. Hence, I have focused attention here on children who began their experience at the Laboratory at four, five or six years of age and who remained in the program for only one academic year (or less). These children gained useful skills and attitudes which, with the help of clinicians, nursery school teachers and others, enabled them to deal somewhat more effectively with pressing individual and social demands.

Another reason for selecting these children was that they make manifest some of the subtleties and complexities of the psychodynamics and sociodynamics of learning. This may serve as an antidote to the dangerous notion that a responsive environments laboratory grinds out results in a purely mechanical way. The role of the supervisor was highlighted throughout in order to emphasize that a responsive environments laboratory, though phases of it are automated, does not run by itself. It would be equally foolish to assume that well-designed instruments do not have an important part to play in the daily operation of a laboratory.

It was the purpose of this chapter to describe an autotelic responsive environment which facilitates the learning of complex symbolic skills. It was suggested initially that no one aspect of the environment should be thought of as constituting its essence. In part it is a mechanical system, in part it is a social system, and in part it is a cultural system. All of these parts are constituents of the total system—all of them must be taken into account if the Laboratory is to be understood. The task of designing optimal environments for learning is in its infancy, and the theoretical problems of understanding what is going on in the Laboratory are staggering. One would have to be very insensitive to its research possibilities not to imagine quickly a hundred and one experiments that could be carried out within it which might increase our understanding of human beings. For example, the startling similarities between Betty's and Jane's first sessions practically demand further studies of identical twins. The behavior of Billy and Edward may be of special interest to psychoanalytically oriented researchers.

For the present and for an additional year or so I intend to continue to operate my laboratories as a demonstration project rather than as a controlled experiment. I may be mistaken in this policy, but there are hazards connected with focusing sharply on one or another aspect of human behavior before one gets a full sense of its variety in longitudinal perspective. This easily can lead to lopsided theorizing and debilitating polemics. The Responsive Environments Project is endeavoring to remain open and responsive to whatever changes the continuing observations of children's behavior seem to call for, although it is easy to deceive oneself about such matters.

This chapter, in abridged form, was presented at the Second National Northwestern Summer Conference, "The Special Child in Century 21," held in Seattle, Washington, August 1962.

I am indebted to Alan Ross Anderson and Edith S. Lisansky (also see below) for helpful criticisms of earlier drafts of this chapter.

The work reported here has received the generous support of the following organizations: The Carnegie Corporation of New York; The Cooperative Research Program of the Office of Education; The McGraw Foundation; The Murray Foundation; The Office of Naval Research, Group Psychology Branch, Contract No. SAR/Nonr-609(16); The Responsive Environments Foundation; The Higgins Fund of Yale University.

The Thomas A. Edison Research Laboratory of West Orange, New Jersey, a division of the McGraw-Edison Company, bore the entire cost of developing the equipment described here. I wish to thank particularly Richard Kobler, an electronic engineer at the Edison Laboratory, for his valuable contributions.

Special thanks are due to Dr. Burton Blatt, Head, Department of Special Education, Boston University; Dr. John Martin, Superintendent of Schools, Freeport, Long Island; and Edward I. McDowell, Jr., Headmaster, Hamden Hall Country Day School, for their initiative and administrative skill in establishing responsive environments laboratories.

Recognition should be given to the many essential contributions of the Project's supervisory staff at the various laboratories: Caroline Colby, Mary Coogan, Ann Ferguson, Dorothy Johnson, Ruth Moore and Ruth Wong. Also to Blanche Pierpont Blanchard, supervisor of the laboratory-connected classrooms at Hamden Hall Country Day School.

Last, but just as important, I wish to thank the following persons for their professional services: Dr. Edith S. Lisansky, who is in charge of the Project's work in clinical psychology; Dr. Robert F. Newton, for general physical examinations; Dr. Robert F. Nagel, Clinical Instructor of Otolaryngology, Yale University, for speech and hearing evaluations; Dr. Meyer Samson for eye examinations.

References

Anderson, A., and Moore, O. K. 1959. Autotelic folk-models. Technical Report No. 8, Office of Naval Research, Group Psychology Branch, Contract SAR/Nonr. 609(16), New Haven. Reprinted in *Sociological Quarterly,* 1: 204–16.

Anderson, A. R., and Moore, O. K. 1957. The formal analysis of normative concepts. *Amer. Soc. Rev.* 22: 9–17.

Mead, G. H. 1934. *Mind, self and society.* Chicago: Univer. of Chicago Press.

Moore, O. K. *Dictation.* (Motion picture). Will be available through the Responsive Environments Foundation, Inc., 20 Augur Street, Hamden, Connecticut.

Moore, O. K. 1958. Problem solving and the perception of persons. In *Person perception and interpersonal behavior,* ed. R. Tagiuri and L. Petrullo. Palo Alto: Stanford Univer. Press. Pp. 131–50.

Moore, O. K. 1960. Orthographic symbols and the preschool child—a new approach. Proceedings of the third Minnesota conference on gifted children, Minneapolis: University of Minnesota Press. Pp. 91–101.

Moore, O. K. *Automated Responsive Environments: Part 1.* (Motion picture). The Responsive Environments Foundation, Inc., Hamden, Connecticut.

Moore, O. K. *Automated Responsive Environments: Part 2.* (Motion picture). The Responsive Environments Foundation, Inc., Hamden, Connecticut.

Moore, O. K., and Anderson, A. R. *Early Reading and Writing, Part 1: Skills.* (Motion picture). Basic Education, Inc., Hamden, Connecticut.

Moore, O. K., and Anderson, A. R. *Early Reading and Writing, Part 2: Teaching Methods.* (Motion picture). Basic Education, Inc., Hamden, Connecticut.

Moore, O. K., and Anderson, A. R. *Early Reading and Writing, Part 3: Development.* (Motion picture). Basic Education, Inc., Hamden, Connecticut.

Moore, O. K., and Anderson, A. R. 1962. Some puzzling aspects of social interaction. In *Mathematical methods in small group processes,* ed. J. H. Criswell, H. Solomon & P. Suppes Stanford Univer. Press. Pp. 232–49. Also, *Rev. of Metaphys.* 15: 409–33.

Moore, O. K., and Anderson, A. R. 1961. The structure of personality. Read at the ONR symposium on the "Social Self," University of Colorado, October 7–9, 1961. Also, *Rev. of Metaphys.* 16: 212–36. Also, in *Cognitive determinants of motivation and social interaction,* ed. O. J. Harvey. University of Colorado: Ronald Press, 1963.

Moore, O. K., and Lewis, D. J. 1962. Learning theory and culture. *Psych. Rev.* 59: 380–88. Also in *Current perspectives in social psychology,* ed. E. P. Hollander & R. G. Hunt. New York: Oxford University Press.

Pierce, J. R. 1961. *Symbols, signals and noise: The nature and process of communication.* New York: Harper & Brothers.

Terman, L. M. 1925–1959. *Genetic studies of genius,* Vols. 1–5. Palo Alto: Stanford University Press.

29 / Technical Note: A Reliable Wrist Counter for Recording Behavior Rates
OGDEN R. LINDSLEY

The reader will have noted early in the reading of this book that a primary kind of datum gathered in the studies is number of responses during, usually, a specified period of time. Elery L. Phillips counted agressive statements and use of the word "ain't"; Betty M. Hart and Todd R. Risley tabulated adjective use; Ann Dell Duncan's teenagers gathered frequencies on use of swear words and in-between-meal snacks; Don R. Thomas's data came from such discrete events as chair-scooting, getting out of one's seat, chair rocking, and so on.

Judgments after the fact have frequently been found to be inaccurate when compared to frequency counts as events are occurring. The two following technical notes consist of simple, inexpensive counters that the teacher may use while in the classroom.

Over the past three years, a wrist-type golf-score counter has been found helpful in recording movement rates for behavior modification and

Source: Ogden R. Lindsley, "Technical Note: A Reliable Wrist Counter for Recording Behavior Rates," *Journal of Applied Behavior Analysis* 1 (Spring 1968): 77–78. Copyright © 1968 by the Society for the Experimental Analysis of Behavior, Inc. Reprinted by permission of the author and the *Journal of Applied Behavior Analysis*.

analysis. Several different types are available from local sporting goods stores. The most cosmetic and reliable model located to date is the "Domatic Score," which is manufactured in Switzerland and can be obtained from the Hoffritz Cutlery Company, 20 Cooper Square, New York, New York for $8.00

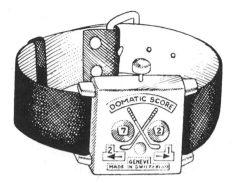

Over the past two and one-half years I have worn three of these, each operating at least 100 times a day. Table 1 summarizes their operating properties.

Over 100 behavior modifiers have purchased and worn these counters, with only a few replacing the supplied plastic band with a more attractive commercial watch band. They are highly recommended as the best two-digit wrist counter available.

Table 1   Operating Properties

Counter number	Date worn	Months worn	Number of counts	Operational malfunction
1	9/65	14	over 42,000	Occasionally jams as tens digit turns.
2	11/66	7	over 21,000	Too hard to push as tens digit turns.
3	5/67	8+	over 24,000	None

30 / Technical Note: A Manual Counter for Recording Multiple Behavior

ROBERT L. MATTOS

Hand-held digital counters are widely used to count behavior. The simultaneous recording of multiple behavioral categories on a single subject or a single behavioral category for multiple subjects necessitates the use of a counter with more than one channel. A compact (5.25 by 1.5-in.) five-channel manual counter ("Multi Counter" #99C9031) is available from Lafayette Radio and Electronics, 111 Jericho Turnpike, Syosset, L.I., New York 11791, for $12.95. The "Multi Counter" fits comfortably in the palm of the hand and after some practice, can be operated rapidly and reliably using the fingers of the same hand. . . . Limiting characteristics are the audible click that accompanies each operation and the fact that the five, three-digit channels cannot be reset independently; the reset knob resets all channels simultaneously.

Source: Robert L. Mattos, "Technical Note: A Manual Counter for Recording Multiple Behavior," *Journal of Applied Behavior Analysis* 1 (Summer 1968): 130. Copyright © 1968 by the Society for the Experimental Analysis of Behavior, Inc. Reprinted by permission of the author and the *Journal of Applied Behavior Analysis*. This work was supported under NICHHD Grant No. 00183.

DATE DUE